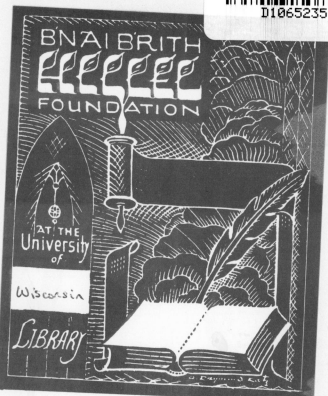

JEWISH REACTIONS TO GERMAN
ANTI-SEMITISM, 1870-1914

COLUMBIA UNIVERSITY STUDIES IN JEWISH
HISTORY, CULTURE, AND INSTITUTIONS

EDITED UNDER THE AUSPICES OF THE
CENTER FOR ISRAEL AND JEWISH STUDIES,
COLUMBIA UNIVERSITY

NUMBER 3

ZVI ANKORI, GENERAL EDITOR

Jewish Reactions to German Anti-Semitism, 1870-1914

ISMAR SCHORSCH

NEW YORK AND LONDON
COLUMBIA UNIVERSITY PRESS

PHILADELPHIA
JEWISH PUBLICATION SOCIETY OF AMERICA

Ismar Schorsch is Assistant Professor of Jewish History at the Jewish Theological Seminary and Visiting Assistant Professor of Jewish History at Columbia University.

This study, prepared under the Graduate Faculties of Columbia University, was selected by a committee of those Faculties to receive one of the Clarke F. Ansley awards given annually by Columbia University Press.

2435

Copyright © 1972 by Columbia University Press
Library of Congress Catalog Card Number: 74-190193
ISBN: 0-231-03643-4
Printed in the United States of America

PREFACE

THE ANNIHILATING JEW-HATRED of the Nazis had deep roots in German history. Since the Holocaust, a number of studies have illuminated some of the complex manifestations of German anti-Semitism prior to the Weimar Republic.* To date, however, historians, with the exception of Uriel Tal, have neglected to pay the same careful attention to the responses of German Jewry. Yet the subject is of transcending importance for the understanding of the Jewish experience in modern Germany. Few developments in German Jewish life since the beginning of the emancipation struggle were unaffected by the constant and widespread anti-Jewish sentiment of the environment. The very incompleteness of the emancipation process in Germany sustained an atmosphere of creative tension which repeatedly called forth the men, the ideas, and the institutions that bestowed on German Jewry its indisputable leadership of world Jewry. We have hardly begun to explore the involved interaction between a disturbing but tolerable level of anti-Semitism and Jewish creativity in modern Germany.

The present study is hopefully a beginning in this direction, though limited mainly to the most obvious level. Since the subject of Jewish reactions to anti-Semitism, properly understood, encompasses

* Paul Massing, *Rehearsal for Destruction* (New York, 1949); Eva G. Reichmann, *Hostages of Civilisation* (London, 1950); Eleonore Sterling, *Er Ist Wie Du* (Munich, 1956); Fritz Stern, *The Politics of Cultural Despair* (Garden City: Doubleday Anchor, 1965); George L. Mosse, *The Crisis of German Ideology* (New York, 1964); Peter G. J. Pulzer, *The Rise of Political Anti-Semitism in Germany and Austria* (New York, 1964); Uriel Tal, "Anti-Semitism in the Second German Reich" (Hebrew) (unpublished Ph.D. dissertation, Hebrew University, 1963); *idem, Christians and Jews in the 'Second Reich' (1870–1914)* (Hebrew) (Jerusalem, 1969). For a review of Tal's book, see my essay in *Judaism,* XIX (1970), 373–377.

so much of the Jewish experience in Germany, it is clearly too involved and still too amorphous a subject to be tackled in a single
venture. For this reason I decided rather early in my research to concentrate on the institutional response during the crucial period of Imperial Germany.

The unanticipated resurgence of anti-Semitism shortly after national unification compelled German Jewry to reappraise its
situation. The ultimate outcome was a fundamental shift in defense
strategy, away from a reliance on silence, Christian spokesmen, and
Jewish courtiers. German Jewry came to realize that emancipation
also required eternal vigilance and accordingly built the institutions
to defend its rights and interests. With this decision German Jewry
set the example for other emancipated Jewish communities. A new
status dictated new policies in fighting an old enemy.

But my intention was never merely to write a narrow organizational history. The far larger subject of the interrelationship between
a hostile society and Jewish behavior forms the indispensable background to the otherwise isolated and meaningless facts of organizational history. Thus I have consistently tried to probe this background in order to sketch the social setting which alone can properly
illuminate the developments recounted here.

The present work, I admit unashamedly, is the revision of a doc-
toral dissertation completed at Columbia University under the exacting supervision of Professors Gerson D. Cohen and Fritz Stern. They
guided me into the arcane world of historical method and research,
and their insightful questions prodded me to go further with my material than I had imagined possible. Whatever merit this work may
exhibit is in no small measure due to the concerned involvement of
these men with whom I had the privilege to study. I should also like
to express my gratitude to Professors Salo W. Baron, Peter Gay, and
Louis Lusky who participated in my defense of this dissertation and
from whose critical comments I benefited.

At the outset of my research I received some welcome personal
direction from Professor Uriel Tal of the Hebrew University, whose
own seminal studies of German anti-Semitism constantly informed
and stimulated my own thinking. My utilization of the Jewish Historical General Archives in Jerusalem was enormously facilitated by the

expertise and kindness of Mrs. Rahel Blumenthal, whose untimely death in July 1969 is a great loss to the scholarly community she served so unstintingly. My trip to Jerusalem in the fateful summer of 1967 was financed in part by a travel grant from the Memorial Foundation for Jewish Culture. Above all I should like to express my gratitude to the Leo Baeck Institute whose unfailing interest, rich library resources, and unique memoir collection immeasurably aided my work. I hope the final product to some extent has merited the assistance of those to whom I owe so much.

New York City
July 1971

CONTENTS

Preface v

Introduction 1

1 The Initial Reaction: Deutsch-Israelitischer Gemeindebund, 1869–1881 23

2 Continued Ambivalence: The 1880's 53

3 Help from Outside: Verein Zur Abwehr des Antisemitismus, 1891–1914 79

4 Time to Act: 1893 103

5 Self-Defense: Centralverein deutscher Staatsbürger jüdischen Glaubens, 1893–1914 117

6 A Second "Front": Verband der deutschen Juden, 1904–1914 149

7 Internal Discontent, 1897–1914 179

An Appraisal 203

Notes and Bibliography 211
  ABBREVIATIONS 212
  NOTES 213
  BIBLIOGRAPHY 269

Index 285

JEWISH REACTIONS TO GERMAN ANTI-SEMITISM, 1870-1914

INTRODUCTION

THE PRICE OF EMANCIPATION

THE MAJOR DEFENSE ORGANIZATION built by German Jewry during
the period from 1870 to 1914 was the Centralverein deutscher
Staatsbürger jüdischen Glaubens (the Central Union of German Citizens of the Jewish Faith). In retrospect, the Centralverein's formation in 1893 can be seen to have heralded a turning point in the prolonged "identity crisis" of German Jewry, a crisis brought on and
constantly aggravated by the battle for full emancipation which
spanned the first three quarters of the century. This bitter struggle
decisively affected the self-esteem and self-image of the German Jew.
He had not failed to grasp the message that his admission into society demanded the suppression of every external trace of Jewishness. To fight anti-Semitism at the end of the century inevitably required a public affirmation of Jewish identity. But such a display of
Jewishness was precisely what the extended battle for equal rights
had conditioned Jews to fear and loathe. Their deep aversion to self-
defense epitomized their commitment to abide by the terms of their
admission. Jewish reactions to anti-Semitism in the Second Reich
must be studied against the background of the interminable struggle
to remove Jewish disabilities inaugurated by the publication in 1781
of Christian Wilhelm Dohm's epoch-making book, *Über die bürgerliche Verbesserung der Juden.*[1]

The common denominator of the endless debate after 1781 was the extent to which Jews would have to surrender their Jewishness to gain full citizenship. Both the advocates and the opponents of emancipation agreed that Jewish separatism was the major problem; they differed on the possibility of correcting the situation. The opponents contended that neither the Jew nor Judaism could be changed. They charged that Christian persecution in the Middle Ages had not formed the debased character of contemporary Jews, for Jews had already displayed the same deficiencies in the Biblical period.[2] They had always manifested an extraordinary inclination for commerce, theft, fraud, and usury.[3] Judaism likewise posed an insurmountable obstacle. With its hatred of Christianity and its separatistic law, it reinforced the alien character of the Jew. Communal autonomy preserved a state within a state, while Judaism's political messianism restricted the Jew's loyalty to his people and his land.[4] By the 1840's the conservative sector of the political spectrum fought emancipation on the grounds that a Christian state could not tolerate Jewish citizens, while the radical sector behind Bruno Bauer contended that the Jews were unsuitable because they lacked the capacity for historical development.[5]

The advocates for Jewish admission were no less adamant in their opinion about the need to change the contemporary Jew and his religion. Christian Wilhelm Dohm, the young councilor and archivist at the War Office in Berlin, was but the first in a long line of German liberals who fought for emancipation while insisting upon the radical revision of Judaism. In 1781 he became the first Prussian official to speak out for the immediate unconditional extension of almost full equality to the Jews.[6] To answer his critics, he published a second volume two years later, in which he openly expressed what he expected of the Jews. The very title of his book, *Concerning the Civil Improvement of the Jews,* he proclaimed, should have established that he was not an uncritical defender of the Jews. He attributed the survival of Judaism to the hostility of the environment, and stressed the radical changes in Judaism that emancipation would effect. With a touch of prophecy, he predicted how quickly Jews would discard all burdensome, uncomfortable, and alien differences, and how hastily the rabbis would justify the changes to stem the exodus from the synagogue. Despite all reforms, many would still depart to convert or simply to profess a religion of reason.[7]

In 1809 Wilhelm von Humboldt reiterated the same hope that emancipation would hasten the total disintegration of organized Jewry. In a thoroughly liberal memorandum on a proposed draft for the emancipation of Prussian Jewry, the humanistic statesman revealed his illiberal expectations only once. To ensure ecclesiastical decentralization, he strongly opposed the appointment of a chief rabbi. The inevitable result would be that "Individual persons will realize that they have merely a ceremonial law and really no religion, and will feel impelled to turn to the Christians out of their own desire, motivated by the inherent human need for a higher faith." [8]

During the 1830's and 1840's the liberal advocates of emancipation in Baden spelled out what they expected of the Jews. At the time, Baden enjoyed the most liberal constitution in Germany, for it alone had created a second chamber elected by all resident citizens rather than by estates.[9] In 1831 this liberal-dominated Chamber of the Diet considered revoking the disabilities that remained. But the opponents easily succeeded in convincing the majority that Jews had still not shed their separate nationality. They continued to use Hebrew, to observe such divisive religious practices as the Sabbath and the dietary laws, to accept the authority of the rabbis, and to await the messiah. The tenor of the discussion clearly indicated that if the Jews would convene a synod to discard their separatistic practices the Diet would respond with emancipation. In the meantime the Diet decided to leave their present status unchanged. Baden Jewry rejected the proposal outright. During the next fifteen years the Baden Diet debated the issue five more times. Each time, after a torrent of anti-Semitic oratory, the liberal lower house reaffirmed its *quid pro quo* offer of 1831. When in 1846 the Diet finally adopted a resolution advising the government to complete the emancipation, the Crown simply ignored it.[10]

In sum, both the opponents and the advocates desired conversion or, at the very least, the abandoning of Judaism. They differed only on the question of timing. The former refused to extend emancipation prior to conversion, while the latter generally argued that emancipation would eventually lead to the baptismal font. The manner in which the Prussian government subverted its heralded emancipation edict of 1812 in the years after the Congress of Vienna should have dispelled whatever illusions Jews might still have harbored about the price of admission.

The emancipation of Prussian Jewry was part of the reconstruction of the Prussian state undertaken by Baron vom Stein and Prince Hardenberg in the wake of the debacle of Jena in 1806 and the subsequent French occupation of Berlin. The edict of 1812 granted citizenship to all formerly protected and tolerated Jews living in Prussia, and it removed all Jewish disabilities, except the holding of civil service positions outside of teaching and the special Jewish oath demanded of Jews appearing in court.[11] But during the reactionary period which followed the defeat of Napoleon, the promise of emancipation suffered the same fate as the other liberal reforms of the short-lived Stein era.

The Prussian government refused to extend the emancipation to the new territories acquired at the Congress of Vienna. While the rejuvenated absolute state of Frederick William III, resting securely on the twin pillars of the army and the bureaucracy, labored to unite its sprawling lands judicially, administratively, and economically, it merely confirmed the different existing Jewish statutes of every annexed territory. In violation of its own absolutist principles, the government tolerated a situation in which twenty-one different sets of laws were allowed to govern the status and conduct of the disparate Jewish communities of the realm.[12] Only 58,000 of the 124,000 Jews living in the enlarged Prussia of 1815 were citizens.[13] In the Rhineland the government continued to subject some 20,000 Jewish inhabitants to the numerous disabilities reimposed by Napoleon's "Infamous Decree" of 1808, which even the French Emperor had intended to remove after a decade. When the Provincial Assembly in 1843 became the first representative body in Germany to recommend full equality, Frederick William IV of Prussia squelched the proposal.[14]

In the old Prussian provinces the government curtailed the emancipation of 1812 administratively. Despite Section 8, which expressly admitted qualified Jews to teaching positions, the Cabinet, in August 1822, ordered that henceforth no Jew was to be appointed. The conversion three years later of Eduard Gans, the former president of the ephemeral Verein für Cultur und Wissenschaft der Juden, and a brilliant young legal historian, bespoke the desperation of many frustrated young Jewish intellectuals. The government likewise refused to open any public office to Jews, thus effectively sealing off another large and prestigious area of employment. In 1826 the Minister of Interior specifically denied state employment even to Jewish veterans of the War of Liberation.[15] The Jewish community remained legally only a tolerated private corporation. It could not purchase land or build a synagogue without royal approval nor compel individual members to pay their communal taxes. In contrast to its treatment of Christian clergy, the government did not recognize Jewish religious leaders as ecclesiastical officials, and would not exempt them from communal and personal taxes.[16]

Through its unofficial but close affiliation with the Gesellschaft zur Beförderung des Christentums unter den Juden, the Prussian government actively endorsed the effort to convert the Jews. It granted the society free use of the mails, and Frederick William III personally enriched its coffers annually with the sum of 300 thalers. Until 1861 a Prussian general always served as its president.[17] Finally, in the 1840's, Frederick William IV concluded that the Jews actually constituted an unassimilable minority for a Christian state. Accordingly, he tried to turn the clock back entirely by depriving the Jews of their citizenship and reintroducing the medieval corporate structure, a move bitterly and successfully contested by Prussian Jewry.[18]

This unrelenting pressure to assimilate and convert, effectively expressed in the first half of the nineteenth century by the withholding of full emancipation, was the decisive force in shaping the relationship between the modern German Jew and his ancestral religion. Because Judaism loomed as the insurmountable barrier to equality, Jewishness suddenly became an inescapable condition of painful self-consciousness. Ludwig Börne, who converted to Christianity in 1818 to evade the effects of the revoking of emancipation in Frankfurt, testified: "It is like a miracle! I have experienced it a thousand times and still it remains ever new. Some accuse me of being a Jew, others forgive me for being a Jew, still others praise me for it, but all of them reflect upon it." [19]

Continued disabilities alienated Jews from Judaism more rapidly than the persuasive allurements of reason and culture. The actual number of conversions to Christianity remained very small. In Prussia, between 1812 and 1846, an average of 108 Jews converted annually, and many of them, including a sizable number of intellectuals, used baptism merely as an entry into German society.[20] But short of conversion, the only alternative left to the individual who valued emancipation was to suppress every external mark of Jewishness. In 1843 a Leipzig Jewish paper reported: "A Berlin Jew is blissfully happy when he is told that there is no longer anything Jewish about him." [21] With neurotic sensitivity, countless insecure and perplexed Jews indiscriminately appropriated the negative judgments about Jews and Judaism which were shared by friend and foe alike.[22]

The most significant Jewish response to this unabated German pressure was an organized movement for religious reform. There is no doubt that the very desire for emancipation presupposed a certain willingness to alter the basic autonomy of the medieval Jewish community. What determined the future course of events in Germany, however, was the partial nature of the emancipation, the fact that, unlike the Jews of France, England, and America, German Jews were compelled to battle for an entire century to complete and implement the emancipation promised since the Napoleonic Wars. The same tense decades during which German Jewry fought to win full emancipation also gave rise to a growing movement for religious reform. The efforts at reform of the major institutions of Judaism reflected the extent to which Jews had internalized the eighteenth-century rationalist and nineteenth-century nationalist critiques of Judaism and amounted to a desperate attempt to placate the formidable anti-Jewish sentiment that continued to thwart emancipation. Unwilling to abandon Judaism, the spokesmen for reform struggled to salvage as much as an intolerant society would suffer.[23] What distinguished the early Reform Movement in Germany from the indigenous reform efforts by American and English Jews in the 1820's and the 1840's, which were concerned mainly with an abbreviated, decorous and edifying service, was precisely this willingness to tamper with the major institutions of Judaism. In marked contrast to German Reformers, the Charleston advocates of reform in 1824 insisted "that they entirely disclaim any idea of wishing to abolish such ceremonies as are considered land-marks to distinguish the *Jew* from the *Gentile*. . . ." [24]

At the outset of the emancipation debate in Germany, Moses Mendelssohn had publicly declared that Jewish religious law would never be bartered for the rights of citizenship. The law constituted the very essence of Judaism and remained binding in all its manifoldness. Moreover, Mendelssohn propounded an elaborate political theory to deny the state any theoretical right to demand changes in Judaism in return for emancipation. [25]

But already David Friedländer, his major disciple and one of the acknowledged leaders of Prussian Jewry, rejected both Mendelssohn's definition of Judaism and his political posture vis-à-vis the prospect of emancipation. Reducing the statutory nature of Judaism to a transient stage of history, Friedländer located the essence of Judaism in its concurrence with the basic tenets of natural religion and its lofty ethical injunctions. Politically Friedländer, who in contrast to Mendelssohn engaged the Prussian authorities unsuccessfully in protracted negotiations for the alleviation of Jewish disabilities, accorded the state the right to interfere in the religious practices of its citizens. Only matters of conscience remained outside the jurisdiction of the state. [26] Consequently, Friedländer openly advocated religious reforms that would allay the reservations of those contesting emancipation and establish the fitness of the adherents of Judaism for full citizenship. [27]

The next generation of proponents for religious reform generally adopted the positions delineated by Friedländer, and in accord with the *Zeitgeist* marshaled an impressive array of historical arguments to legitimize the accommodations demanded by German society. Abraham Geiger, one of the seminal figures of nineteenth-century German Jewry, did not deny that in the periods of the Bible and the Second Commonwealth Judaism exhibited national traits. But he vigorously contended that the depravity of pagan society dictated this temporary national protection, behind which the new theological concepts revealed at Mount Sinai might take root among the people in their pristine purity.[28] Geiger depicted these early periods of Jewish history as mere preparation for the day when the Jews would be summoned from Palestine to teach their ethical monotheism to mankind:

Besides, it was not its mission to establish a nation; its nationality was but a temporal hull, a necessary means for fortifying the belief and so deeply rooting it in the constitution of the individual members that it would continue to live with full vitality, even in their dispersion.[29]

Samuel Holdheim, a former Orthodox rabbi who in the 1840's became the spokesman for the radical wing of the German Reform Movement, made the same historical distinction between the religious and national roots of Judaism, but he was far less reluctant than Geiger to apply the theory. He appears to have acted on the assumption that whatever German nationalists found offensive in Judaism might in fact be a vestige of Jewish nationhood and ought to be renounced:

Before the religious consciousness, prejudice can make no claim to special treatment and toleration. Here the question must be frankly and scrupulously examined; perhaps in fact this or that which we have till now practiced as a religious observance is actually according to its origin and significance a national institution. Perhaps this or that in our ethics or observances which obstructs our intimate union with our fatherland —and perhaps without our awareness—is, precisely because of this antagonism, not of universal, unconditional value, but rather is political and national in character.[30]

Armed with this theory, Holdheim attempted to convince his rabbinic colleagues that authentic Judaism does not forbid marriage to Christians. German anti-Semites fulminated against rabbinic refusal to sanction mixed marriages. This putative Jewish horror of intermarriage preserved the Jews' national identity as effectively as the isolation imposed by the medieval ghetto. Holdheim agreed. He insisted that the Biblical and Talmudic injunctions against marriage with non-Jews were not motivated by religious values, but by a determination to guard the holiness and purity of the Jewish people; and such nationally rooted laws must not be allowed to prevent Christians and Jews living in Germany from forming a single *Volk*.[31] Holdheim urged Jews to recognize that "the unifying power of the state manifests itself precisely in that it succeeds in overcoming the nationalities stemming from different origins and binding them into a single national community." [32]

The character of Prussian marriage law increased the pressure on the rabbis to issue a declaration permitting intermarriage. Besides denying civil marriage to any member of the Evangelical Church, Prussian law explicitly prohibited any Christian from marrying a non-Christian whose religion did not recognize the validity of the Christian wedding ceremony.[33] Thus at the first German rabbinical conference in Brunswick in 1844, the rabbis declared after considerable deliberation that "the marriage of a Jew with a Christian, marriage with adherents of monotheistic faiths in general, is not forbidden, if the laws of the state permit the parents to raise the children of such a union also in the Jewish faith." [34]

The concluding condition was demanded by those who hoped thereby to contribute to diminishing the allegedly widespread religious indifference among Jews.[35] But its addition at least partially nullified the legal import of the statement, since Prussian law called for the children of a mixed marriage to be raised in the religion of the father till age fourteen.[36] In 1847 a Königsberg court declared the marriage of a German Jewish man with an English Christian, which had been performed by a Christian minister in England, as invalid, because contemporary Judaism did not recognize it.[37] Even after a Prussian law of 1874 allowed Jews and Christians to marry by civil ceremony, the issue of Judaism's opposition to intermarriage continued to arouse intense interest.[38]

The problem of intermarriage is merely an extreme example, but therefore highly instructive, of the intimate connection between political pressure and religious reform in nineteenth-century German Jewry. The religious rhetoric and canons used to reexamine the validity of the dietary laws, circumcision, the role of Hebrew, the Sabbath and festivals, and the messianic concept often concealed political fears.[39] In 1844 William Freund, the editor of a short-lived political periodical entitled *Zur Judenfrage in Deutschland,* openly advised his readers that the fight for emancipation had an undeniable religious dimension. Judaism had to be remodeled according to German views and values. As the Protestant Reformation overcame the Romanism in Christianity, so the contemporary Jewish analogue, the

Reform Movement, had to eradicate the Orientalism left in Judaism. The large number of articles devoted to religious reform which appeared in Freund's political journal reflect his broad view of the emancipation battle.[40] Reform leaders themselves were not entirely unaware of the nexus. In 1835 the young Geiger warned:

Civil equality should and must be won, but not at the price of religious independence. If you are willing to pay the price, that would be the easiest means for attaining what we seek. Thus there are those who are afraid to utter even one word that might displease some Christian, and who abandon any custom that seems to them to jeopardize their chance for reaching this goal.[41]

The relentless pressure on the Jews affected the course of Orthodox Judaism in Germany as well. While the Old Orthodoxy attempted to salvage as much of the judicial autonomy and separatism of the medieval Jewish community as was possible under an unwelcome emancipation,[42] the Neo-Orthodoxy advanced by Samson Raphael Hirsch enthusiastically embraced the multiple opportunities it would provide.[43] Like the spokesmen for reform, Hirsch dropped all demands for judicial autonomy and continuance of Jewish civil law.[44] He insisted upon the wholly religious character of Judaism,[45] reduced the significance of the periods of Jewish national independence,[46] and divested the messianic concept of political overtones.[47] With a rationalism and Hegelianism that he fully shared with the reformers, whom he detested, Hirsch too emphasized the ethical content and universal mission of Judaism.[48] Without a doubt, his vigorous defense of the divine origin and obligatory character of Jewish law infuriated the Reform, but one should not lose sight of the substantial agreement in the area of theology imposed by the same external pressures.

The first penetrating critique of this common effort by the leaders of German Reform and Neo-Orthodoxy to divest Judaism of all national traits came from the young Heinrich Graetz. In 1846, seven years before he published the first volume (i.e., Vol. IV) of his monumental *History of the Jews,* Graetz outlined his philosophy of Jewish history in a bold and perceptive essay titled "The Structure of Jewish History." Alarmed by the proliferation of arbitrary definitions of Judaism, Graetz proposed to tackle the question "What is

Judaism?" by an examination of Jewish history.[49] From its inception and throughout its long history, Judaism was twofold in character. It comprised both theology and politics, matters of religion and matters of state. Its body politic was the indispensable soil upon which the creedal abstractions would be transformed into social justice. The soul of this peculiar national organism was the Torah, but its body was the land of Israel. All later Jewish history revolved around these two axes of Judaism. One period might manifest the political or the religious aspect alone, but both constituted the irreducible content of Judaism. In characteristically vigorous fashion, Graetz related the import of his view of Jewish history to the contemporary Jewish scene:

Judaism without the firm soil of national life resembles an inwardly hollowed-out and half-uprooted tree, which still produces foliage at the top but is no longer capable of sprouting twigs and branches. You may subject Judaism to a process of refinement, extract modern thoughts from the fullness of its contents and trumpet forth this essence as the heart of Judaism with stupefying, resonant phrases and brilliant clichés; you may build a church and accept a creed for this refined and idealized Judaism "in a nutshell"; nevertheless, you still will have embraced only a shadow and taken the dry shell for the succulent fruit.[50]

At the end of 1879, after Graetz had completed the translation of his youthful program into a meticulously researched and passionately narrated eleven-volume history of the Jews, he became the target of a bitter broadside by Heinrich Treitschke. The work had aroused the nationalistic wrath of the Berlin professor. He denounced Graetz as an unassimilable national Jew, who adamantly refused to pay the price of emancipation. The attack was not unmerited. Graetz had devoted a lifetime of scholarship to proving that Judaism was anything but an abstract and inconspicuous set of beliefs. As Treitschke rightly sensed, his work amounted to a repudiation of the reformers for knuckling under to German pressure.[51]

In the third quarter of the nineteenth century, German resistance to full emancipation gradually subsided. The Prussian Constitution of 1850 theoretically granted equality before the law, and opened all public offices to qualified applicants regardless of religion. In the early 1860's both Württemberg and Baden removed the last Jewish disabilities. On July 3, 1869, the Reichstag of the North German Confederation extended equal civil and political rights to all citizens, and upon the establishment of the Empire in January of 1871, the Act of July 3, 1869, became Imperial law.[52]

However, the long controversy over equal rights had bequeathed a potent legacy of anti-Semitic sentiment and literature to the new Empire. Every sector of the German political spectrum from the Hegelian radicals to the Junker conservatives had at some time vented its deep-seated animosity to Jewish claims. Most of the arguments so fully developed by the anti-Semites of the Second Reich had already been articulated or adumbrated.[53]

Equally portentous for the future of German Jewry, the long struggle had psychologically taken its toll. The tremendous pressure on the Jews to establish their German identity by repressing every religious, social, and ethnic distinctiveness had transformed being Jewish into a wholly internal matter. Jews had at least made a large downpayment on the price of emancipation. Many had substantially altered the form and content of their religion. No regional or national Jewish organizations existed to irritate German sensibilities. Jewish life did not extend beyond the confines of the local corporate community. When anti-Semitism exploded again but a few years after the halcyon days of emancipation and unification, the Jews stood singularly defenseless. Nearly a century of German pressure had rendered them incapable of any public affirmation of their Jewishness. To fight anti-Semitism would violate the terms of the emancipation. Reassured by what they felt to be the very limited extent of this German regression and their own inveterate faith in progress, they emphatically opposed every suggestion to resist.

Seen in this light, the formation of the Centralverein in 1893 signaled the beginning of a Jewish revision of the terms of emancipation. The defense of Jewish honor by an open fight against anti-Semitism embodied a repudiation of concealment as the price for equality. The Centralverein undertook to recondition the German Jew to assert his Jewishness publicly. In place of traditional behind-the-scenes appeals to the seat of power for special protection, the Centralverein waged its battle against anti-Semitism before the eyes of the German public. The Centralverein's historical importance in the context of the Second Reich, therefore, lies not in its nominal success in combating the forces of German anti-Semitism, but rather in its impact upon the mentality of German Jewry. By means of a mass organization, it labored during the two decades before the war to revive the self-esteem and self-image indispensable for survival which German Jewry had sacrificed in the fight for equality. In time, as we shall see, it also came to revise the narrow and vapid definition of Judaism that intimidated Jews had adopted as the price of emancipation.

DEMOGRAPHIC AND OCCUPATIONAL DISTRIBUTION

In the course of the nineteenth century, German states had granted their Jewish subjects economic freedom far earlier than civil equality, with the result that by the beginning of Bismarck's Empire the urban and occupational concentration and the prosperous economic circumstances of German Jewry decisively offset its numerical insignificance. In 1871 Germany's 512,153 Jews constituted only 1.25 percent of the total population. By 1910 German Jewry had grown to 615,021, but, because of the enormous increase in the general population, it now amounted to slightly less than 1 percent of the total. The major reason was the steadily declining birthrate of the Jewish sector. Between the years 1881 and 1909, the number of yearly births declined from 10,269 to 7,123, giving German Jewry a birthrate that was only half that of the German population.[54]

The majority of Germany's Jews resided in Prussia, and during the period of this study it was Prussian Jewry that registered the largest absolute increase. As the following table indicates, with the excep-

State	1871	1910	Percentage of Total in 1910
Prussia	325,587	415,926	1.02
Bavaria	50,648	55,065	.8
Alsace-Lorraine	38,937	30,483	1.62
Baden	25,703	25,896	1.2
Hesse	24,050	24,063	1.87
Saxony	3,346	17,587	.36
Württemberg	12,425	11,982	.49

tion of the Jewish populations of Saxony and Bavaria, those of the other states either remained stable or declined.[55]

Several important factors operated to offset this numerical insignificance. First, the Jews were far in advance of the general migratory trend to the cities, with the result that they were disproportionately concentrated in the rising urban centers. In Berlin in 1881, the nearly 54,000 Jews represented 4.8 percent of the city's population. By 1885, 32.7 percent of Prussian Jewry lived in cities with populations of at least 100,000 while in 1910, 54.5 percent of Prussian Jewry was to be found in cities of 100,000, and more than 71 percent resided in cities of 20,000 or more.[56] The 1910 figures were nearly double those of the Prussian population. In that year slightly less than 25 percent of the general Prussian population lived in cities of 100,000 or more, and only about 37 percent in cities of 20,000 and over.[57] Obviously, the Jewish percentage in many of these urban centers exceeded the national ratio. Thus in 1925, when half of German Jewry lived in the seven major metropolises of Berlin, Frankfurt-am-Main, Breslau, Hamburg, Cologne, Leipzig, and Munich—cities that contained only 13 percent of the German population—Jews represented 4.3 percent of the population of Berlin and 1.8 percent of the population of Hamburg. Since Jews tended to settle in only a few of the districts of these cities, within these districts their percentage was still higher.[58]

Secondly, the occupational distribution of the Jews exhibited an extraordinary concentration in sectors not highly valued by a society still rooted in the values of a pre-capitalistic age. In 1881 the statistical yearbook of Berlin published for the first time employment figures for the city according to religious affiliation as well as occupational distribution, evidently in response to the intense anti-Semitic pressure of the time. With state employment almost wholly closed to Jews, they represented less than .4 percent of the civil servants in the municipal, state, and national governments and less than .3 percent in the Berlin branches of the railroad, post office, and telegraph systems. In contrast, Jews represented 7.9 percent of the city's legal profession, 8.6 percent of its writers and journalists, 11.7 percent of its medical personnel, 21.3 percent of its wholesale dealers, 25.1 percent of those involved in the shipping of goods and in small business, and 25.8 percent of those engaged in the money market. The Jewish correspondent who reported these statistics laconically observed that "everyone who reads this work will readily perceive at what points we must still improve the situation." [59]

This concentration resulted in an occupational distribution for the Jews that differed markedly from that of the Germans. In 1895 the fields of business and commerce employed 56 percent of the Jews earning a living, while only 1.4 percent worked in agriculture, and 19.3 percent in industry. In contrast, 36 percent of the German labor force worked in agriculture; another 36 percent in industry; and only 10 percent in business and commerce. By 1907 some mutual assimilation had begun in the direction of industry, where now nearly 22 percent of the Jewish labor force, and 37 percent of the German, were employed. But the differences in business and commerce remained substantial. While 50.6 percent of the Jewish labor force earned their livelihood in these branches, only 11.5 percent of employed Germans still did. [60]

This commercial concentration at the end of the nineteenth century represented the culmination of an occupational shift among German Jews that had begun during the Thirty Years' War. The dire economic straits of the German princes, aside from spawning the last great period of the court Jew, also created opportunities for an increasing number of Jews to abandon moneylending and penetrate trade and even industry. The trend was substantially accelerated by the economic freedom granted by the various emancipation edicts in the first half of the nineteenth century as well as by the continued exclusion of Jews from all branches of the civil service. [61] The result was that Jews were to be found mainly in economic groups whose income greatly exceeded that of civil servants and craftsmen. And even among those engaged in commerce, relatively more Jews than Christians were self-employed. In 1907 three-fifths of the Jews in business were independent, as compared with only one-fourth of the Christians. [62]

The income taxes paid by Jews at the beginning of the twentieth century indicate the extent of Jewish prosperity. In Berlin in 1905–1906 the average Jewish taxpayer paid 357.42 marks; the average dissenter (i.e., an individual without religious affiliation),

270.11 marks; the average Lutheran, 132.91 marks; and the average Catholic, 111.27 marks. Phrased differently, the Jews of Berlin in 1905 constituted 4.84 percent of the total population; yet they amounted to 14.27 percent of the householders liable to an income tax of more than 21 marks (which meant having an income of at least 1,500 marks). The amount paid by this 14.27 percent of the taxpayers came to 30.77 percent of the total income tax collected that year in Berlin. In the light of all these figures, it is apparent that of the nearly 30,000 Berlin Jews gainfully employed, few earned less than 1,500 marks annually.[63]

The same high income among Jews is suggested by the figures from Frankfurt-am-Main. In 1900 Jews represented 63.1 percent of those earning more than 3,000 marks. According to Werner Sombart, in 1905 the Jews of many cities paid a percentage of the total taxes collected in the city far greater than their numbers warranted.[64]

City	Percentage of Population	Percentage of Taxes
Posen	4.2	24.0
Breslau	4.3	20.3
Beuthen	4.0	26.9
Bromberg	2.8	13.7
Gleiwitz	3.2	23.9
Wiesbaden	2.6	8.2
Düsseldorf	1.1	3.5
Elberfeld	1.1	3.8
Magdeburg	.8	3.6

The predominantly rural Jews of southern Germany were less comfortably situated than their coreligionists in the north though still a lot wealthier than their immediate neighbors. In 1907 the average Jewish income in Catholic Baden was 1,229 marks, as compared with 244 marks for the Protestants, and 117 marks for the Catholics. The average total wealth per individual in Baden was figured at 13,829 marks for Jews, 2,806 marks for Protestants, and 1,646 marks for Catholics.[65]

COMMUNAL STRUCTURE

From the viewpoint of communal structure, German Jewry of 1870 was about as fragmented as Germany had been before the advent of Bismarck. Although among emancipated Jewish communities German Jewry had indeed pioneered in the development of the Reform Movement and the historical study of Judaism, it had not produced a single permanent regional, national, or international organization. In part, the relentless pressure to assimilate exerted during the battle for emancipation accounts for the organizational lag. Most Jews were unwilling to support separatistic concerns which accentuated their Jewishness. However, an equally decisive factor was the traditional parochialism of Jewish life which the legislation pertaining to Jews by German governments like Prussia helped to reinforce.[66]

In the Second Reich the individual states and not the Imperial government controlled religious affairs. Consequently, the official status and treatment accorded by the state to its Jewish community before 1870 remained unchanged. In southern states like Württemberg and Baden, the local Jewish communities were united in officially recognized central councils, an arrangement that accorded Judaism a status approximating that enjoyed by Catholicism and Protestantism, and in Württemberg even included an annual government subsidy to the Jewish budget. In other states, like Bavaria and Prussia, Judaism enjoyed no official status. No central authority governed the local communities and no recognized spokesman represented them before the government.[67]

In Prussia the Jewish community received no financial assistance from the state. Unlike the French government, which assumed responsibility for a large part of the religious expenses of its Catholic, Protestant, and Jewish communities, the Prussian government generally contributed only to the maintenance of the national institutions of its two established churches, the Catholic and Evangelical. Although Protestants outnumbered Catholics in Prussia by two to one, the size of the subsidies was determined on the basis of need. Thus the 1870 budget of the Ministry of Religion provided only 615,522 thalers for the Evangelical Church, but 858,657 thalers for the Catholic. In contrast, the school budget for that year allocated 75,576 thalers for the salaries of sixty-three professors in nine Evangelical theological faculties, but only 17,200 thalers for twenty-two professors in three Catholic theological faculties. The difference in educational subsidies resulted from the fact that all Protestant clergy received their education at a university, while most priests were trained in seminaries. Throughout the period of the Second Reich not a single German university opened a Jewish theological faculty.[68]

Even within Prussia no single legislation regulated all six hundred of its Jewish communities. The law of July 23, 1847, controlled the structure and internal affairs of Prussian Jewry. But it was never extended to the territories annexed in 1864 and 1866. In these provinces the existing Jewish legislation continued in effect. Despite the resulting diversity in details, the twelve different sets of legislation governing the various sectors of Prussian Jewry all granted the local Jewish community the status of a public corporation, empowered it to tax, and recognized the principle of compulsory membership.[69]

The upshot of this legislatively encouraged decentralization, particularly in Prussia, was the formation of a powerful local Jewish community which jealously guarded its financial resources as well as the right to determine its own religious practice. In the larger cities, the Jewish community had no difficulty in financing its variety of religious, educational, and welfare services. For example, the Berlin community reported in 1872 an income of 309,347 marks from the tax receipts of its members.[70] Ten years later that figure had risen to 461,000 marks, and by 1890 it reached the sum of 727,000 marks.[71] Proportionately the smaller urban Jewish communities also had adequate resources available to finance their programs. In 1874 some 3,800 members of the Breslau community paid about 180,000 marks in religious taxes, while that same year the far smaller Jewish community in Leipzig collected almost 36,000 marks.[72] In general the Jewish community assessed its members on the basis of income, and collected the taxes itself.[73]

The real financial problem existed in the countless small Jewish communities of rural Germany, where the departure of even a single family to the city meant a substantial loss of revenue. In 1872 two-thirds of Prussia's 600 Jewish communities maintained 768 synagogues and 481 schools, and employed 1,206 personnel.[74] But the lack of information about the remaining one-third suggests that their resources were too limited to run any independent institutions. Outside of Prussia the number of impoverished small communities was still greater. In 1872 a Jewish population slightly more than half that of Prussia (183,013) was distributed among nearly twice as many Jewish communities as existed in Prussia (1,150).[75]

At the beginning of the Empire, German Jewry lacked a network of national organizations which could supplement the diminishing services of these countless small communities. Despite the financial crisis facing these communities, the larger communities were generally reluctant to hand out funds from which they would not benefit directly. As we shall see, much of the resistance from large communities encountered in the 1870's by the Deutsch-Israelitischer Gemeindebund, the first national organization committed to alleviating the plight of the small community, rested on such pecuniary considerations.[76]

Deep religious differences augmented the centrifugal forces fostered by the decentralized communal structure of German Jewry. As we have seen, both the Reform and the Neo-Orthodox wings of German Judaism welcomed emancipation, and transformed Judaism into a confession. But they differed sharply over the authority to accommodate the details of Jewish law to the needs of an integrated society. As a growing number of Jewish communities embraced Reform in the second half of the nineteenth century, the apprehension and discomfort of the Orthodox minority steadily mounted. One contemporary observer estimated that by the beginning of the twentieth century only 10 to 15 percent of German Jewry could still be classified as Orthodox.[77] Under the leadership of Samson R. Hirsch in Frankfurt-am-Main, the Orthodox had already begun to exert pressure before 1870 to break the principle of compulsory membership which often forced them to belong to Jewish communities governed by the Reform.[78]

Bismarck's Kulturkampf presented the Orthodox with the opportunity for which they had waited. In a move to weaken the control of the Catholic Church over its members, the Prussian legislature

passed a law in 1873 permitting a Christian to withdraw from his de-
nominational church without having to renounce Christianity (i.e., to
convert).[79] In a final section, the law also extended to Jews the right
to renounce Judaism without conversion, which till then had been the
only means to exit from the local Jewish community. Hirsch immediately began to lobby for specific legislation that would allow his followers to withdraw from the local Jewish community without having
to renounce Judaism. He contended that Judaism like Christianity
was composed of wholly separate denominations, and was in truth divided by conflicts more fundamental than those dividing Christians.
Moreover, compulsory membership in a Reform-dominated community constituted an intolerable violation of freedom of conscience.[80]
Reform Jewry repudiated both contentions passionately. Fearing a
mass exodus of indifferent Jews, Reform leaders viewed any such
legislation as a direct threat to the survival of an organized Jewish
community. They did not hesitate to accuse the government of overt
discrimination. Not only did the Jewish community not receive any
financial assistance from the state, but now the state was prepared to
deprive it of the compulsory membership upon which its continued
viability so heavily depended.[81] Over their repeated objections, the
Prussian government in April 1876 submitted to the Landtag the
draft of an *Austrittsgesetz* in order to extend religious freedom to the
individual Jew. Supported by the Liberals and Progressives, the bill
became law a month later.[82]

This three-year controversy exacerbated the already strained relations between Orthodox and Reform. Mutual suspicion and bitterness
stood in the way of every future proposal for cooperation on common interests. For the followers of Hirsch, who now withdrew from
the local Jewish communities, the defense of their newly acquired religious freedom became an obsession.[83] Coupled with the aforementioned communal decentralization, these divisive forces effectively
fragmented German Jewry into a conglomerate of isolated and self-
centered local units. In addition to the inhibitions produced by the
pressures to assimilate, this chaotic situation still further impeded the
organizational response of German Jewry to anti-Semitism. In this regard too, the Centralverein foreshadowed a triumph over the conditions created by emancipation, for it slowly succeeded in uniting

Jews of all persuasions and from every sector of the country in the fight against a common enemy. It opened the way for a rapid succession of powerful national organizations which marshaled the resources of German Jewry to withstand the multiple forms of German intransigence.

1

THE INITIAL REACTION: DEUTSCH-ISRAELITISCHER GEMEINDEBUND, 1869-1881

THE DEUTSCH-ISRAELITISCHER GEMEINDEBUND (German-Israelite Community League) represented the first successful attempt to create a national organization, although decades were to pass before it would win the support of the majority of the Jewish communities in Germany. This frigid response epitomized the centrifugal forces splintering German Jewry. Thus the early history of the Gemeindebund sheds some valuable light upon the communal and religious tensions that stood in the way of any effective organized self-defense. At the same time, the Gemeindebund also represented the first instance of such a defense. Its very creation manifested the apprehension of its founders over the vestiges of anti-Semitism that had surfaced during the Franco-Prussian War. And as the only national Jewish organization on the scene when anti-Semitism erupted explosively in the mid-1870's, it cautiously took up the defense of Jewish interests. At the end of 1881 the hostile intervention of the Saxon government quietly crushed this first stumbling effort by German Jewry at organized self-defense.

THE FOUNDING OF THE GEMEINDEBUND

The involved series of events which eventually led to the formation of the Gemeindebund began in 1869. That year Emil Lehmann, a politically active Dresden lawyer and an advocate of extreme religious reform,[1] called for the regular meeting of communal representatives to cooperate in solving mutual administrative problems. His long essay, "Hear, O Israel," which examined the needs of German Jewry upon the threshold of full emancipation, is a striking example of the political considerations that motivated so many of the religious reforms proposed during the battle for emancipation. "Precisely because we demand and enjoy relatively full freedom of religious practice as well as civil and political equality, we must adhere carefully to what is expected in return [*Gegenleistung*]: civil responsibilities must not suffer on account of religious practice." [2]

For this reason, as well as to accelerate integration, Lehmann raised again many of the reforms considered by the rabbinical conferences of the 1840's. His essay proposed dropping circumcision, rabbinic jurisdiction in matters of marriage and divorce, and the second day of the three seasonal festivals. He insisted that the Sabbath be observed on Sunday. He contended that Judaism did not forbid marriage to a Christian, and he vigorously encouraged such unions as an effective means to eradicate anti-Jewish prejudices. He also appealed to the various German governments to adopt legislation allowing civil marriage between Jew and Christian.[3] In sum, Lehmann struck the same compromise agreed to by his Reform predecessors. While he conceded that many of the visible traces of Jewish distinctiveness should be erased for the sake of integration, he insisted on retaining and strengthening the organized Jewish community. To that end he proposed building a framework in which local communities could share their experiences on problems of mutual concern.[4]

Lehmann's suggestion for a national organization won the quick support of the Board of the Leipzig Jewish Community, which decided to use the forthcoming synod of liberal rabbis and laymen in Leipzig to convene a simultaneous assembly (Gemeindetag) of communal leaders.[5] On April 22, 1869, the board sent the Jewish communities a circular inviting representatives to Leipzig on June 29, for the purpose of "uniting the communities of German Israel [*des deutschen Israels*] for the protection of common interests and the pursuit of common objectives." [6] Despite the fact that the synod and the Gemeindetag met simultaneously, the latter rejected a motion by the dean of the liberal rabbinate, Abraham Geiger, that the two conferences constitute a single body and instead declared itself an entirely separate institution. From three sessions an agreement emerged to form a national organization of German Jewish communities as soon as a membership of one hundred communities paying an annual total of 2,000 thalers (6,000 marks) had been reached. A provisional board was elected, with Moritz Kohner, the president of the Leipzig Community, as its chairman.[7]

The Gemeindetag considered a second problem, which reveals one of the reasons why Lehmann's proposal received such quick attention. Cholera and famine had recently aggravated the chronically impoverished condition of Russian Jewry imprisoned in the Pale of Settlement, and the illegal emigration of destitute Jews, unable to obtain a passport, mushroomed accordingly.[8] The delegates at Leipzig felt compelled either to organize this chaotic flight into and through Germany into an orderly transfer of Jews abroad or to attempt to negotiate with the Russian government their settlement in the Russian interior. They appointed Ludwig Philippson, the venerable editor of the weekly *Allgemeine Zeitung des Judentums,* to head a committee to elicit the cooperation of world Jewry.[9]

But it was not only the desire to stem the flow of Eastern Jews into Germany that moved the Gemeindetag to grapple with the complex problem of Russian Jewish emigration. A spirit of German nationalism also permeated the deliberations. For the Gemeindetag's initiative amounted to an effort by German Jews to supersede the French Alliance Israélite Universelle. This international Jewish defense organization had been founded in 1860 by seventeen French Jews in the wake of the kidnapping by papal police of Edgar Mortara, a six-year-old Jewish boy in Bologna who had allegedly been baptized by his governess during an illness some years before. Its objectives were to accelerate the emancipation and moral improve-

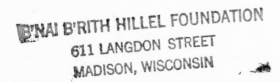

ment of "Israelites" the world over, and to assist those still subjected to persecution. By 1869 the Alliance had a membership of 11,364 Jews. Although its members were always organized into local chapters of ten or more, rather than into national bodies, the 1,712 German Jews constituted a national contingent surpassed only by that of the French. Nevertheless, with the seat of the Central Committee in Paris, the Alliance remained a distinctly French organization.[10] The tone of the deliberations in Leipzig in 1869 was unmistakably nationalistic. Not only were German Jews to guide the efforts to solve the Russian problem, but the prospective union of German Jewish communities in the future would aid Jews abroad independently. The Gemeindetag expressed its gratitude to the Alliance for its achievements, but, henceforth, its objectives would be incorporated in the program of the German association.[11]

The Alliance reacted swiftly. On October 12, 1869, several of its leaders met in Berlin with a few dozen notables of German Jewry to consider action on the problem of Russian Jewry. The outcome was an agreement to establish a committee in Königsberg (Hauptgrenz-comité) to alleviate conditions inside Russia and to organize all emigration. Although ten of the fifteen members were to reside in Königsberg, the committee would be financed by the Alliance.[12] Philippson, who had been diligently trying to organize local committees to raise funds for Russian Jewry in accord with the Gemeindetag's directive, was not even invited to the Alliance meeting. Not until November did the Königsberg Committee finally invite him to join, and then the two committees were merged.[13]

By January of 1870 the Alliance and the board of the prospective Gemeindebund had agreed upon their respective areas of operation. The Alliance would remain international in scope, while the Gemeindebund would confine itself to Jewish affairs in Germany.[14] Thereafter, the Gemeindebund treated only the internal manifestation of the Russian Jewish problem: the widespread and uncontrolled vagrancy of East European Jews over the German countryside which threatened to blemish the public image of Judaism and provided potential ammunition for anti-Semitic agitation. Almost immediately after the Alliance had put Philippson's committee out of business, his paper took up the problem of vagrancy, and its control became one of the major objectives of the Gemeindebund. During its first decade, the organization strove to close the doors of individual Jewish home-owners to pleas from unknown vagrants for charity. By establishing a central fund in each community, conducted along rationally accepted guidelines, and by carefully examining each applicant, the Gemeinde-bund hoped that it would be possible to aid the deserving while put-ting an end to begging as a permanent livelihood.[15]

Several disconcerting experiences during the Franco-Prussian War decisively altered the mood and motivation of the men still working to create the Gemeindebund. The deliberations before the war had focused exclusively upon defending and assisting Jews abroad. A similar concern for the status and rights of German Jewry at the time no longer seemed warranted. On July 3, 1869, the Reichstag of the North German Confederation had finally ended the long struggle for full emancipation by declaring the rights of citizenship and the hold-ing of public office wholly independent of religious affiliation.[16] Yet, at the very hour when Jewish soldiers were honorably serving the fa-therland, German Jewry was abruptly reminded that the ancient ani-mus still survived. Whereas the government had provided its Protes-tant and Catholic troops with military chaplains, it refused the same service to its Jewish soldiers, claiming that their small number were too widely dispersed for effective coverage. Only after the High Hol-idays of 1870 did the government finally agree to appoint three rab-bis as chaplains, and to provide them with free transportation, food, and quarters in enemy territory, although it refused to give them mil-itary rank or remuneration.[17] After the war the government again ig-nored the Jewish community in the conduct of official thanksgiving services.[18]

Still another incident at the beginning of 1871 provoked vehement Jewish protest. Aroused by the conversion of seven Berlin Christians to Judaism in one year, the highest authority of the Prussian Evan-gelical Church, the Oberkirchenrat in Berlin, had issued a declara-tion, "Concerning Conversion to Judaism." It instructed every minis-ter henceforth in case of a conversion to Judaism to announce the name of the apostate from the pulpit, to reprimand him for violating the words of the Gospel, and to move his people to pray that God might have mercy upon his soul. The Supreme Council asserted that the Church was not merely angered by the loss of a member, but far more by his conversion to a community that rejected God's son in his lifetime and continued to hate him to this day. The pronouncement was picked up and disseminated by the daily papers. The leaders of German Jewry were outraged at this revival of medieval religious hatred. The Board of the Berlin Jewish Community published an immediate protest. On February 25, 1871, a number of Berlin Christian notables, including nineteen city councilmen, followed suit with a public assurance to the Jewish community that the Christian population in no way shared the reprehensible sentiments of the Supreme Council. The widespread critical response finally compelled the council to explain that its action intended no attack against Judaism, but only against conversion, especially if motivated by materialistic reasons, as had allegedly been the case in the conversions that had originally aroused its ire.[19]

When the deliberations for the founding of the Gemeindebund were resumed after the war, the impact of these experiences was quite discernible. On April 20, 1869, Moritz Kohner addressed a meeting of communal representatives in Leipzig, and the major part of his speech dealt with what he felt ought to be the first objective of the new organization: to represent the interests of Jewry and Judaism before the various German governments and legislatures. With evident anger, Kohner depicted the disillusioning incidents that had emphasized the still unequal position of Judaism and the inadequacy of individual efforts to correct the situation: "If indeed according to the law we have the same rights, if in fact Jewry is emancipated, Judaism is still entirely ignored." [20]

Only a recognized spokesman for German Jewry could effectively remonstrate against such discrimination. Kohner contended that Judaism was entitled to the same government support as that given to the Evangelical and Catholic Churches. As long as the government ignored the principle of a free church in a free state, and Jewish taxes helped to fill church coffers, Jewish spokesmen should and would insist upon equal treatment.[21] Consequently, the 1872 constitution of the Gemeindebund declared its first objective to be the "protection of common interests by attention to all common concerns relating to the public legal status of the Jewish faith and its adherents in the German states." [22]

Despite this shift in motivation, a still more fundamental consideration permeated the deliberations both before and after the war. The idea of unity was in the air. Bismarck's skill had transformed an elusive dream into an intoxicating reality.[23] Other emancipated Jewish communities had already succeeded in uniting to defend their interests. Besides the Alliance Israélite Universelle, French Jewry still enjoyed the benefits of Napoleon I's consistorial system. The Board of Deputies of British Jews, a cooperative effort between the Sephardic and Ashkenazic communities, dating back to 1760, defended the political status of English Jewry. It had received official government recognition in 1836. In response to the Mortara case, even the small Jewish community of the United States had established in 1859 a Board of Deputies of American Israelites.[24] These precedents formed the background to the recurring appeals to unite, which punctuated the literature and deliberations on the Gemeindebund between 1869 and 1872.[25] Only German Jewry seemed unable to achieve any organizational unity under emancipation, and the consequences of its decentralized and fragmented structure were ominous. At the beginning of 1870, Kohner had stressed to a meeting of his provisional committee that the small and middle-sized communities were increasingly unable to meet the demands made upon their limited resources. The need for a national organization to subsidize their programs was urgent.[26]

This consideration was not prompted by the threat of any external enemy, but rather by genuine anxiety about the survival of an organized German Jewry. It was a concern that the leaders of the Gemeindebund articulated openly and passionately a few years later in their vigorous three-year campaign to thwart the pressure of German orthodoxy to weaken the 1847 requirement of compulsory membership in the local Jewish community. Although unequivocally forbidden by its own statutes to handle religious questions, the board of the Gemeindebund felt compelled from its inception to act in order to prevent a step that it believed threatened countless Jewish communities with dissolution.[27] In its final appeal of April 16, 1876, to Rudolph Gneist, the chairman of the Petitions Committee of the Prussian House of Deputies, the Gemeindebund delivered a moving affirmation of Jewish solidarity:

Viewed historically, the Jews are not only a religious community, but also a community of fate.

A several-thousand-year history of suffering has woven a band of solidarity around the Jews and created a feeling of unity in sorrow and joy in the heart of every Jew, as long as he still feels himself to be a Jew. This feeling of solidarity prepared and still prepares one for every sacrifice which the group [die Gesammtheit] requires.

Be this group inclusive or that which concerns a geographic fragment of the whole, i.e. the local community, whoever is a genuine Jew will make every sacrifice for the preservation of the whole, whether he is personally involved or not. He who is not capable of this sacrifice is spiritually bereft of that intensive historical feeling, and is in truth estranged from Judaism.[28]

CENTRIFUGAL FORCES

Although the very formation of the Gemeindebund embodied the intention to preserve Jewish group identity, the extended period required to form it, and the subsequent fluctuations in membership, reveal how little this sense of identity was shared by German Jewry at large. Between 1869 and 1872 the provisional board of the Gemeindebund had managed to win the promise of 113 communities to affiliate with the forthcoming organization, although only 49 sent representatives to the founding ceremonies in the Leipzig synagogue on April 14, 1872. At the second national convention of 1875, the attending delegates represented only 35 communities.[29] By the time of Kohner's death in 1877, the number of affiliated communities had fallen to 25, and only after intensive deliberation did Jacob Nachod, Kohner's successor as president of the Leipzig Community, who had assumed the leadership, decide against dissolving the ailing organization.[30] But even after the ensuing reorganization, the Gemeindebund recovered very slowly. Two years later the membership had risen to 131 communities, at a time when Germany may have harbored close to 2,000.[31] Writing an official history, in 1879, of the organization's first decade, Bernhard Jacobsohn, its secretary since March 1, 1874, noted how few Jewish communities knew anything about the only organization committed to their vital interests.[32] He concluded his account, obviously written to attract new support, with a direct plea to the "Israelite communities of Germany" to unite behind the Gemeindebund and defend the endangered rights of German Jewry.[33]

Organizational problems contributed to this unimpressive first decade. Essentially a community organization, whose representatives met in a national convention only once in three years, the Gemeindebund, as originally conceived, was to be led by a board whose seat would rotate among the large communities. Thus, five of the six members of the board came from Berlin, Dresden, Breslau, Nuremberg, and Fürth. In fact, however, the board never left Leipzig, and the major responsibilities devolved upon Kohner.[34] Moreover, the first president, a self-assured and domineering personality, rather intolerant of differing points of view, preferred to work alone.[35] This excessive concentration of responsibility proved almost fatal to the organization during Kohner's long terminal illness. The revised statutes adopted at the special convention convened in Leipzig on September 19, 1877, sought to correct the problem by making Leipzig the de jure seat of the board and stipulated that at least three of its five permanent members were to live in Leipzig.[36] The more accommodating character of Jacob Nachod, elected by the new board at its first meeting as the successor to Kohner, made a cooperative effort more likely.[37]

However, the centrifugal forces atomizing German Jewry would have undermined even the most effectively organized collective enterprise. The very location of the Gemeindebund in Leipzig epitomized the fragmented structure of German Jewry, whose obvious center of gravity lay in Berlin with a Jewish population of nearly 36,000 in 1873, and not in Leipzig which in 1873 had only 1,739 Jewish residents.[38] The meeting of communal representatives on April 20, 1871, had in fact entertained the notion of making Berlin the seat of the Gemeindebund, but Moritz Lazarus, the well-known ethnologist representing the Board of the Berlin Jewish Community, declined the honor. He reported that Berlin's earlier efforts to cooperate with other Jewish communities on issues of mutual concern had proven utterly fruitless.[39] In 1877 after Kohner's death, Nachod tried again to persuade the Berlin Board to permit the organization to settle in the German capital and to allow one of its members to assume the vacant presidency, but to no avail.[40] Only after the Saxon government had decreed that the Gemeindebund as then constituted would have to cease operating in Saxony, did Nachod succeed, and then only after arduous negotiations, in overcoming the still considerable opposition in Berlin. At the special convention of February 1882, the Gemeindebund finally found a permanent home in Berlin.[41]

Although direct evidence to explain the reservations of the Berlin Board is lacking, it appears likely that its consistent reluctance was a patent instance of the suspicion and jealousy exhibited by several large Jewish communities toward the Gemeindebund. One observer explained their refusal to join as stemming from the conviction that the large communities were fully capable of handling their own administrative, educational, and welfare needs, and therefore quite unenthusiastic over the prospect of financing an organization whose main benefactors would be the small Jewish communities.[42]

Beyond such pecuniary considerations, there operated also a jealous concern to protect the cherished religious autonomy of the local community. Every community zealously defended the freedom to interpret Judaism and to regulate its own religious practice and educational system. Indeed, even when local resources proved inadequate, few communities were eager to unite in a common cause at the expense of even the slightest degree of autonomy. According to one Leipzig correspondent in 1878, what had destined the Gemeindebund to such an inauspicious start "was its inherent tendency toward resolute centralization, which ran so counter to the character and actual conditions of the Jewish communities of Germany, that it was rendered ineffectual from the beginning." [43] Not only the program of the Gemeindebund, but every subsequent attempt at voluntary consolidation, had to contend with this ingrained and legally encouraged decentralization.[44]

The overwhelming majority of Germany's small Jewish communities likewise did not respond affirmatively to the appearance of the Gemeindebund. Not until the end of the 1880's did its membership begin to reach impressive proportions. According to its periodic *Mitteilungen,* in 1888 the Gemeindebund totaled 350 communities. A year later the figure had climbed to 399, and, with an additional fifty communities by 1892, the organization could claim to represent more than two-thirds of German Jewry. In 1893 the membership stood at 500 Jewish communities.[45] During these decades Orthodoxy still dominated the religious life of countless small Jewish communities. In the villages and hamlets, particularly of southern Germany, traditional observances continued to regulate the daily life of those who resisted the powerful attraction of the urban magnets.[46] Since the leaders of German Orthodoxy responded warily to the appearance of the Gemeindebund, their widely scattered rural adherents obviously refused to affiliate.

Both branches of German Orthodoxy—that led by Esriel Hildesheimer of Berlin and the other by Samson Raphael Hirsch of Frankfurt—opposed the formation of the Gemindebund. The fundamental obstacle proved to be the Reform associations connected with the original conception of the organization and its subsequent implementation. To Orthodox spokesmen, the unadulterated religious radicalism of Emil Lehmann's 1869 essay, the conjunction of the first assembly that same year with the liberal synod and the Reform leanings of the men who labored to bring the Gemeindebund to life, proved beyond a doubt the actual religious character of the organization. Kohner's direct written appeals in 1870 to Markus Lehmann, the editor of the weekly *Israelit,* which usually echoed the views of Hirsch, and a personal visit to Hildesheimer in 1871 did not allay these suspicions.[47] Consequently, Orthodox leaders absented themselves from the constituent convention of April 14, 1872. The *Israelit* in particular repudiated the convention's address to Bismarck, which expressed approval of the Chancellor's attack against Germany's "internal enemy", the Catholic Church. How could the Gemeindebund presume to interfere in an affair which did not concern it? How could it justify such unabashed hostility toward the members of another religion? Besides being astonishingly tactless, the declaration endangered the welfare of Jews living in the Catholic sections of the country.[48]

Moreover, from the Orthodox point of view the Gemeindebund's constitutional commitment to preserve compulsory membership in the local community implicitly contradicted the constitutional exclu-

sion of all religious questions from its competence. The deliberations
leading to the Gemeindebund had coincided with mounting Orthodox
agitation against compulsory membership, encouraged by an 1869 judicial decision in Baden which allowed several Orthodox members to
withdraw from the Reform-controlled community of Karlsruhe.[49]
Thus, from its inception, the Gemeindebund had assumed an anti-
Orthodox position on an issue the Orthodox passionately felt to be
religious.[50] Later the Gemeindebund openly intervened to counter
the assertions of Samson R. Hirsch regarding the existence of denominations in Judaism.[51] It asked the non-Orthodox rabbinical seminaries in Breslau, Berlin, and Vienna whether the religious differences dividing Jews could be construed as forming distinct
denominations. All three institutions agreed that the internal situation in Judaism was entirely different from that in Christianity, and
that existing conflicts could not be regarded as creating antagonistic
denominations.[52] In the judgment of the leaders of the Gemeindebund, the future of organized Judaism in Germany was at stake, and
the crisis fully justified this temporary sacrifice of the Gemindebund's
avowed religious neutrality. For three years the Gemeindebund pressured the Prussian bureaucracy and legislature with letters, resolutions, and petitions to maintain the legal unity of the individual Jewish community.[53]

The intervention of the Gemeindebund into this acrimonious
debate obviously did not enhance its appeal to the Orthodox. In
1877, when the Gemeindebund had almost died with its first president, Markus Lehmann offered neither aid nor consolation. Its imminent demise was sad, but there were too many basic disagreements to
permit cooperation.[54] A closing statement to his lengthy evaluation
exemplified the obstacles that awaited future national ventures in self-
defense:

If we come to speak of the difficulty of making positive suggestions for
the formation of a union of Jewish communities, we must limit this statement to the observation that we regard it as difficult, in fact impossible,
to find ways and means through which all Jewish communities could be
united in one body.[55]

By the 1880's the relations between the Orthodox and the Gemeindebund had improved considerably. German Orthodoxy was by

no means a monolithic body, and, as the recriminations over the Law of Withdrawal (*Austrittsgesetz*) subsided, the moderate wing led by Hildesheimer came to view more favorably at least some of the projects of the Gemeindebund.[56] Hildesheimer had been especially eager to cooperate when the Gemeindebund was being reorganized in Berlin in the winter of 1882. He insisted only that the new leadership must be truly representative of all religious groups and not merely a coterie of irreligious Berlin notables. But aside from Jacob Nachod, whom the *Jüdische Presse,* the Hildesheimer weekly in Berlin, had always respected, the new board evoked little confidence.[57] After Nachod's death, Samuel Kristeller, a personal friend of Hildesheimer, became the third president, a post he occupied till 1896. Although a knowledgeable Jew, who had translated didactic medieval Hebrew poetry and the *Ethics of the Fathers,* he was a devoted member of the Society for Ethical Culture and was heard by Hildesheimer to have said that he did not attend the synagogue even on the Day of Atonement.[58] By October 1885 Hildesheimer, in contrast to Hirsch, had become convinced that the administrative projects of the Gemeindebund—such as a pension for religious schoolteachers and the placing of Jewish apprentices with masters who would permit them to observe the Sabbath and festivals—were worthy of support. At the sixth national convention of the Gemeindebund in 1892, in which the representatives of Berlin Orthodoxy participated, Hildesheimer's son Hirsch, a lecturer at his father's rabbinical seminary in Berlin and an extraordinarily active participant in the organizational life of German Jewry, declared, "The points that unite us are plentiful; those that separate us, few." [59]

Thus, the divisive forces confronting the Gemeindebund in the early 1870's were formidable. It took two decades of selfless effort for the cause of national cooperation to finally overcome the resistance. The founders of this first nationwide organization were not unaware of the tortuous road that lay ahead. They acknowledged that in the near future the Gemeindebund would be unable to alleviate some of the most urgent communal and welfare needs—controlling Jewish vagrancy, strengthening Jewish education in the small communities, and creating pension funds for the families of deceased rabbis and teachers. The greatest achievement, in their view, was the formation

of the Gemeindebund itself, whose very existence offered a center
from which united action could be undertaken in vital matters of
common concern.[60]

RESURGENCE OF ANTI-SEMITISM

The recrudescence of anti-Semitism which accompanied the economic crash of 1873–74 created precisely such an issue. This international economic crisis began with the collapse of the stock market
in Vienna and New York in May and September of 1873. When it
hit Berlin in the Fall, it abruptly ended the industrial overexpansion
and proliferation of stock companies that had been set in motion by
the French indemnity of five billion francs. Stocks plummeted, companies closed, goods remained unsold, speculators lost their investments, and workers their jobs. It took the German economy fully six
years to recover at least part of its momentum.[61]

The dominant anti-capitalistic sentiment of German society indicted the Jews. The overwhelming majority of German Jewry had
fervently cheered the achievement of national unification,[62] and now,
but a few years later, anti-Semitic diatribes again singled out the
Jews as swindlers, aliens, and subversives. For the first few years the
anti-Semitic campaign against the evils of Jewish prominence was
confined to an intensive literary polemic. In 1873 Wilhelm Marr, an
unsuccessful journalist, published a pessimistic appraisal of German
chances, titled *The Victory of Judaism over Germanism.* It went
through twelve editions by 1879. Otto Glagau, a far more talented
journalist, followed in 1875 with a series of articles on "The Stock
Exchange and Speculation Fraud in Berlin" in the widely circulated
popular magazine, *Gartenlaube.* Glagau articulated the grievances of
the lower middle class whose livelihood was jeopardized by capitalism and liberalism. The culprit was the Jew, that alien parasite who
represented 90 percent of all speculators on the stock exchange and
dominated the Reichstag. These initial rumblings of Marr and Glagau soon reverberated in the pages of the *Kreuzzeitung* and *Ger-
mania,* the organs of the right wing of the Prussian Conservatives
and the Catholic Center, respectively.

On September 19, 1879, Adolf Stoecker, William I's court chaplain, took the issue directly to the people in a blistering attack upon the arrogance of German Jewry. Alongside his conservative Christian Social Party, there now sprang up a spate of new political groups committed solely to racial anti-Semitism: Marr's League of Anti-Semites (1879), whose name introduced to the German public the recently coined term, anti-Semitism; Ernst Henrici's Social Reich Party (1880); Alexander Pinkert's German Reform Party in Dresden; and Förster's and Sonnenberg's German People's Association (1881).[63] Several academic personalities added a useful aura of intellectual respectability to the spreading political movement. Since the 1850's Paul de Lagarde, the brilliant and irascible Biblical scholar, had called for the birth of a Germanic Christianity cleansed of all Jewish dross. Cassandra-like, he now thundered against the ominous "Judaization" of Germany.[64] At the end of 1879 the nationalist historian of nineteenth-century Germany, Heinrich Treitschke, vindicated the current agitation in the *Preussische Jahrbücher* by accusing the Jews of failure to fulfill the terms of emancipation. Two years later Eugen Dühring, a lecturer in philosophy and economics, provided the first important theoretical statement of racial anti-Semitism in his book, *The Jewish Question as a Question of Race, Morality and Culture.*[65]

During 1880 and 1881 Förster, Sonnenberg, and Henrici circulated a petition entitled "The Emancipation of the German People from the Yoke of Jewish Rule," and ultimately intended for Bismarck. It demanded the suspension, or at least the limitation, of Jewish immigration, the exclusion of Jews from government positions of authority, the preservation of the Christian character of the *Volksschule,* and the revival of a Jewish census. Thousands of copies were sent to editors, mayors, judges, economic associations, and district and local government officials throughout Germany, while members of the Social Reich Party and the German People's Association gathered as many signatures as possible.[66]

The increasing momentum of the anti-Jewish campaign finally forced the liberals to break their silence. On November 13 and 14, 1880, the leading Berlin papers carried a declaration, inspired by Maximilian Forckenbeck, the Lord Mayor, and Theodor Mommsen, the great authority on the history of ancient Rome, inveighing against the rampant hatred which threatened to shatter the urgent process of national and religious reconciliation. Its seventy-three esteemed Christian signatories included the Lord Mayor and Mayor of Berlin, seventeen university professors, fifteen members of the Berlin Chamber of Commerce, ten municipal officials, nine lawyers, six legislators, five higher bureaucrats, four school directors, three Evangelical clergy, and two physicians. A few days later a Progressive interpellation in the Prussian House of Deputies on the attitude of the government toward the petition provoked a two-day debate on the "Jewish Question." Although the government refused to take a specific stance on the particulars of the petition, since it had not yet been submitted, it did reaffirm its commitment to the constitutional guarantee of religious equality.[67]

To refute the anti-Semitic assertions that the majority of Germans were rapidly losing confidence in the judgment of their representatives, the Landtag members from Berlin decided to convene the body of Berlin electors. Elections to the Prussian lower house, the Chamber of Deputies, were indirect. The electorate of a district, unevenly divided into three classes according to the level of personal income tax, elected, without secret ballot, a body of electors who in turn chose the representatives to sit in the Chamber. On the evening of January 12, 1881, 2,500 Berlin electors condemned the anti-Semites for defiling the honor of the German capital and Empire. They declared that only the harmonious cooperation of all sectors of the society, regardless of religion, could ensure the welfare of the German Reich.[68]

Despite these countermeasures, the signatures for the petition continued to accumulate. On April 13, 1881, the petition was delivered to Bismarck with an alleged total of 225,000 names, including 45,-000 from Silesia, 30,000 from Brandenburg, 27,000 from Westphalia, 20,000 from the Rhineland, and 9,000 from Bavaria. But the Chancellor did no more than acknowledge its receipt.[69]

The months of verbal agitation finally incited a series of anti-Jewish outbursts. On February 18, 1881, the old but unsightly synagogue of the small Jewish community in Neustettin (Pomerania) was put to flames. The anti-Semitic agitators accused the Jews of burning their own synagogue to collect the insurance to pay for a new one. Several months later, in July, anti-Jewish riots erupted in Neustettin and spread rapidly to other communities in the provinces of West Prussia, Pomerania, and Brandenburg. This time the government intervened decisively. The Minister of Interior forbade all anti-Semitic speeches in Pomerania and West Prussia. Rioters were arrested and punished, and the municipalities were ordered to compensate their Jewish residents for damages suffered.[70]

JEWISH COUNTERMEASURES:
LEGAL DEFENSE

The first objective, broadly stated in the statutes of the Gemeindebund—to protect the common interests of German Jewry —had suddenly assumed a painfully specific relevance. A common danger had transformed this single national organization into the likely headquarters from which a coordinated defense could be mounted.

But in the mid-1870's the leaders of the Gemeindebund were deeply embroiled in the fight over the impending *Austrittsgesetz,* and they responded slowly to the emergence of this new danger. More than two years after the initial explosion, in September 1875, they finally adopted a resolution to implement the intention of their statutes: As the only overall representative of the Jewish communities of Germany, the Gemeindebund must utilize every legal recourse to end the vituperation of the anti-Semitic press.[71] The same resolve characterized the slightly revised statutes of 1877, which called for "attention to all common concerns relating to the legal and social status of the adherents of the Jewish faith and defense against attacks upon the same." [72]

To their dismay, the leaders of the Gemeindebund soon learned how ineffectual a protection the legal system actually provided. Between the Gemeindebund and the courts stood the Office of Public Prosecution (Staatsanwaltschaft), an institution stemming from the French Revolution. Its original objective had been to divide the roles of prosecutor and judge, which the medieval inquisitorial system had

united, and its adoption in Germany was one of the basic planks in
the program of the liberals during the first half of the nineteenth century. By 1860 nearly every state had incorporated some modified
form of the institution. The Imperial Code of Criminal Procedure,
which became effective on October 1, 1879, created a uniform procedure of public prosecution in criminal cases throughout the Reich.
Thereafter, the public prosecutor exercised a near monopoly on the
right to bring charges (*Anklagemonopol der Staatsanwaltschaft*),
which meant that, in order to prosecute, a plaintiff had first to demonstrate to the public prosecutor that a crime had indeed occurred.
Only after having been apprised and convinced of a possible crime
was the public prosecutor bound by law to press charges (*Legalitäts-
prinzip*). In the event of failure to satisfy the public prosecutor, the
plaintiff could bring charges himself, but only in a very limited number of criminal cases, such as libel and bodily injury. Although theoretically such a direct appeal to the courts was of equal weight, it
clearly entailed greater financial and personal risks to the plaintiff.[73]

It soon became apparent to the leaders of the Gemeindebund that
the public prosecutor loomed as the major obstacle to bringing anti-
Semites into court, for in most appeals he found no evidence of a violation. Only in the most serious instances did the Gemeindebund actually submit a number of appeals, but the majority of these were
rejected with a legal reasoning its leaders felt would never have been
risked with another religious group. In one instance the Gemeindebund challenged pamphlets that had been distributed in Berlin before
an election and which condemned voting for Jewish candidates. The
public prosecutor contended that the pamphlets in question contained
no provocation to class riot, that Jews were attacked as a race or ethnic group and not as a religious community, and that the law did not
consider derision as defamation.[74]

In the beginning the Gemeindebund did occasionally register a victory. In 1876 it won a conviction against a Paderborn publisher for
the publication and distribution of an anonymous anti-Semitic pamphlet revealingly titled *Not a Jew-hunt but a Christian-defense*. On
the basis of Section 166 of the Criminal Code, which prohibited the
defamation of the institutions (*Einrichtungen*) or practices of an incorporated religious group, the court confiscated those copies it could

locate and sentenced the publisher to a stiff six-month confinement. But the pamphlet was immediately republished in a corrected second edition.[75] As the anti-Jewish hysteria spread, public prosecutors became noticeably less responsive to the briefs of the Gemeindebund.[76]

In 1878 Emil Lehmann clashed with the board of the Gemeindebund over the best way to fight the multiplying defamations. Since prosecutors and judges were now rarely returning favorable decisions, he recommended pushing for a legislative revision of the press laws. The minutes of the meeting at which Lehmann offered his suggestion do not record the reasons for the board's disagreement. What is entirely apparent, though, is the board's deepening perplexity over what action to take. Some advised resuming a more aggressive judicial assault against the national organs of the anti-Semitic press; others urged the Gemeindebund to concentrate upon appealing to Jews to avoid any provocative behavior that could feed or justify gentile animosity. The meeting ended without decision.[77]

At the third national convention in Leipzig on April 11, 1880, Lehmann spoke bitterly of the government's indifference toward the agitators, contending that it was the responsibility of the government to punish those who incite to class riot (Sec. 130) or slander the sacred practice and heritage of a corporate religious body (Sec. 166); that when the government was unwilling, private initiative was useless, and even dangerous if it resulted in acquittal.[78] According to Jacobsohn writing in 1879, the official defense policy of the DIGB was now "without appealing to the public prosecutor . . . to influence the large masses solely through educational and enlightening materials." Private suits were entirely rejected as an affront to the dignity of Judaism and the Gemeindebund.[79] Not all accepted the board's increasing caution. In the Spring of 1881 a Leipzig lawyer who had sent from Berlin a number of legal briefs to the board for endorsement finally condemned its policy. The board, he indicated, had recently refused to sign a denunciation against an anti-Semitic weekly. Accusing it of a timidity which rendered it worthless in the fight against anti-Semitism, he rejected further cooperation because their views on the subject differed so radically.[80]

Despite their apprehension over the contagious character of the unrest, the leaders of the Gemeindebund, during the closing months of 1880 and the first months of 1881, became steadily more reluctant to fight anti-Semitism publicly.[81] At the end of November 1880, the board sent to its representatives throughout Germany a confidential circular advising that municipal and state authorities be contacted personally to convince them not to aid, but rather to oppose, the anti-Semitic petition. Local representatives were also advised to try to prevent the public airing of the "Jewish Question" in newspapers and meetings, and particularly to prevent any self-appointed spokesman from indiscretion. The board advised personal exchanges with individual Christians as a more effective alternative.[82]

A few months later, in July 1881, the board again advised restraint. It had been encouraged by the reports of its men throughout the country, who generally agreed that anti-Semitism had failed to strike roots except in a few politically and religiously conservative centers like Berlin, Breslau, Dresden, and certain districts of Westphalia and Pomerania. Nevertheless, the close relations with government circles enjoyed by the anti-Semites gave the movement considerable strength. The repudiation of anti-Semitism by the Crown Prince and Christian liberals had not yet stemmed the tide. The Gemeindebund proposed, therefore, that Jews should not appeal to the Kaiser, Chancellor, Reichstag, or any minister, nor should they precipitate any further debate in the legislatures. The prospects for favorable action appeared too slim. Similarly, all public discussion of the problem was to be avoided, because such attention tended to distort the dimensions of the movement.[83]

APOLOGETICS

A far less controversial measure of public defense, which the Gemeindebund continued to employ in the 1880's even after it had relinquished its active role in fighting anti-Semitism,[84] concentrated upon enlightening public opinion about the history and religion of the Jews. In stating the significance of this measure at the 1882 convention in Berlin, David Honigmann, one of the founders of the Gemeindebund and an admirer of Geiger, recapitulated what had been one of the fundamental objectives in Germany of the scientific study of the Jewish past:

What is most important for me is not the promotion of scholarship for its own sake, but rather the promotion of scholarship as a means for spreading correct opinions about Judaism in Jewish and non-Jewish circles; and in this regard I believe that all the attacks and persecutions of the last years essentially have their roots in the ignorance about the actual conditions, fundamentals, and achievements of Judaism.[85]

Pamphlets were commissioned and distributed. Thus, in 1879, the Gemeindebund produced a seventeen-page pamphlet titled *Has Judaism Abetted the Disgraceful Practice of Usury?*, which surveyed the relevant passages from Jewish literature from the Bible to the modern era. The board sent it to local authorities, clergymen, teachers, and some leading citizens, and even managed to have lengthy excerpts published in such local newspapers as the *Schlesische Presse* in Breslau and the *Württembergische Landeszeitung*. The Orthodox *Israelit,* however, objected. It insisted that the Talmud was not a development of Biblical law, nor had the rabbis of the Middle Ages intended to abrogate the Biblical prohibition against lending on interest to another Jew, as the pamphlet proclaimed. The review warned German Jewry not to entrust its holiest possessions to irreligious spokesmen.[86]

The Gemeindebund also invested a considerable amount of money in the distribution of apologetic literature written by Christians. In an 1876 issue of Westermann's *Illustrierten deutschen Monatsheften* there had appeared an unusually sympathetic article by a renowned German Christian botanist, Matthias Jakob Schleiden, on "The Significance of the Jews for the Preservation and Revival of Science in the Middle Ages." The Gemeindebund had the essay reprinted, and by 1877, 1,500 of the 2,250 copies had already been sold. Two years later in the same journal, Schleiden published an equally favorable treatment on "The Romance of Martyrdom among the Jews in the Middle Ages," which, at the suggestion of Heinrich Graetz, the dean of contemporary Jewish historians, the Gemeindebund reprinted and circulated.[87]

David Kaufmann, one of Graetz's most gifted students, explained the importance of Schleiden's two essays in an article written in 1878, but not published until 1891. Despite the fact that Jewish scholars had labored in the scientific study of the Jewish past for more than half a century, the Christian academic world stubbornly continued to ignore their conclusions. Not a single chair of Judaica existed in all of Germany, and few Christian savants were qualified to speak on the subject. For gentiles, the main sources on the Talmud and Judaism remained the prejudiced works of sixteenth- and seventeenth-century Christian Hebraists. The work of Jewish scholars entered the purview of Christian students only when it was restated by a sympathetic Christian spokesman, and this was the function of Schleiden's essays. Inadvertently discovering the role the Jews had played in medieval intellectual history, he undertook a serious study of medieval Jewish history. His own research was not original, but he did introduce the pioneering studies of Zunz, Steinschneider, and Graetz to the learned Christian world. Kaufmann closed with the hope that some day ignorance in Jewish matters would be held as contemptible as any other form of ignorance. From the academic world such informed views would then percolate down to the people to effect an ultimate reconciliation.[88]

By far the most ambitious and substantive effort made by the Gemeindebund to improve the public image of German Jewry came in 1885. On October 19 three members of the board met with three Christian medieval historians—Wilhelm Wattenbach and Julius Weizächer of the Royal Academy of Science, and Otto Stobbe, Professor of Law at the University of Leipzig—and three Jewish medievalists —Harry Bresslau and Ludwig Geiger of the University of Berlin, and Hermann Bärwald, the Director of the Jewish *Realschule* in Frankfurt-am-Main. This group constituted itself as the Historical Commission of the Deutsch-Israelitischer Gemeindebund with Bresslau as its president. That same month the Gemeindebund issued a pronouncement drafted by Bresslau, which explained the purpose of the commission. Since Stobbe's 1866 history of *The Jews in Germany During the Middle Ages,* no progress had been made. The regional and communal histories that had appeared were not the work of trained historians. Their authors had failed to utilize all the available sources, and lacked the critical tools to evaluate those they did.

In addition, their works suffered from the same shortcoming exhibited by all Jewish histories to date; namely, the failure to treat the history of German Jewry as an integral part of the overall history of Germany. Only within this framework could it in fact be correctly understood and evaluated. The objective of the commission, the statement concluded, was to make the writing of such a history eventually possible by systematically collecting, translating, and interpreting all Hebrew and non-Hebrew sources dealing with the history of the Jews in Germany, along the model of the *Monumenta Germaniae Historica*. The more immediate relevance of such a collection, one may surmise, was to provide irrefutable evidence of the antiquity of Jewish life in Germany. The allegedly alien character of the German Jew was to be proven a charge without substance, and in the process Jewish sources might even offer material on the medieval history of Germany as well.[89]

The conspicuous omission of any reputable German Jewish medieval historian of the stature of Heinrich Graetz, David Cassel, or Abraham Berliner not only provoked immediate controversy in Jewish circles, but also provided a hint at another objective of the project. A few years later, in 1889, at the fifth national convention of the Gemeindebund, Bresslau explicitly declared in a report that the commission sought to end the domination of Jewish historiography by theologians and orientalists; that the writing of Jewish history lagged three hundred years behind modern historiography, because it was still subservient to theological guidelines. He also decried its esoteric character, adding that Jewish historians consistently failed to translate their Hebrew sources, and the texts consequently remained unavailable to German historians. But he reserved his harshest words for the tendentious, apologetic nature of the enterprise. Echoing the criticism of Treitschke against Graetz, he denounced the practice of judging great non-Jewish figures on the basis of their attitude toward Judaism: "That created a lot of bad blood, and I can assure you that within the learned circles of historians it was one of the factors which led many into the camp of anti-Semitism." [90] In order to demonstrate immediately the objectivity of the commission, both Christian and Jewish scholars had been invited.[91]

The conception of the commission was therefore inextricably related to the Treitschke-Graetz controversy of 1879–80, especially since Bresslau, its president, had at the time conceded to Treitschke, in an obsequious essay, that many Jews were still not Germans. He had reminded his academic colleague, however, that the Jews had been fully emancipated only in 1869, and one should rather marvel that so many had already become good Germans. In a later response, Bresslau admitted that the unhealthy elements of German Jewry did indeed contribute to the spread of anti-Semitism—a conclusion which had prompted Treitschke to speak out in the first place—and he promised that Jewish efforts to eradicate them would continue.[92]

Graetz was obviously unacceptable to a commission determined to overthrow the ruling clique of German Jewish historians. Pressure by the Board of the Berlin Community to expand its membership yielded only a change in name to the Historical Commission for the History of Jews in Germany. Thereafter, the Gemeindebund's involvement was limited to administering its funds.[93]

In trying to mediate the conflict over Graetz, Samuel Kristeller, the president of the Gemeindebund and a close friend of Graetz, expressed yet a third objective of the commission. For the first time, he wrote to a friend in October 1885, a field had been found in which Jewish and non-Jewish scholars could work together for the benefit of both scholarship and fatherland; amid the present tensions this was a partnership of social and political significance. Later that month, in another letter, he reiterated the point. To preserve this harmonious relationship, all polemics had to be excluded, and thus neither the presence of Treitschke nor Graetz could possibly further the work of the commission.[94]

The life span of the commission was brief. At the end of 1892 Bresslau announced in the last number of its historical journal that the commission was about to disband, because the necessary funds were no longer forthcoming. Although few had risen to defend Graetz back in 1880, the Jewish community had generally not approved of the plan to oust the present "apologetic theologians" who dominated the field of Jewish history, with the result that the contributions steadily diminished.[95] Nevertheless, the commission did succeed in conceiving and promoting a number of important textual studies, which unquestionably enriched the sources available to later historians of German Jewry.[96]

SELF-CRITICISM

The Gemeindebund endeavored to reach three distinct groups with the tactics it gropingly developed to combat anti-Semitism. The appeal to the courts aimed at silencing the anti-Semites. The apologetical literature stated the Jewish case to the still large body of uncommitted Germans. In addition, the Gemeindebund periodically addressed itself to the Jewish community. The tenor of this address to the Jews was largely determined by the widely shared conviction that the tactless and insolent behavior of many Jews precipitated much of the current anti-Semitic furor.[97] The self-criticism which suffused this message reflected the self-image that German Jews had come to adopt during the battle for emancipation.

Ludwig Jacobowski's 1891 novel, *Werther, der Jude,* sharply delineated the details of this self-image. It is the story of a young uprooted and assimilated Jewish student at the University of Berlin, who cringes at the financial operations of his father, a small-town banker, and his Eastern European cousin. How grievously must the young generation suffer for the sins of its fathers! With angry shame he berates the character defects and unscrupulous practices of his uncultured family. Anti-Semitism is indeed based upon fact and can only be overcome by a drastic ethical reformation of the entire Jewish community. It would take another decade of disillusionment before a more militant generation of defense leaders would jettison this self-accusing assumption.[98]

At the peak of the anti-Semitic agitation in December of 1880, the Gemeindebund sent out a document titled "An Address of the Board to Co-religionists in Germany" on the subject of "how a Jew is to handle himself in regard to the anti-Semitic movement." In nine statements (in the original draft written by Emil Lehmann there had been ten) the German Jew is advised as to the proper behavior during the present crisis. He must avoid every display of arrogance, su-

periority, aggressiveness, and ostentation. If possible, he should take
up a craft; if not, he should support efforts to see that others do. All
business is to be conducted honestly and conscientiously, regardless
of the customer's religion. Any deceit or lie is a desecration of the
name of God, and those guilty should be ostracized. One should not
associate exclusively with Jews: yet in seeking Christian company
one should not be aggressive. Conflicts and disputations are to be
avoided; when unavoidable, one should answer without insult. Duels
are despicable, the vestige of medieval barbarism. The religious beliefs and practices of non-Jews are never to become the object of jest
or sarcasm. Jews must remain faithful and active sons of the fatherland, working for the common good personally as well as financially.
Above all, let Jews see in their present pain a touch of Providence
guiding them toward self-improvement.[99]

The address did not please all members of the board. As on an
earlier occasion, some feared that the document would supply the
anti-Semites with ammunition. But this time the majority accepted
the opinion of Nachod that its effect would indeed be salutary, because Christians could now see that Jews were not oblivious to their
own shortcomings. The address was intentionally given the widest
circulation. By January of 1881, 5,000 copies had been sent out. Its
reception in non-Jewish circles was favorable. A number of papers
reported its content with praise; some even printed the entire text.
Nachod urged the members of the Gemeindebund to influence their
local papers to do likewise. He hoped thereby to bring it to the attention of many Jews who never read a Jewish newspaper.[100]

DEPARTURE FROM LEIPZIG

Since its earliest deliberations on how to counter German anti-Semitism, the Gemeindebund had been anxious over its lack of corporate
status. At the 1875 meeting in Kohner's house, at which the board
resolved to resort to the offices of public prosecution and the courts,
Emil Lehmann succeeded in having a second resolution passed to the
effect that, as long as the Gemeindebund lacked the status of a juridical person, it would cooperate closely with the sole Jewish body that

did—the individual Jewish community.[101] Two years later Lehmann wrote to the Saxon Minister of Interior on behalf of the Gemeindebund, formally requesting incorporation so that his organization could increase its financial resources by inheriting legacies. Lehmann argued that its present limited income prevented the Gemeindebund from effectively aiding the local institutions of Jewish education. It is very likely that another motive was to strengthen its hand against anti-Semitism. In any event, the Minister of Interior denied the request. He added ominously that according to a Saxon law of 1850 any organization handling public matters could form local chapters and enter into relations with organizations elsewhere in Germany only after being incorporated. In a personal meeting with the Minister, Lehmann argued that the term "public matters" used in the law meant politics. The Minister disagreed, implying that the Gemeindebund's occupation with anti-Semitism was a public matter.[102]

From the surviving documents, it seems as if the issue was ignored by both sides until the Summer of 1881, when the Minister of Interior again pressed for compliance. This time Nachod submitted a revised constitution in an effort to convince the authorities that the Gemeindebund deserved incorporation. On December 16, 1881, the Saxon Minister sent a final decisive rejection which was buttressed by four wholly new arguments. First, it was not at all apparent why the already incorporated Jewish communities of Saxony needed such an organization. Secondly, it was clear even from the suggested revisions that the Gemeindebund was operating in certain areas of public life that the government had already placed under the supervision of its own agencies, and such competition was not welcome. Thirdly, the fact that many of the Gemeindebund's members lived beyond the borders of Saxony made it impossible for the Saxon authorities, who were being requested to grant the corporate status, to supervise them. And, finally, the government was concerned that an organization of this type might disrupt the religious harmony of society.[103]

At the special convention convened in Berlin in February 1882 to approve a new constitution, Nachod attempted to counter the widely held impression that anti-Semitism had motivated the decision. He insisted that the Saxon government could not legally permit the Gemeindebund to continue functioning in Leipzig without incorpora tion. However, Nachod's defense convinced no one.[104] Lehmann, Jacobsohn, and the author of an unpublished fifty-year history of the Gemeindebund, when they came to speak of this episode later, readily attributed the decision to anti-Semitism.[105] Corroboration of their opinion comes from an unexpected source.

In 1879 the Gemeindebund had appealed to the Saxon Minister of Justice to prosecute Alexander Pinkert (writing under the pseudonym, Egon Waldegg) as the author of a widely circulated anti-Semitic pamphlet.[106] But the public prosecutor in Dresden found no grounds for legal action. The indictment of Jews and Judaism for a low standard of morality, he contended, was confirmed by respectable German authorities and the welfare of the state dictated that the situation be corrected. In June of 1881, the Gemeindebund submitted a second request for prosecution, this time citing mainly the passages taken from Rohling's notorious *Talmudjuden*. The publisher responded with a brief which included opinions offered by, among others, Stoecker and Rohling. This time the case reached the State Court in Dresden before it was lost. What is relevant to the problem at hand is that the publisher in 1883 printed a small volume of some of the documents pertaining to the case. In the introduction he suggested in underlined print that the fruitless efforts of the Gemeindebund to acquire the rights of a juridical person were not unrelated to the accusations brought against Waldegg's pamphlet.[107]

In fact, it seems entirely likely that the Gemeindebund's decision to challenge Pinkert a second time in the Summer of 1881 proved fatal, for by then Pinkert had succeeded in building a solid political base for his cause. In 1880 he had founded in Dresden the German Reform Party, whose mixture of anti-liberalism, anti-capitalism, and anti-Semitism attracted those sectors of the middle class who suffered most directly from the financial crash and the swift industrialization which characterized the Saxon economy in particular.[108] In the Landtag elections of July 1881, the new party emerged as a political force to be reckoned with. Emil Lehmann, running as a Progressive candidate for the Dresden seat that he had held since 1875, lost to an anti-Semitic-backed Conservative opponent, and Pinkert's party triumphantly claimed credit for a victory which no anti-Semitic party in Berlin had yet achieved.[109] Thus, when the Gemeindebund moved against Pinkert again in the Summer of 1881, it was now contending with a political figure whose party claimed title to the leadership of the anti-Semitic movement in Germany. Very likely, in response to pressure from Dresden's growing anti-Semitic forces, the Saxon government resolved to invoke an old statute against the Gemeindebund which it had formerly chosen to ignore.

That Saxony became a center of German racial anti-Semitism at the beginning of the 1880's was certainly not due to the size of its Jewish population, which in 1895 amounted to only .26 percent of the total,[110] but rather to its composition. Of all German states, Saxony consistently harbored a Jewish population with the largest percentage of foreign-born Jews. In 1880, 15.3 percent of its Jewish inhabitants were born abroad, and by 1910 the percentage had risen to 59 percent.[111] A rapidly industrializing state in eastern Germany, and long a center of international fairs, Saxony loomed as an attractive haven to oppressed Jews further east. To make it less inviting, the Saxon government in 1892 became the first and only German state to deny Jews the right of kosher slaughtering by ordering that all animals must first be stunned.[112] The composition of Saxon Jewry, therefore, provided a specious validity to the xenophobic motif of German anti-Semitism, and it comes as no surprise that Dresden and Leipzig were the only large urban centers where anti-Semitism steadily thrived.[113] In the 1893 Reichstag elections in which the anti-Semitic parties registered their most impressive gains to date—a total of 263,861 votes out of 7,673,976, and 16 candidates out of 397—Saxony supplied more than one-third of each— 97,246 votes and 6 candidates.[114] Slightly more than one-third of the Saxon anti-Semitic vote came from Dresden.[115] Thus, the first organized Jewish defense effort fell victim to the ominous alliance between political anti-Semitism and the German authorities.[116]

Nachod had anticipated the negative reply of the Minister of Interior, and in October of 1881 he approached the president of the Board of the Berlin Jewish Community about shifting the home of the Gemeindebund. Berlin responded with doubts and objections. As will become clear from its policy toward the Lazarus Committee, the Berlin representatives were reluctant to support any public opposition to anti-Semitism. One can surmise that the treatment of the

Gemeindebund by the Saxon government only confirmed their apprehension. Nachod's plea was finally heard, but when the Gemeindebund reappeared in Berlin in February 1882, its sole avowed purpose had become the strengthening of the administrative, educational, and welfare institutions of the German Jewish communities.[117]

2

CONTINUED AMBIVALENCE:
THE 1880's

GERMAN JEWS ATTEMPTED yet a second coordinated response to the first widespread eruption of anti-Semitism in the Second Reich. Das jüdische Comité vom 1 Dezember 1880, formed in Berlin at the end of 1880 under the direction of Moritz Lazarus, proved to be an even less effectual venture than that of the Gemeindebund. It soon collapsed without the need for outside interference. What distinguished both ventures was the striking gap between the intensity of the assault and the modesty of the response. Both the Gemeindebund and the committee were undermined by an ambivalence which German Jewry would resolve only when confronted by yet a second unexpected wave of Jew-hatred in the early 1890's. The historical significance of these early unsure countermeasures is the insight they provide into the factors inhibiting a perplexed Jewry from resorting to determined resistance. The records of the Gemeindebund during the first decade and the short-lived Lazarus Committee suggest the communal problems and intellectual reservations which paralyzed German Jewry. Both factors together effectively thwarted any decisive response.

THE BERLIN MOVEMENT

The most successful early penetration of organized anti-Semitism into the arena of German politics came in Berlin at the end of the 1870's. Adolf Stoecker, the politically minded court chaplain of William I, provided the indispensable leadership. Having failed to woo the Berlin proletariat away from the Social Democrats with the gospel of Christian Socialism, Stoecker directed the attention of his Christian Social Workers' Party to the Jewish question. On September 19, 1879, he began his courtship of some of the other discontented elements of society—traders, artisans, shopkeepers, and civil servants—with an address to a party rally demanding of German Jewry "a little more modesty, a little more tolerance, a little more equality." Buttressed in November 1879 by the grave diagnosis of Treitschke, and flanked by the racial agitators, Stoecker founded the Berlin Movement, a loosely organized anti-Semitic body of Christian and Conservative state socialists. Its coordinating body was the Central Committee of the Conservative Party. The Movement transformed the atmosphere of the city. On several occasions during the excited months of 1880–81, Stoecker delivered his harangues to mass meetings of two to three thousand cheering supporters. Scenes of disorder and violence greeted the new year of 1881.

The Reichstag elections of 1881 brought still further gains. For four of the six Reichstag seats of Berlin the Conservatives ran well-known anti-Semites, including Stoecker. Although the Progressives won all six seats, Stoecker managed to raise the Conservative vote in Berlin from 14,000 in 1878, to 46,000. The Progressives clearly retained control over their Progressive stronghold in the capital, but the Conservatives did replace the Social Democrats, restricted by Bismarck's discriminatory laws, as the second largest party in the city. Stoecker himself was beaten by the eminent Progressive, Rudolph Virchow, though he captured another Reichstag seat in Siegen, Westphalia.

During the next three years, Stoecker reached the peak of his turbulent career, and the Junker-dominated Conservatives, by appealing to anti-Semitic prejudices, seemed on the verge of building a grass-roots political organization. But the Reichstag elections of 1884 presaged the Movement's loss of impetus. In Berlin the Conservatives dropped again to third place, behind the Progressives (71,000) and the Social Democrats (68,000)—though they increased their vote to 56,000—and Stoecker lost for a second time to Virchow in a dramatic run-off election.[1]

MOUNTING ANXIETY

The reactions of many Jews to this revival of medieval hatred betrayed anxiety and disillusionment. The decade that had heralded Jewry's fondest hopes for complete acceptance closed with a painful German backlash. The most assimilated were the most aggrieved. Many of the old Jewish families of Berlin had abandoned all forms of Jewish observance. They had raised their children with a Christian religious education or no religious instruction whatsoever. Every trait that marked one as a Jew was expunged and the rebuke that "that is Jewish" was taken as the most severe kind of criticism. And now suddenly they were bluntly reminded that they were still Jews and still unacceptable. Years later a sensitive observer recalled the diametrically different Jewish responses.

The effect on the relationship of the individual Jew to Judaism was to a certain extent a radicalizing one. Many who till then had given little thought to their origins remembered them once again, turned back to their people [Stammesgemeinschaft] again out of a sense of injured pride and honor, interceded for them and sought out again the old forgotten values. Others preferred to hide their head in the sand, not to let themselves be recognized. Only now a really dishonorable assimilation began which ended either in getting baptized or having one's children baptized.[2]

Hermann Robinow, a wealthy and fully assimilated Hamburg importer-exporter, momentarily exemplified the first type. His diary betrays not the slightest attachment to Judaism. The only religious holidays to be noted were Christmas and Easter. And yet on March 14, 1880, he recorded his perplexity at the outburst of an irrational hatred which "people in our *soi disant* enlightened age and in our *soi disant* enlightened Germany scarcely considered still possible . . .

nonsense which people long figured as buried, without foundation, without a goal, without a purpose." The result was that "people like us, who have actually not identified themselves as Jews for a long time and considered themselves as successfully assimilated, are naturally again compelled to assist those being oppressed." [3]

Gustav Maier, a Jewish writer from southern Germany, confessed that his former optimism about the possibility of rapid integration had been severely tempered. Freed from the oppression of the Middle Ages, many idealistic Jews had stood ready to enter the temple of the universal religion of the heart, to which the sundry religions formed mere vestibules. They rushed in only to find it empty. Their friends had intended that their entry be but a passage into yet another vestibule. Now it was abundantly clear that Jews would still have to wait a few centuries in their particular anteroom before they would be greeted by others in the common sanctuary of mankind.[4]

The intensely personal disillusionment of Berthold Auerbach received wide attention in the contemporary Jewish press, for the anguish of this gifted Jewish chronicler of German peasant life in the Black Forest seemed to speak for many.[5] To have devoted sixty-four years of work for Germany only to be told at the end that one is not German, to have lived and labored in vain—these were the thoughts that punctuated the correspondence of the three years before his death on February 8, 1882.[6] In January 1880, he had even thought of convening a large public gathering to protest against the swelling agitation. Shortly before his death he told Fritz Mauthner, the drama critic and one of the editors of the *Berliner Tageblatt:* "Life no longer charms me; I conceal in my heart untold grief and sorrow. When I am gone, then tell them all: B. Auerbach died from shame in deep pain." [7]

In his theoretical and somewhat obscure rebuttal to Treitschke in 1880, the young Marburg professor of philosophy, Hermann Cohen, defended the expectations of highly assimilated Jews with Olympian idealism. Despite the bitterness he felt at being forced again to confess his faith publicly, Cohen tried to reduce the religious differences separating German and Jew. The essence of his answer to Treitschke amounted to the assertion that the religious unity which Germany's political union dictated already existed. In the scientific sense of religion, Israelite monotheism and Protestant Christianity were identical. By humanizing God, Christianity had humanized religion and guaranteed the Kantian ideal of ethical autonomy, without repudiating the Prophetic insistence on the wholly spiritual nature of God. Since Cohen considered a common religious foundation as the basic criterion of a modern *Kulturvolk,* the Jewish minority had to give evidence of the extent to which it shared the religious world view of the German people. And this evidence, Cohen felt, German Jewry could readily offer.

Our Israelite religion, as it exists in our midst today, has already begun in fact a cultural, historical union with Protestantism. Not only that we have more or less definitely and openly thrown off the tradition of the Talmud as binding just as they have [discarded] the tradition of the Church. But in a much deeper sense, in all spiritual questions we think and feel in accord with the Protestant spirit. Thus this common ground in religion is in truth the most powerful and effective unifying force for a genuine national fusion.[8]

But the situation which provoked the essay proved to be a turning point in Cohen's life. In 1914 he dated his own return to Judaism from the year 1880, and, as we shall see, the numerous essays on Jewish subjects which were to pour forth from his pen since that fateful year dwelled almost exclusively on the profound differences that still separated Judaism and Christianity.[9]

There is evidence to suggest that at least some Orthodox Jews shared the deep disappointment of their more assimilated and often alienated coreligionists. Juda Oppenheim was the devoted Orthodox teacher and rabbi of a small Jewish community in Westphalia. Filled with national fervor by the Franco-Prussian War and German unification, Oppenheim began to write a textbook on German history for children in Jewish schools in which he attempted to incorporate into the narrative also the history of the Jews in Germany. When the Stoecker movement loomed on the horizon, he had already invested ten years on this labor of love. To reassure himself that his work was not in vain, he anxiously hurried off the still unfinished manuscript to the Prussian Ministry of Education for the required official approval. The bulky manuscript was promptly rejected. Sadly Oppenheim buried it in his desk with the following eulogy:

In the first promising days of the new German Empire I imagined that peaceful co-existence and the annulment of old enmities were assured. As the writer of a German history I ought to have known better, seeing what its course has been like hitherto. But fool that I was, I believed in all seriousness in the outstretched brotherly German hand.[10]

The alarm which spread through the Jewish community in the wake of the anti-Semitic movement gave rise to a number of Jewish countermeasures. Gerson von Bleichröder, the Berlin agent of the Rothschilds, Bismarck's financial confidant and the first Prussian Jew to have been raised to the ranks of the hereditary nobility without first converting to Christianity, appealed directly to the seat of power.[11] At a rally on June 11, 1880, Stoecker had advised his Social Democratic hecklers to alleviate the social ills of Germany by tapping the inexhaustible resources of wealthy Jews rather than by harassing an impoverished Church: "Herr von Bleichröder has more money than all the Evangelical clergy together." A week later Bleichröder, who two years before at the Congress of Berlin had successfully used his unique position for the cause of Rumanian Jewry, wrote directly to the Kaiser stressing the dangers inherent in the movement. Endowed with a practical sense not yet manifested by the Socialists, Stoecker's party could potentially foment much greater social unrest. The isolated attack against Jews could readily assume the dimensions of a social revolution.

Shortly thereafter Bleichröder received a private audience with William I, at which the Kaiser admitted his disapproval of the current unrest. Bleichröder's appeal precipitated some sharp differences of opinion between the untroubled Minister of Religion and Education, a friend of Stoecker, and Bismarck, who seemed genuinely concerned about the socialist overtones of the polemic and at one time expressed a willingness to invoke the anti-socialist laws against Stoecker. The result was a reprimand from the Kaiser delivered on December 29, 1880, of which Bleichröder was informed, in which Stoecker was rebuked for arousing expectations among the workers which he could not fulfill. It concluded: "I expect that you will henceforth on every occasion when you appear in public, even in an unofficial capacity, constantly bear in mind your office's responsibility to preserve the peace among all classes of my subjects." [12]

Bleichröder's success overshadowed the futile efforts undertaken by the Board of the Berlin Jewish Community toward this same end. On October 17, 1879, it addressed a request to the Prussian Minister of Interior that steps be taken to halt the malicious harangues which threatened to endanger public order and social harmony. That appeal plus two later ones on April 20 and May 31, 1880, went unanswered. Subsequently the president visited the ministry personally, but failed to get an appointment with the Minister of the Interior. Finally he wrote a personal letter directly to the Minister, and this time merited the answer that the appeals were ignored because the Minister refused to consider the Berlin Jewish Community as authorized to speak for German Jewry. Moreover, no action could be taken against the Christian Social Worker's Party, because it was not at all certain that any laws had been violated.[13]

THE JEWISH COMMITTEE OF
DECEMBER 1, 1880

Several months later Moritz Lazarus, a successful academician, who still actively identified with the Jewish community, proposed a more open and direct plan of attack than that secretly ventured by the cautious board. His scholarly reputation rested upon his contributions to the field of ethnology. A discipline which he had helped create, *Völkerpsychologie* sought to fathom the patterns and features of a people's national life by studying its constellation of geographic, ethnic, physiological, psychological, and historical conditions. In 1859 Lazarus and Heymann Steinthal, his brother-in-law, started the *Zeitschrift für Völkerpsychologie und Sprachwissenschaft,* which they edited for more than thirty years and raised to one of the leading scholarly periodicals in Germany. In 1873 he was rewarded with an honorary professorship at the University of Berlin.

Unlike many of his Jewish colleagues, however, he remained active in Jewish life. Lazarus was born in 1824 in Filehne, a Posen community of some 3,000 German, Polish, and Jewish inhabitants. There he received a thorough traditional Jewish education, evidenced by his continued Hebrew correspondence with his learned father. Although he recalled his traditional childhood with affection, he was deeply disturbed by the increasing irrelevance of Jewish practice and became one of the leading lay spokesmen for Reform Judaism. A fine orator, he had been elected as president of both the 1869 and 1871 Reform synods in Leipzig and Augsburg respectively. He had also served as president of the Berlin chapter of the Alliance Israélite Universelle and had chaired the convention in 1872 that had tried unsuccessfully to create the Israelitische Alliance in Deutschland. That same year Lazarus helped to open the liberal rabbinical seminary in Berlin, and in 1877 he joined the board of the Gemeindebund.[14]

By the beginning of 1879 Lazarus had become convinced that the unabated advances of the anti-Semitic movement dictated an immediate organized Jewish response. In March 1879 twenty-five Jewish notables met to consider the advisability of organized resistance. They represented two small groups of notables who had been searching independently for a viable course of action. By letter Lazarus urged the combined meeting to adopt a policy of organized resistance. He deplored the Jews' incapacity to unite to defend their vital interests, and warned that fear of publicity must not again intimidate Jews to suffer in silence. To his dismay, the meeting took no action, because the majority still found the idea repugnant.[15]

He himself had been one of the first to issue a public protest. On December 2, 1879, he delivered a speech on "What Is National?" before the general assembly of the Hochschule für die Wissenschaft des Judentums in which he challenged Treitschke's indictment in the November issue of the *Preussische Jahrbücher,* to the effect that German Jewry had broken the agreement upon which its emancipation rested by remaining conspicuously and aggressively un-German. Defending a concept of *Volk* which he and Steinthal had presented in the first volume of their journal, Lazarus attempted to transcend the usual physical criteria of land, ancestry, and language. Animals and plants are classified by objective criteria, but men are asked to which people they belong. Philosophically committed to reasserting the role of ideas in history, Lazarus argued that the concept of *Volk* is the expression of a will to belong to a *Volk*. A *Volk* is created by individuals who want to live together. It is always preceded by the will to be a *Volk*. The quotation of a Tübingen professor who also stressed this subjective criterion enabled Lazarus to relate the theory to the immediate problem: "My *Volk* are those whom I regard as my *Volk*, whom I call mine, with whom I know myself to be tied by unbreakable bonds." [16] Armed with this definition of nationality, Lazarus could unequivocally and eloquently identify the German Jew as an integral member of the German people:

Gentlemen, what are we then? Germans! We are, wish to be, and can be nothing else. Language alone does not make us Germans. The land we inhabit, the state we serve, the law we obey, the scholarship which informs us, the art which inspires us—they are all German. Mother tongue and fatherland are German, both the creators of our innermost being. Here stand our cradles; here are the graves of those from whom we descend over many generations. Thus the beginning and the end of our lives is here.[17]

A year later a spate of ineffective individual responses to Treitschke's indictment convinced Lazarus that he must act again. He sensed that many were waiting for him to take the lead. On December 11, 1880, he wrote to a friend in Munich about the compelling urge to do something:

So your old friend is again Moses in the wilderness where the pillars of smoke are thicker than the pillars of fire. Your old friend, who loves and needs peace as fish need water, is again at the front, because I must be. If there were only no categorical imperative! and this rascal would not sit exactly in my heart of hearts, going about and ruling as if I had nothing to say.[18]

On the evening of December 1, 1880, Lazarus convened an assembly of two hundred Jewish notables and persuaded them to establish a committee of twenty-eight which was to be known as Das jüdische Comité vom 1 Dezember 1880. Among the members were such well-known figures of German Jewry as Berthold Auerbach; Professors Jakob Barth, Emil Breslaur, Harry Bresslau, Julius Hirschberg, and Heymann Steinthal; Deputies Ludwig Loewe, Emanuel Mendel, and Wolf Strassman; and Samuel Kristeller, the later president of the Gemeindebund. Two weeks later, on December 16, Lazarus ad-

dressed an assembly of six hundred Berlin Jews on the objectives of
the committee. In the course of these two meetings, Lazarus presented his case for organized self-defense.[19]

Without going into detail, Lazarus announced that the objectives
of the committee would be to stem the current outbreak of animosity,
to disseminate information about Judaism, and to take action against
those Jews whose behavior contributed to anti-Semitism. Lazarus
went on to assure his audience that the committee would scrupulously avoid slurring the heroes and relics sacred to Christians and
Germans alike. This had been the egregious mistake of Graetz,
whose history of the Jews evaluated renowned non-Jews solely from
a parochial Jewish point of view, for which he had been rightly cen-
sured by Treitschke. Lazarus openly dissociated himself from
Graetz's tactless approach: "We condemn whatever wrongs a few
Jewish litterateurs have committed against the sancta of another religion by presumptuous, tactless, even worse, by unjust or sarcastic
criticism as strongly as if they had done the same against Judaism; in
fact, we condemn it more." [20]

However, Lazarus insisted that the committee's work would be carried out in public. Many who recognized the need for counter-action
would cooperate only if such an undertaking were initiated behind
the scenes, ostensibly for fear of inciting still further unrest. At least
this had been the conclusion of the aforementioned meeting of Berlin
Jewish notables in March 1879. Lazarus contended that clandestine
measures were an affront, implying that Jews could not defend themselves. Like minors, they required protection. Furthermore, what was
there to hide? The committee intended to attack no one. Self-defense
was the sole object.[21]

On the other hand, Lazarus was not calling upon those present to
fight as Jews. The emancipation stood in no danger of being revoked.
The enterprise to combat anti-Semitism was not a narrow Jewish interest; it actually served the entire nation. The very discussion of
Jewish status was a national disgrace; the anti-Semitic disorders
sweeping Berlin were a national blemish. Jews were uniting to defend the purity of the German spirit. They had gathered as patriotic
sons of the fatherland to defend the rights of all Germans against

movements seeking to divide them according to religion or race. These were Jewish meetings devoted to a German cause.[22]

But Lazarus did not mean to reject the position that he had assumed in 1879. Then he had asserted that being a German did not require discarding Judaism. Contrary to the claim of Treitschke, great nations harbor a mixture of racial stocks. Nor did the Christian character of European civilization necessitate conversion, as Mommsen advised. Racial and religious diversity, corresponding to the multiplicity of forms in nature, yielded an unexpected qualitative richness. Lazarus believed that the uniqueness of Judaism and some of the spiritual traits of the Jewish character would fructify the quality of German life. Consequently, in 1880 he had no reservations about advocating a dual loyalty for every Jew. "Loyal toward our religion, because loyalty is in itself something in which we, perhaps before others, in the course of thousands of years have distinguished ourselves a bit; and loyal at the same time toward the fatherland and the nation." [23]

Lazarus did hasten to add that this continued loyalty to Judaism did not imply withdrawing behind a network of Jewish organizations. He had been deeply disturbed by the concluding illiberal remarks of Mommsen's famous reply in 1880 to Treitschke's essay in which the latter held the Jews responsible for the current anti-Semitic turmoil. After having defended the German character of the Jews, Mommsen had called for the dissolution of separate Jewish societies committed to the same ends as secular and integrated associations. He regarded such obstinate preservation of Jewish identity for essentially secular purposes as an affront to the Christian tone of contemporary civilization. Integration had its price, and the first to pay it ought to be those Jews alienated from their own religious tradition.[24] Lazarus retorted that these organizations were the very product of discrimination. When Jewish students were unable to receive financial aid from the German authorities and societies set up for that purpose, a Jewish scholarship association became indispensable. In 1872 Lazarus had been president of a Berlin Association for the Support of Jewish Students. He reminded his audience in 1880 that eight years before at a dinner following the general meeting of the association, at which a number of important Christians were present, he had proposed a toast that in the future a constitutional change would be in order to drop the word "Jewish" from the name of the association. When Christians were ready to meet Jews half way, then they could form an association together to help the students of all religious persuasions. Eight years later he felt justified in asserting that as long as Jews participate in the genuinely charitable organizations of the entire community, even in some purely Christian ones, then there could be no objection to their maintaining exclusively Jewish organizations as well.[25]

Beyond the two meetings in December of 1880, the committee arranged one more public function. On Friday evening, April 1, 1881, two thousand Jewish soldiers and reservists, many wearing battle insignia and the Iron Cross, met to consider a resolution reminding the German people that Jewish blood had also been shed for the fatherland, and that Jewish soldiers intended to defend the emancipation earned on the battlefield. But the resolution was not adopted. Some objected to the very convening of Jewish veterans, who had not been attacked directly either by their Christian comrades or by any military association. Others felt that the resolution would make no impression on the anti-Semites. Moreover, the Jews had already received the support of the press and the legislatures. The meeting ended with a trio of thundering cheers for the Kaiser.[26]

This was the extent of the committee's public performance. Thereafter it continued to operate for some time quietly behind the scenes. Its leaders considered the chances of any legal action or direct appeal to the government as slim, and they attempted to forestall any rash outbursts by zealous individual Jews. Its main positive thrust seems to have been in the distribution of apologetica, especially copies of the two Lazarus speeches and Mommsen's response to Treitschke.[27] Its silent efforts drew so little attention that contemporaries scarcely noted when the committee ceased operations. Already at the end of September 1881, the Berlin correspondent of the *Allgemeine Zeitung des Judentums* admitted that he knew nothing of its activities. Again in February of 1883 Philippson had no information to report, and by 1887, when Lazarus published a collection of his speeches on Jewish subjects, including those delivered on behalf of the committee, he chose to pass over its activities in silence. "As the name of the Committee was merely borrowed from that time, so may its activities disappear with that time." [28] Those who subsequently came to evaluate its work could find little to praise. [29]

RELUCTANCE TO RESIST

When compared with the intensity of the anti-Semitic campaign, the response of the committee is most noteworthy for being so nominal. Despite the alarm sounded in many Jewish quarters, the fact remains that German Jewry did not organize to defend its interests. The brief and ineffectual history of the committee points unmistakably to the deep aversion of German Jewry to open resistance, an aversion best exemplified by the policy of the board of the largest Jewish community in the country. As its urgent appeals to the Prussian Minister of the Interior at the peak of the unrest in 1879 and 1880 imply, the Berlin Board did not consider inconspicuous measures amiss. What it consistently rejected outright was overt Jewish action. Thus in August of 1879 the board refused to support a project organized by Ludwig Philippson. The latter had invited the boards of the Jewish communities of Berlin, Breslau, Frankfurt, and Hamburg to send delegates to a meeting at which some form of united resistance would be considered. Philippson had in mind official appeals on behalf of Jewry to various German governments, as well as a try at the publication of anti-defamation literature. Hamburg and Frankfurt accepted; Breslau chose to await further developments; and Berlin alone did not even bother to send a reply. [30]

The measures proposed by Moritz Lazarus likewise failed to win the cooperation of the Berlin Board. At the boisterous meeting of the two thousand Jewish veterans, a representative of the board justified its inactivity. The board had desisted from lending support because it was convinced that a favorable reaction would not be forthcoming. In fact none was needed, for in due time the present disorder would correct itself; meanwhile Jews could take comfort in the support they had already found. The board therefore objected to the purposeless, self-glorifying resolution that the veterans proposed to adopt. [31]

Again in 1884 the board reaffirmed its opposition to any form of public defense. That year sixty-eight rabbis assembled in the capital to discuss, among other things, an official declaration on the attitude of Judaism toward the non-Jew, a step clearly meant to counter the endless distortions and defamations. The Berlin Board objected. Its representative welcomed the visitors on behalf of the entire board, but urged them not to issue a declaration. Had such a statement appeared a few years earlier, it might have prevented much harm. At this late stage it seemed quite useless.[32]

It may well be that this consistent reluctance to fight anti-Semitism openly was the major reason for the board's initial unwillingness to welcome the Gemeindebund after its expulsion from Leipzig. Only after extensive negotiations had struck from the revised statutes every trace of involvement with defense did the board finally agree to allow the Gemeindebund to reopen its offices in Berlin.[33]

The timid policy of the Berlin Board epitomized the inhibitions paralyzing German Jewry. For nearly a century Jews had labored to win German citizenship by diminishing their differences. As late as 1890 they were still consciously suppressing every conspicuous and distinctive Jewish trait. In the words of one candid observer: ". . . a religious community that constitutes only a small fraction of the population must carefully avoid all outward, public practice of its ritual commandments and must strive mightily to adapt itself in its external life to the general customs of the society." [34] The repeated encouragement by many Jewish spokesmen of intermarriage with or without the conversion of the Christian partner reflects the lengths to which at least a sizable section of the Jewish community was ready to go to overcome the oft-cited ancestral and racial differences excluding Jews from German society.[35] But in the process of "self-improvement," Jews had become emotionally and ideologically incapable of defending their "Jewish persuasion," the last remaining objective difference.

It is to Lazarus' credit that he correctly perceived the issue to be the adoption of a policy of public self-defense and not mere self-defense. With a long history of precarious existence in non-Jewish societies, the Jews had certainly developed an often effective defensive policy centered around the court Jew. And there is no doubt that emancipated German Jews continued to approach and implore the seat of power behind the scenes in the best medieval tradition of intercession. During the very years when German anti-Semitism surfaced again, men like Lazarus, Bleichröder, and Kristeller, along with the Berlin Board, had registered a brilliant success in winning Bismarck to the cause of Rumanian Jewry and thereby influencing the Congress of Berlin in 1878 to demand of Rumania that she grant religious liberty to all her citizens.[36] But the same tactics against the endemic forces of German anti-Semitism proved far less effective. The appeals of Bleichröder and the Berlin Board produced no decisive government intervention against anti-Semites.[37] The mass character of the movement and the sympathetic neutrality of the authorities, plus the new legal status bestowed on Jewry by the emancipation, combined to dictate a fundamental revision of Jewish policy. The failure of the Lazarus Committee reflects the fearful reluctance of German Jewry to discard the defense policy of another era.

The aversion to any public display of Jewishness also partially accounts for the deep-seated Jewish preference for Christian spokesmen. Berthold Auerbach, aging but volatile, articulated the longing succinctly when his spirits momentarily rose following the declaration by seventy-three Christian notables in November of 1880. In a letter to his lifelong friend, Jakob Auerbach, he wrote:

In this instance one is joyously revived; here one sees that the concern of the Jews is not their own concern but at the same time that of freedom and humanity. What we have so long wished and hoped for, that we Jews should not have to defend ourselves, that instead Christians would take the initiative, has happened and in the best manner.[38]

Just three days before he had reported to his friend how the anti-Semitic petition had almost driven him to convene a large protest rally of the leading figures of Berlin. The unanimous objection of those to whom he spoke convinced him to drop the project. Despondently, he concluded that the only hope remaining was that a group of respected Christians, who still knew what humanity was, might rise against the present infamy.[39]

During the first two decades of the Second Reich, Jewish weeklies manifested the same preference by quoting extensively from Christian works to refute the arguments and allegations of anti-Semites. Often they reviewed or reprinted a Christian rebuttal despite the unfavorable attitude of the writer toward Judaism. For example, in 1890 the *Allgemeine Zeitung des Judentums* published an 1882 letter of Queen Augusta, the wife of William I and steady adversary of Bismarck, in which she expressed her embarrassment at the unchristian behavior toward Jews. The paper chose to ignore the fact, openly stated in the same letter, that she was also disturbed by the prospect that the agitation might obstruct the continued conversion of the Jews.[40]

It is thus entirely evident that this first wave of anti-Jewish sentiment to sweep the Empire failed to compel the Jews to abandon their traditional reliance upon accommodation, silence, and Christian intervention. On the contrary, the manner in which the majority of Jews interpreted the current unrest tended to reinforce and even vindicate that reliance. Many took comfort in what they considered to be the very limited extent of the turmoil. The sudden resurgence of Jew-hatred did not appear to be the spontaneous outburst of mass discontent. It certainly did not represent a popular reaction by the people to national danger, as suggested by Treitschke. Rather one could objectively date its origins to the anti-Semitic polemics of the press in 1875. The current disorders were clearly produced by certain political parties exploiting medieval prejudices for their own immediate advantage. Stoecker and his cohorts had merely shifted the scene into the public assemblies. It was obviously a disorder dictated from above. Even men like Nachod and Lazarus did not reject this interpretation. Lazarus could assuage his pain with the consolation that only a minuscule group of bigots was responsible for the disturbances that were disgracing the name of Germany. Under no circumstances would he accuse the entire German people for the sins of a few.[41]

With such an estimate of the dimensions of the movement, it is not surprising that the overwhelming majority of German Jews reacted passively. They sensed no danger to their legal status. Emancipation was not about to be revoked or redefined. Resistance would only serve to give publicity to the anti-Semites, whose cause enjoyed little popularity and whose distortions were too blatant to convince anyone. Silence recommended itself not only as the most honorable, but also as the most effective, course.[42]

A second notion, widely shared, helped to place the current explosion within a larger perspective and thereby again to diminish its immediate significance. Ludwig Philippson, who certainly viewed the Berlin Movement as gravely as any contemporary Jewish observer, and offered a number of trenchant analyses, often reminded his readers of the inevitability of human progress. Though frequently troubled, he never condoned the despondency of a Berthold Auerbach. A proper reading of history, he declared, demonstrates that nothing human fails to progress. Writing in the wake of Prussia's lightning military victories of the 1860's, Philippson cited the character of modern warfare as a striking example. It had eliminated personal hatred between combatants, shortened the duration of war itself, and thereby limited the amount of destruction to the civilian population. He countered the despair of Leon Pinsker's anonymously published *Auto-Emancipation,* which diagnosed anti-Semitism in the wake of the 1881 Russian pogroms as a fully irrational "Judeophobia," with the declaration that mankind had already overcome a long series of similar aberrations.[43]

The import of this dogma was considerable. It offered consolation to those distressed at the eruption of an issue thought resolved, and again it tended to diminish the seriousness of the outbreak. Though Philippson refused to underestimate the gravity of the crisis, many of his Jewish contemporaries who enthusiastically shared the belief in progress certainly did. It permitted them to view the current episode of Jew-hatred as merely the final epidemic of a medieval plague that would soon yield to treatment by reason. The legal and social integration of the Jews in Germany had advanced so rapidly during the preceding two decades that people often failed to recognize that age-old prejudices were not eradicated quite as quickly as the legislation which institutionalized them.[44]

There was still one other widely shared point of view that served to militate against organized self-defense. Too many German Jews, including figures like Lazarus and the leaders of the Gemeinde-bund,[45] considered the anti-Semitic backlash as at least partially justified. As late as 1910 Martin Philippson, a professional historian and dedicated leader in German Jewish communal affairs, echoed this sentiment when he tried to account for the anti-Semitic eruption of the 1870's in his *Neueste Geschichte des jüdischen Volkes:*

> The scope, depth and duration of the anti-Semitic movement have, however, actual causes inside the Jewish community. The bitter violence of its fate during so many centuries produced in the character of its people uncertainty, lack of harmony and rough contrasts. From this stems the unrest, the formlessness, and loud, volatile nature, the scrambling after external distinction and the approval of others; from this [stems] the rapid fluctuations between deep despondency and excessive joy; from this stems the most intimate family love, the purest acts of charity, genuinely ideal selflessness, as well as unrestrained selfishness and hedonism.[46]

Others were distressed by the financial role Jews continued to play in the long-ailing agrarian sector of the economy. The involvement of Jewish middlemen and moneylenders in the steady impoverishment of the peasants seemed to account for areas like Westphalia and Hesse becoming hotbeds of virulent anti-Semitism. When peasants could no longer pay back the credits extended to them, their creditors, who were often Jewish, would parcel up their property and sell it at considerable profit. Denounced as *Güterschlächter* (the butchers of property), these prosperous Jewish businessmen of the declining agrarian economy were hated by the peasants and disapproved of by the local Jewish communities.[47]

Many Jews were dismayed at the lack of discretion exhibited by Heinrich Graetz. It is remarkable that, in all the ink spilled over Treitschke's attack against Graetz, not a single important Jewish spokesman defended the Jewish historian, a fact that rankled Graetz deeply. The consensus was unmistakable: Graetz had tactlessly blundered in his condemnation of the anti-Semitic sentiments of German heroes like Luther and Fichte. Even the support Graetz received from the graduates of the Breslau Seminary, where he taught, dealt more with the principle of standing united in the face of a common enemy than with the substance of the issue.[48] It may well be, as one historian of the debate has conjectured, that Graetz fell silent after his second rebuttal in order to play down the deep divisions that had emerged within Jewry over the merits of his case.[49]

In the light of such provocations, many Jews felt anti-Semitism to be a legitimate German protest. If action were in order, it should be taken against Jews who precipitated the reaction. Accordingly, in 1890, as a second storm of Jew-hatred hit the Reich, one Jewish critic proposed the idea of an Association for the Social Reform of Judaism in every Jewish community. Loosely united in a central office in Berlin, these local associations would direct their efforts toward the ethical improvement of the Jews as well as their integration into German society by a reform of Judaism.[50]

AN UNDERTONE OF APPREHENSION

The apparently limited and ephemeral impact of this initial anti-Semitic incursion into the German political scene seemed to vindicate the optimistic analysis of most Jews. The racial groupings that had sponsored the famous petition did not win a seat in the Reichstag elections of 1881. Stoecker, who did win, joined the Conservative faction, and even his star declined rapidly when Bismarck moved closer to the National Liberals in 1887. Jews now praised their initial passivity as having effectively disproven the anti-Semitic allegations of Jewish solidarity and power. Above all, their quiescence had not fed a fire destined to burn itself out.[51]

Nevertheless, an undertone of concern persisted for the remainder of the 1880's. Periodically a worried voice warned that the calm surface concealed a deeply rooted and rapidly spreading malevolence. While the majority repeatedly reassured itself that the worst was over and the movement was bankrupt,[52] a minority felt that only the symptoms had subsided; the malady itself persisted. For example, the opening statement of a memorandum submitted from Breslau, probably by Graetz, in the beginning of 1882 to the group of men deliberating on the reorganization of the Gemeindebund professed apprehension over the future:

In the depth of the German people there still rages the hatred against Judaism and the Jews which undermines the roots of our participation in civic and political life. The apparent returning surface calm will not deceive those who know the fate of the Jewish people and who care not only for themselves and the immediate future.[53]

A still more forceful pronouncement of the same anxiety came from Breslau four years later. On October 23, 1886, a group of eleven Jewish medical students, along with one rabbinical student, formed the first Jewish fraternity in Germany at the University of Breslau. In a forthright manifesto they justified their bold undertaking. They rejected the illusion that anti-Semitism was on the wane. On the contrary, it was damaging the very fiber of the German people. Most disconcerting and ominous was the extent to which the university students, the future leaders of the nation, had embraced anti-Semitism, with the result that Jewish students were socially ostracized. Often the first bitter experience of prejudice for a young Jewish student accompanied his entrance into the university, and unable to cope with its organized character, he desperately concealed his Jewish identity. To regain their self-respect and the respect of their Christian peers, Jewish students must organize. A sense of Jewish identity must be cultivated through a study of Jewish history and the ability of self-defense developed through extensive physical training. Fearing anti-Semitic repercussions, the Jews of Breslau vigorously disapproved. In contrast, Graetz, who taught both at the University and the rabbinical school in Breslau, openly encouraged their enterprise. The one rabbinical student involved, Benno Jacob, was one of Graetz's favorite students. The founders named their fraternity Viadrina, after the name of the University, Leopoldina Viadrina, and it represented the first of what in 1896 became a small network of nationally affiliated Jewish fraternities, the Kartell Convent. But in the 1880's its warnings went unheard and its example unheeded. As late as 1889 it was still the only Jewish fraternity of its kind.[54]

Elsewhere the anxiety over German anti-Semitism expressed itself in a preoccupation with the defense of Jewish ethics. Numerous attempts were made to counter the endless distortions and fabrications which maliciously and ominously attacked the wisdom of granting Jews full equality as long as they continued to adhere to an inferior and misanthropic moral system. In August 1883 representatives of the Jewish communities of London, Paris, Vienna, and Berlin met in Koblenz and commissioned Moritz Lazarus to undertake a comprehensive exposition of Jewish ethics. However, neither the financial nor scholarly support for which Lazarus hoped and labored ever materialized. Some fifteen years later the first and only volume which Lazarus lived to complete finally appeared, a classic apologia of Judaism under emancipation, successfully expunging every trace of the particular, the irrational, and the historical from what Lazarus held to be the essential unity of Jewish ethics.[55]

To counter the charge that Jewish law countenanced an internal and external morality, that is, permitted actions toward non-Jews that it would not tolerate toward Jews, David Hoffmann, the outstanding Talmudic scholar at the Orthodox rabbinical seminary in Berlin, published a learned analysis in the pages of the *Jüdische Presse,* which later appeared as a book, on the position of Jewish law regarding the relationship of Jews toward non-Jews.[56] The 1884 declaration of sixty-eight liberal rabbis had the same purpose. It declared that Judaism commands Jews to treat all men who exercise love, practice justice, and walk humbly before God (Micah 6:8) with love (Leviticus 19:18) and justice (Leviticus 24:22), regardless of their religion. Whatever statement in Jewish literature contradicted this inviolable principle must be construed as the opinion of an individual and understood in light of the sufferings of his generation. This formulation did not satisfy the Orthodox rabbis who refused to attend the conference, and Esriel Hildesheimer issued a modification signed by fifty-nine rabbis which limited the principle of universal love to those men who live according to the seven ethical laws prescribed to the sons of Noah. The later statements of authorities contradicting the principle must be understood to refer to men who do not observe even this minimum ethical standard.[57]

A somewhat more ambitious project to define the ethical content of Judaism was set in motion by a number of Berlin notables in December 1883. They formed a committee chaired by Lazarus which two years later submitted to the Board of the Berlin Jewish community a statement comprising the fifteen ethical principles of Judaism. Although published immediately by the board, the Gemeindebund undertook to buttress this statement with the approval of leading German Jews. By 1891 some 350 rabbis and religious teachers, including the faculty of the Hochschule für die Wissenschaft des Judentums and the chief rabbis of France and England, and some 270 lawyers had affixed their signatures to the document. Furthermore, a second committee had substantiated each of the principles with proof texts drawn from the normative texts of Jewish literature. This concise summation of Jewish ethics was then vigorously disseminated in thousands of copies to the far corners of the land, either with or without the validating documentation.[58]

As a number of contemporary observers warned, this unabated vilification of Jewish ethics directly jeopardized the political status of emancipated Jewry. The real objective was the circumscribing or revoking of emancipation itself. Leopold Auerbach, a very knowledgeable critic of Prussia's Jewish policy, asserted that these attacks provided a convenient way by which to justify the exclusion of Jews from certain key areas of public employment. Auerbach recognized that the Conservative government of Germany rested on the concept of the Christian state, that is, according to Auerbach, a conviction that the state must be grounded in a divinely revealed ethical system, whose principles are unchangeable, stand beyond political and rational questioning, and guide its future development. The concept did not imply, however, a specific form of revelation or worship. Having defined the concept, Auerbach could now argue pursuasively that ethically Judaism and Christianity demanded the same standards of conduct. Hence Jews were equally qualified to serve in positions of public administration and authority. This qualification was precisely what those who maligned Jewish ethics denied, and the indifference to the truth on the part of the German government abetted their cause.[59]

Hermann Cohen submitted that the ramifications were still graver. The repeated scholarly assertions that the Old Testament excludes the non-Jew from its commandment to love thy neighbor and the general claim that neither the Old Testament nor the Talmud ever reached the ethical universalism of Christianity made of the modern Jew a Don Quixote whose stubborn preservation of Jewish identity meant obedience to an inferior ethic. By rejecting Christianity with its superior ethical system, the Jew remained an alien and contemptible element in German society. Such inferior strangers did not deserve the full protection of the constitution. From a higher vantage point, no official would be guilty of injustice in violating their legal rights in practice. Cohen warned that this academically supported

charge of ethical inferiority allowed the racial anti-Semites an air of
self-righteousness, lent their polemic a modicum of veracity, and hallowed their hatred as a healthy national impulse.[60]

During the 1880's these periodic expressions of concern completely failed to shatter the sense of security of the vast majority.
Certainly the occasional appeals for a collective defense were consistently ignored. The evident decline in overt anti-Semitism only reinforced the traditional communal and conceptual reservations. Toward
the end of the decade, one worried observer denounced the apparently insurmountable disunity by applying the ancient condemnation
of Jeremiah: the number of Israel's gods still corresponded to the
number of its towns. Local autonomy had become the fetish of every
German Jewish community.[61]

The most cogently argued appeal to unite, and also the most debated, came in 1889 from Leopold Auerbach, a legal historian, who
resided in Berlin. Twenty years earlier Auerbach had produced a
huge systematic and comparative study in German on the nature of
personal obligation in Jewish law. He also included a lengthy introductory sketch of the entire history of Jewish law. Decades later this
learned tome was to find its most appreciative reader in Werner
Sombart, who relied upon it for his own methodologically shoddy
study of *The Jews and Modern Capitalism*.[62] The appeal of 1889 was
incorporated in a thoroughly researched treatise, noticeably intended
for the consideration of Prussian officials as well, tracing the development of Prussian policy toward the Jews since emancipation. The
main thesis was that since the emancipation edict of 1812, which
transformed the formerly corporate Jewish communities into private
religious organizations, the Prussian government, guided by its concept of a Christian state, had steadily pursued a policy designed to
ignore, fragmentize, and dissolve German Jewry. Even the legislation
of 1847 which restored corporate rights to the individual communities, Auerbach maintained, granted no official status to Judaism. The
intention of a century of Prussian policy had been to obstruct the development of a non-Christian religious minority.[63]

The Jews, he contended, shared some responsibility for this situation. Their strategy since the emancipation had been to demand
equality as individuals and not as a community. But Prussia was a

state in which the church was not separate. The Prussian government extended support and protection to, and exercised supervision over, the recognized Christian churches, and they in turn exerted considerable influence in public affairs. Within this context, the consistent ignoring of Judaism by the government saddled the Jews with serious disadvantages. Yet the Jews so cherished the freedom to determine their particular religious practices that they warmly approved Prussian policy,[64] at least until the anti-Semitic assault and siege of the last fifteen years. Only when the Jews witnessed the futility of their recourse to the offices of public prosecutor, the courts, and the government ministries did they begin to fathom how defenseless their position actually was. The cost of local autonomy had proven high: national disunity and the absence of any officially recognized spokesman.

The time had come, and this conclusion was the ultimate objective of Auerbach's presentation, for Prussian Jewry to create a central body of rabbis and laymen elected by the individual communities to preserve the unity and maintain the level of Judaism in Prussia. Above all, this body required the official recognition and support of the Prussian government.[65] Besides implementing its decisions, the government ought generally to extend financial assistance to Jewish education, including the opening of institutions for the training of rabbis and teachers. Had such an official body existed at the time of the anti-Semitic eruption, the agitation would never have reached the proportions it did. In its wake the Prussian government was left with only two alternatives. If it regarded Judaism as capable of raising moral human beings and useful citizens, then it had to concern itself with the welfare of both Judaism and the Jews. If the government did not believe Judaism capable of educating such citizens, then it ought to return the local Jewish communities to the status of private religious associations.[66]

The historical significance of the deservedly wide attention that Auerbach's book received is that the discussion summarized some of the considerations that had obstructed efforts to erect a defense establishment since 1875. The agreement of most critics ended once they had praised the impressive factual content of the book. The Reform, of course, were not at all pleased by the unfavorable judgments

Auerbach had pronounced upon their endless attempts to bring Judaism into conformity with the dictates of the age. Though expressing sympathy for the proposal of a central authority, they did not consider it seriously, for neither the Prussian government nor the Jews seemed willing.[67]

Auerbach had proposed a traditional orientation for his suggested central authority, and he explicitly stipulated that it would regulate the religious practices of Prussian Jewry. The differences between the various currents of Prussian Jewry did not appear to him substantial enough to prevent such unification.[68] The reactions of both the moderates (i.e., the Breslau School) and the Orthodox exposed his judgment as naïve. The spokesmen of the Historical School and the separatistic Orthodox in Frankfurt rejected the idea as a violation of freedom of conscience. Anarchy was preferable to such control. Isaac Hirsch, the son of Samson R. Hirsch and author of the long review in the *Israelit,* berated Auerbach for belittling the differences between Orthodox and Reform. The disagreements were so fundamental and the animosity so intense that no cooperative effort was possible. Moreover, Hirsch insisted that the existence of such an official authority would not have helped in combating anti-Semitism. The presence of a central consistory for French Jewry had not thwarted the vicious propaganda of Drumont. Finally, Hirsch repudiated Auerbach's interpretation of Prussian policy. He insisted that the government had extended equality to Judaism as well. Auerbach spoke as if the conditions prior to 1869 still existed.[69]

The more moderate Orthodox *Jüdische Presse,* a paper that had vigorously battled anti-Semitism for the entire decade, likewise did not embrace the suggestion for a government-recognized central authority. Despite the importance of the book, the Berlin paper endorsed a proposal published a few months earlier in its own pages calling for local initiative to set up a defense committee in every Jewish community. Their operations would be coordinated by a central office in the capital of each province. A decentralized and privately initiated enterprise would skirt the problems raised by a centralized and state-initiated organization.[70]

Auerbach's proposal even drew the disapproval of Eugen Richter, one of the leaders of the Progressives. In an article entitled "The

Federalization (*Verstaatlichung*) of Judaism," which appeared in the party's *Freisinnige Zeitung,* he rejected the assertion that the decentralization of Prussian Jewry had been intended to accelerate its demise. It was precisely this enormous freedom that helped to stimulate a vibrant religious life on a local level. In contrast, the centralization of the Evangelical Church had effectively deadened religious life in the local churches. The review also cautioned Auerbach not to defend Judaism by demanding special rights. All the privileges binding medieval Jewry to the royal courts did not protect them from persecution. The only defense of Judaism was the equality of all religions.[71]

The debate made explicit what had been implicit for a long time. It delineated the course to be taken in the eventual formation of a permanent defense organization. When the external pressure would become sufficiently intense, the initiative would have to be private, and limited solely to the objective of self-defense. There was not much eagerness and even less hope for government assistance, and the religious antagonisms had again proven themselves so bitter that any common effort would have to be based upon a rigorous neutrality between the Orthodox and Reform sectors of German Jewry.

3

HELP FROM OUTSIDE: VEREIN ZUR ABWEHR DES ANTISEMITISMUS, 1891-1914

THE PREFERENCE OF GERMAN JEWS for the intercession of Christian spokesmen on their behalf predated the anti-Semitic backlash of the 1870's. In this regard, as in so many others, the behavior of Moses Mendelssohn in the eighteenth century constituted a weighty precedent. When Alsatian Jewry appealed to the renowned sage of Dessau at the end of the 1770's to aid them in gaining some alleviation of Jewish disabilities from the French government, he succeeded in attracting the services of the young Prussian bureaucrat Christian Wilhelm Dohm. A few years later Mendelssohn spelled out in a letter to a Christian chemist the rationale behind his consistent refusal to undertake a campaign for emancipation. Baron Hirschen had invited Mendelssohn to join with him and a Christian professor of philosophy in a literary project to defend the Jews. Mendelssohn was delighted with their venture, for, as he wrote, he had always believed that only a recognized Christian authority could effectively combat the anti-Jewish prejudices of the common man. To be convincing, the writer had to be above the slightest suspicion of self-interest:

In order to advance this noble project, therefore, Jews must certainly not mix in. As soon as they do, it will be misunderstood and misinterpreted. Thus the Right Honorable Lord now understands the reason why I as a Jew may not become involved with this matter. . . .[1]

Two additional considerations further enhanced the appeal of this passive reliance upon Christian goodwill. With concerned Christians in the forefront of the battle against the antagonists of Jewish equality, Jews could continue to deemphasize their religious identity for the sake of integration. To defend Judaism themselves meant to play up the last feature which still distinguished Jew from Christian.[2] Secondly, Christian assistance provided some much-needed reassurance to countless insecure Jews that their zealous cultivation of German identity had not been an exercise in self-delusion or futility. At times even committed Jews felt that German patriotism dictated demonstrative acts of self-transcendence. Thus in the Reichstag elections of 1887 Professors Moritz Lazarus and Levin Goldschmidt advised voting for anti-Semitic candidates who supported the government's case for a seven-year rather than a three-year military budget to counter the French menace. The periodic pronouncements of favorable Christians seemed to vindicate such displays of selflessness.[3]

A CHRISTIAN DEFENSE ORGANIZATION

The formation of the Verein zur Abwehr des Antisemitismus (the Association for the Defense Against Anti-Semitism) at the beginning of 1891 provided a dramatic fulfillment of this long-standing preference for Christian intervention. The Verein expressed the apprehension of a handful of liberal and progressive Christian politicians concerning the appearance of a new specter on the political scene.

While Stoecker's conservative anti-Semitism had held national attention for most of the 1880's, a far more radical racial anti-Semitism firmly established itself in such states as Waldeck, Hesse, Saxony, and Thuringia, and in the Prussian provinces of Hesse and Saxony. Its unnoticed progress attained political significance in 1887 when the "pure" anti-Semites succeeded in electing a twenty-six-year-old librarian and student of German folklore, Otto Boeckel, in a poor and rural election district of Hesse, long an uncontested Conservative preserve. In the Reichstag he refused to join the Conservative faction. In the next Reichstag elections of February 1890, the anti-Semitic People's Party of Boeckel and the German Social Anti-Semitic Party of Sonnenberg ran candidates in thirty-one election districts, winning in five of the districts in the Grand Duchy of Hesse and the Electorate of Hesse and polling about 48,000 out of more than 7 million votes. The four victors of Boeckel's party formed an "anti-Semitic group" in the new Reichstag.[4]

These portentous results alarmed Heinrich Rickert, a prominent leader of Germany's dwindling number of Progressives. In March 1890, shortly after the elections, he rose to defend the Jews in the Prussian Chamber of Deputies against the harangues of Stoecker.[5] At the suggestion of an equally disturbed Jewish friend, Edmund Friedemann, a Berlin lawyer, Rickert convened a private meeting of concerned German notables in Friedemann's house on March 30. There he succeeded in convincing those present of the need for a systematic defense against anti-Semitism, and proposed a plan to that end.[6] A few months later he took up the theme again in an article on "The Persecution of the Jews in Germany at the End of the Nineteenth Century," in the Nation, the Progressive journal founded in 1883 by Theodor Barth.[7] Rickert warned that the election returns of 1890 had finally shattered the optimistic illusion that the anti-Semitic disturbances would quickly subside, that countermeasures were unnecessary because Germans were too civilized to be moved by such appeals. The anti-Semites had successfully switched their tactics. Whereas in 1880 they had attempted by means of a petition to influence the entire country simultaneously, they were now concentrating their energy upon a few regions in an effort to saturate them with their ideology. Unfortunately the last decade of German history demonstrated that man's lowest passions could still thrive if unopposed by public opinion. Rickert suggested that it was the duty of Christians to rise in protest against the un-German and un-Christian polemic which had poisoned public life and that it was the duty of Christians to ensure that Jewish citizens finally receive the equality which had long been legally enacted.[8]

By the end of the year, twelve Reichstag deputies were negotiating the formation of such a Christian defense organization, and in January 1891 the Verein appeared before the public with a declaration signed by some five hundred leading Christians from a variety of political, academic, literary, religious, business, legal, and industrial circles. Among the signatories were Professors Karl Biedermann, Theodor Mommsen, Albrecht Weber, and Otto Caspari; the author Gustav Freytag; Reichstag Deputies Theodor Barth, Hans Haehnle, and August Maager; and Mayors Forckenbeck of Berlin and Funk of Dessau, to name just a few. The statement condemned the campaign of hatred against the Jews as contrary to the character of the German people, its historical development, and its place among the civilized nations of the world. As Germans and Christians they had united to form an organization to oppose what had long been denounced by German princes and statesmen.[9]

At first the Abwehrverein (as it was known) grew rapidly. By the middle of March its membership had risen to 3,000; by June, to 8,-000. At the time of its first general assembly held in Berlin in November 1893, the membership numbered 13,338 individuals from 963 localities. However, since this seems to have been the last public reference made before the war as to the number of members, it would appear that the figures never surpassed that peak and, in fact, probably declined.[10]

Certainly the available information on income corroborates this suspicion. According to its statutes, each member was obligated to pay dues annually, though he could determine the amount. This arrangement, including one-time contributions, netted 68,905 marks in 1891; the following year the figure fell to exactly one-half, 34,282 marks; and by November 1, 1893, the income had dropped for the third year to 14,794 marks. Nevertheless, the 1897 report indicated that the Berlin bureau had collected 19,722 marks and the Frankfurt bureau, 17,821 marks from their respective members. By 1901 the income of each bureau seems to have leveled off at about 20,000 marks.[11]

The membership figure of 13,338 was distributed across Germany. Of these members, 4,831 came from 397 places in northern Germany, while 8,441 came from 562 localities in southern and western Germany. In order to be more sensitive to local conditions, the Abwehrverein tried at first to encourage decentralization, and these figures may reflect the initial success of that effort as well as the areas of anti-Semitic concentration. In February 1891 a second fully independent bureau was opened in Frankfurt. The original Berlin office was to cover the North and East while the new bureau would be responsible for the South and West. In 1893 the decentralization was carried still further, with regional offices in Marburg and Cologne, although they seem to have eventually disappeared from the scene.[12]

The formation of the Abwehrverein in Berlin seems to have prompted a number of important Viennese Christians in June 1891 to organize a similar Verein zur Abwehr des Antisemitismus to combat Austrian anti-Semitism. Its honorary president was Dr. Hermann Nothnagel, a professor of medicine at the University of Vienna, while Baron von Suttner, a novelist whose better-known pacifist wife, Bertha, won the Nobel Prize for Peace in 1905, served as its active president. Although by 1895 the Verein had only some 4,520 members, the composition of this membership differed markedly from that of its German counterpart, insofar as its membership included quite a few representatives of the Austrian nobility. By 1899 the Viennese Abwehrverein had been forced to reduce its program to little more than a literary campaign against anti-Semitism. In 1908 the two organizations began to cooperate for the first time.[13]

THE SEARCH FOR TACTICS

With little previous experience available to draw upon in its search for tactics to fight organized anti-Semitism, the initial efforts of the Abwehrverein were bound to be exploratory. At first it considered sending speakers into anti-Semitic rallies to counter the charges directly, but it soon dropped the plan as futile and even detrimental. If its men ever got to speak, they were granted only the briefest rejoinder. In most cases the anti-Semitic sponsors exploited the presence of a spokesman from the Abwehrverein to draw still larger crowds, which they would then inflame with their own hateful oratory. The Abwehrverein soon realized that it was more effective to organize separate meetings in the locality where anti-Semites were operating.

Even in areas into which the anti-Semites had not yet penetrated, such meetings would be held as a precautionary measure. However, after a few years, lack of funds and demand forced the discarding of this tactic as well. The usual local response was that harmony reigned supreme.[14]

The formation of a "protective association against the usurious exploitation of the people" was another tactic on the local level initiated by individual members of the Verein. The most successful seems to have operated in Karlsruhe, Baden, which by 1893 had a membership of 1,124. It sought to provide legal advice and loans at honest rates, to supervise the business practices of clothing peddlers, and to counsel villagers and peasants on how to sell their cattle and produce.[15]

Such associations were in effect a throwback to the prejudices of an earlier period. They presumed to tackle again the rehabilitation of the debased Jewish stereotype disseminated throughout the long battle for equal rights. The "civic improvement" of the uneducated and immoral Jewish peddler or moneylender was the indispensable prerequisite for emancipation. Jewish leaders accepted the condition, and throughout the nineteenth century invested large sums of money to effect the vocational redistribution of their "undesirables." [16] The recrudescense of Jew-hatred at the end of the century convinced assimilated Jewry, as we have already seen, that many of their coreligionists still remained vocationally and morally defective.[17] It is evident that both the leaders and the rank and file of the Abwehrverein assumed this allegedly objective cause of anti-Semitism,[18] although the leadership tended to discount its significance and soon lost interest in these associations.

From the very beginning the Abwehrverein had rejected the strategy of fighting anti-Semitism in the courts. To prosecute men like Ahlwardt, whom Barth considered sick, was a losing proposition. The Abwehrverein feared that court cases would merely serve the anti-Semites as a sounding board for their ideas while transforming the defendant into a hero or martyr. Moreover, the authorities repeatedly displayed an aversion to punishing agitators, and there was little the Verein could do to alter the impression that the courts' restraint somehow vindicated the anti-Semites. In 1892 Theodor Barth, a Progressive Deputy in the Reichstag, asserted that the real problem was not the inaction of the authorities but the exaggerated reliance of the people upon the government in the formation of their opinions. It was this extraordinary dependence upon authority that led Germans to conclude that an anti-Semitic demagogue must be at least partially right if the authorities ignored him. Barth insisted that freedom of speech requires a certain lack of sensitivity, a tolerance for the preposterous, a capacity for judgment without the paternal guidance of government. Germans were still wanting in the courage and maturity to exercise the right of free speech without official guidance.[19]

A tactic which the Verein adopted as early as the Reichstag campaign of 1893 and continued to employ thereafter was open opposition to anti-Semitic candidates. It published large numbers of posters and pamphlets, provided speakers, and urged liberals not to vote for an anti-Semite under any circumstances. When it proffered funds directly to the campaign of a candidate, it demanded not only his personal repudiation of anti-Semitism, but also a promise that, in the event of a run-off election in which an anti-Semitic candidate was involved, he would always support the other candidate, even if he were a Social Democrat. By 1903 the Verein's policy had solidified to the extent that it called upon the voters to vote against every anti-Semite running, even if it meant voting for a Conservative or Social Democrat. Anti-Semitism was the greater danger in either case. The Verein's leaders were particularly distressed by instances of local Progressive organizations openly supporting an anti-Semite, and defeated Progressive candidates who were helping the cause of an anti-Semite in a run-off election. In the 1907 Reichstag campaign, two members of the enlarged board of the Verein even called for the victory of an anti-Semite in one run-off election. Both were asked to withdraw from the Verein. At the time Barth, who was now president, reasserted that, for the sake of higher interests or public welfare, his organization would never support the election of an anti-Semitic candidate. Anti-Semitism remained the most dangerous enemy of the principle of civil equality.[20]

From the start the major effort of the Abwehrverein was invested in publication. On November 1, 1891, it issued the first number of its *Mitteilungen,* a weekly paper devoted to a comprehensive coverage of anti-Semitic activity in Germany. After January 1, 1911, it appeared only biweekly.[21] The abundant information on the scope and character of anti-Semitism has made the *Mitteilungen* the primary source for any study of the subject. In addition, its pages included innumerable rebuttals. The objectives were to place this material in the hands of those fighting anti-Semitism, as well as to give some of it still wider circulation by getting it reprinted in local newspapers. But the program proved to be of limited effectiveness. At a time when the Verein enjoyed a membership of 13,338, only about 6,000 subscribed to the *Mitteilungen*. Local newspaper editors were frequently reluctant to use the material. The organization encouraged its members to exert personal influence when possible, and later developed a weekly digest of material taken from the *Mitteilungen* and sent directly to editors across the country. As the years passed, the Verein's energies were increasingly limited to the publication of the *Mitteilungen* and periodic pieces of counterpropaganda. Friends criticized the effort as too academic and thereby failing to reach the circles most seriously infected. But its spokesmen contended that the publications disseminated essential information for the eventual enlightenment of the German people.[22]

LEADERSHIP AND IDEOLOGY

The leadership of the Abwehrverein remained in the hands of nationally known political figures deeply committed to the realization of the *Rechtsstaat* and generally identified with the Progressive left of the German political spectrum. The partial exception to this description was the organization's first president, Rudolph von Gneist, an important liberal historian of law and an active member of the middle-of-the-road National Liberal Party. Although regarded by contemporaries as a cofounder of the Verein, Gneist had already passed his seventy-fourth birthday when it was formed, and one suspects that his most valuable contribution was the lending of his universally respected name. It was a reputation acquired in service to the Liberals' sacred concept of the *Rechtsstaat*. Like many German liberals of the nineteenth century, Gneist preferred the historically rooted system of English self-government to the rationally contrived constitutions of the French Revolution. He was also in the forefront of a campaign to translate political theory into practice by pushing for the reform of the Prussian bureaucracy, the formidable stronghold of absolutism. The objectives were twofold: to transfer many of the administrative powers exercised by the state bureaucracy to local organs of self-government, and to protect the rights of the individual against arbitrary bureaucratic decisions by placing the bureaucracy under the jurisdiction of administrative courts to which he could appeal. Thus Gneist provided until his death in 1895 a figurehead for the Verein which, as will become clear, immediately identified its major concern.[23]

His successor was Heinrich Rickert, whose initial apprehensions had provided the impetus to create the organization. Until Gneist's death he served as vice-president. By the time he assumed the presidency, he had already been a member of the Reichstag for twenty-one years. His political career began as a National Liberal deputy from Danzig, but in 1880 he seceded along with twenty-eight other deputies, in protest against his party's support of Bismarck's tariff and anti-socialist legislation. In 1884 he joined the newly formed German Progressive Party, and when this coalition disintegrated in 1893 he formed his own party, the Progressive Union (Freisinnige Vereinigung, as opposed to Eugen Richter's Freisinnige Volkspartei). In the chambers of the Reichstag he consistently defended the right of Jews to complete equality, so that at his death the *Allgemeine Zeitung des Judentums* unreservedly asserted: "Never before was there a Christian who defended Judaism so vigorously, more convincingly and more enthusiastically than many Jews." The anti-Semites in turn honored him with the epithet "director of the Jewish mercenaries." [24]

When Rickert died at the end of 1902, he was succeeded by another confirmed Progressive, Theodor Barth. Through four visits to the United States he had gained a genuine understanding of the nature of American democracy, as well as an honorary doctorate from Harvard University. His admiration also extended to the British political system, and he worked hard to counter German prejudices against both countries. He obviously undermined his efforts toward that end by simultaneously supporting the policies to enlarge the German army, navy, and colonial empire. In 1883 he had started the *Nation,* which he continued to edit until 1907. The circulation never surpassed three thousand, and with his departure it ceased to appear. The loss in 1903 of the seats that he held in the Reichstag and the Prussian Chamber of Deputies decidedly diminished Barth's effectiveness as president of the Abwehrverein. He never returned to either, and thus lost a national platform from which to plead the cause of his organization.[25]

The last president of the Verein before the war was Georg Gothein, who succeeded to the office at the death of Barth in 1909. Like Rickert and Barth, he too was a member of the Progressive Union and had sat in the Reichstag uninterruptedly since 1901. A recognized student of the German economy, in 1901 he published a massive survey of Germany's foreign trade. He was also a severe critic of the government's protectionist policy.[26]

It is thus apparent that the leadership of the Abwehrverein shared the heritage of nineteenth-century German liberalism, a political movement which at the end of the 1870's had been condemned by Bismarck to the fate of a perpetual opposition with little hope of gaining power. Deprived of such hope, and without the responsibility and discipline attending it, the liberals during the ensuing decades broke into ever smaller splinter groups so that none was much more effective than a political club.[27] Nevertheless, the traditional allegiance to the ideal of the *Rechtsstaat* remained unbroken. Since the beginning of the nineteenth century German liberals had struggled to realize a national life in Germany governed by a written constitution that would express the will of the German people and safeguard the fundamental rights of every citizen. The essence of such a document had to be the separation and delineation of powers between what ought to be three independent branches of government. Particularly crucial was the successful limitation of the executive branch and its ubiquitous bureaucracy. The ultimate goal was a parliamentary monarchy as it had developed in eighteenth-century England. Bismarck, however, had effectively terminated German development at the far less satisfactory stage of a constitutional monarchy, which liberals

had agreed to accept only as a transitional stage in order to accelerate unification.[28]

During the Second Reich even this latter stage required defense
against the incursions and subversions of reactionary forces. The
Prussian Constitution of 1850 and the North German Constitution of
1867 did produce a *Rechtsstaat* of sorts that guaranteed many of the
fundamental rights indispensable for individual development. What
moved the founders and leaders of the Abwehrverein to act was the
threat that anti-Semitism posed to this imperfect *Rechtsstaat*.

The major concern of the Verein was the character of the German
state. As a *Rechtsstaat* it rested upon the principle that citizens
bound by the same obligations are entitled to the same rights. By at-
tacking the emancipation of the Jews, the anti-Semites weakened the
very fabric of the German state. At issue was the absolute civil and
political equality of all citizens. To circumscribe the rights of Jews
would be a violation of the Constitution and a betrayal of the
Rechtsstaat. Since both the emancipation and the *Rechtsstaat* were the
achievements of nineteenth-century German liberalism, spokesmen of
the Abwehrverein warned that ultimately the assault against the Jews
was also a repudiation of liberalism. Anti-Semites contended that liberalism had unleashed a swarm of Jewish capitalists, usurers, and
foreigners to impoverish the German masses. They did not hesitate
to identify liberalism with Judaism and to excoriate both for defiling
the purity of pristine German values. The Abwehrverein railed
against those liberals who either failed to perceive this danger or
chose to remain indifferent, and who on occasion even supported an
anti-Semitic candidate in a run-off election for the Reichstag.[29]

The leaders of the Verein viewed the victories of the anti-Semitic
parties during the Reichstag elections from 1893 to 1907 as a political expression of economic discontent. The anti-Semitic deputies, in
their view, represented a protest vote by economic groups unable to
adjust to the rapid transformation of the German economy. Peasants,
artisans, and Junkers were ready to employ demagoguery to influence
the government to assuage their plight. Anti-Semitism was therefore
the epitome of a reactionary hatred fed by the conspicuous economic
success of the Jews themselves. Men like Treitschke and Stoecker

merely served to legitimize the hatred by sanctifying it with the vir-
tues of religious and national passions; they did not create it. The
source was to be found in the victims of capitalism, who desperately
attempted to alter the system that afflicted them and rewarded the
Jews.[30]

Barth held the Junkers directly responsible. "Antisemitism is a
kind of socialism of the Junkers . . . by the Junkers and for the
Junkers." In a reckless gambit to reverse the economic trend which
entailed their own destruction, they skillfully incited the masses
against the Jews, the most evident and vulnerable symbol of the capi-
talistic system. Hopefully the resulting disorder would intimidate the
government to discard its hated economic policies. For the Junkers,
group interests were prior to the welfare of the nation.[31]

Thus, the Abwehrverein was not formed to defend Jewish interests. Its spokesmen frequently reiterated that their perspective was
greater than the special concerns of a single confession. Their effort
was not the expression of any subjective philo-Semitism.[32] Accordingly, at a meeting of the board in 1901 Rickert rejected the suggestion that the fight against anti-Semitism was a Jewish matter and
ought to be left to the Jews. On the contrary, it constituted a vital
German interest, and as German Christians the members of the Verein were preoccupied with a problem that directly affected the quality of their lives.[33] Defining the issue thus in legal and political
terms, the Verein could ignore the social forms of anti-Semitism during its first decade. It was not about to tell anyone with whom he
should associate. This could legitimately be considered a Jewish concern. Only after the turn of the century, when political anti-Semitism
visibly subsided only to be replaced by multiplying forms of social
exclusion, did the Verein begin to address itself to this pernicious
manifestation. The exclusion of the Jew now seemed but another
form of the divisive particularism that was splintering German society into selfish and antagonistic castes and interest groups.[34]

That the defense of the *Rechtsstaat* was the major objective of the
Abwehrverein emerges indisputably from its increasing polemic
against the German and Prussian governments' consistent reluctance
to admit Jews to various branches of state employment. With the decline of overt political anti-Semitism, especially after the Reichstag

elections of 1907, the Verein steadily intensified its efforts to publicize this long-standing policy of bureaucratic subversion of the Constitution. It demanded the appointment of Jews to the judiciary, the
teaching staffs of secondary schools, the civil service, and above all,
the officer corps. The leaders of the Abwehrverein raised the issue of
Jews in the military almost annually in the Reichstag. According to
the *Frankfurter Zeitung,* not one Jew had become a reserve officer
out of the twenty-five to thirty thousand Jewish volunteers (i.e., secondary school graduates who had to serve only one year and who
alone could become officers) who had served since 1880. During the
same period, of the twelve to fifteen hundred Jewish converts serving
in the military, about three hundred were accepted as reserve officers.[35]

Spokesmen of the Abwehrverein fought such covert discrimination
as an intolerable violation of imperial law (*Reichsgesetz*) and the
Prussian Constitution which rejected religion as a qualification for
office. A Conservative-dominated bureaucracy had effectively cir-
cumvented them. The revoking of emancipation for which the
anti-Semites were clamoring in the 1890's had now been partially
won by administrative fiat. When a Prussian Minister of Justice
could openly admit that Jews were not appointed as judges, in order
not to offend the religious sensibilities of the people, then the Constitution had truly been rendered meaningless. Germany had regressed
from the rule of law to the arbitrary rule of bigoted bureaucrats.[36]

The defense of the Jews against government discrimination, of
course, was part of the larger struggle against the Conservative-
Junker hegemony over the Second Reich. There is no doubt that, especially in Prussia where the overwhelming majority of German
Jewry lived, Jews enjoyed little success in entering the diplomatic
service, the general state administration, the officer corps, the office
of public prosecution, and the state primary and secondary schools,
or in penetrating the upper echelons of the judiciary, the civil service, and the faculties of universities.[37] But then large numbers of
other Germans made little headway in many of these same areas. Regardless of the Constitution, the Prussian government in particular
was determined to preserve the Conservative and Christian character
of the state, and it carefully examined the extra-official qualifications

of religion, title, family, military rank, and political affiliation of aspirants to the bureaucracy. Even though the Junkers may not have been numerically the predominant social and political group in the Prussian Administration, they still exercised formidable power because they dominated the strategic offices that possessed the greatest political authority. Since the end of the Kulturkampf Catholics had been appointed in proportion to their number in the population, although virtually excluded from any high office in the Imperial or Prussian bureaucracies. Liberals and Social Democrats were almost totally excluded from all echelons of the system. To a certain extent the campaign of the Abwehrverein against the government reached its peak at the end of the first decade of the twentieth century, when a reunited and rejuvenated Progressive Party simultaneously was making a concerted effort to wrest control of the German Empire from Junker domination. Both maneuvers failed completely.[38]

JEWISH INVOLVEMENT

The reaction of German Jewry to the formation of the Verein zur Abwehr des Antisemitismus seems to have been unanimously favorable. Both Reform and Orthodox Jews united in their praise for what they regarded as a significant event, and they expressed gratitude at the display of Christian concern, for which they had hoped so long. They spoke approvingly of the tactics being developed and were quick to point out signs of their effectiveness. The *Allgemeine Zeitung des Judentums* was ready to attribute the decline in the number of anti-Semitic votes cast in Hesse in the Reichstag elections of 1893—from 30,468 to 26,470—to the impact of the bureaus operating out of Frankfurt and Marburg. (At best, such a claim of effectiveness was debatable, since this reduced vote returned five anti-Semitic deputies, three more than had been elected in 1890.) The Jewish papers advised Jews to contribute generously to the organization's campaign fund. Above all, they urged Jews to become members.[39]

Initially there had been some doubt as to whether Jews would be accepted. As soon as the Abwehrverein appeared, Jews inquired about the possibility of joining. In a circular dated February 19, 1891, the board responded affirmatively whereupon the board of the Frankfurt Jewish Community issued an appeal for Jewish members. The following month Charles Hallgarten, the first Jewish member of the Verein Board, addressed a confidential circular to the presidents of the Jewish communities of Germany, stating his conviction that the Jews must take an active role in the fight against anti-Semitism, and that every Jew must become a member of the defense organization. He asked the presidents to enlist the members of their communities.[40]

The Verein not only welcomed Jewish members; it actively sought Jewish support. Indeed, it soon began to criticize what it regarded as the staggering indifference of German Jewry in the face of a dozen years of uninterrupted provocation. During this period, its publications declared, the German Christian had witnessed the passive submission of Jews to an interminable barrage of invective and defamation. Eventually the uncontested assertions began to sound convincing. A Christian observer was forced to conclude that guilt or cowardliness motivated Jewish silence. The fight against anti-Semitism must not be comfortably left to Christians. Jews have the right and the duty to defend themselves. And yet many were so oblivious of their duty that they continued to buy anti-Semitic papers and tracts to satisfy their curiosity, thereby helping to finance the propaganda. Although such criticism tended to encourage separate, organized Jewish initiatives, the main intention was merely to bring Jews into the Verein.[41] Writing to Edmund Friedemann in 1893, Rickert expressed his disappointment at the results:

I have unfortunately had to correct my judgment in several respects about the willingness of your coreligionists to make sacrifices. I could tell you stories that completely depressed me. When millionaires consider it a bargain to redeem themselves in this question of existence and life with minimal contributions, then one indeed loses all pleasure and courage. Particularly Berlin and the North are conspicuous by their indifference.[42]

Despite Rickert's annoyance, the available evidence suggests that the major portion of the Verein's annual budget of about 40,000 marks actually did come from Jewish sources. Certainly efforts were constantly made to attract such support. In an 1894 circular the Abwehrverein proposed that every Jewish community include an annual contribution in its budget, and as late as 1902 Hallgarten was still sending out personal appeals to individual communities such as Regensburg.[43] The figures of Königsberg in East Prussia and Neuwied along the Rhine do indicate a steady decline in contributions, but if a single large community like Königsberg with a population in 1895 of 4,228 Jews raised well over 1,000 marks annually for the Abwehrverein for the entire last decade of the century, it is likely that the combined contributions of the large Jewish communities provided most of the income. The figures from Königsberg are shown in the accompanying tabulation.[44]

Year	Contributions (Marks)	
1891	3,477	
1892	2,701	
1894	1,696	(until April 1, 1896)
1896	1,400	
1897	1,488	
1898	1,350	
1899	1,233	
1901	850	(until June 1, 1901)

The few figures left from Neuwied, a much smaller community of only 480 Jews, reveal an even sharper drop.

Year	Contributions (Marks)
1893/1894	318
1894/1895	84.50
1895/1896	30.50

The Abwehrverein's initial success in Neuwied may well have been related to the resurgence of anti-Semitism in the area. In 1893 agitators in Xanten had revived the charge of ritual murder against a Jewish butcher, who had already been acquitted of murder in July 1892. In September 1893, a circular from the recently opened Cologne bureau of the Verein reported that the populace was again being incited.[45] The case of Neuwied indicates that contributions may have fluctuated according to the intensity of local anti-Semitism. Generally, however, the amounts declined steadily, partially because local money was now also going into the coffers of the Centralverein.

The extent of active Jewish involvement was likewise considerable. Hallgarten, who in 1875 had returned to Germany a wealthy man after a successful banking career in the United States, helped open the Frankfurt bureau of the Verein and played a commanding role in its operations until his death in 1908.[46] During the first decade of the Verein's existence, young Ludwig Jacobowski [47] served as a member of the board and deputy treasurer. A prolific writer, committed to fusing the German and Jewish components of his background, he enriched the *Mitteilungen* with many articles. His most famous novel, *Werther, der Jude,* published in 1891, went through seven editions and six translations by 1920. The response to anti-Semitism of this alienated Jew was thus marked by extreme vacillation between severe criticism of his coreligionists and defiant reaffirmation of Judaism. He died in 1900 at the age of thirty-two.[48] Some of the more notable among the other Jewish members of the board of the Verein at various periods before the war were Hirsch Hildesheimer, Paul Nathan, Rudolf Mosse, Senator Fischer, Heinrich Meyer-Cohn, and Martin Philippson.[49]

VIEWS ON GERMAN JEWRY

This substantial amount of Jewish support and involvement did not imply that the Abwehrverein's Christian leadership held an entirely uncritical attitude toward the Jews of Germany. Although somewhat muted in the beginning, the attitude became increasingly explicit and may in time have alienated many of those Jews who formerly contributed generously. The Verein seemed to harbor no doubts about the nationality of the Jews. Nationality was a quality determined by language, culture, and mentality, not by the length of residence or ancestral origins. The Germans of Jewish persuasion were nothing less than Germans. The racist arguments about the alien Semitic character of the German Jew were as contemptible as the efforts to transform the figure of Jesus into an Aryan prototype. Not racial purity or distinctiveness but religion and a history of persecution formed the common denominator of present-day Jewry, and if Jews still continued to exhibit a certain cohesiveness and clannishness, that was mainly the achievement of the current anti-Semitic hostility.[50]

The Verein was certainly not ready to deny that the behavior of many German Jews did exhibit numerous shortcomings. It simply insisted, as had pro-Jewish spokesmen since Dohm, that they were the product of history rather than of race. Only time and honest self-criticism would effect a correction of the character deformities produced by the extended humiliation of the Middle Ages. Moreover, it refused to countenance the insidious generalizations that anti-Semites drew from the errors of a few. Genuine self-criticism had all but ceased as a result of anti-Semitic distortions and fabrications, and occasionally a member of the Verein would urge that the organization not relinquish this corrective to the inept hands of the anti-Semites.[51]

The first explicit statement of what the Abwehrverein expected of German Jewry came in an 1893 article in the *Mitteilungen* by Professor Albrecht Weber, a pioneer in the study of ancient Indian literature and one of the founders of the Verein. After admitting that anti-Semitism had no place within the Evangelical Church, in view of Jesus' undeniably Jewish background, Weber encouraged the increase of mixed marriages as the most effective mission to the Jews, since the children were usually raised as Christians. Turning to the Jews, he advised them to discard those practices of Judaism he felt to be offensive. A genuine religious reform was required to drop those oriental rites which were among the actual causes of anti-Semitism. Not only was their very strangeness abrasive, but they continued to give expression to the old Jewish claim of being God's chosen people.[52]

The article provoked anger and indignation in Jewish circles. Heinrich Meyer-Cohn, a Berlin lawyer and banker, condemned the illiberal demands of liberals like Mommsen and Weber, who failed to recognize the differences between state and nationality, and who advised the discarding of customs only because they seemed exotic, as well as the adoption of a religion in which they themselves no longer believed. The rabbi of the Jewish community in Freiburg, Baden, asserted that Jews who had so often been maligned as hucksters and hustlers (*Schacherjuden*) were not ready to barter with their religious beliefs, sensitivities, and rites.[53]

The protest evoked an official declaration of policy. The Verein underscored that it had no intention of interfering in the affairs of another religious group, unless its practices offended the accepted standards of morality. It definitely would not take issue with harmless rites that might irritate some by their strangeness. With regard to Weber's specific reference to the practice of kosher slaughtering, the Verein was satisfied with the judgments of the numerous experts who regarded it as the most humane method in use. In conclusion, the declaration explained that Weber's article was published to elicit discussion and not to enunciate official policy.[54]

This concern to diminish the extent of Jewish separateness was still more openly articulated several years later in reaction to the appearance of several Jewish fraternities and clubs. The growing exclusion of Jews from the various circles of German social life, especially from the university fraternities, provoked a Jewish organizational response, of which the Abwehrverein did not approve. In commenting on the 1896 formation of a national organization of Jewish fraternities known as the Kartell Convent, the Verein regretted the appearance of social fraternities along religious lines. It deplored the formation in 1895 of the Verein jüdischer Studenten (Association of Jewish Students) at the University of Berlin, and especially denounced the Association's intention in 1900 to fight for the election of a Jewish member to the official representative organ of the student body. Jews had begun to give up the common fight for equality. Such action could only strengthen the anti-Semitic campaign to force all Jews out of integrated fraternities. Several years later the Abwehrverein expressed the same disapproval at the creation of the Union of National Jewish Sports Clubs (Verband national-jüdischer Turnvereine), which was a response to the growing exclusion of Jews from German sports groups. In an editorial pejoratively entitled "Separate Jewish Games" ("Jüdische Abschliessungsspielerei"), the *Mitteilungen* tried to convince Jews not to respond by withdrawal. Without justifying its position, the editorial simply advised Jews to join those clubs that still raised no religious or racial barriers.[55]

By far the most outspoken expression of opinion on the internal affairs of the Jewish community came on the issue of Zionism. With the acceptance of the Basel Program, the Abwehrverein insisted that Zionism had ceased to be an internal Jewish matter, because it now threatened to jeopardize Jewish citizenship throughout Western Europe. However, even before 1897 the Verein considered Zionism to be a formidable danger to the Jews, and it therefore felt compelled to discuss the issue. Zionism served to reawaken all the doubts and reservations about the possibility and quality of Jewish patriotism that had undermined the commitment to total emancipation for nearly a century. One could certainly be an equal German citizen without stemming from one of the original Teutonic tribes, but not even the Abwehrverein was prepared to admit that one could simultaneously be both a German and a Jewish nationalist. Being a German citizen required more than just paying taxes. The Verein reminded the Jews of Germany that each had to prove himself a reliable member of the German people.[56]

Verein spokesmen did not regard Zionism as the reflection of any historical truth; rather it was the disillusioned reaction of the victims of anti-Semitism. The irony of the situation was that the first Zionists were of course the anti-Semites themselves, who had never doubted the alien character of the Jew; the tragedy lay in the fact that Zionism vindicated the entire anti-Semitic movement.[57] In addition, it presented a regrettable obstruction to the ultimate assimilation of German Jewry. Zionists had sanctified another ineradicable difference between German and Jew, and thereby reduced still further the chances of harmonious integration.[58]

The evidence concerning the Verein's attitude toward German Jewry is sufficiently consistent to warrant the conclusion that what its spokesmen ultimately expected was an integration that would result in the dissolution of Germany's organized Jewish community. The open displeasure at all manifestations of Jewish life beyond the act of public worship and the intimated desire to diminish differences even in this area implied a conviction that emancipation had its price. The Verein's sustained opposition to Zionism sprang not only from anxiety about the quality of Jewish patriotism, but also from fear of the revival of Jewish consciousness.

The Abwehrverein embodied, therefore, the latent intolerance of

German liberals for Jewish survival, which had manifested itself periodically since the end of the eighteenth century.[59] Assimilation meant conversion, and their liberalism operated only to the extent that they advocated the immediate extension of full emancipation, in the hope that it would hasten the trip to the baptismal font. The spectacle of Jewish obstinancy impelled them at intervals to spell out their position.

In 1880 Theodor Mommsen had again reminded German Jews of their unpaid debts. His famous response to Treitschke did condemn anti-Semitism, but not because he viewed it as a threat to the character of the *Rechtsstaat*. He was far more troubled about prospects for achieving a thoroughgoing national reconciliation and thereby strengthening the unity of the Empire. His overriding fear was that the bitterly feuding latter-day descendants of the various Teutonic tribes would destroy in peacetime the political unification they had won on the battlefield. The immediate need was for overcoming the ethnic, sectional, and religious antagonisms that still seethed beneath the veneer of political unity. Mommsen did not criticize the substance of Treitschke's remarks about Jews as much as he questioned the sagacity of raising them at that moment, a blunder that merely intensified the existing divisiveness. The overcoming of German particularism required sacrifices even of the Jews, and Mommsen agreed with Treitschke that the Jews were partly to blame for the present unrest, especially those countless liberal Jews who refused to convert to Christianity long after they had ceased to believe in and practice any form of Judaism.[60] Thus the Abwehrverein was heir to a German liberal tradition that begrudged the Jews any organizational separateness and ultimately any religious individuality.

In retrospect, this ideological legacy of the Abwehrverein perforce disqualified the organization from speaking on behalf of German Jewry. Whether Jewish leaders intuitively sensed the intolerance as early as 1893, and therefore moved to form a Jewish defense establishment, is doubtful. As shall be suggested in the next chapter, it was rather a second wave of anti-Semitism that overcame the deep-seated reluctance of Jews to fight openly. In either case, once founded, the Centralverein seems to have maintained a consistently formal and distant relationship with the Abwehrverein. Before 1911

the only cooperation between the two defense organizations was limited to the annual contributions of the Centralverein to the coffers of
the Abwehrverein. In 1900 the board raised the sum from 100 to
300 marks, still a trifling sum, though now the largest single contribution given by the Centralverein to any organization. Finally in
1911 the two bodies expanded their cooperation by setting up a common election fund to finance the campaign against anti-Semitic candidates in the coming Reichstag elections.[61] This limited relationship
may well reflect the growing awareness among Jewish leaders of the
ideologic antagonism between the two organizations and their corresponding disillusionment with liberal motives. Though both fought a
common enemy, the Abwehrverein was exclusively committed to the
defense of the *Rechtsstaat,* while the Centralverein increasingly saw
the problem in terms of the survival of Jewish identity.

Within the context of the Second Reich, the attitude of the Abwehrverein toward Jewish survival is a striking instance of a thesis
cogently argued in recent years by Uriel Tal. Armed with extensive
research, Tal has contended that German Jewry's quest for full integration coupled with a determination to maintain a separate group
identity never won the backing of German liberals, whether political
or religious. Political liberals responded to Jewish efforts at communal survival with the same disregard that they had shown for Dan-
ish rights in 1864. With their profound reverence for authority, a
mentality which they shared with the rest of their countrymen, the
liberals vacillated between condoning direct government intervention
to impose Germanization or advocating a process of internalization
whereby the citizen would come to identify voluntarily with the will
of the state.

Liberal Protestants were no more sympathetic. Though they repudiated the Conservative's notion of the Christian state and fought for
a separation of church and state, they had every intention of
strengthening the exclusively Christian character of Germany. Despite their abhorrence of clericalism, dogma, sacraments and institutionalized religion, they hoped to Christianize society by permeating
every facet of life with the spirit of the Gospels. That spirit was to
pervade especially the educational institutions so that eventually the
example and message of Jesus would shape the character of every

citizen. Thus in the very sector of German society where the Jews should have found their staunchest allies, they confronted a vision of a state which replaced equality with uniformity and pluralism with a cultural-religious monism. [62]

4

TIME TO ACT: 1893

THE INITIAL EFFORTS of the Abwehrverein exerted no immediate influence upon the course of German anti-Semitism. On the contrary, in the two years following the creation of the Verein, anti-Semitism reached alarming proportions. A burgeoning hostility had shattered the relative calm of the 1880's, and the recent political successes of the anti-Semitic parties seemed to defy the inveterate optimism of the most assimilated observers. This rapidly deteriorating situation drove German Jewry to reevaluate some of its most vigorously defended convictions. In a mood of profound distress, many embraced an alternative that German Jewry had dismissed for nearly two decades.

A SECOND WAVE OF
ANTI-SEMITISM

In the Summer of 1891 German Jewry was again confronted with the ugly charge of ritual murder. At the end of June the corpse of a five-year-old Christian boy with a deep gash in the throat had been discovered in Xanten, a predominantly Catholic community along the lower Rhine. Systematic anti-Semitic exploitation succeeded in forcing the arrest of a Jewish butcher, whom the authorities released in December for lack of evidence. Unperturbed, the anti-Semites in February 1892 took the issue to the Prussian Chamber of Deputies through an interpellation accusing the authorities of succumbing to Jewish pressure. The accused was again incarcerated, this time to be tried for murder. Five months later, with the public prosecutor demanding acquittal, the jury after an eleven-day trial returned a verdict of not guilty. But continued local animosity forced the defendant and his Xanten coreligionists to evacuate their homes. Only the condemnation of the charge by the Bishop of Cologne and his order to preach against it finally helped to quell popular unrest.[1]

On another front the sporadic campaign against the practice of kosher slaughtering seemed on the verge of yielding results. On October 1, 1892, a directive of the Saxon Minister of Interior became effective that henceforth all animals to be slaughtered, except poultry, were to be stunned first. Similar directives were issued in 1893 by various local Prussian authorities, although the Prussian Minister of Interior revoked them. Jews began to fear ministerial curtailment of the religious freedom guaranteed by the Constitution.[2]

Still more ominous was the impact of the anti-Semitic forces upon the course of German politics. In the Reichstag elections of 1893, whose main issue was the government's intention to enlarge the army, the anti-Semitic parties had increased their vote from 47,000 to 263,000, and the number of their delegates from 5 to 16, one more than the number of deputies required to form an independent Reichstag faction. Not only had the Social Democrats and the anti-Semites registered the most impressive gains, but the Progressives, who had divided over the army bill into two independent organizations, dropped from 67 to 37 seats.[3]

Even before the election the growing anti-Semitic sentiment had induced the Conservatives to become the first major German party to adopt an anti-Semitic plank in its revised Tivoli platform of December 8, 1892. Against only seven votes the boisterous, radical-dominated convention had agreed to drop the modifying addition, "We repudiate the excesses of anti-Semitism," so that the remaining condemnation of Jewish influence was unequivocal: "We fight the multifarious and obtrusive Jewish influence that decomposes our people's life." The convention's political instinct had been sound, and in the Reichstag elections of 1893 the Conservative Party, with a million votes, had won seventy-two seats. Thus the second largest bloc in the Reichstag was now openly anti-Semitic.[4]

URGENT REASSESSMENT

This succession of anti-Semitic triumphs aroused fear and consternation within the Jewish community. The German Jewish papers took the lead in reevaluating the situation. They agreed that German anti-Semitism suddenly appeared to be a far more frightening specter than originally imagined, that it still had not reached its peak, and that the time had come for Jews to fight back. They rejected any further attempts to account for the hostility by recourse to Jewish shortcomings. Anti-Semitism had proven itself to be quite independent of Jewish behavior.[5] Both the Reform *Allgemeine Zeitung des Judentums* and the Orthodox *Jüdische Presse* urged their readers prior to the Reichstag elections of 1893 to vote against all anti-Semitic candidates, and during the campaign for the Prussian Landtag later that year they even called for the election of at least one Jewish deputy to defend Jewish interests.[6] That both these predominantly religious papers should independently offer the same political counsel, opening themselves to charges of bloc voting and a Jewish "Center," charges to which German Jews were exceptionally sensitive, reflects the gravity of the moment. But the influence of the four major Jewish papers was too limited to make them effective organs of self-defense. Not one could claim a circulation of 3,000 subscribers.[7]

The consternation at the spectacle of another blood libel manifested itself in the immediate publication of two important studies intended to counter this irrational and unscrupulous witch-hunt. Hermann Strack, the renowned Lutheran authority on Judaism, and editor of *Nathanael,* the literary organ of the Church's mission to the Jews, had been engaged for some time in researching the subject of blood in Christian and Jewish literature. The occurrence of a ritual murder case in Korfu in April 1891 induced him the following July to bring out the first edition of his *Der Blutaberglaube bei Christen und Juden.* In the wake of the Xanten charge in October 1892 he published an enlarged second edition.[8]

That same year Paul Nathan, the Progressive Jewish journalist, published his detailed account of the Hungarian ritual murder libel at Tisza-Eszlár. Although this *cause célèbre* went back to 1883 and Na-

than's study had been finished shortly thereafter, he had refrained
from publishing it under pressure from friends who believed that the
case would surely be the last instance of a blood libel being hurled
against the Jews. The events in Xanten, which Nathan covered for
Nation, abruptly proved that opinion naïve. Especially alarming was
the fact that the Prussian Chamber of Deputies, with the hearty backing of the Conservatives, saw fit to entertain the discredited accusation seriously. Still Nathan's sense of history and belief in progress
enabled him to conclude his sober report on the Xanten affair on a
note of consolation.

The Crusaders (once) slaughtered the Jews in Xanten; that occurred on
June 27, 1096. On June 29, 1891, exactly 795 years and two days later, a
poor child with his throat slit was found in that same Xanten, and fanaticism raged again. But they demolished only one house and they dragged
a single innocent, suspected Jew no further than the vicinity of the scaf-
fold. That certainly amounts to some difference, and who would deny
that in the course of 795 years we have not made progress? [9]

Also in 1892 a number of angry Leipzig Jews composed a series
of six essays to rebut a variety of anti-Semitic allegations. First published separately in local newspapers, they later appeared as a sixty-
page pamphlet. The opening address, "to our Christian fellow-
citizens," accurately conveys the mood:

Our forbearance, our confidence in the automatic collapse of the
anti-Semitic edifice, built upon lies, defamations, and distortions, is gone.
We are resolved to tear asunder the fabric spun with unheard of effron-
tery [*Unverfrorenheit*], to present before our Christian fellow citizens
the most essential, shameless lies of the anti-Semites. [10]

As 1893 opened, Hermann Strack again volunteered an important
contribution entitled *May the Jews Be Called "Criminals on Account
of Their Religion"?* Convinced that only decisive judicial intervention could dam the endless stream of anti-Semitic invective, Strack
and four Evangelical theologians had asked the public prosecutor in
Berlin to prosecute several pieces of anti-Semitica accusing Jews of
crimes allegedly committed in compliance with Jewish law. Not only
was this request denied, but two additional appeals, to a higher office
of prosecution and to the Prussian Minister of Justice himself, had
received the same treatment. Finally Strack printed both the appeals

and denials in pamphlet form in order to invoke directly "the sense of justice of the Christian German people." The performance to date of the Prussian judiciary had convinced both Jews and Christians, both anti-Semites and philo-Semites, that the legal system lacked firm leadership. The very refusal to prosecute such literature posed the state with an unavoidable dilemma: "If the assertions of the broadsheet [*Flagblattes*] are true, then measures must be taken against Judaism by the state; however, if they are not true, their dissemination cannot continue unhindered." [11]

A militant, anonymously published, essay at the beginning of 1893 purported to convey the shifting mood of the majority of German Jewry. The rumored intention of the worried board of the Berlin Jewish Community to appeal urgently to the Kaiser for protection provoked the irate author to articulate his critical opinion. The resulting essay included a significant repudiation of the traditional Jewish defensive strategy which relied upon a special and mutually beneficial relationship between Jewry and the ruling power. The author denounced the intention of the Berlin Board as the typically medieval recourse of a "protected Jew" whose emancipated descendants had still not learned the difference between privilege and right. A new legal status dictated a new defensive policy, and it was this inevitable consequence that the author pleaded with his coreligionists to recognize. After refuting the practical value of the appeal, he elaborated further:

The request for protection, however, also has its moral significance. The man who has no rights, or whose rights are being curtailed, is the one who pleads for protection. But we are in full possession of our civil rights and the boisterous crowd of anti-Semites has no power to reduce them. However, in a free society every opinion may be freely expressed; he who wishes to contest should enter the lists with the weapons of the spirit and should not call for outside help. If we do more, we lower ourselves. Then we silently renounce the means which our rights grant us and sink back into the medieval wretchedness which made our ancestors protected Jews.[12]

But the writer also shared the widely held conviction that at least part of the anti-Semitic fury was justifiably directed against the unwholesome groups still left within German Jewry. He urged, therefore, that the Jews themselves immediately take effective action against those harmful elements within the Jewish community: the Orthodox, whose stubborn separatism rested on the Talmud, a work which the overwhelming mass of German Jews neither knew nor lived by nor cared to defend; the parvenus, whose tasteless ostentation evoked disgust; and the uneducated.[13]

In conclusion, he proposed to base the public challenge of the anti-Semites on the following principles shared by the majority of German Jewry:

1. We are not German Jews, but German citizens of the Jewish faith.

2. We need and demand as citizens no other protection than the duly constituted system of justice.

3. As Jews we belong to no political party. Political views, like religious, are the concern of the individual.

4. We stand firmly upon the soil of the German nationality. We have with the Jews of other countries no other relationship than have the Catholics and Protestants of Germany with the Catholics and Protestants of other countries.

5. We have no other morality than that of our non-Jewish fellow citizens.

6. We condemn the immoral behavior of the individual, regardless of his religion; we deny all responsibility for the behavior of the individual Jew; and we protest against the generalizing with which careless or malicious critics charge the entire body of Jewish citizens for the behavior of the individual Jew.[14]

These principles won the attention of the German press and brought an avalanche of letters to the publisher from enthusiastic Jewish readers, with the inevitable result that the identity of the author, Raphael Löwenfeld, a prominent theatrical figure, soon became a well-known secret.[15]

Löwenfeld's anti-Orthodox diatribe did not break new ground. It was but another instance in an increasingly vituperative debate between German Reform and separatistic Orthodoxy in the face of mounting external pressure. Each side repeatedly asserted that the other alone was the designated object of anti-Semitism or at least contributed to its virulence. Reform spokesmen fulminated against the anachronistic religious practices of Orthodoxy which they contended obstructed assimilation and disrupted the harmony of public life.[16] The Orthodox camp of Samson R. Hirsch, particularly in the pages of the *Israelit,* cited anti-Semitism as proving the bankruptcy of Reform. Having discarded the institutions of Judaism as the price of emancipation, Reform Jews were left with neither, and unhappily were forced to defend that which they no longer believed or practiced. To retain their identity, Reform leaders were compelled to elaborate upon the superiority and mission of Judaism, and thereby succeeded only in irritating Christian sensibilities.[17] For the *Israelit,* unified resistance to anti-Semitism was impossible. The original unity of the Jewish community had been shattered only by the Reform, who remained the most dangerous enemy of Judaism.[18]

The more moderate wing of German Orthodoxy, led by the Hildesheimer Seminary in Berlin, viewed the German scene far more gravely than its Frankfurt ally and did not repudiate collective action. In response to a four-day debate on the Talmud in 1893 in the Prussian Chamber of Deputies, Ezriel Hildesheimer and Marcus Horovitz joined a representative group of rabbis to issue a declaration on the nature and importance of this legal, ethical compendium. The statement depicted the Talmud as a rich combination of authoritative interpretations of both the Written and Oral Laws, as well as a multiplicity of individual opinions, with no binding status. Within the latter classification belonged especially the infrequent hostile outbursts against pagans (*Akum*), to be found in Talmudic and later Rabbinic literature, which must be understood in light of the trying circumstances of the time.[19] Clearly intended to reaffirm the suitability and trustworthiness of Judaism for the modern state, this declaration was subsequently sent to members of German legislatures, government officials, and newspaper editors. Nevertheless, the separatistic Orthodox, represented by the *Israelit,* rejected what it regarded as a misleading distinction between Written and Oral Law and refused to endorse the apologetic efforts.[20]

But even among the followers of Samson R. Hirsch some were intensely worried by recent events. Perhaps the most perceptive analysis to appear in the anxious months of 1893 came from Marcus Hirsch, a son of the founder of German Neo-Orthodoxy. Hirsch, a physician, warned that the revoking of emancipation was not incon-

ceivable. It had only recently been granted, and political anti-
Semitism had already begun its assault. Two conditions encouraged
its prospects. First the government had obviously permitted the anti-
Semites to operate as a legitimate political force, although the Jews
did not constitute a political entity and the anti-Semitic parties offered
no other platform than their anti-Jewish proposals. Even more disconcerting was the support that the radical anti-Semites were quietly receiving from that large cultured, liberal sector of society that
abhorred the excesses of the extremists, while conceding that their
charges contained a modicum of truth. Why should the uneducated
masses reject anti-Semitism when the upper strata of society were
crypto-anti-Semites? Hirsch believed that Jewish efforts at self-
defense would be useless. The cultural lag of German society could
be overcome only by a revolutionary change in attitude, which had
to be initiated from above by the educated and liberal leaders of
Germany.[21]

It was the opinion of Leopold Auerbach that an improved public
image of Judaism would in fact help to dispel some of the miscon-
ceptions nourishing official and popular prejudices about Judaism. In
an essay published shortly before the Reichstag elections of 1893, he
argued that the courts were hampered by confusion as to what genuinely constituted Judaism. One could not expect them to convict
without precise information on the nature of the subject. To provide
such authoritative material, Auerbach called for the formation of a
national committee of religious leaders. Furthermore, to repudiate
the prevailing impression that Judaism was the religion of an exclusive racial stock, Auerbach urged that converts be sought actively.
The requirements for conversion, including circumcision, ought to be
relaxed. The result of both these theoretical and practical measures
would be to project an attractive image of a denationalized and ethical religion that would be qualified for integration into German society.[22]

The very terminology of two other essays which appeared in 1893
testifies to the declining optimism. Both James Simon, a leading cot-
ton manufacturer and personal friend of William II, and Fritz Auerbach spoke of German anti-Semitism as a disease reaching epidemic
proportions. The irrational character of the animosity would not be

cured by time alone; the Jews themselves had to undertake the treatment. Simon particularly stressed that self-respect dictated such action. Jews had to equip themselves with knowledge of their history
and organize to employ every legal means to terminate the unchallenged validity of the anti-Semitic fabrications.[23]

A new tone of militancy marked this literary outburst. Anger had
shattered the self-conscious restraints of the 1880's. The policy of silence had failed catastrophically. The anti-Semitic movement seemed
to endanger the very position of German Jewry, a prospect that few
had considered possible a decade before. Most of the writers con-
curred in the conclusion that Jews must act in their own defense. A
number of German Jews had already begun to translate the growing
consensus into action.

FROM WORDS TO ACTION

When Gustav Karpeles, a talented literary historian, became editor
of the *Allgemeine Zeitung des Judentums* at the beginning of 1890,
he began to work for the formation throughout Germany of adult
study groups committed to the mature examination of the Jewish past
and present. One could not expect Jews to love and defend a heritage
to which they were strangers. Despite its network of welfare organizations, German Jewry was in dire need of organizations for its
healthy members.[24] Karpeles recurrently focused on the two-front
war in which German Jewry was caught: simultaneously fighting intense animosity outside and massive indifference within. Every Jewish community required an Association for Jewish History and Literature (Verein für jüdische Geschichte und Literatur) in order to
inculcate the individual Jew with the pride and knowledge to withstand the daily pressures of anti-Semitism.[25]

Karpeles was by no means the first to realize the social function of
adult Jewish education. In the last quarter of the nineteenth century
the number of German Jews who had reached maturity without the
slightest exposure to even a minimal Jewish education was increasing
at an alarming rate. Mordechai Eliav has recently estimated that by
the end of the century only 35 percent of the Jewish children in Ber-

lin, and up to 60 percent in the rest of Germany, were receiving
some kind of Jewish education.[26] During the 1880's a handful of
such associations for adult education appeared in Germany.[27] Karpeles' contribution was that he organized these sporadic individual
attempts into what became an impressive and sustained nationwide
effort.

In the beginning of 1893 he joined in forming such a group in
Berlin.[28] By December 26, 1893, he had succeeded in bringing to
Hanover delegates from the existing associations in order to establish
a national Verband der Vereine für jüdische Geschichte und Literatur. The first issue of its *Mitteilungen,* which appeared that winter,
defiantly announced: "The storm of enemies rages against us outside,
but we have, like our ancestors of old, with one hand prepared ourselves for defense and with the other begun the construction of the
great work which should secure the holiness of our scholarship." [29]

The objectives of each Verein were threefold: to build a library
and reading room for Jewish books and periodicals, to hold a
number of evening discussions preceded by a report on the subject to
be discussed, and to hold at least three public lectures a winter. The
scope was to include the Jewish past and present, and the Verband
stood ready to aid smaller communities with resource material and
eventually with speakers.[30] The growth of the Verband was dramatic.
By 1900 Karpeles could report that about 1,000 lectures were being
given in 150 Jewish communities during the average winter season of
six months. In 1903 the membership stood at 180 Vereine, with over
15,000 individual members. By 1914 the number had risen to 230
associations.[31]

In 1898 the Verband also began to publish a yearbook devoted to
Jewish history and literature. In actuality, its scope was more limited. Emphasizing German Jewish history and Jewish theology, the
Jahrbuch provided a respectable vehicle for low-keyed apologetica
pitched for an educated Jewish audience. Thus the yearbook was one
more manifestation of the response by Jewish scholarship to the challenge of anti-Semitism, a connection that forms a leitmotif of German Jewish history in the modern period. Between 1898 and 1938
the Verband published some thirty-one volumes, containing a rich
variety of enduring contributions.[32]

Anti-Semitism not only precipitated the formation of the Verband; it directly influenced its growth. In 1900 Karpeles admitted: "We wish merely to confess openly that it was not our toil and labor alone which called forth this movement; without the alliance of our foe we would scarcely have succeeded to shake our coreligionists out of their lethargy." [33] The behavior of a Jewish community in an unidentified small Prussian town documents this observation. When anti-Semitism erupted locally, the Jewish community formed a Literaturverein to fortify itself. During the ensuing three years of unrest, the Verein prospered. When the agitation subsided so did the support for the Verein, and after the election of the first Jew to the town council, a general meeting of the members decided to disband the Verein entirely. [34] Other Jewish communities refused even to form a local Literaturverein for fear of inviting criticism of another instance of Jewish separatism. [35]

The approaching Reichstag elections of June 1893 finally produced two simultaneous initiatives to organize a Jewish defense effort. In January 1893 nearly one hundred Berlin Jewish notables issued an urgent appeal for money to mount a counterattack against the steady barrage of anti-Semitic defamations. Deeply troubled by the specious validity which such vilifications gained through Jewish silence, they proposed to fight back with broadsheets, pamphlets, and speakers. The legal equality of Jewry had to be defended by every legitimate means available. [36] The most immediate result of the appeal was the formation at the end of January 1893 of a Comité zur Abwehr antisemitischer Angriffe (Committee for Defense against anti-Semitic Attacks). Edmund Friedemann and Paul Nathan assumed the responsibilities of president and vice-president of the committee, which included among others Adolf Ginsberg, Heinrich Meyer-Cohn, Hirsch Hildesheimer, Salomon Neumann, James Simon, Julius Isaac, and Samuel Kristeller. [37]

Although the committee enjoyed the open endorsement of the Abwehrverein, [38] some Jews at least were disturbed by the apparent duplication. On Feburary 14, 1893, the Board of the Königsberg Jewish Community addressed an irate letter to Paul Nathan: What was the purpose of another defense organization? Königsberg had already contributed large sums to the Abwehrverein, and a second organization would only split the forces fighting anti-Semitism. Moreover, the board contended, the involvement of Christians in the fight against anti-Semitism was vital. In his response, Nathan justified his group's entry into the battle:

Our Committee was formed with the knowledge and agreement of the Abwehrverein, especially of Rickert. It has become clear that for certain jobs the Abwehrverein is not properly organized, and that above all, according to its statutes, it cannot intervene in political battles. However, it is also necessary to fight directly the election of anti-Semitic candidates, and only *to that extent* will we be politically active. We will thus assume certain tasks that the Abwehrverein cannot assume, and we are in closest contact with it, for Dr. Heinrich Meyer-Cohn, who is one of the most active workers of the Abwehrverein, is at the same time a member of our Committee.[39]

However, the committee never became the instrument to realize its announced objectives. Its organizers almost immediately found themselves confronted by a competing group of Berlin notables, who moved swiftly to establish a Jewish defense organization. This second initiative was led by Raphael Löwenfeld, whose bold declaration had struck a sympathetic chord. Löwenfeld was the son of an Orthodox educator who had received his rabbinic ordination from the illustrious Talmudic sage Rabbi Akiba Eger. His father had prevented him from studying law, fearing that a legal career would make a strict observance of Judaism difficult. Instead he studied Slavic languages, became the first authorized German translator of Tolstoy, and eventually founded a German *Volkstheater* to produce classical drama at low prices for the masses. A humanist and active member of the Society for Ethical Culture, he believed in the effectiveness of education and the perfectibility of man.[40]

After preliminary deliberations with members of the committee, Löwenfeld met on February 5, 1893, with some two hundred Berlin notables at the home of Julius Isaac, one of the founders of the committee, to discuss the formation of a new defense organization.[41] An official letter to the *Allgemeine Zeitung des Judentums* a few days later reported the decision to create a mass organization to demonstrate the determination of German Jewry to defend itself and to assist the individual victim of discrimination. The fight would be waged

in public, for at stake was the support of the neutral and uncommitted majority of German Christians.

We intend to express openly before the whole world how we feel and
what we think. The systematic slanderers will not cease therewith to
cover us with their poison. But the neutral will not deny their sympathy
to a serious and respectably conducted defense, and those who today do
not know us, who are unable to get to know us because our entire life is
strange to them, will testify for us: these Jews of Germany are not less
loyal citizens than we, just as self-sacrificing patriots, just as noble human
beings.[42]

On March 26, 1893, the committee selected by the two hundred notables officially constituted itself as the Centralverein deutscher
Staatsbürger jüdischen Glaubens.[43]

Once the Centralverein had been formed, the committee headed by
Friedemann and Nathan confined itself to the occasional publication
of substantive studies refuting specific anti-Semitic allegations, while
the more powerful Centralverein took over the daily struggle against
the anti-Semitic forces. This division of labor may not have been
agreed upon quite as smoothly as Paul Rieger, an active member of
the Centralverein and its first historian, implied in his twenty-five-
year history.[44] At least according to the letter of Paul Nathan to Königsberg, which was written sometime after February 14, that is, more
than two weeks after the discussions between Löwenfeld and members of the committee, the latter still intended to implement its entire
program.[45] But the momentum of the Centralverein proved decisive,
and the committee, perhaps reluctantly, turned to the more circum-
spect task of preparing resource material. In the following years it
produced three major publications on the practice of Kosher slaughtering, the incidence of crime among German Jews, and the number
of Jews in the armies of eight European powers and the United
States.[46] The committee operated quietly for about a decade, mostly
under the direction of Nathan, who remained conspicuously unin-
volved in the work of the Centralverein.[47]

In 1893 an independent defense organization, the Vereinigung
Badischer Israeliten (Union of Baden Israelites), also appeared in
southern Germany. With its seat in Karlsruhe, and with its own peri-

odical, it maintained a separate identity until 1908, when it constituted itself as the Landesverband of the Centralverein.[48]

The year 1893 thus manifested the beginning of a fundamental change in the mood of German Jewry. Many had at last resolved to abandon the psychological fetters imposed by emancipation. They stood ready to reveal and defend their Jewishness in public. The tenacity and virulence of German anti-Semitism had driven them to overcome their deep-seated reservations about self-defense and to reject what increasingly appeared as a humiliating reliance upon Christian intervention.

5

SELF-DEFENSE:
CENTRALVEREIN DEUTSCHER
STAATSBÜRGER JÜDISCHEN
GLAUBENS, 1893-1914

THE HISTORY OF THE Centralverein before the First World War reveals a progressive assertion of Jewish consciousness. At first limited to a defiant determination to challenge every instance of scorn and harassment, the assertion of Jewish consciousness steadily assumed more positive forms as the Centralverein took up the battle to stem the rising tide of defections from Judaism. As a direct consequence of this new role, the Centralverein, during the final decade before Sarajevo, groped cautiously for a more inclusive definition of post-emancipation Judaism.

This assertion of Jewish identity did not signify a repudiation of the desire for integration. The very name of the organization protested the conviction that German Jews were full-fledged Germans, separated from their countrymen solely by religious persuasion.[1] According to the opening paragraph of the Constitution, the cultivation of a sense of German identity was incumbent on every member.[2] But in the face of rampant anti-Semitism, self-respect dictated a fearless recourse to public self-defense.[3]

ORGANIZATIONAL INNOVATION

In contrast to the earlier efforts of the Gemeindebund and Moritz Lazarus,[4] the founders of the Centralverein intended to try another type of organizational framework. The Centralverein was to be a mass organization composed of the largest number of German Jews possible rather than a coterie of notables working clandestinely to protect the interests of a disorganized and passive community.[5] The founders had learned from the contemporary German scene that effective representation required the backing of an imposing and well-organized pressure group.

The year 1893 witnessed the formation of three of the most powerful lobbies to operate in the last two decades of the Second Reich. In February a number of Conservative landowners, despondent over their party's inability to prevent the government from lowering tariffs on agricultural produce, moved to create a mass agrarian organization that would ensure the election of deputies to the Reichstag ready to defend the interests of the farmer. Two general conventions in Berlin that month drew an attendance of about 10,000 supporters, and by May 1893 the membership of the Bund der Landwirte (Agrarian League) had soared to 162,000 members. Between 1894 and 1902 the Bund obtained an average annual income of about 500,000 marks. Its ideology was astutely enriched with an eclectic brand of anti-Semitism composed of traditional agrarian hatred for Jewish moneylenders, the anti-liberal and anti-capitalistic sentiment of the Conservatives, and the virulent racism of the *völkisch* nationalists.[6]

Equally nationalistic and anti-Semitic were the Alldeutscher Verband (Pan-German League) and the Deutscher Handlungsgehilfen Verband (German Federation of Commercial Employees). After floundering for some years, the former was successfully reorganized in the summer of 1893. It soon emerged as a potent force in the formulation of German foreign policy. The German Federation of Commercial Employees was also founded in 1893 to combat the danger of its members' sinking into the proletariat. By 1912 it numbered over 148,000 commercial employees.[7] That the appearance of such contemporaneous pressure groups influenced the organizational structure of the Centralverein is suggested by the allusion of Eugen Fuchs, its leading ideologist prior to the war, in his address to the first public meeting of the Centralverein in June 1893: "What the individual cannot do can be done by a strong, large body. Authorities will pay heed to the voice of an imposing organization." [8]

In addition to exerting pressure on the authorities to move against the anti-Semites, a mass organization would provide the opportunity for an effective internal mission to Jewry. By insisting that defense was the responsibility of every Jew, the founders of the Centralverein hoped to transform German Jewry into a self-respecting and self-disciplined community.[9]

Accordingly, the Centralverein invested heavily to marshal German Jewry. Despite the cost, propaganda meetings for the acquisition of new members were held frequently both in Berlin and elsewhere.[10] Every German Jewish citizen was eligible, and membership required only the paying of a self-determined quarterly contribution.[11] Besides individual members, frequently an entire community or organization would affiliate itself. Thus by the beginning of 1896 the Centralverein consisted of 5,359 individual and 39 corporate members. At the end of its first decade, in February 1903, the membership had risen to 12,000 individuals and 100 affiliated bodies totaling more than 100,000 Jews. By 1916 the Centralverein claimed to represent some 200,000 German Jews, of whom more than 40,000 were individual members.[12]

Such steady growth necessitated some reorganization. During its first decade the Centralverein consisted of little more than its Executive Committee located in Berlin and mostly unorganized members and delegates scattered mainly in northern Germany. By 1905 the leadership began to tighten this loose organization in order to effect closer cooperation between the central office and local members as well as to increase local membership. Local chapters were officially organized in communities having seventy-five members, and in those lacking that number efforts were made to reach it.

Ernst Herzfeld, the last president of the Centralverein, recalls briefly in his unpublished memoirs how as a young lawyer in Essen

he labored to found Centralverein chapters throughout the Rhineland. An outspoken critic of the organization's excessive centralization, he successfully advocated the formation of regional branches to
give greater voice to the multiplying local chapters in their affairs
with the central office. In January 1906 at the age of thirty-one,
Herzfeld became the youngest member of the national Executive
Committee. In 1909 the Centralverein adopted a revised Constitution
envisioning local chapters united in regional associations whose delegates would meet annually in Berlin. The Executive Committee,
which chose the president of the organization, consisted of eighteen
members, half of whom had to reside in Berlin. This reorganization
allowed for some decentralization, greatly increased the number of
Centralverein meetings throughout Germany, and intensified its propaganda campaign. By 1911 the Centralverein had activated regional
associations in the Rhineland, Westphalia, Hesse-Nassau, Württemberg, Upper Silesia, and the Kingdom of Saxony.[13]

To increase both the amount of publicity for the Centralverein and
the communication between the central office and the membership,
the Executive Committee decided in March 1895 to publish a
monthly journal. A month later it selected the title *Im deutschen
Reich,* intending thereby an unequivocal expression of German national sentiment. Sent free of charge to a cross-section of important
German leaders and libraries, the periodical reached a circulation of
11,200 copies by 1902. A decade later it had become by far the largest representative of the German Jewish press with a printing of
some 37,000 copies per issue.[14]

Information about the financial foundation of this defense establishment is unfortunately sparse. Its income for 1894 was reported
by an unfriendly source to be 17,500 marks, more than 4,000 marks
less than expenditures, although by the end of December 1896 its
treasurer reported holdings worth 11,500 marks.[15] Such growth was
probably the result of numerous and sizable single contributions to
the Centralverein rather than of annual dues.[16] By the end of 1903,
however, the resources and expenditures of the Centralverein still
trailed far behind those of some of the other major national Jewish
organizations, as the following table indicates.

Organization	Assets	Budget	Year
Hilfsverein	688,000	295,000	1903
Gemeindebund	600,000	100,000	1903–1904
Centralverein	42,042	51,987	1903

Toward the end of the decade its yearly income was reputed to stand between 50,000 and 60,000 marks.[17]

THE RESPONSE OF GERMAN JEWRY

The response of German Jewry to the appearance of the Central-verein was cautious. The Orthodox were particularly suspicious because of the tone of Löwenfeld's diatribe and his personal involvement in its formation. The leaders of the Centralverein insisted that their organization was strictly neutral regarding the religious divisions within the Jewish community. They explained that the term "Jewish faith" in its name designated only the character of the membership and not the purpose of the organization. They also moved quickly to dissociate themselves from Löwenfeld's anti-Orthodox bias, accepting only his closing principles as guidelines. The *Jüdische Presse* of Hirsch Hildesheimer had denounced Löwenfeld as a coward who was ready to disown his brother to guarantee his own safety. Yet it had warmly endorsed Simon's appeal to organize, and by 1895 Hildesheimer had become an active member of the Centralverein, thus encouraging the participation of other Orthodox Jews.[18]

The more immediate followers of Samson R. Hirsch in southern Germany were decidedly unenthusiastic. Needless to say, the *Israelit* had condemned the Löwenfeld pamphlet and the Reform origins of the Centralverein, but even after the Centralverein had convinced Hildesheimer of its religious neutrality, the *Israelit* remained stridently critical. It returned to a position that it had defended for most of the 1880's. Approaching anti-Semitism theologically and historically, the *Israelit* identified it as the divine rod sent to shatter Jewish indifference and thwart assimilation. God had always employed persecution to cleanse His people. Jews would survive this punishment as they had earlier ones. Self-defense was futile and detrimental. The polemics of the Centralverein were decidedly anti-Christian; its consistent defeats in the courts only encouraged the anti-Semites, and its very character projected the image of a political party. If anti-Semitism had to be fought, the fight could be waged only in cooperation with the liberals, and it was precisely the Abwehrverein, the expression of this alliance, that the Centralverein threatened to undermine. By 1913 the arguments had changed somewhat, but the basic opposition remained.[19]

Even less Orthodox newspapers like the *Allgemeine Zeitung des Judentums* and the *Israelitische Wochenschrift* felt radical Reform Jews like Löwenfeld and Lehmann to be a liability. In the face of a common enemy all internal dissension had to cease. The *Israelitische Wochenschrift* applauded the creation of the Centralverein, but warned against the danger of centralization in Berlin. Anti-Semitism could be resisted effectively only on the local level. The *Allgemeine Zeitung des Judentums* withheld its approval until the end of 1894. Its silence mirrors the general lack of coverage by the Jewish press from which the Centralverein suffered during its initial years.[20]

Old prejudices were not easily overcome. Many continued to assert that anti-Semites could not be taught, and objective Germans needed no instruction. Particularly disturbing to many was the intention to carry the fight into the open. Intellectuals objected running to the courts at every instance of libel. As late as 1910 some of the more frequently cited reasons for not joining the Centralverein were the conclusion that its presence made no difference, the wish not to irritate German Christians by a display of Jewishness, and a reluctance to identify with any aspect of Jewish life.[21]

Nevertheless, despite the relatively widespread persistence of some of these original critical sentiments, the single most important achievement of the Centralverein before the First World War was its unabated growth. In light of the powerful centrifugal forces which had fragmented German Jewry since 1870 and undermined any large-scale effort at resistance, this was no mean achievement. Against the background of a proliferation of mass-based interest groups within German society generally, the Centralverein labored adroitly and energetically to unite a deeply divided Jewish community in defense of its vital interests. A well-informed Christian observer of the contemporary Jewish scene rightly regarded this organizational success as a turning point in the modern history of German Jewry. In the course of a lengthy objective survey of German Jewish institutional life, which appeared in 1904–1905 in the periodical of the Evangelical Church's mission to the Jews, Paul Billerbeck offered the following assessment:

The most significant achievement of the Centralverein lies . . . in the fact that it has become the bond of unity for all parties within Judaism, that it has sharpened and strengthened the sense of togetherness among the Jews of Germany as no other organization.[22]

LEGAL DEFENSE

To implement its declaration of public self-defense, the Centralverein decided to prosecute anti-Semites in the courts. In December 1893 a legal department composed of six to eight lawyers began to function. Its assignment was to provide assistance to any Jew who suffered abuse or discrimination because of his religion. In instances of a legal violation the Centralverein urged the Jew affected to appeal to the public prosecutor, and if rebuffed to bring charges directly. It stood ready to support him with evidence and money. Whenever the department's continuous scrutiny of the anti-Semitic press turned up the defamation of a specific Jew, it would inform him immediately and urge him to take legal action. If he did not respond, he would be approached a second time.[23]

The legal department of the Centralverein regarded the prosecution of crimes against Judaism and its institutions as far more important and attempted to employ four sections of the 1876 Uniform Criminal Code of the German Reich. Section 130, which had first been enacted in 1849 as an anti-Socialist measure, forbade inciting one class to violence against another. Section 166 proscribed blasphemy as well as the defamation of the institutions and practices of any incorporated religious body. Sections 185 through 200 dealt with libel, and Section 360, paragraph 11, forbade disturbing the peace or committing a gross nuisance, categories that might be extended to

cover instances where anti-Semites harassed individual Jews or Jewish businesses. The Centralverein contended that public prosecutors
had usurped the function of the courts. By consistently refusing to
bring charges, prosecutors had formulated legal interpretations that
might differ sharply from decisions the courts might render were they
given the chance to hear the cases. Public prosecutors had expanded
their procedural role into a judicial one, to the detriment of German
Jewry. The refusal to apply these sections created the impression that
Jews and Judaism were fair game not guaranteed the same protection
extended to individual Christians and incorporated churches.[24]

Since the 1870's public prosecutors had rejected Jewish appeals,
as we have seen, for a variety of oft-repeated reasons. Insults against
individual Jews would not be prosecuted because the case did not involve an issue of public interest, and collective defamations were
likewise turned down because it could not be shown that the individual bringing the charge was included in the intent of the defamer.
Prosecutors exhibited little sympathy in cases of defamation of the
Talmud, because it was not clear that the Talmud was recognized by
all Jews or that it constituted an institution or practice of Judaism.
They preferred to classify it as a body of doctrine. When Judaism itself was the object of defamation, prosecutors maintained that the
Jews were being addressed as a people rather than a religious association. Cases of insult were frequently rejected because the prosecutors simply felt the language not strong enough to prosecute. And finally in instances where anti-Semitic literature seemed to incite to
class violence, the prosecutors argued that the same literature had not
disturbed the peace in the past nor did the Jews constitute a class in
the sense intended by the law.[25]

What disturbed Jewish observers of the judicial system was the
willingness of prosecutors to bring charges and of courts to convict in
strikingly similar cases involving gentile causes. Thus an editor of a
German weekly was sentenced to one month in prison for insulting a
relic of the Catholic Church, irrespective of its authenticity.[26] Elsewhere, a Catholic priest who informed his congregation in a sermon
that all evil came from the Protestants, and admonished it not to imi-
tate them, was convicted under the same Section 166 for insulting the
Evangelical Church. When a German paper spoke of the character-

less and ambitious judges of the Prussian judiciary who revere every ministerial edict as the Gospel, the court held every individual judge to have been affronted.[27] Yet in 1894 the Centralverein received no cooperation in its claims against an article in an anti-Semitic paper entitled "Religious Community or International Association of Deceivers." Its appeals were successively turned down by the public prosecutor in Dresden, his superior, and the Saxon Minister of Justice. This performance provoked the *Nation* to observe that the German judiciary had transformed the relevant provisions of the criminal code into exceptional laws clearly not applicable to Judaism.[28]

Several factors determined this recourse to an instrument that had thus far proven unreliable. In his provocative essay Löwenfeld had advocated discarding the mentality and method of the protected Jew. Jews ought to realize the implications of citizenship. The desire for special consideration was medieval. The judicial system existed to protect the rights of all citizens. By turning to the courts, Jews were simply demanding the protection to which their new status entitled them.[29]

The decision may also have been influenced by Hermann Strack's aforementioned pamphlet of January 1893. At the very time when a number of men were engaged in founding the Centralverein, this significant pamphlet forcefully stated the conviction that only judicial intervention would be effective, and documented the difficulties awaiting any serious effort to procure such intervention. The extent to which Strack's argument and evidence were incorporated by Max Apt [Maximilian Parmod], a member of the Centralverein's legal department, in his 1894 study of anti-Semitism and German criminal justice reveals the influence that the theologian exerted on the lawyers of the Centralverein.[30]

Equally decisive was the professional competence of the Centralverein leadership. In contrast to the leadership of earlier defense efforts, that of the Centralverein rested predominantly in the hands of lawyers. The first head of the legal department was Eugen Fuchs. Although he vacated the post at the end of 1894, he remained the vice-president of the Centralverein until ill-health forced him to retire in 1919. A dynamic speaker, Fuchs was the most profound and articu-

late spokesman of Centralverein ideology. Denied an academic career at the completion of his legal studies, he entered the practice of
law. Still he found time to make a number of scholarly contributions
to the study of German law, and in 1906 was rewarded with an appointment to the commission that supervised the examination of all
candidates for the Prussian judiciary—the first and, up to the time of
his death in 1923, the only Jew to receive the honor. According to
the recollection of one contemporary, Fuchs' fearless and passionate
defense of Jewish rights, his professional achievements, and his idealism and integrity earned him the affectionate respect of German
Jewry.[31]

The president of the Centralverein for most of this period was also
a lawyer. Maximilian Horwitz assumed the presidency in December
1894 when Martin Mendelsohn, a physician, university lecturer, and
the organization's first president, resigned because of professional obligations. Since their first meeting in 1884, Fuchs and Horwitz had
developed a warm friendship, and in 1893 Fuchs prevailed upon his
friend to join the Centralverein. Although impulsive in temperament,
Horwitz was nevertheless disciplined, and proved to be an effective
speaker and energetic worker. He remained a very active president
until his death in 1917.[32]

The Centralverein's legal policy aroused considerable criticism
within the Jewish community, especially in light of the policy's numerous early failures. Each major defeat was accompanied by a cho-
rus of appeals to desist. The ambivalence of the *Allgemeine Zeitung
des Judentums* was typical. Two years before the formation of the
Centralverein, the paper had declared its opposition to judicial defense because nothing would be altered by a fine of 300 marks or an
eight-day prison sentence. Some judicial successes in 1894, however,
began to convince it that the Centralverein's legal policy was a potentially effective weapon. But the reversals of 1895 dampened its
enthusiasm, and the failure to win a conviction in 1896 against an
article in an anti-Semitic paper on "The Most Recent Ritual Murder" provoked the *Allegemeine Zeitung des Judentums* to demand
that the Centralverein cease its fruitless and damaging recourse to the
courts. Yet when the Centralverein managed to win a conviction in a
second try, with the courts declaring the editor guilty of blasphemy

and a defamation of the Jewish community (Sec. 166), the *Allgemeine Zeitung des Judentums* applauded the significance of the decision. Not till 1898, however, was the paper ready to endorse unequivocally the energetic prosecution of anti-Semitic defamations by the Centralverein.[33]

Even within the ranks of the Centralverein, opposition was vocal. In 1895 the aging Emil Lehmann publicly repeated his evaluation of 1880 that the German judicial system failed to cover the Jews. The minimal accomplishments of the Centralverein had only reinforced this conviction. Without daring to impugn the objectivity of prosecutors and judges, Lehmann suggested that they shared the attitudes of their society and could not really appreciate Jewish sensibilities.[34] At a Centralverein meeting in the Fall of 1896 yet another skeptical member rejected the official claims of progress and urged the organization to take its case directly to the public.[35]

The leaders of the Centralverein insisted that there was no alternative. Defamations had to be repudiated; otherwise popular fantasy would accept them as fact. Was that not the lesson to be learned from the medieval trials and executions of witches? How else could a Jewish butcher have been convicted and sentenced to four months in prison in 1894 for allegedly urinating on meat he would sell to non-Jews? Furthermore, Jewish self-respect demanded action, regardless of the result. Verbally the anti-Semitic agitation had reached its peak. Any adverse judicial decision could not possibly lead to any more vulgar vilifications. Appeal to public opinion provided no alternative. The social, religious, and political antagonisms dividing German society gave little hope that public opinion would soon recognize the rights of a minority. Nevertheless, the legal policy of the Centralverein clearly included a subtle pitch to public opinion. By demonstrating conclusively the extent to which the German courts failed to protect a single minority, it hoped to arouse thoughtful Germans to the implicit danger of such arbitrary justice for the entire society.[36]

By 1902 the legal department of the Centralverein was handling an average of one hundred cases annually. Many more were turned down because they failed to meet the guidelines according to which cases were accepted. Originally the Centralverein had contested rather indiscriminately, but its losing record had provoked angry and disillusioned criticism. Moreover, the anti-Semites had quickly learned to accommodate their defamations to the dictates of the law. Thus they now spoke of *Blutmord* (blood murder) rather than *Ritualmord* (ritual murder) to circumvent Section 166, and carefully avoided castigating all Jews to escape the charge of collective libel. As a result, the Centralverein had decided to prosecute only those cases that it stood some chance of winning. Secondly, certain anti-Semites were no longer worth prosecuting. A coarse demagogue like Count Pückler had already been convicted several times, and even the Imperial Court, the highest court of the land, had considered him deranged. Finally, the Centralverein was no longer trying to prosecute the satirical defamations of anti-Semitic periodicals.[37]

In time the legal efforts of the Centralverein did yield a modicum of success. Initially it succeeded in overcoming the obstruction of public prosecutors. After a few years they tended to agree more readily to press charges and even on occasion to initiate action without a request by the Centralverein.[38] German courts also began to extend the protection of certain sections of the Criminal Code to Jews and Judaism. In 1896 a Centralverein spokesman had reported that no anti-Semite had as yet been convicted of inciting to class violence (Sec. 130).[39] But Pückler, a judicial assistant turned agitator, provided the breakthrough. In May 1899 the Centralverein tried to win a conviction against him in the criminal court in Glogau for a virulent anti-Semitic harangue in which he goaded his audience to "grab the Jew by the collar with your bare, strong fist and club him till his bones break." Pückler denied that he meant this advice literally. His picturesque metaphors and rhetoric were intended merely to arouse the stolid peasants he was addressing. The court decided that, although objectively such appeals might easily provoke class violence, subjectively the defendant neither intended this nor realized the potential consequences of his words. Despite the acquittal, the Centralverein was pleased by the court's recognition that the Jews constitute a class in the sense of Section 130. The public prosecutor immediately appealed the verdict to the Imperial Court in Leipzig, which in turn upheld the decision of the lower court, because Pückler truly appeared to be a deluded crusader unaware of the consequences of his actions. But more important, the Court had not disputed the applicability of Section 130 to the Jews.[40]

This implication was stated explicitly by the Imperial Court in November 1899. A lower court in Berlin had convicted three editors of anti-Semitic papers for printing and distributing three Pückler speeches. The Court held that Jewish citizens were Germans but did constitute a separate class within the population. Two of the defendants received fines of 200 marks, while the third was fined 100 marks. The decision was immediately appealed, and this time, in upholding the verdict of the lower court, the Imperial Court enunciated the principle that Section 130 applied to social as well as to economic divisions within the society.[41]

The Centralverein also fought to gain the protection of Section 166 for the Jewish community and its religious institutions and practices. As early as 1882 the Imperial Court had recognized Judaism in Prussia as an incorporated religious community and therefore protected by Section 166.[42] But the real problem was to get German courts to consider specific anti-Semitic defamations as violations of Section 166. One of the most consistently maligned rites was the Kol Nidre prayer solemnly recited at the start of the Day of Atonement. At that time the worshipper implores God to absolve him of the religious vows in which he alone is involved and which he might make inadvertently and be unable to fulfill during the coming year. Since the thirteenth century, anti-Semites had contended that this absolution indiscriminately nullified all Jewish oaths. The special humiliating oaths for Jews demanded in the Middle Ages were only slowly discarded by the various German states during the first half of the nineteenth century and by Prussia not till 1869.[43] In 1895 the editor of a Hanover newspaper had been convicted and sentenced to fourteen days' confinement for an article in which he claimed that the recitation of Kol Nidre exonerated the Jew of all guilt in cases of false oaths. However, the Imperial Court overturned the decision, because neither the Jewish community nor an institution of Judaism had been directly attacked as the law required, but only indirectly.[44] It was this reversal that had prompted the aforementioned criticism of the Centralverein's legal policy by Emil Lehmann. His dismay was widely shared.[45]

But by 1899 the Imperial Court had become more sympathetic. In one case that year the Court turned down an appeal from an anti-Semitic group that had been convicted by a lower court for having mistranslated the Kol Nidre to prove the worthlessness of a Jewish oath. The appeal had contended that, since the broadsheet in question juxtaposed Jews with Germans rather than with Christians, it had spoken of them as a race and not a religious body.[46] That same year the Imperial Court ordered a retrial of an editor whose paper had carried an article asserting that a Jew can free himself from any oath by simply going to a rabbi. The lower court had acquitted the defendant because the defamation lacked the necessary invectives. The Imperial Court declared that such words of abuse were not required by Section 166, and in the subsequent retrial the editor was convicted.[47]

A dramatic instance in which the courts vigorously applied Section 166 occurred in 1901. The anti-Semites had transformed the murder of a Christian Gymnasium student in Konitz in March 1900 into a blood libel. On the first anniversary of the murder, whose perpetrator had still not been found, an anti-Semitic publisher circulated a postcard with a painting depicting eleven Jews in a cellar witnessing the brutal ritual slaughter of the young student. The card bore an admonition warning brothers to protect their unmarried sisters, and parents, their children. Charges were leveled by the public prosecutor and the publisher received the unusually stiff sentence of six months in prison.[48]

In the area of collective libel, however, the Centralverein consistently failed to win a conviction. Judges usually maintained that the term "Jews" was by no means as limited as terms like "the Prussian Army" or "the Officer Corps," in whose defense convictions for collective libel had been returned. Even when anti-Semites occasionally stressed the all-inclusive nature of their defamation, no conviction was forthcoming. In one such case the judge was reputed to have said that he could not imagine that the accused meant to insult all Jews. In his 1902 report on the work of the legal department, Julius Brodnitz declared:

If we, gentlemen, would at some time wish to collect for you out of the thick files at our disposal what one can say with impunity against the

Jews, provided one is not too clumsy, according to the opinion of our courts, even the highest court, and according to the opinion of our public prosecutors, you . . . would scarcely believe it.[49]

The entire legal effort by the Centralverein to combat anti-Semitism was seriously handicapped by the fact that in most instances a deterring sentence did not reinforce the conviction. Punishment rarely exceeded a few hundred marks or a few days or weeks in prison. In 1899 the Düsseldorf court, which had convicted the aforementioned editor for defamation of the Jewish community for the article that asserted that every Jewish oath could be nullified by a visit to a rabbi, sentenced the accused to but two days' confinement.[50] Convictions against anti-Semitic street vendors who harassed Jewish passers-by (Sec. 360, par. 11) carried nominal fines of less than 150 marks. One such repeater was finally arrested for eight days.[51] When Theodor Fritsch, perhaps the hardiest of the anti-Semitic agitators in the Second Reich, was sentenced in 1911 to one week's imprisonment for blasphemy (Sec. 166), some of the Progressive papers observed that the blasphemer received only one week while a defendant convicted about the same time for insulting a Prussian official was sentenced to a year's confinement. That sentence was exactly what Fritsch had received for the same crime back in 1888.[52]

Despite successes in bringing the courts to recognize that Sections 130 and 166 of the Criminal Code also covered German Jewry, it is extremely doubtful that the legal policy of the Centralverein affected the course of anti-Semitism in the Second Reich. Recent scholarship attributes the rapid decline of the anti-Semitic parties, especially after the Reichstag elections of 1907, to a variety of national developments. The rising level of prosperity, the growing menace of the Social Democrats, and the increasing preoccupation with foreign affairs diminished the electoral appeal of anti-Semitism. To a large extent the anti-Semites simply shifted their base of operation. While losing political strength, anti-Semitism continued to flourish in the influential parapolitical organizations of the Agrarian League, the Pan German League, and the Federation of Commercial Employees, as well as in wide circles of the Prussian and Imperial governments. At best Centralverein spokesmen could point to their achievement in forcing anti-Semitic papers and demagogues to moderate their denunciations.[53]

Despite its vigorous recourse to the German courts, the Central-verein did not discard the more traditional and less publicized means of fighting anti-Semitism. It pressured, for instance, to have Jews appointed as jurors in localities where they had been systematically excluded.[54] It lobbied for years to gain equality for German Jewish businessmen traveling and trading in Russia.[55] It protested discrimination in the hiring of Jews by large commercial and industrial firms.[56] It represented Jewish interests on the issues of kosher slaughtering [57] and the Konitz blood libel of 1900.[58] It distributed counterpropaganda,[59] and carefully watched the German scene for new manifestations of anti-Semitism.[60] However, within the scope of the present study, our attention is directed mainly to the Central-verein's major tactical innovations.[61]

POLITICAL POSITION

From its inception the Centralverein had chosen to fight anti-Semitism legally rather than politically.[62] Yet the political dimensions of the phenomenon could not be ignored, and the Centralverein, despite its avowed political neutrality, became increasingly enmeshed in German politics. As early as 1893 it worked to defeat anti-Semitic candidates running for the Berlin City Council. By the 1898 Reichstag election its position had been clearly enunciated. Although all Jews were urged to vote, not one vote was to be cast for a party favoring any kind of exceptional law or for any anti-Semitic candidate. Those candidates who had not as yet revealed their attitude were to be forced to do so. Where possible, the Centralverein encouraged German Jews to work for the nomination of a qualified Jewish candidate. In the Fall election of 1898 for the Prussian Chamber of Deputies, the Centralverein went one step further by actively supporting the election of a specifically Jewish candidate running for Richter's Progressive People's Party, of which both Fuchs and Horwitz were members, in a Berlin election district.[63]

This last development of Centralverein policy did not go unchallenged. On October 16, 1898, the day after it was announced, three members withdrew from the organization. They argued that, since the Centralverein was politically neutral, it should refrain from any campaigning and above all not put forward a religious candidate. In a public defense of the policy, Fuchs defined a confessional candidate as a man whose only qualification for office was his religion. But the support of the Centralverein for the candidate in question was not solely on religious grounds. Two reasons made it imperative that at least one knowledgeable and committed Jew be among the 430 deputies of the Prussian lower house, a chamber that had not seen a Jewish deputy in twelve years. The anti-Semitic slanders so often raised required informed refutation, and on certain pieces of legislation affecting German Jewry the government needed a competent adviser. Fuchs asserted that any Jew who recognized these legitimate needs and still opposed the election of a Jewish candidate for fear of gentile criticism lacked self-respect and courage; his timidity had inhibited him from demanding what the Constitution granted.[64]

The Centralverein's political program remained predominantly negative. To fight anti-Semitic candidates in the Reichstag campaign of 1903, the Executive Committee designated the insignificant sum of 3,000 marks. In the 1907 Reichstag election the Centralverein received enough contributions through its newly organized election fund to intervene in thirty-two election districts. With the money going through Centralverein area representatives into the coffers of the local party organizations, thirteen of the candidates opposed were defeated.[65]

Even relatively speaking, the rising investments of the Centralverein in Reichstag elections compared unfavorably with the far greater involvement of major interest groups. For example, in the crucial election of 1907, the recently founded Imperial Union for Combating Social Democracy campaigned in eighty-two districts, distributing more than ten million leaflets. Businessmen and manufacturers provided the bloc of Chancellor Bülow with an election fund of 600,000 marks. Some 30,000 marks from this fund went to the Navy League, which itself distributed some twenty million leaflets during the campaign.[66] To increase their resources, the Centralverein and Abwehrverein, prior to the next Reichstag election in 1911, agreed for the first time to combine their election funds to fight unacceptable candidates.[67]

Yet even this negative approach faced substantial difficulties. A growing number of Jews were staying away from the polls entirely.[68] With the inclusion of the National Liberals and the Progressives in 1907 in the governmental bloc that included the anti-Semitic parties, Jewish voters were often left with candidates from the Social Democrats or Catholic Center, who both had repudiated anti-Semitism, as the only distasteful alternative. Progressives were not above voting for an anti-Semite rather than a Socialist. In the election of 1907, Progressive votes had in fact won the election for three anti-Semitic candidates.[69] Consequently by 1903, Centralverein speakers were declaring Socialists preferable to anti-Semites, who were to be regarded as the fatherland's most dangerous enemy. Aside from nervous patriotism, some Jews voted for anti-Semites intentionally, for fear of economic retaliation if they did not. In provinces where Jews were intimidated by threats of an economic boycott, the Centralverein representatives would circulate urging them to defend the honor of Judaism.[70] Since voting for the Reichstag was by secret ballot, it is not clear from the available sources precisely how the anti-Semites determined the way individual Jews voted. The withholding of financial or public support from the anti-Semitic candidate during the campaign may have been enough evidence to satisfy the promoters of economic reprisal.

The original neutrality of the Centralverein continued to manifest itself in its steadfast refusal to endorse specific candidates or cooperate with a single party. Perhaps the closest it came to altering this policy occurred in the Fall and Winter of 1906, when representatives from the Centralverein, the German Zionist organization, and perhaps the B'nai B'rith met secretly to negotiate the formation of a political organization claiming to speak for German Jewry. With the Reichstag elections imminent, they sought to formulate a minimal platform and to agree upon several Jewish candidates. This Jewish slate would then be offered to one of the major political parties, on whose ticket it would run, in return for Jewish money and votes. By the Spring of 1907 these talks had irretrievably collapsed.[71]

Jacob Toury has suggested that this political initiative failed to materialize because the Centralverein leadership was unwilling to sacrifice its traditional alliance with the Progressives, which had, in fact, compromised the Centralverein's vaunted political neutrality from the very start.[72] But the evidence for such an alliance is wanting. Toury has succeeded only in establishing that the Centralverein's national leadership in Berlin (i.e., Fuchs and Horwitz) and the local leadership in Posen belonged to Richter's Progressive People's Party, and that in the one race in 1898 in which the Centralverein did endorse a Jewish candidate he had been nominated by the same party.[73] There is no evidence of sustained active cooperation. On the contrary, the Centralverein consistently repudiated such an alliance for fear of alienating members and potential members affiliated with other German political parties.[74] From its very inception the Centralverein had set out to mobilize the largest number of German Jews into a powerful pressure group against anti-Semitism. This was the fundamental reason why it carefully avoided taking positions on controversial questions that would only undermine its continued growth. Thus, until 1913 it steadily refused to polemicize against German Zionism.[75] Nor did it expand its policy of combating anti-Semitic candidates into an endorsement of acceptable candidates. The widespread resistance among German Jews in the opening years of the twentieth century to the formation of the Judentag and the Verband der deutschen Juden, projects which were basically non-political and which enjoyed the open support of the Centralverein, must have forcefully brought home to the leaders of the Centralverein the potentially divisive impact of a purely political venture.[76] It seems entirely likely that the Centralverein's total commitment to uniting German Jewry in its own defense prevented it from embracing a political plan whose only certain consequence would have been to aggravate the existing divisions already hampering Jewry. Instead, the Centralverein encouraged its members to affect political life by making individual Jewish participation and money felt in the local political organizations.[77]

INTERNAL MISSION

Since the first organized efforts to combat anti-Semitism, Jewish spokesmen had accepted the premise that the ill-mannered and unethical behavior of all too many Jews contributed substantially to feeding the anti-Semitic furor. The main thrust of their address to the Jewish community had been to reduce what they regarded as the objective cause of inter-group tensions. At the outset, the Central-verein preserved a trace of this old self-criticism. Incorporating the subjective conception of nationality originally expounded by Lazarus into the opening paragraph of its Constitution, the Centralverein demanded of its members the cultivation of a sense of German identity.[78] Its speakers conceded that there were still segments of German Jewry bearing the scars of the ghetto. There were still too many alien and uncultured Semites living in Germany. They apologized for such vestiges by depicting German Jewry as a maturing community.[79] Particularly detestable were the materialists whose only concern was earning money and who did not hesitate to advertise their wares even in anti-Semitic papers.[80]

The guidelines for German Jewry issued by the Centralverein around the turn of the century, however, suggest the extent to which this theme had been played down. In total contrast to the similar document issued by the Gemeindebund in 1880, which carefully delineated proper Jewish behavior, the ten guidelines of the Centralverein statement dwelt upon the dangers of anti-Semitism and asserted Jewish claims for equality. Only one alluded to the former preoccupation of the Gemeindebund. After denouncing the continuous indictment of all Jews for the shortcomings of a single one, it advised every Jew, in light of this unjust reality, to exercise self-discipline.[81]

If the Jews bore any responsibility for the anti-Semitic agitation, it lay elsewhere. From the beginning, the main thrust of the Centralverein's campaign had been directed against the cherished Jewish policy of silence and concealment. The Centralverein argued forcefully that the self-effacing effort by Jews to conceal their identity earned only Christian contempt. The refusal to read a Jewish newspaper on the train, to hold a public lecture on a Jewish subject, or to announce religious services in the daily newspapers were all acts of cowardliness. They all bespoke the same fear not to provoke an unfavorable response to a display of Jewishness. But such a posture was unworthy of sympathy or respect. A Jew should openly admit his Judaism in strange company before he is, wittingly or unwittingly, compelled to defend it.[82] An appeal in 1907 to "German citizens of the Jewish faith" opened: "The behavior of the Jews itself bears considerable responsibility for the growth of the anti-Semitic movement: their lack of esprit de corps and self-consciousness, their indifference, but above all the lack of timely, forceful defense." [83]

A basic change in the character of German anti-Semitism, which became increasingly evident during the first decade of the twentieth century, decidedly altered the substance and tone of the Centralverein's message to German Jewry. At the very time when anti-Semitism was becoming less of a political factor, its social significance rose ominously. The leaders of the Centralverein were especially distressed by what they regarded as the deteriorating social and economic position of German Jewry. Two decades of anti-Semitic propaganda had not been in vain. The prejudices had percolated down to the broad strata of German society, reversing the trend toward ultimate social integration. The Centralverein pointed out the disturbing symptoms of growing isolation. Social intercourse between Jewish and Christian families had substantially diminished over the last few decades. At high schools and universities Jewish students were excluded from fraternal organizations. In legal and medical organizations, Jewish lawyers and doctors were rarely elected to office. While Jews gave generously to, and worked long hours for, public charities, Christians rarely reciprocated. In Germany no Christian protests condemned the Russian pogroms and no Christian money was forthcoming to help the victims, a reaction which contrasted sharply with the Christian support extended in Western Europe and America. The only official posts to which Jews were appointed were of an honorary character, that is, entailing considerable work with no remuneration.[84]

Discrimination also began to appear in economic life. Christian merchants hesitated to hire Jewish help. In one large unnamed city, only ten Jews were employed by Christian businesses.[85] Some Christian stores advertised that they did not welcome Jewish patronage.[86] Jewish engineers and chemists faced increasing difficulties in finding employment.[87] In small towns Christians often boycotted Jewish lawyers and doctors, driving them into the cities where the concentration of Jews in these professions steadily rose.[88] To these multiplying obstructions in the private sector of the economy must be added the continued discrimination in the public sector, which will be examined more closely in the next chapter, which kept numerous Jews out of careers in teaching and the civil service.[89]

This mounting social and economic exclusion directly increased the number of Jews seeking to circumvent the difficulties by conversion. As in the opening decades of the nineteenth century, under similar circumstances, German Jewry was once again endangered by attrition.[90] The statistics, regardless of discrepancies in detail, attest the growing number disaffiliating from Judaism and actually converting. (The former required merely a declaration before the court; the latter, actual baptism. Many withdrew without converting.) The trend in Berlin, as in the other large cities of Germany, was unmistakable. Between 1873 and 1890, an insignificant total of 218 Berlin Jews departed from the Jewish community. Between 1891 and 1908, the yearly average jumped to 92, while in 1908 alone 186 withdrew. Between 1880 and 1910, a total of 12,375 Jews entered Protestantism in Germany.[91] Many of these dissidents and converts were adults who already as children had participated in Christian rather than Jewish religious instruction. Among Jewish children attending middle and upper schools, it was estimated that about 10 percent were receiving religious instruction from teachers of the Evangelical Church.[92] Another estimate raised the figure to 15 percent of all Jewish school children. Regarding total losses, one observer calculated that approximately 1 to 2 percent of the Jewish children born annually in Germany were being baptized and that German Jewry as a whole was losing about one thousand Jews a year at the turn of the century.[93]

The personal experiences and recollections of contemporaries readily confirm the gist of these statistics. In an age of rampant materialism, dominated by Darwin and Haeckel, transcendant concerns were alien and religious commitment wanting. In his perceptive memoirs, Abraham Fraenkel, the renowned mathematician and former Rector of the Hebrew University, recalled that the practice in many Berlin Jewish families at the end of the century was for the son interested in a university career and the daughter who was about to marry a Christian to convert, while the son who entered business or industry remained a Jew. Flora Meyer, a sensitive observer of the same metropolitan society, married the youngest son of the Chief Rabbi of Hanover in 1907. Of the Rabbi's grandchildren, seven had already converted or married non-Jews.

The celebrated poet and philosopher Margarete Susman married the son of a German admiral. Her future in-laws insisted that she convert before the wedding and she dutifully complied by taking lessons from a pastor. They were, in fact, not her first, for already as a child she, like many others, had participated in school in Protestant religious instruction. Nevertheless, at the last minute she refused to proceed and remained steadfastly Jewish for the rest of her life.

In 1912 Fritz Mauthner, who advocated a form of assimilation that certainly entailed the disappearance of the Jews, summed up his own experience.

It is indeed not impossible that an adult and educated Jew would become a Christian out of conviction. It is only that in my life I have not seen such a case. In the vast majority of cases the adult convert is brought to profess a creed in which he does not believe out of higher or lower reasons of expedience.[94]

In direct response to this attrition, the Centralverein soon expanded its denunciation of the cringing Jew into a scathing polemic against apostasy, which it regarded as the most abhorrent form of cowardice. In tones reminiscent of their medieval Jewish ancestors, Centralverein speakers excoriated "the renegades who sacrifice their honor and conviction to win recognition and the thoughtless who themselves shun apostasy but destroy the harmony of their own family by having their children baptised." [95] The tragic consequence of the inferiority complex from which so many Jews suffered was conversion. Committed to the revival of self-respect, the Centralverein soon came to label the apostate as the most dangerous enemy to Jewish survival in Germany. Three arguments were generally put forth to demonstrate this danger. Conversion for materialistic reasons, and theoretically this was the only type of conversion that the Centralverein condemned, was not only a disreputable and cowardly act, but also substantiated the anti-Semitic contention that Jews worshipped money. Conversion hurt German Jewry also in its fight for complete equality. As long as a sufficient number of Jews stood ready to convert to enter the portals of government service closed to unconverted

Jews, the government would never alter its discriminatory policy; it would always claim that Jews were not really being denied at all. But even from the viewpoint of the state, conversion was undesirable. Current policy placed a premium on lack of character. Those Jews entering public service via conversion represented the most unscrupulous elements of German Jewry. Not only did they project a detrimental image of Judaism; they eventually would exert a deteriorating influence on the quality of public morality.[96]

The deep concern of the Centralverein over the social ramifications of individual conversion had been fully anticipated by Hermann Cohen. Whereas in 1880 he had dwelt exclusively on the fundamental unity of Judaism and Protestantism, taking an equivocal stand on the issue of Jewish survival,[97] during the last decades of the Empire, he emerged as the most profound spokesman for the right of German Jewry to retain its religious identity. Three years before the founding of the Centralverein, Cohen had already forcefully drawn attention to the nexus between the individual act of conversion and the fate of the organized Jewish community.

Treitschke had calmly set forth what one could expect from the emancipation. And I might refer here to the fact that I answered him in an essay for which public opinion at the time was not sufficiently mature. One expects, one assumes conversion. But what if it still does not occur? If the Jewish community should insist on the right to survive? We are witnessing the reaction of society and government to such an eventuality: Jews are not appointed to government service. But why speak of appointment? One seeks to make the separation permanent at its very roots: the specter of the ghetto rises again. And even the most well-meaning deny Judaism the character of a religion. Thus the suspicion clings to those who remain Jews that they cultivate their ethnic group and thereby a state within a state to the detriment of the unity of the Fatherland.

This is the actual harm which conversion inflicts on the abandoned community: it confirms and strengthens society and government in their distrust of and opposition to the legally equal Jewish community.[98]

In attempting to fortify the resistance of German Jewry to conversion, Centralverein speakers now rejected the alleged identity of liberal Protestantism and Judaism cited by Jewish intellectuals who justified conversion. Liberal Protestantism had not simply deepened the

Jewish concept of monotheism with a series of mystical and pantheistic images, nor could baptism justifiably be considered as merely the ritual expression for entering a community that identified with the personality who had exercised the greatest influence on mankind. Unconsciously echoing the rejections by Teller and Schleiermacher of David Friedländer's offer to convert in 1799, young Ludwig Hollaender, the later Executive Director of the Centralverein, asserted that the trinity remained a dogma and baptism was still an ineffable mystery.[99] Other speakers hammered away against child baptism. Gustav Levinstein, a successful entrepreneur who became one of the Centralverein's most impassioned polemicists, reminded his audiences that Jews at one time had considered it an outrageous crime when their children were kidnapped for baptism; now parents willingly committed the crime themselves. At least the earlier crime was motivated by religious fervor, in contrast to the materialistic motives of the present perpetrators.[100] When a 1908 change in German law permitted women to join the Centralverein, they were appealed to as the most effective instrument to prevent the younger generation from discarding Judaism.[101]

It was not easy to do more than polemicize against apostasy. In September 1900 the Executive Committee rejected a proposal to publish a list of converted Jews.[102] Five years later it turned down a more extreme recommendation to expel all adults who baptize their children from the ranks of the Centralverein. Opponents argued that not only was such a policy distasteful because of its inquisitional character, but it was also unfeasible because of the difficulty involved in establishing the fact.[103] In 1908 Felix Goldmann, one of the rabbis who spoke often on behalf of the Centralverein, suggested that Jews avoid all social contact with converts and above all that they prevent their children from associating with them and their children. Two years later the Centralverein began sponsoring a series of mass meetings to dramatize the danger of apostasy. On February 9, 1910, some four thousand attended (many others were turned away) a meeting in Berlin at which three speakers discussed different aspects of the problem. A later meeting drew thirteen hundred, while eight hundred attended a similar demonstration in Munich on January 3, 1911.

Such rallies usually ended with the adoption of a resolution condemning the government for its encouragement of conversion and
calling on Jews to speak out against those who had converted.[104]

Eventually the Centralverein's militancy produced political repercussions. A wholly unimportant Berlin election in 1908 posed an
embarrassing dilemma for the Centralverein. A converted Jew by the
name of Otto Mugdan was running for office on the ticket of the Progressive People's Party against a candidate from Theodor Barth's
Progressive Union. Since neither was an anti-Semite, the Centralverein had assumed its normal position of neutrality. However, a member of its Executive Committee personally endorsed Mugdan as his
party's candidate. The endorsement was greeted with angry criticism,
for the Centralverein suddenly appeared to be supporting a baptized
Jew for office, and the leadership was compelled officially to dissociate itself from the statement. The Executive Committee reiterated
its abhorrence of conversion and criticized Centralverein members
for not having obstructed Mugdan's nomination in the first place.
Nevertheless, the Centralverein's ultimate objective of Jewish unity
dictated a policy of strict neutrality in such cases.[105]

The Mugdan affair revealed the divergence of opinion within the
Centralverein itself. It seems as if the Orthodox members wished to
extend the campaign against apostasy, with which all agreed, to opposition to all baptized candidates. Their opponents within the Centralverein were willing to concede only that this opposition be waged
by Centralverein members during nominations. Thereafter the Centralverein had to maintain its neutrality. Any other course would in-
fringe upon the freedom of its members and shatter the unity of the
organization. Moreover, such a policy would be unfeasible. What
position should the Centralverein assume when a baptized Jew ran
against an anti-Semite? [106] At the convention of 1909 both sides reaffirmed that apostasy was a greater danger than anti-Semitism, but
the delegates refused to bind all members to vote against every baptized candidate. Two years later another convention instructed members to fight the nomination of such candidates, but when the Centralverein tried to thwart the nomination of Mugdan by the recently
organized Progressive People's Party (Fortschrittliche Volkspartei) for

the Prussian Legislature from the first Berlin district, it was defeated by the party leadership. Such action would constitute a form of discrimination incompatible with its liberal principles. Although the Centralverein did not renounce its determination to oppose such nominations, it never went beyond this policy to fight baptized candidates once they had been nominated.[107]

The concurrence of a rising rate of conversion with spreading social and economic discrimination clearly suggests that most of these converts, as their detractors averred,[108] acted to escape the unofficial disabilities reimposed by an intolerant society. The German context did not allow for a comfortable state of religious indifference. But only a handful of troubled and sensitive Jews struggled to vindicate intellectually the act of conversion. Yet the profound alienation which marks these personal statements may shed some light on why many others felt little compunction about giving up their religion for social or economic advancement.

One such aggrieved soul chose the pages of the *Preussische Jahrbücher,* the former podium for Treitschke's pronouncements, to air his painful dilemma. Writing under the pseudonym of Benedictus Levita, he agreed that secular German society had deep Christian roots and that Jews remained aliens because they were religiously different. He desperately yearned to end the unbearable tension that resulted. Only Judaism's lofty concept of God still bound him to his religion. Its ritual he regarded as barbaric and nationalistic, and its ethics, as wholly particularistic. And yet conversion was impossible; a Jew was unable to accept Christianity's concept of God. Its aesthetically attractive rituals and intellectually admirable ethics could never compensate for its irrational theology. Nor was circumvention possible. Even the liberal Protestantism of the lectern and pulpit bowed before the authority of the altar. Equally repelled by the ritual and ethics of Judaism and the theology of Christianity, the emancipated Jew was destined to live a lonely and alienated existence:

And we are so tired, oh so tired of our Judaism, which separates us from our people, without guaranteeing us in return any religious uplift. The precious possession, which nature bestows on the infant in the cradle, peoplehood [*Volkstum*], is denied us. Into Germanism [*Deutschtum*] we cannot enter, to Judaism we do not wish to return. We continue to walk our hopeless road alone. The great crime of the crucifixion is punished to the thousandth generation.[109]

The only remedy available to the uprooted Jew for whom Levita spoke was to convert his children and thereby save them from the same tragic fate.[110]

An equally negative assessment of Judaism was offered a few years later by the librarian of the Berlin Jewish Community. A wayward young married student at a Russian Yeshivah, Jacob Fromer, thristing for knowledge, finally made his way to Germany in the mid-1880's. Amid constant deprivation, which at one point almost drove him to convert and accept the comforts of a Christian mission house near Stuttgart, Fromer struggled for years to acquire a Gymnasium and university education. In 1899 he dramatically succeeded in obtaining German citizenship by appealing directly to the Kaiser. Depressed by the Kishinev pogrom of 1903, Fromer confided to his diary the belief that the Jews must convert because the ubiquity of anti-Semitism proved Judaism to be an aberration, a violation of reason and nature.[111]

A year later he said so publicly. Writing under a pseudonym in an influential German periodical, Fromer urged his emancipated coreligionists to convert. Judaism was a schizophrenic attempt to impose on reality a moral code hostile to every manifestation of reason and art that did not serve some ethical purpose. This ethical fanaticism fatefully pitted Judaism against nature in a struggle that it could never hope to win. True, the Jews had managed to survive and even to imbue their life with the loftiest ethical standards. But at what a price: the suppression of every natural instinct for beauty, the defiance of reason in accounting for their fate and mankind's eternal hatred! The only rational option left the still persecuted modern Jew, who had long discarded the ethical fanaticism and the theological premises which sustained his ancestors, was to disappear.[112]

Having lost his job as well as his legal suit against the Berlin Jewish Community, Fromer reiterated his case in the course of a rambling, sentimental, but gripping autobiography which ended in total despair. The central figure of this pathetic tale was a confused, ambivalent, and tortured young Jew, unable to extricate himself from the accident of his birth. While he counseled his people to abandon Judaism, Fromer designed projects to present the content of Rabbinic literature in scientific form. He regarded Jewish literature as far inferior to that of other nations, yet took delight in ridiculing German rabbis for their ignorance of it. Though he despised the religion and cultural backwardness of his people, he suffered at the spectacle of Russian pogroms. In brief, the attachment to his family and the recollection of centuries of persecution bound him inextricably to his people, despite the enlightened dictates of reason.[113]

This plight, which could not be relieved by the baptismal font, also characterized the early career of Walther Rathenau, the gifted son of the founder of the German electrical industry and later Foreign Minister of the Weimar Republic.[114] In 1897, two years after he had announced before the court his wish to leave Judaism,[115] he still wrote as a Jew, although as one who regarded himself as a German. In that year he published a sardonic analysis of the Jewish question, at least partially provoked by the four-year effort of the Centralverein. Rathenau, writing under a pseudonym, claimed that the Jews alone were responsible for their social isolation and for the feeling of abhorrence, which led to their expulsion from every sector of German society. The Jews had remained an alien and uncultured Asian stock that refused to assimilate. The activity of the Centralverein only aggravated matters:

You have founded organizations—for defense rather than self-examination [*Einkehr*]. You have made life miserable for the best among you, with the result that they turn their backs on you, and as they desert, you do nothing better than curse them; that's why you get along so well.[116]

Although he was convinced that the liberal Protestant minister and the enlightened rabbi were preaching the same deism, conversion was no answer. The present animosity would merely be shifted toward the convert. The only solution was an unprecedented mass effort at self-education, which in time would free German Jewry of its mannerisms, femininity, peculiarities of speech, and patterns of thought.[117]

A few years before the war Rathenau offered a more personal explanation of why his type rejected conversion. Prodded by the plea for conversion by a Christian professor, he again depicted the deistic faith of the modern cultured Jew, which brooked neither dogma nor ritual. He added:

I believe that the four Gospels are as familiar to the educated Jew as the educated Christian, and I have never met a Jew who has rejected the ethics of the New Testament. Some believe they are contained in the Old Testament; others recognize their superiority over all moral teachings known to us.[118]

Still these Jews would not convert, because they were repelled by the coercion of the German government. The policy to open for converts all doors closed to Jews would make their conversion appear motivated by material considerations. They were men of integrity, who did not wish to defile the purity of a spiritual act by material gain.

I know that persons who feel themselves unreservedly attracted to Christianity renounce the external membership because it is connected with reward. This renunciation rests upon the conviction that a spiritual step must lose its purity when it leads to material advantages, a consideration which does not entirely fit the conception that one ordinarily forms of the cool calculating Jewish spirit.[119]

Rathenau himself remained a Jew, but he refused to join the Centralverein. In January 1917 Eugen Fuchs met for more than an hour with Rathenau in an effort to bring him into the organization. He learned that Rathenau believed that Judaism was in need of major reforms. Rathenau also criticized the Centralverein for preoccupying itself with a defense of outmoded rituals. Fuchs left him a package of Centralverein materials, that he might gain a more accurate picture. On January 31, 1917, Rathenau wrote that he was still unable to join. He too was committed to the legal and social equality of the Germans of Jewish persuasion, but he feared that the growth of the Centralverein was incompatible with the radically liberal Judaism in which he believed. Fuchs continued to protest the religious neutrality of the Centralverein, and asserted that its defense of Orthodox practice rested upon the principle of religious freedom and civil equality and not on any proclivity toward Orthodoxy. In a letter more than a year later, Rathenau reiterated his conviction that it was not the task of contemporary Judaism to defend ritual institutions which it found religiously objectionable, and he was therefore unable to support the efforts of the Centralverein.[120]

Nothing demonstrates more clearly than this polemic against apostasy the internal transformation of the Centralverein itself. Founded by a theatrical director whose views of Judaism were not unlike those of Rathenau, and committed by its constitution to a cultivation of German consciousness, the Centralverein had become intensely preoccupied with strengthening the sense of Jewish identity. This concern had been only implicit in the original appeals to duty and self-respect which the Centralverein utilized to galvanize German Jewry. But confronted with a rising rate of attrition caused by ever more external pressure, the Centralverein responded boldly by mounting an aggressive internal mission. To a limited extent its campaign may have been influenced by the example of German Zionism, a movement primarily committed to the revival of Jewish consciousness. Occasionally, Centralverein leaders indicated their indebtedness.[121] But by and large these men recognized both the threat to Judaism and its pernicious cause independently.

Again the relationship to Rathenau provides an indication of the Centralverein's shifting emphasis. When Rathenau's vitriolic essay "Hear, O Israel" first appeared in 1897, the review in the Centralverein's periodical was so moderate that it just about accepted all of his strictures against German Jewry. In 1902 Rathenau reprinted the essay in a personal collection entitled *Impressions*. This time the Executive Committee commissioned a total repudiation. The ensuing review contained not a word of agreement. It assailed Rathenau for his malice, distortions, errors, and unproven assertions.[122]

The leaders of the Centralverein, before and after the First World War, reflected upon this development themselves. In 1913 Fuchs conceded that the Centralverein had begun as a purely defensive organization. However, its leaders had come to realize that at stake was the preservation, and not only the equality, of Judaism. The wavering sense of Jewish identity had to be buttressed with knowledge, pride, and loyalty. Fuchs was not ready to settle for an assimilation that demanded the surrender of all Jewish practices and patterns of behavior simply because they were different. He had grown to recognize that Jews were not merely members of another religious persuasion, as he himself had declared in 1897 and 1903. Jews exhibited their own style, they had their own ancestral and historic roots, and the Jewish home of their parents had marked them with a particular spiritual and physical stamp.[123]

The statement by Fuchs demonstrates the fact that the Centralverein had actually begun to redefine the character of post-emancipation Judaism. In February 1928, Ludwig Hollaender, the Executive Director and ideological heir of Fuchs, likewise admitted the inadequacy of the strictly religious definition that had been so readily adopted to acquire emancipation. It failed to explain the countless unpracticing and unbelieving Jews of the modern era who continued to identify with Judaism. A common origin and history had added a shared fate and culture to the religious unity of the Jews. With this expanded concept of Judaism, the Centralverein committed itself to a relationship of equals, in which the Jewish partner, invigorated by a new self-awareness, was no longer merely a religious factor. The objective had become twofold: an integration that would also allow for preserving a sense of Jewish identity, the practice of Judaism, and the cultivation of Jewish values.[124]

6

A SECOND "FRONT": VERBAND DER DEUTSCHEN JUDEN, 1904-1914

JEWISH LIFE in Germany during the last two decades before the war exhibited a furor of organizational activity. In part, Jewish behavior simply paralleled the organizational ferment in German society, where the number of pressure groups continued to proliferate unabated. In part, Jews became increasingly alarmed by the constant surfacing of anti-Semitism in ever new sectors of the Reich. While anti-Semitism provided the impetus to act, the German scene showed the way. In rapid succession German Jewry built a network of imposing national organizations to supplement the services of the local Jewish community and to counter the consequences of growing isolation. The formation of the Grossloge Unabhängiger Orden Bnei Briss (1888), the Centralverein (1893), the Verband der Vereine für Jüdische Geschichte und Literatur (1893), the Kartellconvent der Verbindungen deutschen Studenten jüdischen Glaubens (1896), the Hilfsverein der deutschen Juden (1901), the Gesellschaft zur Förderung der Wissenschaft des Judentums (1902), the Verband der deutschen Juden (1904), the Vereinigung für das Liberale Judentum (1908), and the Verband der Jüdischen Jugendvereine Deutschlands (1909) attest the urgency with which Jewry marshaled its resources to withstand the multiple forms of German intransigence.

Of these organizations only the Centralverein and the Verband fought anti-Semitism directly. In 1904 the Verband opened a second "front," which it continued to man for nearly two decades until the Centralverein became sufficiently powerful to consolidate the defense effort. What the Verband temporarily supplied was the illusion of an all-embracing defense organization empowered by an official mandate from German Jewry.

IN SEARCH OF A MANDATE

The immediate impetus for the lengthy debate, which eventually culminated in the formation of the Verband, came not from the electoral fortunes of the anti-Semitic political parties, but rather from a number of *causes célèbres* which reflected the pervasive influence of anti-Semitism in the government. In fact in the Reichstag elections of 1898 and 1903 the anti-Semitic parties were unable to match their 1893 showing of 16 deputies. Running almost 90 candidates in 1898, they managed to raise their total vote to over 284,000, although they won only 13 seats. In 1903 their total remained about the same, while the number of seats dropped to 10. The significance of these figures becomes apparent the moment it is recalled that during the same decade the electorate grew by nearly 2,000,000 voters and the Social Democrats nearly doubled their vote.[1]

But if the danger subsided in one area, it immediately cropped up in another. A few months after the turn of the century, Jewry was again shocked by the explosion of a major ritual murder scandal. Again the anti-Semites effectively exploited the murder and quartering of an eighteen-year-old Gymnasium student in Konitz (West Prussia) to bring Judaism to trial. A Jewish butcher was accused, and kept under arrest for five months. Medical experts were called in to examine the cut running from the chin to the trachea and to explain the absence of blood in all parts of the corpse. The local synagogue was searched for traces of a ritual murder. And even after the acquittal of the accused butcher, two other Jews were convicted of perjury and sentenced to terms of one and four years.[2]

Equally disconcerting for German Jewry was the position taken by the Prussian Minister of Justice, Karl Heinrich von Schönstedt, in response to an interpellation in the Chamber of Deputies, on January 31, 1901. Noting that Jewish lawyers in Berlin were compelled to wait an average of eight years longer than their Christian colleagues for appointment as notary publics, Martin Peltasohn, a Progressive Jewish Deputy from Bromberg, asked the Minister what criteria were employed for selecting a candidate. Schönstedt was somewhat surprised by the implied attack, for the Department of Justice was the only department left "in the entire monarchy in which Jewish judicial assistants (*Assessoren*) were even appointed. All other departments refuse to employ Jewish men." [3] He defended the discriminatory policy of his own office by invoking the religious sensibilities of the German masses, who would not tolerate having their most intimate affairs handled by Jewish notaries. The same consideration applied to appointment of Jews as judges. There were countless localities in Prussia where it was simply impossible to send a Jewish judge. Schönstedt admitted that the Constitution opened all public offices to Jews, but, he added quickly, "I do not recognize that passing an examination gives every candidate the right to a state appointment." [4] Predicting that Jewish candidates in the future might have to wait still longer, he concluded emphatically: "I cannot, and I will not, change this, and I believe thereby to be serving the entire people [*Gesammtheit*]." [5]

It was not merely the chronological proximity of these incidents that prompted Eugen Fuchs to treat them together in a speech delivered, on February 28, 1901, to a Centralverein protest rally of seven hundred in Berlin. Both testified to the continued effectiveness of "the terrorism of the anti-Semitic agitation." In each instance the government had submitted to anti-Semitic pressure. In Konitz the anti-Semites had demonstrated the extent to which the mob could influence the judiciary. In the Chamber of Deputies, no less an authority than the Minister of Justice conceded that German sensibilities deserved greater attention than German law. Instead of leading and educating its citizens, the government heeded their bigoted wishes. Since when had it become Prussian tradition to interpret the Constitution and conduct the bureaucracy according to the will of the people, Fuchs asked sarcastically. The survival of a beleaguered Germany depended upon the loyalty of all its citizens, but this was a commitment that could be earned only through equality and justice.[6]

In those anxious days between the blood libel and the interpellation began the extended deliberations which finally produced the Verband. A small group of Centralverein men led by Fuchs proposed to the Prussian Minister of Education and Religion the creation, with government assistance, of an official representative of Prussian Jewry from whom the government would receive reliable information on all Jewish matters. Uppermost in their minds was the desire to establish an officially recognized organ that could allay, at least in government circles, the suspicion that the manifold charges against Jewish texts and practices contained a touch of truth. But the proposal was buried in the files of the Ministry without action.[7]

During the same period a more radical alternative was brought to the attention of the Centralverein leadership by Bernhard Breslauer, a Berlin lawyer active in the Jewish community, and Martin Philippson, a former professor of history at the University of Brussels who had apparently been forced into retirement in 1891 because of his German sympathies. Since then he had lived in Berlin and devoted himself to Jewish communal work and the study of modern Jewish history. The thinking of both men was partially stimulated by the annual convention of German Catholics (Katholikentag), an institution first created in 1848 to inform the Frankfurt National Assembly of Catholic interests. In 1900 German Catholic representatives were meeting for the forty-seventh time in such a national session to articulate their hopes and grievances. Breslauer and Philippson suggested that the time had come for German Jewry to convene its own Judentag to protest noisily and fearlessly an alarming situation. Horwitz and Fuchs agreed, and in September 1900 Philippson proposed the idea in the Jewish press. He specified the reasons for his apprehension: the social segregation of German Jewry, the ritual murder charge of Konitz credited even by government officials, the bureaucratic subversion of the Constitution, and the flight from Judaism. Jews must resist by every means available. The Centralverein had bravely shown the way, but it could not speak for German Jewry. Only an annual assembly of German Jewry (Judentag) could provide the mandate and platform indispensable for effective protest.[8]

In a second fervent appeal published in 1901, Philippson spelled
out the reasons for the Centralverein's inadequacy:

. . . despite its constantly growing membership, despite its laudable and
courageous activity, the Centralverein lacks—and must lack—two
things: a public mandate to speak in the name of German Jewry, and
consequently a moral authority that compels all its members to [pursue]
the same religious-political course. Only some sort of official mandate
could bestow such authority.[9]

Philippson's proposal precipitated a debate not unlike the one that
had agitated German Jewry back in 1893. Those favoring the Judentag viewed the present pessimistically. The increasing exclusion, the
apparent status of second-class citizenship, the absence of government protection, transformed Jews de facto into an alien class. In his
annual survey of the year's events in the *Jahrbuch für jüdische Geschichte und Literatur,* Philippson depicted German Jewry as an isolated and besieged minority, many of whose educated and wealthy
members were ready to abandon their affiliation for advancement or
honor at the slightest opportunity. Repeatedly he called for united
and open protest: "We live in a time of battle in which all interest
groups unite more tightly in order to guard against damage what concerns them most and to employ their own organizations to press for
their most vital interests." [10] The Jews could expect help from no-
where. They too must organize to exercise pressure on a government
which had ceased to lead.[11]

The followers of Samson R. Hirsch rejected Philippson's proposal
outright. They considered the Judentag an unwelcome first step toward the eventual creation of a central authority for all German
Jews. In 1876 they had won their release from compulsory membership in Reform-dominated communities, and they were unmoved by
a project that might cost them their freedom of conscience. The *Israelit* suggested that Philippson's pessimism was excessive. The position of the emancipated Jew was incomparably better than that of his
medieval ancestor, and the anti-Semitism that remained was God's
way of prodding the Jews back to Judaism. The hypersensitivity of
the modern Jew was the result of his irreligious makeup. Finally, the
Israelit reaffirmed its position of 1893 that anti-Semitism could be
fought only in alliance with the liberals.[12]

Because of the undeniable quasi-political character of a Judentag, the opposition from other quarters was intense. Its opponents insisted that the Jews were solely a religious community and ought not to mix in politics. Their numbers were insignificant, and the deep divisions within German Jewry in any case made the objective unfeasible. Some feared that public demonstrations, especially if boisterous and militant, would only fortify German antipathy, and accordingly they counseled continued patience. So much had already been accomplished. With time anti-Semitism itself would become more amenable to reason. If action was still necessary, let it be taken through the legislatures. Many opposed the idea simply because German Zionists had openly endorsed it. The president of the Breslau Jewish Community and the local Literaturverein irately declared that he would reject a priori every suggestion approved by the Zionists.[13]

On October 8, 1900, several days after Philippson's article appeared, Theodor Herzl had advised the president of the Zionist Federation of Germany (Zionistische Vereinigung für Deutschland), Max Bodenheimer, to pay careful attention to the developments. Should the Judentag materialize, it could provide the fledgling Zionist organization of Germany a chance to present its cause to a wider public. Two days later Bodenheimer, a Cologne lawyer, informed Philippson of his interest. "We [i.e., the Zionists] are particularly interested to emphasize in Germany that we will energetically defend the native rights of the Jews".[14] Philippson replied that he considered the ultimate objective of Zionism utopian, but that he respected the genuine Jewish feeling behind it. He welcomed Bodenheimer's support and asked him to sell the idea within his own circle.[15] In the pages of Die Welt, the official organ of the World Zionist Organization, the Judentag was also warmly endorsed. It appeared to be a serious attempt to overcome the demoralizing dependence upon the Progressives. At last the Jews had resolved to defend their own interests.[16]

Centralverein support for the Judentag did not waver. Its leaders realized that the Centralverein lacked both the mandate and the membership to speak in the name of German Jewry and that as a defense organization it had little to say on German legislation affecting Jews. The Executive Committee agreed to send Fuchs and Horwitz to the forthcoming meeting of notables, scheduled to convene on December 27, 1900, to decide the fate of Philippson's suggestion. They were empowered to propose that representatives of the large organizations and communities should assemble periodically in a Judentag at which two or three main speakers would air Jewish grievances. A permanent committee should also be formed to make the arrangements.[17]

Sixty Jewish leaders met in Berlin on December 27, and their rejection of the Judentag proposal was unqualified.[18] The Zionists tried vainly to revive it by promoting a number of large rallies during the next few months in Berlin and elsewhere. Their speakers denounced the duplicity of the liberals for not running Jewish candidates or defending Jewish interests. They berated the Jews for their timidity and they called for the convening of a Judentag whose delegates would be directly elected by all German Jews.[19] There can be little doubt that the Zionist embrace represented the kiss of death. A Jewish leadership that had effectively prevented the first Zionist Congress from meeting in Munich four years earlier was not prepared to consider a proposal inherently offensive and now propounded by the Zionists.[20]

The meeting of Jewish leaders on December 27, 1900, had not been entirely fruitless. It had decided to create a committee which would consult with the Centralverein and other organizations in order to arrive at new alternatives to be presented to a later general assembly. This committee, which included Breslauer, Fuchs, Horwitz, and Philippson, among others, began now to consider seriously the formation of a comprehensive and permanent organization (*Gesamtorganisation*) to represent the interests of German Jewry, an option that Fuchs had already advocated when Philippson first approached the Centralverein. In September 1901 it issued a circular in which it declared that, if the Jews had manifested their solidarity in such a single spokesman years ago, the anti-Semites would never have succeeded in curtailing their rights. Other groups had long recognized the strength of unity:

There is scarcely a class of society that does not recognize the need for a common representation, does not possess one, or is not striving for it. Should the Jews in Germany wait until the state imposes a common representation on them? The spiritual powers of Judaism in Germany are sufficiently strong to create by themselves an organization that has no other purpose than to demand what the totality of German Jews considers useful for itself.[21]

When the committee proceeded to survey the sentiment of communities and of rabbis in order to measure the support that the new endeavor might enjoy, the response was ambiguous. Out of 1,553 communities polled, 227, including the largest, responded affirmatively; 84 of the 291 rabbis polled likewise endorsed the project. Among the opponents were Hermann Cohen, the Marburg philosopher, who feared that such an organization would be guilty of *Interessenpolitik,* and the association of the separatistic Orthodox in Frankfurt.[22]

Opposition also appeared from an unexpected source. The Jewish Community of Königsberg and its rabbi, Hermann Vogelstein, criticized the very attempt to crowd the German Jewish scene with yet another organization that would only undermine the praiseworthy efforts of the Centralverein, a criticism that Königsberg had already raised in 1893 when the Comité zur Abwehr antisemitischer Angriffe first appealed for funds.[23] They further believed that a legitimate representation of German Jewry had to be based upon the membership of Jewish communities, not upon organizations. They therefore advised expanding the role of the Gemeindebund as envisioned in its original statutes of 1872.

At the ninth national convention of the Gemeindebund in February 1902 Königsberg moved to transform the Gemeindebund into the desired spokesman of German Jewry by readopting the original statutes of 1872. The most vigorous dissenter to the Königsberg suggestion was none other than Philippson himself, the president of the Gemeindebund. In 1898 the Gemeindebund had received the status of a juridical person, a status it had anxiously sought since its expulsion from Saxony in 1881. As a juridical entity it could now inherit estates and own property, and thereby expand its welfare and educational programs extensively. Any change in its constitution required the approval of the government, and Philippson fully realized that transforming the Gemeindebund into a quasi-political organization would hardly evoke much favor in Berlin. The convention agreed and the motion was defeated.[24]

By the end of 1902 the committee seemed on the verge of dissolution. The anxieties aroused by the Konitz affair and the remarks of the Minister of Justice were subsiding, and the resistance to any nationwide enterprise had proved to be substantial. However, the resolve to push for such an organization was revived by the formation of a large committee in Frankfurt to combat the continued flight from Judaism among the better circles of Frankfurt Jewry. Intending to call a convention of notables, this committee first contacted the older body which had been deliberating in Berlin. At a combined gathering in Frankfurt in May 1903 the decision was reaffirmed to pursue the original objective of creating a comprehensive organization. Further deliberations were devoted to writing and approving a constitution. The labors of the two committees culminated on April 25, 1904, when approximately 130 delegates representing many of the larger communities, regional associations, and major organizations of German Jewry (only the Jews of Bavaria and Württemburg were unrepresented) met to found the Verband der deutschen Juden.[25]

The very name of this new organization was significant, for the use of the term *Juden* rather than *Israeliten* marked a defiant readoption of a formerly detested epithet. Ever since the efforts of David Friedländer in Berlin at the end of the eighteenth century, and the deliberations of the Assembly of Notables in Paris in 1806, emancipated Jewry had preferred to mark its new status with a new nomenclature. The switch was the more desirable, because the designation "Jew" had not survived the Middle Ages untainted. Christian polemical literature had transformed "Israelite" into a laudatory term, while saddling the word "Jew" with an invidious pejorative connotation. In 1793 Friedländer had already painfully noted: "The extent to which this general name 'Jude' has hurt us is indescribable. A name which designated the nation or religion was branded a character name and, often contrary to every rule and logical justification, became common usage." Consequently, the major Jewish organizations formed in the West in the third quarter of the nineteenth century all bore the name

"Israelite": The Board of Deputies of American Israelites, the Alliance Israélite Universelle and the Deutsch-Israelitischer Gemeindebund. In contrast to this acceptance of Christian terminology, Gabriel Riesser, the early leader in the fight for the full emancipation of Prussian Jewry, in 1832 dared to call his ephemeral paper *Der Jude,* to the dismay of many. Likewise Graetz boldly entitled his multi-volume history *Geschichte der Juden* (1853–76), while his more timid forerunner, Isaac M. Jost, had been willing to settle for a nine-volume *Geschichte der Israeliten* (1820–28). By the end of the century, the Zionists openly avowed their determination to transform the epithet "Jew" into a title of honor.[26]

This terminological confusion and its underlying psychological ambivalence are dramatized in a typical personal experience related by Sammy Gronemann. When Gronemann became a law clerk (*Referendar*) in Göttingen shortly before the turn of the century, he worked one day with a junior judge (*Assessor*) who was also Jewish. A Jewish witness appeared before them. Asked his name, he answered, "Levinsohn." Asked his religion, he hesitated for a moment and then stammered, "Israelit." The judge also hesitated briefly and then dictated to Gronemann, "Mosaisch." Gronemann, a brash and witty young man, repeated audibly, "Jude," and wrote that feared term into the public record.[27]

HISTORICAL SURVEY

Since the Centralverein had already been fighting anti-Semitism openly for more than a decade, the Verband's role had to be carefully delineated and frequently explained. As the alleged representative of German Jewry, it proposed to deal with institutions rather than with individuals. Whereas the Centralverein defended individual Jews or prosecuted individual anti-Semites, the Verband intended to address the German government. By protesting the discrimination of the bureaucracy, and by presenting Jewish viewpoints on relevant legislation, the Verband hoped to win the equality promised by the Constitution. Its second major function was to mount a literary defense of Judaism, especially against the distortions disseminated by the academic establishment. In sum, the founders of the Verband conceived the new organization to be a valuable supplement to the efforts of the Centralverein. By virtue of its mandate, it was designed to challenge the prestigious institutions of German life: the government and the university, whose practices and pronouncements contributed so decisively to making anti-Semitism respectable.[28]

The membership of the Verband consisted of communities and organizations. At the end of 1904, 116 communities, totaling 234,231 Jews, and 9 organizations with 25,472 members, had contributed 10,447 marks. Four years later the Verband claimed to speak for the majority of large and medium-sized Jewish communities, though some of the large national organizations, such as the Verband für jüdische Wohltätigkeitspflege, the Jüdische Frauenbund, the Grossloge U. O. Bnei Briss, and the Verband der Vereine für jüdische Geschichte und Literatur remained unaffiliated. By 1908 the Verband's income had risen to almost 33,000 marks. However, by 1911 the budget had also risen, to almost 50,000 marks, exceeding income to such an extent that the board decided to ask the communities and organizations to assume the travel and per diem expenses of the representatives they sent to the board meetings, an expense costing the Verband nearly 1,500 marks for every plenary session. During the previous three years the funds of the Verband had dropped by one-third, and the proposed 1912–13 budget was cut back to only 28,200 marks.[29]

The membership met biennially in a national convention that somewhat approximated the Judentag originally put forward by Philippson. With some 300 to 500 delegates and nearly 2,000 observers in attendance, the five conventions held before the war projected a semblance of a Jewish congress, although the Zionists criticized the fact that the delegates were not elected but merely appointed by the boards of the communities and organizations. This representative body of German Jewry did not meet to deliberate, but to protest. It usually listened to two presentations documenting and denouncing the sundry forms of government discrimination and one speech devoted to a forthright defense of Judaism. Government officials were invited after the first convention, and they did in fact attend the next two. Each convention also sent a declaration of loyalty to the Kaiser, and adopted a resolution condemning the denial of full equality to German Jewry.[30]

The actual work of the Verband was planned and executed by the board in Berlin. The biennial convention elected twenty-one of its members. The Centralverein, the Gemeindebund, and the Allgemeiner Rabbinerverband in Deutschland each added another two representatives while the six communities with more than 10,000 Jews sent one representative each.[31] The board elected the president of the Verband, and Philippson fittingly became the first. Fuchs and Horwitz were chosen as the two vice-presidents. Upon Philippson's retirement in 1905 the board elected Edmund Lachmann, an industrialist and vice-president of the Berlin Jewish Community. When he died in 1909 the board was unable to find a replacement until Horwitz agreed to fill the post provisionally. He remained president until his death in 1917.[32]

The difficulty in finding a president again testifies to the declining fortunes of the Verband in the last years before the war. Philippson himself confirmed this impression in an unfavorable critique of the Verband which he delivered to the board on April 3, 1910. He had previously withdrawn from the board in disagreement, and he now indicted the Verband for having failed to achieve its objectives. Its existence had not increased the feeling of identity and solidarity of German Jewry. The number of conversions had not decreased, and in fact the Verband was quite unknown. A coterie of notables conducted its operations, and it lacked entirely the mass support necessary for success. The Verband had failed to establish a relationship with a political party other than the Progressives, and its accomplishments as a pressure group were minimal. Philippson urged three immediate steps: a closer relationship with other political parties, democratizing the board, and holding regular meetings throughout Germany to attract new support.[33]

The board felt that Philippson, while condemning its failures, had ignored its efforts. Some matters such as press coverage, the interest of a political party, or distances from Berlin were simply beyond its control. Nevertheless, the board decided to act upon the last two recommendations. Its intention to involve board members from outside Berlin was soon undercut by financial troubles. The one tangible result of Philippson's critique was a series of large protest rallies against the exclusion of Jews from the Prussian Officer Corps at the end of 1910 and in the first months of 1911, in Berlin, Breslau, Königsberg, and Frankfurt. These rallies were jointly sponsored by the Verband and the Centralverein; they were, however, held principally to advertise the existence and activities of their sponsors.[34]

The Verband never succeeded in becoming the undisputed spokesman of German Jewry. Theoretically, this was to have been its contribution to the defense effort, but it never acquired the approval of all sectors of German Jewry. In its very first representation to the Prussian government in connection with the proposed legislation on public education, it was challenged by the Freie Vereinigung für die Interessen des orthodoxen Judenthums.[35] Admittedly this organization never cooperated or affiliated with the Verband.[36] But even organizations that did continued to approach the Imperial and state governments independently without the slightest prior consultation with the Verband. In a futile attempt to counter this disregard, the board on October 14, 1907, unanimously requested its members to inform the Verband of any intention to address the authorities and to await its advice. A year later the situation remained unaltered. The various sectors of German Jewry still refused to restrict their initiative by allowing the Verband alone to deal with the government on all matters of legislation and administration.[37]

The Verband did not really survive the war. With the separation of church and state, enunciated by Article 137, the Weimar Constitution seemed to abrogate the existing laws regulating Jewish status. The leaders of the Verband, among others, regarded the moment as propitious to create a single, inclusive body to represent German Jewry based upon community membership, and incorporated under public law. However, the leaders of the Gemeindebund claimed that the Gemeindebund potentially already constituted such an organization, and at its national convention in January 1921 the delegates voted to accept a draft constitution prepared by Ismar Freund, the legal historian. The leaders of the Verband doubted whether government approval would be forthcoming. But they had lost the initiative to the Gemeindebund, and when the largest Jewish communities began to withhold their annual contributions to the Verband, its

work was effectively curtailed. Reluctantly the board decided on
April 23, 1922, to dissolve the organization.[38] Thus both the creation and the demise of the Verband were directly determined by policy decisions of the Gemeindebund.

GERMAN JEWRY VERSUS THE STATE

In reality, the Verband had ceased to operate long before its formal
dissolution. Its most fruitful period of activity spanned the decade
prior to the war. During that time it addressed itself mainly to the
prejudices of the German bureaucracy and of Protestant scholarship
on Judaism. The cruder forms of German anti-Semitism had slowly
subsided; the efforts of the Verband were directed against the institutions that nourished the pervasive anti-Jewish sentiment that remained.

In May 1906 the board established a network of eighty-two correspondents throughout Germany who were to submit quarterly reports
on evidence of anti-Semitism in their localities. The objective was to
gain a more accurate reading of local differences while also gathering
the components of a national picture.[39] The correspondents were by
no means trained observers. Of the 133 correspondents cooperating
in 1909, 55 were businessmen and 31 were lawyers. By 1913 the ratio
was still the same.[40] Obviously the quality of the reports differed
greatly, and they were not submitted regularly. Nevertheless, during
the two quarters, from October 1907 to May 1908, fully 77 percent
of the correspondents responded, some of them giving accounts of
exceptional quality. The national picture suggested by the first reports remained substantially unchanged by later contributions. The
reports indicated that in the majority of German communities overt
acts of anti-Semitism had been replaced by a generally cool and
strained relationship with the local Jewish population. The most enthusiastic proponents of anti-Semitism seemed to be found among the
circles of bureaucrats and reserve officers. The relations between
Jews and Christians were best in southwest Germany in areas like
Lorraine, Baden, and the Rhineland. As one moved northeast, the relations deteriorated steadily. However, in northern Germany the Cath-

olics, likewise a minority, were far more sympathetic to the Jews and their struggle for full equality than they were in some of the southern states where they constituted the majority.[41]

In its confrontation with the government, the Verband demanded a twofold equality. It protested the absence of equity in the treatment of individual Jews and Judaism. Regarding disadvantaged Jews, for example, the Verband took up the cause of Orthodox Jews who kept their stores closed on Saturdays. It sought legislation from the Reichstag permitting these owners to use Jewish help to work in their stores on Sunday, albeit behind closed doors.[42] It also fought sporadic ordinances by various local authorities forbidding kosher slaughtering in the abattoirs of their communities, and in 1908 it issued a new collection of 475 opinions defending the humaneness and hygiene of ritual slaughtering.[43]

The Verband likewise protested the periodic expulsions of foreign Jews from Prussian soil. As early as 1881–82 Prussian authorities had expelled Russian Jews from Berlin. In the Spring and Summer of 1884, the government again expelled 667 Russian subjects, nearly all Jews, from the capital. In the following three years some 10,000 Jews were among the 32,000 Russian and Austrian nationals driven out of the eastern provinces.[44] Twenty years later another expulsion of 4,000 Russian Jewish immigrants from Berlin took place. Despite these periodic measures, Germany harbored by 1910 some 79,000 Jews of foreign extraction out of a Jewish population of 615,000. German intellectuals as well as assimilated Jews contended that if the trend were allowed to continue the assimilation of German Jewry would be retarded, if not reversed. Although the borders remained open, individual German states rarely granted citizenship to foreign Jews.[45] In 1910–11 almost the only Jews naturalized were the young men who had volunteered for military service and passed the physical examination. When the Reichstag deliberated upon a new Imperial law for citizenship in 1913, the Verband proposed that it clearly state that the request for citizenship must never be considered on the basis of an applicant's religion. But the proposal was rejected as a limitation of the absolute power vested in the state authorities. The most the Verband achieved was that a Jewish woman who had lost her German citizenship by marrying an alien could regain her citizenship

after his death. Formerly, she and her German-born children remained aliens subject to expulsion.[46]

In 1909 the Verband held its third national convention in the Sile-
sian city of Breslau and utilized the occasion to criticize what it considered the Prussian Administration's discriminatory policy toward
the Jews in the province of Posen. The province with its impoverished Polish majority had been returned to Prussia by the Congress
of Vienna in 1815. During the ensuing decades, the slow emergence
of a Polish middle class intensified the spirit of Polish nationalism.
In response Bismarck after 1870 embarked upon an aggressive policy of Germanization. In 1885 Austrian and Russian Poles were expelled from Prussia's eastern provinces. A year later the government
created a Colonization Commission with a fund of 100 million marks
to buy the lands of Polish nobles for the settlement of German peasants. In addition, the government now assumed direct control of the
public schools in Posen and West Prussia, appointing all teachers
and forbidding the use of Polish as a language of instruction. But the
policy was singularly unsuccessful in stemming the tide of Polish nationalism. By 1908 the Prussian Landtag felt compelled to pass an
exceptional law permitting the government to expropriate some
280,000 acres of Polish land in Posen, though the government failed
to employ it.[47]

Caught in the middle of this bitter struggle was the sizable Jewish
population of Posen, whose numbers dropped from 76,757 in 1849
to 35,327 in 1900. The Verband depicted an isolated minority, hated
by the Poles, and rejected as a force for Germanization by the Prussian government. In fact, the government drove Jews off the land, denied citizenship to any Jewish alien, refused to award contracts to
Jews in proportion to their numbers, and appointed no Jew to the
bureaucracy governing the area. Jews also suffered economically
from the competing Polish and German associations in the province
which dominated the economic life of the area. Both the consequence
and the proof of these grievances, Verband speakers insisted, was the
precipitous emigration of Posen's Jewish inhabitants. Since 1885,
25 percent of the Jewish population in 116 communities and more
than 50 percent in 54 others had departed. The government denied

the charges and dismissed the statistics as merely an instance of the general movement westward to areas of greater economic opportunity.[48]

The Verband invested heavily to prove and protest government discrimination against Jews. It worked to publicize the total exclusion of Jews from the ranks of reserve officers and assiduously compiled statistics to reveal discriminatory practices in other branches of government.[49] Thus in 1911 Breslauer published for the Verband a survey of the number of Jewish full professors at German universities. He found that in 1909–10 of 991 full professors, 25 were Jewish (i.e., 2½ percent of the total) and 44 had been baptized (i.e., 4½ percent of the total). The rate of promotion likewise differed. In that same year, 39½ percent of the Christians teaching and 25 percent of the baptized Jews, but only 12 percent of the unconverted Jews, had reached the rank of full professor.[50] The success of Jews in penetrating the teaching staffs of secondary schools in Prussia was no better. Outside of the two Jewish Gymnasiums in Frankfurt, there were no Jewish school directors in Prussia, and only one baptized Jew. Ninety-six Jews (1.15 percent of the total) had reached the rank of *Oberlehrer,* although these were mainly in the cities of Berlin, Breslau, and Frankfurt. In the provinces of the Rhineland, Westphalia, Pomerania, and Schleswig-Holstein there was not a single Jewish *Oberlehrer.*[51] Aside from limiting the occupational choice, such discrimination from above served to reinforce the anti-Jewish prejudices of the masses, and it was on that account that the Verband considered the data so ominous: ". . . what should the people think of justice, when right and law are trampled by those called upon to protect them?"[52]

The second broad category of grievances that the Verband presented primarily to the Prussian government dealt with the treatment of Judaism by the state, especially in comparison with that accorded to the Evangelical and Catholic Churches. The Verband had returned to a position already articulated by Graetz back in 1870, for which he had been later reprimanded by Treitschke: the full equality of the Jews required the full equality of Judaism.[53] Within the German context, where the Church enjoyed substantial state support, the emancipation of the Jews only as individuals deprived their religious institutions of the same financial and legal assistance extended to the institutions of their Christian neighbors.[54]

In 1911 Ismar Freund catalogued the ways in which the Prussian government denied the Jewish community the same assistance that it extended to the established churches. By law both schooling and religious instruction were compulsory for all children under the age of fourteen. However, only Christian religious instruction was an obligatory part of the school curriculum. In the case of Jewish children, each Jewish community was responsible for providing the required religious instruction. The inclusion of such instruction in the school curriculum was the prerogative of the local school administration, and even then it remained voluntary. Furthermore, the state provided teachers' seminaries only for teachers of the established churches. It also financed the education of clergy by maintaining Catholic and Protestant theological faculties at German universities and by subsidizing seminaries. In contrast, not a single chair for Jewish theology existed in all of Prussia, and the rabbinical seminaries, of course, received no subsidy. The Prussian government liberally, but exclusively, aided the maintenance of Christian churches directly, and granted to Christian clergy alone certain personal rights. The upshot of this discrimination was that the old distinction between approved (*aufgenommen*) and tolerated (*geduldet*) religious communities, theoretically terminated by the Constitution of December 5, 1848, had been perniciously preserved.[55]

The Prussian government employed two tactical arguments to refute these Jewish contentions. On certain occasions it stressed that Prussian Jewry lacked a religious spokesman, recognized by the entire community, who could inform the authorities precisely what constitutes Judaism. How could the government impose compulsory religious instruction upon all Jewish children when there was no agreement upon which version of Judaism ought to be taught? The deep divisions between Orthodox and Reform precluded the instruction of children or the training of teachers according to the precepts of either without violating the freedom of conscience of the other.[56] At other times the government denied the entire charge. In February of 1909 the proposal was made in the Prussian Chamber of Deputies that next year's budget include an appropriation to assist impoverished Jewish communities to pay their clergy and to support the families of deceased clergymen. The government argued that the Jewish community was not entitled to any state assistance because it was not subject to state control, that the corollary of state aid was state supervision. In return for their subsidies, the Catholic and Evangelical Churches had relinquished considerable freedom in the conduct of church life, especially in the education and appointment of their clergy. Prussian Jewry suffered no inequality because it submitted to no comparable supervision of its religious affairs.[57]

The efforts by the Verband to rectify these inequities were limited to two main issues. When confronted shortly after its creation with a prospective revision of Prussian public school legislation, the Verband, from 1904 to 1906, submitted several petitions to rectify a number of undesirable features. In 1903 there were still some 241 Jewish public elementary schools in Prussia with an enrollment of close to 6,000 children. Of these, 28 were maintained by municipalities; 103 by societies of parents; and 110 by Jewish communities. The prospective legislation intended to grant the local school board the exclusive power to decide whether to allow the local Jewish school to continue operating. It also would have empowered it to decide whether a new one could be opened. On these two provisions the Verband succeeded in convincing the government to leave the status quo unchanged. On a third provision of the draft the Verband effected no change. The government draft explicitly required Evangelical elementary schools in which there were at least twelve Catholic children or Catholic schools in which there were at least twelve Protestants to provide the minority with appropriate religious instruction at the school board's expense, if necessary. The Verband was unable to have this provision extended to cases where the number of Jewish children reached or exceeded twelve.[58] However, in 1908 the government did agree to set aside 40,000 marks for indigent Jewish communities to finance their educational programs, but only when the number of children involved was twelve or more.[59]

The second issue concerned state subsidies to the Catholic and Evangelical Churches of Prussia. The Verband claimed that in 1912 the government had granted the established churches almost 35 million marks. Since Prussia had a total population of 40 million, each citizen was paying approximately 1 mark toward their support. Consequently, Prussia's 400,000 Jews were providing nearly 400,000 marks annually to help maintain these two institutions. At the same time each Jew was paying in taxes for the maintenance of his own religious community more than ten times the sum being paid by his Protestant or Catholic neighbor to his respective church. The fact that most other German states included some kind of a Jewish subsidy in their budgets (Alsace-Lorraine and Württemburg were the leaders, with 198,550 and 58,060 marks respectively in 1911) made the injustice intolerable. When the Verband's complaint received no attention from the government, the Verband decided to carry the issue directly to the floor of the Chamber of Deputies. In 1914 the Chamber agreed that the next budget ought to include a contribution to impoverished Jewish communities. However, with the outbreak of the war the intention was never realized.[60]

The deeper significance of these repeated, wearisome, and ultimately futile clashes with the government was articulated with typical vigor and incisiveness by Hermann Cohen, whose own return to Judaism foreshadowed the slow but definite transformation of German Jewry. Reflecting on the broader meaning of Dreyfus' final pardon in 1906, Cohen summed up Jewry's case against the German state.

In the final analysis, what has been at stake in all the battles which Judaism had to fight in its history was the distinction between grace and justice. . . . [In a secular age] toleration takes the place of grace and love. Toleration is not a disreputable way of achieving peace, but it is not entirely free of a touch of deprecation and condescension. People tolerate what they can't or don't want to destroy; they tolerate something for the sake of the improvement which hopefully may stem directly from the policy of toleration. . . . Toleration does not presuppose equal value or birth; it grants equal ethical import as little as it grants equal political power. . . . Christian nations still view Judaism in terms of toleration. This must change. Their overall, universal cultural superiority must not prevent them from recognizing our right to exist in the realm of religious culture and thereby in general culture as well. . . . Thus when it will become clear that the pressure on Jews to convert, which is exerted by state and society by means of discrimination, has as little effect on the better part of Jewry as did the stakes of the Middle Ages, then people will finally have to replace toleration with justice and truth.[61]

RELIGIOUS POLEMICS

Government discrimination was not the Verband's only concern. It also took up the cudgels against Protestant scholarship on Rabbinic Judaism and the Old Testament, which Jewish leaders sadly viewed as a revival of religious polemics. In the opening years of the twentieth century the debate raged with fierce intensity far outside the confines of the university.

Since 1880 New Testament scholars like Ferdinand Weber, Emil Schürer, and D. Wilhelm Bousset had produced a series of studies on Judaism and Jewish history in the inter-testamental period to determine the relationship between Jesus and his Jewish environment.[62] Many of their unfavorable judgments on Rabbinic Judaism were incorporated by Adolf Harnack in a series of six public lectures on "What Is Christianity?" delivered before six hundred students at the University of Berlin in the Winter of 1899–1900. Harnack attributed to the Judaism of the first century an oppressive particularism and ritualistic legalism devoid of social justice.

Subsequently published, this thoroughly rationalistic and wholly subjective reinterpretation of Christianity by a noted authority of Christian history provoked a bitter and widespread controversy within Protestant circles, which in turn gave still greater currency to the deprecatory characterization of Rabbinic Judaism propounded by recent Protestant scholarship. Although Jewish critics did not fail to point out with a touch of glee that Harnack himself had repudiated just about everything that Jews had always found unacceptable in Christianity,[63] his book precipitated a general Jewish assault upon the quality and objectivity of modern Protestant research on Judaism.

Spearheaded by both older and younger members of the German-speaking non-Orthodox rabbinate, this considerable volume of Jewish criticism focused upon several key issues. Regarding methodology, Jewish critics challenged the competence of scholars who were unable to work with the Hebrew sources. Such scholars were limited to earlier Latin and recent German translations of a fraction of the Hebrew or Aramaic originals, often repeating the mistakes of their translators. This handicap forced them to rely excessively upon the Greek apocalytic and apocryphal literature of the period, rather than upon the far more normative Hebrew sources of Rabbinic literature. The result was a distorted image of their subject which they rarely tried to correct by recourse to the works of German Jewish scholars like Abraham Geiger, Levi Herzfeld, and Heinrich Graetz, who had already produced some substantive research on the period.[64] On a more fundamental level, Jewish critics questioned the validity of defining the subject under investigation in terms of the New Testament. The period of the New Testament corresponded to no intrinsic chronological demarcation within Rabbinic Judaism, which certainly deserved to be studied in terms of its own development. In fact, the subject of both Schürer's and Bousset's studies ranged far beyond the period of Jesus and the New Testament, yet the titles of both rigidly preserved the original perspective.[65]

The use of Christian criteria for defining the period in which Rabbinic Judaism was to be studied suggested to Jewish critics that the characterization that emerged was not solely the product of faulty methodology. They did not hesitate to impugn the objectivity with which Protestant theologians pursued their investigations. The work of these theologians remained fundamentally tendentious, because all consciously operated on the theological assumption that Judaism constituted merely a precursor to Christianity (*praeparatio evangelica*). Consequently, the major objective of their research seemed to Jewish critics to be an illumination of Jesus' Jewish background that left no doubt as to the originality of his message. Even scholars like Julius Wellhausen and Harnack, who were ready to admit that Jesus offered the world nothing fundamentally new, condemned the Pharisees for having contaminated the essential with the trivial and the holy with the profane. Generally Protestant scholarship portrayed Rabbinic Judaism in terms of the unbearable yoke of the Law, the transcendence of God, the abandonment of prophetic religion, national particularism, and soulless piety. Jewish critics denounced the portrait as a grotesque caricature.[66]

In January 1902 the religious polemic was further intensified when Friedrich Delitzsch, one of the founders of Assyriology, opened a personal campaign to vindicate the originality and superiority of Babylonian religion as compared with Biblical monotheism. In a lecture to the German Oriental Society on the subject of "Babel und Bibel," attended by the Kaiser, Delitzsch challenged the cherished assumptions of Christians and Jews alike, who had consistently exaggerated the contrast between Biblical religion and contemporary polytheism by unconsciously depicting the latter solely in the critical terms used by the Prophets. Utilizing the materials discovered in the excavations at Nineveh and Babylon, Delitzsch tried to show the enormous indebtedness of the literature, institutions, and faith of the Old Testament to Babylonian culture, a dependence already indicated in the very sequence in the title. A year later he defended his collection of hypotheses against the angry attacks of Christians and Jews, laymen and scholars, in a second lecture, again attended by the Kaiser, before the same society.[67] Within the already religiously charged atmosphere of the Second Reich, many Jews instinctively regarded Delitzsch's pan-Babylonian lectures as yet another anti-Jewish maneuver, directed this time at Judaism's most original contribution to mankind. Besides disputing many details of Delitzsch's argument, such as the identity of the Biblical Sabbath with the Babylonian *shapattu,* or of Yahweh with a Babylonian deity, Jewish critics like Benno Jacob and Leo Baeck also insisted that Israel's originality was to be found in its transformation of the ancient materials that it incorporated.[68]

Criticism of German Protestant scholarship on the Biblical and Rabbinic periods was by no means limited to German Jews. Their judgment was warmly endorsed by English Jewish scholars like Israel Abrahams, Claude Montefiore, and Solomon Schechter, who used the pages of their learned periodical, the *Jewish Quarterly Review,* to repudiate such disguised polemics.[69] In 1903 Schechter, who had in the meantime assumed the presidency of the Jewish Theological Seminary in New York, openly condemned such scholarship as "Higher Anti-Semitism." Clearly alluding to the "Babel und Bibel" controversy, he observed that "this Higher Anti-Semitism had now reached its climax when every discovery of recent years is called to bear witness against us and to accuse us of spiritual larceny." [70] Later Christian students of the Rabbinic period like R. Travers Herford and George Foot Moore were to vindicate the general Jewish indictment of Prot-

estant research during the Second Reich on the inter-testamental period.[71]

To contemporary Jewish spokesmen, the issue far transcended the
mere question of historical truth. They were as deeply dismayed by
the source of the challenge as by its substance and intention. Liberal
Protestant academicians, whose own rationalistic version of Christianity so closely approximated the essence of liberal Judaism, now
seemed intent on destroying Jewry's historical claim to continued
survival. Their reconstruction of the history of Judaism readily reinforced the low estimate of Judaism shared by all too many Germans
with the nimbus of learning and served to vindicate government discrimination against Jews. Above all, the critical treatment accorded
Judaism in the prestigious institutions of higher learning thinned the
ranks of Jewry. It effectively justified the indifference or conversion
of the uninformed and uncommitted who were unequipped or unwilling to endure the multiple forms of external pressure. As on other
occasions, the blunt words of Hermann Cohen in 1907 conveyed the
somber assessment of the present situation by the leaders of German
Jewry.

What is new in our present crisis is that our opponents, as unlikely as it
may seem, reckon in fact with bringing about our destruction in the fore-
seeable future. And it is by no means only the outspoken anti-Semites
who cherish this hare-brained idea, but it must be openly stated that this
idea is now widely shared in the liberal sector of German society and by
many whom we consider our personal friends. It is not regarded as arro-
gant or even as objectionable on humanitarian grounds, but rather people
condone and defend it with a veneer of humanitarianism, that in this way
this interminable misfortune of "our poor Jews" would finally be brought
to an end. It is only sympathy and concern for the Jews which gives rise
to the wish that they might disappear as Jews.[72]

Since the first half of the nineteenth century, Jewish scholarship
had repeatedly been invoked in the contemporary battles for emancipation.[73] At the end of 1902 the scientific study of the Jewish past
was again summoned to defend Judaism and reassert the worthiness
of Jewry. At the initiative of Rabbi Leopold Lucas of Glogau, a large
number of Jewish scholars met on November 2, 1901, in Berlin to
found the Gesellschaft zur Förderung der Wissenschaft des Juden-

tums (the Society for the Advancement of the Science of Judaism). At subsequent meetings the Society developed an ambitious program to unite the talents of Jewish scholars in an organized effort to present the totality of scientific Jewish studies to the German academic and educated communities. It assumed the cost of publishing the *Monatsschrift für Geschichte und Wissenschaft des Judentums,* the leading Jewish scholarly journal in the world; it outlined a multivolume presentation of the synthesized results of a century of Jewish research (*Grundriss der gesamten Wissenschaft des Judentums*); it proposed to subsidize further research, attract young scholars and publish both primary sources and original studies. Martin Philippson served as its first president.[74]

The Society's first publications reflected the preoccupation of its leaders with the character of Protestant scholarship on Judaism. In 1905 it published Leo Baeck's *Das Wesen des Judentums* and Joseph Eschelbacher's *Das Judentum und das Wesen des Christentums.* With only an occasionally overt polemical aside, Baeck tried to present the essential nature and ideology of Judaism. Yet the sum and substance of his reconstruction was determined by a deep aversion to Lutheran Christianity. To Luther's justification by faith, Baeck posed a Judaism that challenged man with the task and the commandment. With his novel philosophical defense of the totality of Jewish law, Baeck became the first non-Orthodox Jewish thinker in Germany since the emancipation willing to take up the defense of Judaism on the issue of law as well as ethics and theology. In relation to the specific controversies of the moment, Baeck countered the assumption of a dichotomy between early Israelite religion and later Judaism with an explication of the basic unity of Judaism despite its continuous adaptation and development. He disarmed the pan-Babylonians by basing prophetic religion upon the unique category of religious experience. On the other hand, Eschelbacher's study was a more prosaic rebuttal to Harnack's ideas on both Christianity and Judaism as well as a survey of the history of Christianity from a Jewish point of view.[75]

One year later, the Society published Moritz Güdemann's *Jüdische Apologetik,* a far more comprehensive polemic against Protestant scholarship on the Bible and Rabbinic Judaism. Again the fundamental unity of Judaism was stressed. Likewise, Güdemann sought to counter the assertion that the law was imposed by the Rabbis from above by marshaling evidence to show the extent to which the people contributed to the development of Judaism.[76]

The Society had thus clearly begun the task of recruiting Jewish scholars for an organized effort to provide a firsthand objective study of the Jewish past. Most of its subsequent publications were fortunately far more substantive and hence more enduring.[77] Yet the underlying apologetic intention was beyond dispute. In context, then, the campaign waged by the Verband der deutschen Juden against the academic establishment was but another manifestation of the rising antagonism between the Protestant and Jewish sectors of German society before the war.

The Verband provided another opportunity to institutionalize the counterattack. Although its constitution had declared the Verband religiously neutral, it did countenance the discussion of purely religious matters in defense against attacks by non-Jews.[78] At its first national convention in 1905, following an outspoken address by Rabbi Werner of Munich on "Judaism in the Light of Modern Criticism," the delegates adopted a resolution that expressed their concerns:

The national convention of the Verband der deutschen Juden repudiates categorically the attacks against the integrity of the Jewish religion and repeats the long-known truth that Judaism, the mother of the monotheistic religions, on the basis of a pure faith in God, teaches a love of one's neighbor that embraces all men, commands total devotion to the fatherland, and construes the fulfillment of social duties as a religious ideal.[79]

The liberal, Jewish-owned and edited *Berliner Tageblatt* applauded the convention as a justified political protest, but it condemned the inclusion of theological disputations in the program of the convention.[80]

Occasionally the polemic reached such intensity that it obstructed the political work of the Verband. After the first convention in 1905, state officials were invited to attend the biennial assemblies so that they might personally witness the presentation of grievances. While a representative of the Regierungspräsident (Administrator of the Provincial District) attended the second convention in Frankfurt, the

third one in Breslau in 1909 was honored by the presence of the Oberpräsident (the Governor) of the province of Silesia. Shortly after
Jakob Guttmann, the renowned scholarly rabbi of the Breslau Jewish
Community, began a speech on "The Idea of Atonement in Judaism," Count von Zedlitz-Trützschler entered the hall.

In the course of his address, Guttmann attacked the pseudo-schol-
arship of Protestant theologians whose sole objective was to depre-
cate the teachings of Judaism. He insisted that Judaism possessed a
concept of genuine salvation and denied that such a concept was
given to mankind first by Jesus. Moreover, the Christian concept involved the cruel theological fiction of original sin. Yet Christians
dared to accuse Jews of believing in a God of wrath! The polemic
was sufficiently aggressive to offend the honored guest, who enjoyed
a reputation of fairness toward the Jews. When Horwitz introduced
the Oberpräsident to the assembly after Guttmann's speech, the
Count, who had served as the Prussian Minister of Religion in
1891–92, felt compelled to remind the audience that he was also a
believing Christian whose faith rested upon both the Old and New
Testaments and whose public service was wholly free of religious
prejudice.[81]

The embarrassing incident precipitated considerable criticism.
Some members of the board felt that apologetic speeches ought to
be excluded from the agenda of the national conventions. The majority found nothing offensive in Guttmann's address, and contended
that such public polemics were important for both Jews and Christians. The board agreed only to examine henceforth a copy of the
speech before allowing it to be delivered. But the damage was ir-
reparable. No state official, of any rank, attended the last two conventions before the war in 1911 and 1913.[82]

Since the effectiveness of apologetics is obviously related to the organs of dissemination, the board of the Verband explored various
ways to reach larger and more important audiences. For example, at
the end of 1905 it received a proposal from Benno Jacob, a well-
known Biblical scholar and learned Rabbinical polemicist, to build a
permanent center for Jewish apologetics in Berlin in which Jewish
university students would study the history and substance of the subject during a four-semester program. The suggestion bespoke the

feeling of many that the future leaders of German Jewry had to be equipped with "a systematic, scientific, and practical apologetical education." The board, however, refused to pursue the proposal. It considered such a center beyond its jurisdiction and feared that erecting it would force the Verband to identify with a specific interpretation of Judaism.[83]

In 1907 the Verband undertook the publication of a modest periodical essentially devoted to the dissemination of apologetics to a lay audience. The articles were to be intelligible for a Christian audience as well. They were to treat matters of immediate relevance rather than historical interest, and they were to avoid all questions over which the Jewish community itself was split. During the seven years before the war only fourteen issues appeared. Some of these essays were reprinted in a small series of pamphlets entitled *Vom Judentum,* of which six issues appeared, for still wider distribution.[84]

The Verband's most substantive apologetic undertaking began with the opening in 1910 of an archive for material to be employed in future polemics. Its director was Simon Bernfeld, a Jewish historian whose main contributions to date had been in the modern period. Divided into eight major categories such as the content of Judaism's religious teachings, the flexibility of its ecclesiastical structure (*Kirchenverfassung*), and the origins of monotheism, the archive intended to gather and classify all relevant sources from ancient, medieval, and modern Jewish literature. The last category particularly reflected the hostile atmosphere. It was to include material relating to areas in which Christianity was allegedly inferior to Judaism, such as the role and nature of dogma, the tendency toward superstition and magic, the character of the ethical system, and ecclesiastical organization. The rabbis of Germany were requested to contribute whatever they had available.[85]

In the remaining years before the war the archive managed to put out only a small volume of essays purporting to summarize the social ethics of Judaism.[86] In the 1920's, after the Verband had ceased operations, the archive finally printed five volumes of *Die Lehren des Judentums,* an ambitious attempt to present in German translation the theological and ethical content of Judaism. The fifth volume was a toned-down modification of the last category of the original archive, dealing with the attitudes of Judaism toward the religions and cultures of its various environments and the influence it had exerted upon them. The project drew upon the talents of many of the most noted scholars of the German Jewish scene. Every one of its carefully organized sections consisted of an introductory explanation, a cross-section of passages from Jewish sources, and a bibliography. It could readily serve as a useful resource for both the defense and the teaching of Judaism.[87]

As overt anti-Semitism became a chronic feature of Wilhelmine society, Jewish leaders devoted ever more energy to the long task of enlightenment. They labored under few illusions. Success was not imminent. In the meantime German Jewry itself had to be strengthened. As with the medieval disputations, a good deal of the apologetical literature was intended primarily to fortify the faithful.[88]

7

INTERNAL DISCONTENT, 1897-1914

THE PROBLEM

SINCE ITS FOUNDING, the Centralverein had steadfastly pursued a policy of neutrality on all internal issues dividing the Jewish community. It had quickly divested itself of any association with Reform Judaism, and thereafter it carefully avoided taking sides on purely internal Jewish matters in order not to alienate any sector of German Jewry. The policy expressed the Centralverein's earnest effort to unite German Jews in the task of self-defense. This position was dramatically discarded in March 1913, when the national convention of the Centralverein adopted an anti-Zionist resolution designed to expel at least one type of German Zionist from its ranks. The resolution reiterated the demand that Centralverein members cultivate a sense of German identity, and it pointedly declared that the Jewish problem could not be solved internationally. As long as Zionists had worked merely to find a homeland for the Jews of Eastern Europe and to fortify the self-respect of German Jewry, the Centralverein had welcomed their membership. "But we must separate ourselves from the Zionist who denies any feeling of German nationality, who feels himself a guest among a host people and nationally only a Jew." [1]

This resolution marked an equally sharp departure from the Centralverein's earlier position on Zionism. For nearly two decades its leadership had consistently refused to combat the movement inspired and organized by Theodor Herzl. To be sure, in 1896 the Centralverein journal rejected Herzl's *Judenstaat* as an ugly dream, and warned that his declaration of Jewish nationality was fraught with danger.[2] A year later, after the First Zionist Congress the Centralverein issued a statement supporting the colonization of Palestine, but criticizing "the fanatics of a Jewish state." [3] In December 1897, Fuchs elaborated the position slightly, reaffirming his own German nationality and his conviction that the Jews were no more than a religious community.[4] However, the leaders of the Centralverein never expanded this initial declaration of differences into a sustained anti-Zionist polemic. Having articulated their position, they welcomed every Zionist willing to join the Centralverein. The very desire to affiliate was sufficient proof of his German patriotism.[5] At a meeting of the Executive Committee on October 20, 1902, it was decided that the Centralverein should avoid any official criticism of Zionism unless provoked by a direct attack. Although repeatedly pressured by individual members and chapters, the Executive Committee abided by its neutrality.[6] When it broke silence on rare occasions, it was usually to praise Zionist efforts to shatter the indifference of German Jewry, and to bolster its self-respect.[7]

In sum, the restraint and moderation of Centralverein policy toward Zionism were based upon the recognition that its policy differed from that of the Zionists only on ultimate and not on immediate objectives. Their common commitment to the revival of Jewish consciousness made cooperation possible, and the overriding need to unite the resources and manpower of the entire Jewish community made it desirable.

This policy of consistent moderation, moreover, stood in marked contrast to the undiminished hostility that the majority of organized German Jewry, and even a Christian association like the Abwehrverein,[8] exhibited toward Zionism. In the course of its extended struggle for full emancipation, German Jewry had grown extraordinarily sensitive on the issue of German nationality. No charge provoked a more visceral denial than that Jews were a distinct nationality. Herzl's intention to hold the First Zionist Congress in Munich had been quickly frustrated. After examining the nature of Zionism and the potential repercussions of a congress, the Board of the Munich Jewish Community wrote Herzl demanding that he convene his congress elsewhere. It feared above all providing grist for the propaganda mills of the anti-Semites.[9] At the same time Rabbi Mose Cossmann Werner of Munich urged his colleagues on the Executive Committee of the recently reactivated Allgemeiner Rabbinerverband in Deutschland (National Association of Rabbis in Germany), which included members from all three branches of German Jewry, to issue a public repudiation of Zionism. They obliged with an official declaration propounding that Zionism contradicted both the messianic concept of Judaism and the patriotic responsibilities of citizenship. The five signatories (Rabbis Maybaum, Horovitz, Guttmann, Auerbach, and Werner) added that the colonization of Palestine violated neither, but they counseled German Jews not to attend the Congress.[10]

Often the first public meeting in a Jewish community on the subject of Zionism was arranged not by the Zionists but by the opposition, which hoped in this way to squelch the idea before it gained a following. Usually the most formidable spokesman for the ideology of the establishment was the local rabbi. Some meetings became so raucous that the local police felt compelled to intervene. Individual Zionists also became the target of group pressure. Sammy Gronemann, the son of the rabbi in Hanover who joined the Zionist movement after a period of intense deliberation, settled as a young lawyer in his home town in 1904 only to be boycotted by his German coreligionists. His clients were mainly Christians and Jews from Eastern Europe. Because of his commitments, he experienced great difficulty in gaining membership in the local lodge of the B'nai B'rith and was often denounced by the local anti-Zionist forces.[11]

This initial animosity toward Zionism did not subside with time. Since many of the German Zionists came from the ranks of Eastern European immigrants, various Jewish communities in subsequent years attempted to deprive all non-German members of the right to vote in communal elections.[12] Liberal rabbis with Zionist leanings experienced great difficulty in finding employment in the larger Jewish communities.[13] In 1907 Berlin dismissed young Emil Cohn as preacher and religious instructor for having aired his Zionist convictions in the course of a three-hour discussion with the Christian director of the Mommsen Gymnasium in Charlottenburg. The board had originally hired him on condition that he would not misuse the pulpit, classroom, or public platform for Zionist propaganda. When it was informed by the aroused director of their rabbi's views, the board immediately suspended him without a hearing. The action quickly mushroomed into an embarrassing *cause célèbre*.[14]

The problem confronting the historian then is to account for the Centralverein's rejection in 1913 of its long-standing independent policy toward German Zionism. The repercussions were immediate and far-reaching, for the decision precipitated an acrimonious conflict that soon engulfed most of German Jewry. The internal development of the Centralverein seems to offer no adequate explanation. If anything, the increasing attention to Jewish consciousness by the Centralverein should have enlarged the area of agreement between itself and the Zionists. Therefore, the controversy must be examined against the background of the nature and growth of the Zionist movement itself in Germany.

THE TRANSFORMATION
OF GERMAN ZIONISM

Organized political Zionism appeared in Germany in the months preceding the First Zionist Congress, which convened in Basle on August 29, 1897. At the behest of Herzl, Max Bodenheimer, a thirty-two-year-old Cologne lawyer who had already independently conceived the idea of a Jewish state in Palestine, brought together a small number of like-minded German Jews to form the National jüdische Vereinigung für Deutschland (National Jewish Organization of Germany).[15] By the end of September 1897, fewer than one hundred German Jews had joined.[16] The fact that at least half of the thirty-three German delegates who attended the Basle Congress came originally from Russia reflects the preponderance in the embryonic organization of Eastern European Jews living in Germany.[17] In order to diminish the irritation of German Jewish sensibilities and accelerate the affiliation of native Jews, the third convention of German Zionists at the end of October 1897 unanimously changed the name from National-jüdische to Zionistische Vereinigung für Deutschland (Zionist Federation of Germany).[18] Nevertheless, growth proceeded slowly. In 1901 the membership had reached only 2,200, of whom 421 came from Berlin. Three years later it stood at about 6,000, divided into more than 65 local chapters. By 1914 a membership of nearly 10,000 made the German branch the third largest Zionist organization in the world, trailing only its Russian and American counterparts. The number of Russian nationals, however, continued to remain substantial.[19]

The Zionists searched steadily for suitable vehicles of propaganda. Their deep involvement in the campaign to create a Judentag was not free of self-interest. Bodenheimer had sensed the opportunity that such a platform would provide for propounding Zionist ideology. On April 6, 1901, he wrote to Adolf Friedemann, one of the very few young German Zionists of wealth, about its potential value: "We must for the present concentrate our entire strength on it, in order to assume perhaps a leading role in the matter and thereby to gain a firm footing in Germany." [20] An official party newspaper was lacking until 1902, when the German Zionist Federation negotiated the purchase of the *Israelitische Rundschau* ("Israelite Review"). Its name was promptly changed to the *Jüdische Rundschau,* and under the dedicated editorship of Heinrich Loewe, the paper conscientiously tried to cover the entire spectrum of Jewish life, as well as to deal extensively with immediate Zionist concerns. It doubled in size to sixteen, and occasionally even to twenty, pages during the next two years; measured by the number of copies printed, the *Jüdische Rundschau* became the third largest Jewish paper in the country.[21]

Constant financial problems beset the Zionist Federation in its first decade. The budget for 1899 was a mere 3,500 marks. As late as 1909 income did not cover the annual budget; and Hans Gideon Heymann, the son of a wealthy Berlin banker, and Arthur Hantke, soon to replace Bodenheimer as president, made up the deficit personally. But by 1912 the financial picture had improved immeasurably. Over the previous two years German Zionists had collected some 350,000 marks for a variety of Zionist causes, and there was no longer fear that an operating budget of even 24,000 marks could not easily be met.[22]

The appeal of the German Zionist Federation was, of course, determined by its ideological posture. The doctrine of political Zionism meant essentially a belief in the reality of a Jewish nation and in the necessity for a Jewish state, but the dilemma of how this was to be most effectively presented to an emancipated, partially integrated, and prosperous German Jewry demanded careful reflection. During the presidency of Max Bodenheimer, from 1897 to 1910, the German Zionist Federation tended to present a non-doctrinaire ideology which carefully toned down the national character of Jewry and the political character of the homeland. The change in the name of the organization already adumbrated the policy. Its proponent, Rudolf Schauer, a young attorney, reminded the convention in October 1897 of the sensitivity of German Jews to the issue of their nationality. To exaggerate the fact of Jewish nationality and to speak prematurely about the idea of a Jewish state would serve only to intimidate or infuriate. In particular Schauer addressed himself to the large contingent of non-German Zionists in the organization who might be unable to appreciate the difficulty.[23]

The early literature of the German Zionist Federation followed his advice. It countered the endless charges of disloyalty by insisting that nationality and citizenship were distinct and not mutually exclusive concepts.[24] More significant was its nonracial, subjective definition of nationality. An official publication of 1903, titled *What Does Zionism Want?*, proposed that a nation comes into being only when a sufficient number of ancestrally related individuals are united by a common will: "On the day when the representatives of hundreds of thousands of Jews driven by the feeling of common ancestry, common history and a common suffering declared: '*We want to be a people*,' did they become a people." [25]

Furthermore, Zionist spokesmen restricted themselves to the subject of acquiring Palestine for the Jewish masses of Eastern Europe. There was little mention of statehood, and it was repeatedly made unmistakably clear that Western Zionists were laboring for the rescue of their persecuted kinsmen. Migration from the West was not expected, encouraged, or demanded. For the physically emancipated but spiritually enslaved Jews of the West, Zionism offered a revival of Jewish knowledge, pride, and consciousness.[26]

This deliberately restrained propaganda confronted its first serious internal challenge at the 1904 Zionist convention held in Hamburg. The delegations from Berlin, Breslau, Munich, and Regensburg submitted a resolution condemning Bodenheimer for the diluted ideology of Zionism that his administration projected. Political Zionism had been reduced to philanthropy. The resolution insisted that the national idea constituted the essence of the movement, that Zionism was a matter of direct and personal import to the Western Jew, and that both these doctrines must be urgently disseminated by Zionist propaganda. Bodenheimer defended his policy vigorously. He asserted that he recognized no other concept of Zionism than the one outlined, and that his Jewish nationalism was no less intense than that of his critics. But again he invoked the sensibilities of German Jewry.[27]

The problem of tactics actually concealed a more basic confusion as to what made a Zionist. Membership was acquired by the annual payment of a shekel (in Germany the Biblical denomination was defined as one mark), but were there no ideological prerequisites? Should the shekel be accepted indiscriminately? The German Zionist Federation had not provided its local chapters with any guidelines, and each one solved the problem independently. Two extreme approaches had apparently emerged: one group accepted the shekel regardless of personal conviction; the other, only after examination proved the prospective member to subscribe to the proper ideology. Sammy Gronemann, who delivered a long discourse on the meaning of the shekel at the same Hamburg convention, depicted the act of paying the shekel as a confession of faith. He insisted that the shekel should be taken only from a man who accepted the Basle Program of 1897, though he rejected the suggestion that a Zionist must also intend to settle in Palestine. This final choice was not a question of doctrine but of personal preference. What distinguished the genuine Zionist was the conviction that his labors were based upon the national character of the Jewish people, and directed toward rescuing the people as a whole, not merely its less fortunate members.[28]

Though the debates in 1904 revealed considerable dissatisfaction with the Bodenheimer regime, it gained at least an apparent vote of confidence. The indictment in the resolution on propaganda was dropped. Also directed at the leadership was a resolution calling for the transfer of the Central Committee of the German Zionist Federation from Cologne to Berlin. Bodenheimer had long been reluctant to sacrifice his modest legal practice in Cologne by moving to Berlin. The compromise, engineered in 1904, left the Central Committee in Cologne, but established an administrative Central Bureau in Berlin under the supervision of Arthur Hantke, Eduard Leszinsky, and Emil Simonson. Ultimate control was to remain in the hands of Bodenheimer until 1910 when he retired.[29]

The most forthright defense of this modest mixture of political and philanthropic Zionism came in 1910, the very year the German Zionist Federation changed its course radically. Franz Oppenheimer, a renowned economist who had been brought into the movement by Herzl, published in the pages of *Die Welt* a spirited analysis of the difference between the Zionism of Eastern and Western Jewry. He submitted that the Jews of the East possessed a genuine sense of belonging to a living Jewish people (*Volksbewusstsein*), for both culturally and nationally they were exclusively Jews. The Jews of the West possessed merely a sense of ancestral kinship (*Stammesbewusstsein*). Like the United States citizens of German descent, the Western Jews were proud of their Jewish origins, despite the irreversible extent to which they had assimilated. The real idealists of the Zionist movement were the Jews of the West. For those in the East, a Jewish homeland meant physical survival. But emancipated Zionists in the West, with neither the intention nor the need to emigrate, had nothing to gain. Only a vital sense of history motivated them to join the movement. To demand that they settle in Palestine was unrealistic and detrimental. Their Zionism lay in their commitment to the revival of the entire Jewish people.[30]

This moderate interpretation of Zionism, which underplayed the potentially divisive elements, created the possibility for amicable relations with the Centralverein. Equally important was the extent to which both organizations acknowledged their agreement upon some fundamental issues. They shared a sober evaluation of the dimensions of German anti-Semitism, although the Zionists alone tried to explain the phenomenon on the basis of irremediable national differences.[31] They fully agreed in their vitriolic critique of the ignorant, indifferent, and self-effacing practice of Judaism that marked the lives of far too many assimilated Jews.[32] Above all, they were equally committed to a revival of Jewish life generated by a mass renewal of knowledge and self-esteem.[33]

Consequently, expressions of mutual respect and cooperation punctuated the period before 1910.[34] The Zionists resented the status of second-class citizenship no less than the Centralverein, and hence their endorsement of the Judentag was entirely consistent.[35] In 1900 and 1902 Die Welt carried articles by Zionists from Berlin and Posen praising the Centralverein as a preparatory school for Zionism.[36] When the Centralverein celebrated its tenth anniversary in the Berlin Philharmonic with two thousand well-wishers, Alfred Klee, representing the Berlin Zionist chapter, rose to commend its fight against indifference and to offer Zionist support in the efforts to complete the emancipation of German Jewry. At the 1908 convention of the German Zionists, Klee contended that had the Centralverein not existed the Zionists would have had to create it. To be sure, Zionism attacked the problem of anti-Semitism at its roots; still it could not ignore the necessity of immediate relief sought by the Centralverein. The fact that similar sentiments were repeated by the official German Zionist Handbook of 1908 indicates that Klee's attitude was not a minority opinion.[37]

Some friction of course did persist. Zionist spokesmen tended to be most critical of the Centralverein's position on German politics. They repudiated what they considered to be an alliance with the dwindling number of Progressives, and they called for the defeat of every baptized Jewish candidate.[38] On local levels, relations between Centralverein and Zionist chapters occasionally were a lot less amicable than those between the national offices. This was particularly true in Hamburg and Posen. In 1908, after several years of intermittent friction, the Zionist groups in both cities refused any further cooperation with the Centralverein. The Hamburg Zionist chapter even passed a general resolution calling upon German Zionists to refrain from joining the Centralverein until it removed from its program all points at variance with the principles of Jewish nationalism. But the national leadership merely took cognizance of the action; it did not endorse it.[39]

By 1908, however, the rhetoric of a new generation of young German Zionists was growing increasingly aggressive. Their clandestine criticism of Bodenheimer's allegedly compromising and directionless leadership now became strident.[40] They lamented the dilution of Zionist ideology for the sake of non-Zionist sympathy and support. The rebirth of the Jewish people and the solution of the Jewish problem required fidelity to a radical diagnosis and policy. Compromise alienated the Jewish students attracted only by genuine Zionism, and assured the demise of the national movement which alone could create a Jewish state. It certainly yielded no additional income for Zionist causes. Jewish capital would only follow the Zionists to Palestine; it would never precede them.[41]

At the end of the first decade of the century, this second generation of Zionists assumed the leadership of the German Zionist Federation. The 1908 convention at Breslau had decided to create the post of Party Secretary in order to organize and expand the conduct of Zionist propaganda. The Central Committee finally selected Kurt Blumenfeld, a twenty-four-year-old law student, to fill the post in the Fall of 1909. An impassioned and perceptive orator, he spent three quarters of the year traversing Germany to preach a practical Zionism which called for an authentic return to Judaism and a personal decision to settle in Palestine, as opposed to the political Zionism of Herzl, Wolffsohn, and Bodenheimer which concentrated upon the immediate acquisition of a charter for Palestine from the Turkish government.[42] In 1910 Blumenfeld's hand was strengthened when Hantke, another practical Zionist, replaced Bodenheimer as president.[43]

The radicalization of Zionist policy ensued forthwith. At the convention of 1910 the delegates adopted a resolution, submitted by Blumenfeld, to the effect that Zionist propaganda must never conceal the national character of the movement.[44] At a plenary session of the Central Committee in February 1912, Blumenfeld spelled out the reasons for the shift. The Zionists were facing an invigorated assimilationist camp whose disintegration through apostasy was not progressing as rapidly as Zionists had expected. On the contrary, a new generation of assimilationists was proudly parading its Jewish identity in a proliferation of powerful Jewish organizations. Blumenfeld still believed in the eventual collapse of the assimilationist position, but in the face of its temporary vigor Zionism had to reassert boldly its own uniqueness. Zionism alone could guarantee the survival of Judaism, and this was its primary objective; saving Jews was secondary. The revival of the assimilationists had elevated the debate to a new level.[45]

At the Posen convention of May 1912, the rhetoric culminated with a far-reaching resolution that obliged "every Zionist—in the first place the economically independent—to incorporate settling in Palestine into his life's program. In any case every Zionist ought to create for himself personal interests in Palestine." [46] This controversial resolution provoked a passionate debate within German Zionist circles that extended over the next two years. The old guard of first-generation Zionists was by now a minority, but it mounted a concerted resistance. Some confessed their total estrangement from Palestine. They had come to Zionism merely to help the persecuted of Eastern Europe.[47] Others stressed their attachment to Germany. Oppenheimer protested: "My Germanism is for me a hallowed thing. Germany is my fatherland, my home, the land of my yearnings, the land of my [ancestors'] graves, the land of my battles and my goals, and when I return from foreign soil, I am coming home." [48] Friedemann scorned the suggestion that Zionists learn Hebrew and develop a national culture in Germany as a "bloodless ideal, an empty abstraction of a theorizing mind." One ought to give his children

a good Jewish education with some knowledge of Hebrew and of course German culture. When they acquire a sense of Jewish ancestry, a love of their people, then that must suffice to educate them to be true sons of their people. Should a Jewish community arise later in Palestine, then they can become Hebraists there; not here. That is our basic viewpoint.[49]

Above all the old guard condemned the resolution for having provoked an organized counterattack by German Jewry. In a plenary session of the Central Committee on November 3, 1912, the consequences of the Posen resolution were heatedly discussed for nearly eleven hours. But the leadership was not to be dissuaded; it neither feared nor regretted the conflict.[50]

In preparation for the Leipzig convention of June 1914, a group of moderate older Zionists led by Friedemann, Bodenheimer, Oppenheimer, and Carl Lewin organized themselves to gain support for a resolution that would order Zionist leaders and spokesmen to abide by the Basle Program, to further understanding of the intimate bond between German Zionists and German Jewry, and to respect the dictates of German nationalism. But they had clearly been reduced to a manageable minority; the resolution was not even introduced.[51] When Hantke closed the general debate on the Posen resolution, he observed that the minority had marshaled its arguments essentially from the past, whereas it was the future that inspired the vision of the majority.[52]

There is little doubt that the transformation of German Zionism was part of a general revision of the policies of the World Zionist Organization itself. Despite the first plank of the Basle Program, which endorsed the colonization of Palestine, Herzl had deprecated a policy of gradual settlement. Driven by concern for the plight of Eastern European Jewry, Herzl had fought for the prior acquisition of a charter. Without such a legal guarantee, immigration could always be arbitrarily terminated when the native population began to fear its dimensions. But from the beginning, Herzl had been challenged by Ahad Ha-Am, the learned and trenchant Hebrew spokesman for the pre-Herzlian Zionism of *Hibbat Zion*. Paradoxically, the Russian-born Ahad Ha-Am was far more distressed by the fate of Judaism in the West. The surrender to non-Jewish values and the rapid disintegration of Jewish unity that had accompanied emancipation could be resisted only by creating a national Jewish culture firmly rooted in Palestine. Thus Ahad Ha-Am, who remained outside the Zionist Organization, advocated precisely the program dismissed by Herzl. In place of futile and demoralizing efforts at the immediate establishment of a state, he steadfastly pleaded for the gradual restoration of Jewish national life in Palestine.[53]

After Herzl's death in July 1904, the pressure of the followers of Ahad Ha-Am, the practical Zionists, for a reversal of the preoccupation with diplomacy steadily increased. They proposed a synthesis of political and practical work both in Palestine and within the Diaspora. They denounced the compromise of the political Zionists dictated by expediency; they emphasized the national character of Zionism, and called for a deepening of Zionist ideology. They finally took control of the Zionist Organization at the Congress of 1911, by forcing David Wolffsohn, Herzl's successor as president and faithful disciple, into retirement. The actual governing body of the organization, the Inner Actions Committee, was now composed of five practical Zionists, including two Germans: Otto Warburg, the new president; and Arthur Hantke, the president of the German Zionist Federation.[54]

The radicalization of German Zionist ideology before the war meant an urgent appeal to every German Zionist to implement the program of Ahad Ha-Am by settlement in Palestine. But the real historical problem is to account for this fundamental and unique change, for the Posen Resolution of 1912 far exceeded the demands of the Basle Program. Not even the Austrian and Russian Zionist organizations, let alone those of the West, had adopted anything of equal consequence for the individual. The extreme character of the Posen resolution is ultimately explicable only in terms of the circumstances peculiar to the German scene. German anti-Semitism had profoundly altered the course of German Zionism. The difference between the Zionism of the first and second generations of German Zionists is an expression of their respective reactions to the personal experience of anti-Semitism.[55]

Many of the first generation of German Zionists had come to Zionism not so much in reaction to German anti-Semitism as out of compassion for the Jews of Eastern Europe. The pronounced philanthropic character of the political Zionism of this generation reflected the basic concern that had originally motivated them to affiliate. They had stepped forward not to solve a deeply personal Jewish problem, but to help alleviate the international one. Some, like Bodenheimer, had already participated in earlier German efforts to colonize Palestine. They fully realized their own deep attachment to German culture and society, and their autobiographical accounts are generally free of anguished protest against the experience of personal discrimination. The existence of a Jewish state might ultimately assuage the intensity of German anti-Semitism, but its immediate objective would be the ingathering of the physically persecuted.[56]

Equally significant was the fact that many of these early Zionists were still firmly rooted in a knowledge of Judaism. Childhood experiences, synagogue affiliation, study, and practice had prepared them for a nationalistic reaffirmation of Judaism. Zionism had not represented as great a personal transformation for them as it did for the totally alienated majority of the second generation. Thus the concern for Eastern Jewry and the familiarity with Judaism, sometimes one alone, destined the Zionism of men like Bodenheimer, Wolffsohn, Isaac Rülf, Löwe, Klee, Schauer, Gronemann, and Oppenheimer to be a form of moderate protest.[57]

In contrast, the turn to Zionism of the second generation of middle-class university students and young professionals [58] represented an intensely personal reaction to the circumstances of Jewish life in the Second Reich. Men like Blumenfeld and Lichtheim came from completely and successfully assimilated homes. Blumenfeld's father was a learned and liberal judge in East Prussia; his mother was an accomplished pianist; German culture had banished every trace of Jewishness from the home, and his parents associated solely with Christian friends.[59] In Lichtheim's family nearly all the members on his father's side had converted to Christianity, while his mother's family stoically preserved its Judaism in name only. But at the age of fifteen Lichtheim was already convinced that conversion offered no solution. German society had come to believe in the ineradicable nature of racial and national characteristics. Yet he could not adjust to the fact that he would never be regarded as an equal. The theoretical and practical denial of equality affronted his pride. He desperately yearned for a way of life that would satisfy the whole man, stubbornly refusing to placate his self-respect with wealth and culture. This in fact was the gnawing discontent that provoked the revolutionary turn of both men to Zionism, a revolution that Blumenfeld called "post-assimilation Zionism." [60]

Blumenfeld depicted Zionism as the only way by which the German Jew could escape his destructive self-estrangement. Emancipation had compelled him to think in alien concepts and speak in a foreign language. Judaism had been reconstructed according to German criteria, methods, and values, and every action was performed with one eye on the non-Jew. In the final analysis the fight against anti-Semitism was really a fight against Judaism, a desperate attempt to efface all distinctly Jewish traits and practices that might give offense to the non-Jew. Zionism offered release from an intolerable spiritual bondage; but it required uprooting oneself from German society. The first step was the bold proclamation of 1912 which meant fundamentally that the German Zionist considered himself already a citizen of the future Jewish state.[61]

Blumenfeld's remarkable influence over the direction of German Zionism in the last years before the war was possible only because so many of its young members shared his sense of alienation. Often the experience of anti-Semitism in the student life of the German university precipitated the realization.[62] One young Zionist, reflecting upon his own career, suggested that with the emancipation the Jew had been transformed from a state of being into a flux of eternal becoming. At the university the rootless Jewish student desperately pursued the acquisition of culture. With a nervous, voracious intensity, he read more, thought more, and matured faster than his secure and calm Christian peer.[63] Often it was the seemingly authentic Jewish life projected by the students from Eastern Europe that offered a meaningful alternative.[64]

Martin Buber added the theoretical analysis of this widely shared experience. He had become a Zionist as a twenty-year-old student at the University of Berlin. In an effort to expose Western Jews to the culture of Eastern Jewry, and to demonstrate the possibility of an indigenous Jewish culture, he formed in the Winter of 1900–1901 a committee within the Berlin Zionist Chapter for Jewish art and scholarship. Buber, Chaim Weizmann, Berthold Feiwel, and Davis Trietsch also tried unsuccessfully to move the Zionist Congress of 1901 to finance a Jewish publishing house in order to stimulate and print works of Jewish poetry, drama, art, and music.[65]

In 1910 Buber diagnosed the inner Jewish question which every Western Jew eventually had to face. The physical identity of a man is the consequence of his membership in a community sharing land, speech, and custom. But the human need for permanence brings a man eventually to seek his spiritual identity, and this is to be found only when he becomes conscious of the community of blood which has preceded him and to which he is substantively bound. For most men these two communities of space and blood are identical; for the Western Jew they are tragically separated. Since ancestry and not citizenship determined the deepest level of a man's soul, a painful internal dualism racked every Jew. Buber, in contrast to Blumenfeld, was not asking for an end to this composite character. He submitted only that the objective was to decide which was supreme. The Jew who courageously identified with his community of blood would become fervently and harmoniously Jewish.[66]

For several years the feelings of disillusionment and estrangement had been aired within the confines of the Zionist Federation or the Jewish community. In the Spring of 1912 a young German Zionist, Moritz Goldstein, published a confession of total resignation in one of the important German cultural periodicals. Inevitably a bitter debate erupted. Goldstein's father had been an observant Jew who felt compelled, as a European, as a German, and as a liberal, to forego the ritual practice of Judaism. Only circumcision, the High Holidays, the Passover Seder, and Hanukah were preserved. Goldstein first experienced anti-Semitism at the University of Berlin, and he soon became a shy and rather inactive Zionist. As a student of German literature, he became the editor of a series of German classics at the age of twenty-seven.[67]

In his cathartic essay of 1912, Goldstein posed the problem that had been agitating him since his student days. The Jews of Germany were guiding the intellectual and cultural life of a people who bore an intense and irrational hatred for them. Despite the most extraordinary exertion to become German and to conceal every vestige of Jewishness, despite the indisputable contributions of Jews to every field of German culture, the Jew was still considered an alien, an intruder. Jewish efforts to deny this truth were equally extraordinary. Zionism, on the other hand, offered no real alternative for the present generation. The facts of life were too obstinate. Producing a national literature in Hebrew within a living Jewish society would be an opportunity only for their children. The language and culture of the present generation were irrevocably German. The only feasible and self-respecting alternative to resolving the insufferable tension, dualism, and lack of identity was to withdraw from all participation in German culture. The rest of their lives could be devoted to creating a Jewish literature in German based upon Jewish material and committed to projecting a new Jewish image.[68]

Thus, a new generation of Zionists had transformed Zionist ideology. Beneath the intensified rhetoric lay the stark fact that this generation no longer believed in the possibility of ultimate integration. One hundred years of diligent effort had not fulfilled the Jewish dream, and the continued daily experience of rejection proved the futility of the endeavor. All the self-criticism and self-correction, the protests of love and loyalty, the endless refutations of anti-Semitism, had not convinced a single sector of German society that Jews were Germans. Even liberal Christians continued to regard the Jews as a body apart. Living in Germany had become an agony of unrequited love. Jews remained a tolerated alien group in the land of their hosts. The young Zionists contended that they neither created nor aggravated the situation; they simply had had the courage to recognize it. Their declaration of disillusionment came in Posen during the very year when Prussian Jewry was celebrating the hundredth anniversary of its original emancipation. In essence it was a declaration of mood. Few intended to leave for Palestine. But its ideological implications could not be ignored. Only a total spiritual and physical return to one's own people could ultimately relieve the sense of unfulfillment and rootlessness.

THE CONFLICT

This declaration challenged the fundamental conviction of German Jewry that integration was a matter of time and education. Even the leaders of the Centralverein with their sober assessment of German anti-Semitism never doubted that integration was achievable without self-extinction. Once the declaration had been proclaimed, collision with the entire German Jewish community loomed ahead inevitably.

What predictably unnerved and infuriated German Jewry was the disconcerting identity between the Zionist and anti-Semitic diagnosis of the Jewish problem. Much of its long-standing disapproval of Zionism had stemmed from this potential confirmation of anti-Semitism. However, as long as the major concern of German Zionism had been directed toward a political solution of the Jewish problem in Russia, the animosity remained somewhat muted.[69] It now intensified steadily. The Centralverein, for example, repudiated Goldstein's mood of resignation. To follow Zionist advice would mean to capitulate to the anti-Semites, who had always maligned the Jews as alien and unassimilable. To deny a thousand years of Jewish history would be an unpardonable act of cowardice. Zionism was a viable alternative only for the Jews of Eastern Europe, who lived in a cultural vacuum. Culturally destined to remain Germans, Jews must reaffirm their faith in their German fatherland.[70]

A series of lectures by Werner Sombart in December 1911 on the future of the Jews, published the following year as a book, again documented this feared identity of Zionism and anti-Semitism. Sombart had earlier been ostensibly inspired by Max Weber to deal provocatively with the role of Jews and Judaism in spawning modern capitalism, though the value of the work is sharply reduced by a shortage of evidence, numerous errors, an abundance of conjecture, and unmistakeable racial categories. Now he dropped the guise of scholarship and addressed himself openly to contemporary issues. Throughout his lectures he treated the Jews as a distinct racial and national entity. He considered a Jewish state in Palestine as the only possible means of alleviating Jewish suffering in Eastern Europe. The United States would soon follow England in closing its doors. However, Palestine was not for the Jews of the West. Their ethnic differences did not make them intolerable, and, furthermore, expulsion of this gifted people would be an irreplaceable loss, as it had proven to be for Spain. To remain, though, required tact and wisdom from the Jews; antipathy toward them would never fully disappear, but with self-imposed limitations, they could remove its venom. Sombart lamented the Judaizing of so many sectors of Germany's public and intellectual life. He applauded the efforts to create an indigenous Jewish culture that might diminish Jewish domination of German culture, and he defended the exclusion of Jews from the bureaucracy and Officers Corps. In sum, he conceded that the state must extend equality to the Jews, but the Jews in turn must exercise the self-control not to use it fully.[71]

In Sombart, the Zionists did not see an anti-Semite, but a Christian scholar who had identified himself openly with Zionism. His endorsement was welcomed as an important vindication. For the first time non-Jewish scholarship had considered the Jewish question in Zionist terms. *Die Welt* even expressed the hope that Sombart might deliver additional lectures on the Jewish problem in other cities.[72]

Fuchs delivered the Centralverein's rebuttal to Sombart in Kattowitz before an audience of about two thousand, including some two hundred Zionists from Upper Silesia. Sombart, he declared, was a new breed of anti-Semite, for unlike the more familiar Treitschke-Hartmann type, he embodied a mixture of philo- and anti-Semitic notions based upon the wholly erroneous supposition that the Jews constitute a race. Despite the expected defense of Centralverein policy, Fuchs carefully avoided criticizing Sombart's Zionist passages, and in conclusion he pleaded that Sombart must not precipitate a fight between the Centralverein and the Zionists, for they were equally committed to fighting assimilation. But Fuchs failed to convince even the other Centralverein speakers sharing the platform. They attacked the Zionists belligerently, and the meeting, to Fuchs' dismay, ended in near riot.[73]

The Zionists could not have chosen a more inauspicious moment to publicize their disillusionment. In a period of feverish German nationalism, their pronouncements raised the feared specter of dual loyalty. The second Moroccan crisis of 1911–12, resulting from the unilateral French abrogation of the agreement which had settled the first crisis in 1906, produced an outburst of militant patriotism. The press of the powerful Pan-German League yelled for war. The halls of the Reichstag reverberated with saber-rattling denunciations of the final settlement, which gave Germany some additional French Congo territory in return for the recognition of full French political control in Morocco. Admiral Tirpitz and the Kaiser utilized the favorable atmosphere to gain approval from the Reichstag for still further naval expansion, which was granted in May 1912, the same month in which the Zionists adopted their Posen resolution. As an apprehensive minority in a nation arming to counter a growing international isolation, German Jewry was visibly shaken by such ill-timed declarations of Jewish nationalism.[74]

In a circular to its local representatives at the beginning of February 1912, the Zionist Federation reiterated its argument that citizenship in the modern state was wholly independent of religion and nationality. It further endorsed again the Centralverein's fight for full equality as a legitimate concern. However, equality was not to be purchased at the price of extinction, or even in return for the drastic remodeling of Judaism. Such a Judaism would be neither capable nor worthy of survival.[75]

Nevertheless, the Zionists realized that a break with the Centralverein was imminent. At an eleven-hour session of the full Central Committee on November 3, 1912, Blumenfeld admitted that open conflict was unavoidable. The Centralverein had ceased being purely a defense organization. Preoccupied with integration, it had come to represent a specific interpretation of Judaism which directly opposed the one expounded by Zionism. Hantke supported the radical posture adopted by the Zionist Federation as the only effective form of propaganda. However, he advised Zionists not to withdraw from the Centralverein, because its meetings granted them a public platform for their own cause. Klee, an old Centralverein member who criticized the Posen resolution as a tactical blunder, admonished his more radical colleagues. The Centralverein was the largest organization in the Jewish community and a political factor on the German scene. Cooperation was advisable and he suggested a meeting of leaders from both sides.[76]

An attempt at reconciliation took place on December 18, 1912. Fuchs, Horwitz, and Hollaender represented the Centralverein, while the Zionists sent Hantke, Blumenfeld, Heymann, and Leo Motzkin, four men who supported the Posen resolution. The Centralverein representatives complained that the Zionists had been systematically sending their speakers to disrupt the propaganda meetings of the Centralverein. They also objected to the unfair criticism of Die Welt and the Jüdische Rundschau against the Centralverein for its failure to prevent the aforementioned nomination of Mugdan in 1912 by the Progressive Party.[77] For their part, the Zionists requested that the Centralverein drop the anti-Zionist polemic, which had come to characterize both its meetings and its journal. The report on the meeting submitted later by the Zionist representatives was not optimistic. While it praised the moderation of Fuchs, it indicated that neither side seemed willing to make significant concessions. The report concluded:

We do not at the moment consider it expedient to declare war officially against the Centralverein, but it would be a mistake to leave unexploited any opportunity for Zionist propaganda out of consideration for the Centralverein. In time the exceptionally great difference in theoretical views must lead to a more or less open battle. . . .[78]

Other sectors of German Jewry had already organized to dissociate themselves from the unpatriotic proclamations of radical Zionists. In November 1912, a newly formed Antizionistische Komitee, which shared the same Berlin address as the Vereinigung für das liberale Judentum (Union for Liberal Judaism), sent out a confidential letter stating its *raison d'être*. German Zionism had carried its case before the German public. It had ventured to seek the support of anti-Semitic and conservative parties (an unsubstantiated charge for which the only shred of tangible evidence was Zionist approval of the recent Sombart lectures), and it had provoked an acrimonious literary debate which threatened to divide Jew and Christian. The committee feared that even favorably inclined political circles might come to see the solution to the Jewish problem in the separatistic terms of the Zionists. To protect the status of German Jewry, the committee planned to initiate its own literary polemic against Zionism.[79]

An avalanche of anxious inquiries about the Centralverein's attitude toward the new direction of the Zionist Federation finally forced the Executive Committee to assume a position. On March 30, 1913, exactly twenty years to the day after its founding, 220 delegates from all over Germany met in Berlin from morning till early evening to debate the proposed resolution of the Executive Committee. Both Fuchs and Hollaender, who presented the resolution which was eventually adopted unchanged, stressed the transformation of German Zionism. Formerly, being a Zionist had meant that a man was equally conscious of both his Jewish and German nationalities, though his Jewish nationalism implied little more than a realization that he belonged to a community of common ancestry and history. With this type of Zionist the Centralverein could cooperate, especially since it also had matured in its understanding of Jewish identity. However, the new breed of Zionist who now dominated the organization denied being German altogether. They were only Jews temporarily living in Germany. This was a dangerous and unacceptable formulation, because even the Centralverein believed that the equality it sought depended upon the extent to which Jews had become Germans. Regardless of theory, in practice equality was extended only to those who fully identified with the fatherland.[80]

For many at the convention, the resolution, which repudiated only the extreme Zionists, was disappointingly mild. They demanded a resolution against the Zionism of the Basle Program. Both the concept of a Jewish people and the objective of a legal homeland in Palestine were untenable for any member of the Centralverein. They argued that the true nature of Zionism was to be sought in its official documents and not in the opinions of individuals. The two types of Zionists distinguished by the resolution had no basis in the movement's official ideology. Nevertheless, the convention preserved the more circumscribed proposal.[81]

The German Zionist Federation did not fail to take up the gauntlet. On May 1, 1913, some ninety delegates convened in Berlin to adopt a resolution calling upon all Zionists to leave the ranks of the Centralverein, and proposing the formation of a new, truly neutral defense organization. That proposal was certainly an unexpected concern for an organization that was directing its own members toward eventual emigration. Its inclusion in the resolution reflected the pressure exerted by the older generation of Zionists. At the preparatory meeting for the convention of the Central Committee on April 6, 1913, older Zionists like Klee, who himself had participated in the founding of the Centralverein, objected to the withdrawal of all Zionists. They finally agreed, provided the Zionists themselves would establish a defense organization committed to the full equality of German Jewry.[82]

The collision between the Centralverein and the Zionists generated an acrimonious debate that quickly engulfed other sectors of German Jewry.[83] The Zionists, for example, moved to deny the Centralverein its permanent seat on the Board of the Verband der jüdischen Jugendvereine Deutschlands (League of Jewish Youth Groups of Germany), an organization of nearly 14,500 young members. The seat had originally been extended to the Centralverein because the Verband wished to identify itself with the fight for complete equality, but now that the Centralverein had departed from its vaunted neutrality, the Zionists contended, it no longer deserved to sit on the board of a neutral youth organization. The third national convention of the Verband in May 1913 defeated the Zionist motion.[84]

The Zionists and the Centralverein also collided on the issue of the Wandervogel, the loosely organized movement of young bourgeois dissidents. By 1913 anti-Semitism had become a noticeable motif in the rebellious litany of the Wandervogel. The Zionists countered with their own nationalistic *Blau-Weiss Vereine*. They urged Jewish teen-agers to leave the Wandervogel, even where still admitted. The Centralverein condemned this as a counsel of despair. Without denying that anti-Semitism had made inroads into the Wandervogel, the Centralverein advised Jewish youth where possible to remain in order to fight from within. When a chapter became overtly anti-Semitic, appeals were to be made to the local school authorities. Complete withdrawal would simply open the way for the anti-Semities to take over. Above all, those youngsters that were forced to leave were not to join the chauvinistic youth movement of the Zionists, but one of the neutral Jewish *Jugendvereine*.[85]

Toward the end of 1913, the Zionists were unexpectedly pulled into another bitter controversy with the major foreign philanthropic organization of German Jewry, the Hilfsverein der deutschen Juden (Relief Society of German Jews). Founded in 1901 to aid the Jews of Eastern Europe and the Middle East, the Hilfsverein had invested substantial sums of money to provide the growing Jewish settlement in Palestine with teachers and schools. It also had begun to raise money for the eventual construction of an advanced technical school, whose provisional board included three Zionists. Thus, in 1908 the official German Zionist *Handbook* lauded the Hilfsverein's work with evident sincerity. In the Fall of 1913, the board of the Technion, which was to be opened the following spring in Haifa, voted to employ only German as the language of instruction to the total exclusion of Hebrew. The three Zionist members resigned in protest, and spontaneously teachers and students struck against the Hilfsverein schools in Palestine. Inevitably the conflict erupted in Germany as well, shattering the formerly cordial relations between the Hilfsverein and the German Zionists.[86]

The alleged support of the German government for the Hilfsverein's position intensified the isolation of German Zionists within the Jewish community, for the Zionists were now openly flouting the national interest by opposing the potential development of a German cultural sphere of influence.[87] In February 1914, a worried Antizionistische Komitee published a declaration with the signatures of nearly three hundred Jewish notables in the liberal German press. It accused the Zionists of pursuing a "Jewish national chauvinism" within the Jewish community that could only undermine the relations with German Christians, from whom Jews up to this time had been separated by religion alone. Even in areas of mutual interest, cooperation had become impossible.[88]

That same month the National Board of the B'nai B'rith in Germany issued an appeal in its organizational journal for a cease fire. The internal Jewish strife had reached explosive proportions. Even the general public was amazed at the spectacle of a minority group surrounded by enemies being consumed by civil strife. Prior to publication the president sent a copy to a leading Zionist in Mannheim. In a personal letter he added: "Would it not then be possible that the Zionists in Germany might issue a declaration that the doctrines of Zionism definitely do not hinder one from being a loyal German and that in fact the German Zionists are?" [89]

Some of the passion subsided in February 1914, when the board of the Technion, with its American members now present, decided that mathematics and physics were to be taught immediately in Hebrew. The outbreak of the war dissipated the passion that remained. In August 1914 both the Centralverein and the German Zionist Federation called upon the Jews of Germany to volunteer for the defense of the fatherland.[90]

AN APPRAISAL

GERMAN JEWRY'S FIGHT against anti-Semitism obviously ended only
with the fateful assumption of power by the Nazis in 1933. Nevarthe-
less, the outbreak of World War I in the summer of 1914 may serve
as a practical *terminus ad quem* for the present study. The recurring
international crises before Sarajevo and the total national effort necessitated by the conflagration that followed had temporarily reduced the major symptoms of anti-Semitism. The dramatic decline of
the anti-Semitic parties in 1912, during the last Reichstag election
prior to the war, revealed the diminishing electoral appeal of a
purely anti-Semitic platform in a period dominated by foreign concerns. The number of anti-Semitic deputies dropped from seventeen
to three.[1] Even the portals leading to the upper echelons of the government and the Army were jarred open by the explosion of the war.
The Prussian Minister of War appointed Walther Rathenau to organize the vital administration for raw materials, which procured and
stored the natural resources indispensable for extended conflict,
and for the first time since the Napoleonic wars, some two thousand
Jews served as army officers.[2] The urgencies of war temporarily ex-
tracted from the government the last measures of full equality that it
had consistently refused to confer in peacetime, although the protrac-
tion of that war and the prospect of defeat were soon to spawn a still
more vicious specter of anti-Semitism.

German Jewry on the eve of the war bore little resemblance to the

Jewry of 1870. A formidable superstructure of national organizations and an increasingly revitalized Judaism had replaced the fragmented Jewish community and the mass religious indifference which
were the hallmarks in 1870 of a very recently emancipated and insecure Jewry. If this study has shown anything, it is the extent to which
this transformation was due to anti-Semitism. Although the study has
addressed itself mainly to the efforts at organized self-defense, it
soon became apparent that few developments on the German Jewish
scene, from the formation of adult study groups to trends in scholarship and theology, were unrelated to the constant pressure of a hostile environment.

This connection was already stressed shortly after the turn of the
century by the perceptive pastor and scholar, Paul Billerbeck. Despite his dedication to converting the Jews, his aforementioned survey of the institutional structure of German Jewry was a masterpiece
of informed and objective reporting. He speculated:

We won't go so far as to say that anti-Semitism is solely responsible for
the awakening of the Jewish spirit and the uniting of all those who are
seized by it. That uniting would have occurred anyway, even if anti-Semitic pressures had not been operating; it has its roots in the denomina-
tionalism which in our day prevails in all religious communities. But that
this unification of Jewry would have been accomplished as quickly and as
securely as it was, that we can unquestionably credit to the account of
the anti-Semites.

To his chagrin, this organizational rejuvenation would render the
Christian mission to the Jews of Germany all the more difficult.[3]

The historical significance of the defense effort is that it took place
at all. To appreciate this deceptively obvious fact, one must compare
the rising militancy of German Jewry during the last two decades
prior to the war to the unswerving course of inaction pursued by organized French Jewry in the face of the relentless vituperation initiated by Edouard Drumont and sustained by the Dreyfus Affair.
French Jewry never made the same transition to self-defense. Despite
intense provocation for more than a decade, culminating in nationwide anti-Jewish riots in January and February 1898 in which synagogues and Jewish stores were burned and individual Jews beaten,
French Jewry never relinquished its basic policy of silence. It dis-

dainfully refused to counter the torrent of anti-Semitic propaganda; it tenaciously continued to hope for and rely on the assistance of concerned Christians. And above all, it feared giving the appearance of defending another Jew. Even the respected Alliance Israélite Universelle, which had since 1860 bravely fought the enemies of emancipation abroad, maintained a rigorous silence on the Affair, so as not to open itself to the charge of defending Jewish interests to the detriment of France. Thus, unlike its German counterpart, French Jewry could not bring itself to admit and combat the existence of an internal and indigenous anti-Semitic enemy.[4]

The manifestly different reaction of German Jewry, after a prolonged period of painful vacillation, serves to challenge the blanket judgment of Hannah Arendt that Jewish leadership steadily exhibited an amazing degree of political naiveté and submissiveness during the era of emancipation. She contends that the Jews' long history of political powerlessness had destroyed any sense for the political realities of modern society. The only alliance they knew how to strike was one with the ruling authorities to whom they submitted unquestioningly.[5] In the light of the history of the Centralverein before 1914, this evaluation certainly stands in need of revision. The policies and tactics of the Centralverein amount to more than an exercise in "mild pressure for minor purposes of self-defense." [6]

Measured against the former silence of German Jewry and the continued passivity of French Jewry, the Centralverein represents a watershed in the history of emancipated Jewry. Its appearance institutionalized the twin objectives of German Jewry. Under intense pressure, German Jews served notice that they still demanded full integration into German society as well as the right to preserve their unique religious heritage. In 1912, on the occasion of Prussian Jewry's centenary celebration of the first emancipation edict, Hermann Cohen summed up the aspirations of his coreligionists.

Our patriotic celebration has an indivisible twofold meaning. Without participation in our state we would cease to be within the present cultural context living persons (i.e. legal persons in the sense of Roman law). But without the fusion of this political right with our religious life and character, we would lose the rootedness, the unity, the security, the natural frankness, the truthfulness and the valour of historical men.[7]

But what is even more important, the existence of the Centralverein served notice that German Jewry had rejected acquiescence or emigration, that instead it had decided to fight for those rights to which it was politically and legally entitled. To this end, the Centralverein worked with courage, skill, and ingenuity. It campaigned to form the largest Jewish pressure group possible. It persistently invoked the courts to the maximum advantage possible under the politically influenced judicial system of the Reich. It fought anti-Semitic candidates during election campaigns, without taking the divisive and doubtful step of forming or openly aligning with a political party. It tried to increase pressure upon government circles by founding a still more imposing all-inclusive Jewish organization, the Verband der deutschen Juden. Finally, the Centralverein correctly perceived the growing menace of conversion precipitated by the exclusion of Jews from more and more sectors of German society, and boldly set out to strengthen the will to resist. In the process, it came to reconsider the content of the Judaism it so tenaciously defended. To characterize this record of the Centralverein as mild, naive, or submissive, is simply to ignore the evidence.

Perhaps the most favorable testimony in behalf of the Centralverein was inadvertently submitted by the Zionists. Despite occasional criticism of the Centralverein for not forming a political pressure group, the Zionists never broke with the Centralverein over tactics. The most radical group in German Jewry did not find the Centralverein inept or timid in its fight against anti-Semitism. In the pursuit of their respective objectives, they were equally militant. When the break finally came, it was on the most fundamental question possible: whether integration within the German context was still feasible.

Our study has also indicated the extent to which the entire defense effort was organized and led by Reform Jews. Men like Moritz Kohner, Jacob Nachod, Emil Lehmann, Samuel Kristeller, Moritz Lazarus, Paul Nathan, Raphael Löwenfeld, Maximilian Horwitz, and Eugen Fuchs were often theologically at odds with the institutions or practices of Judaism that they defended. Notwithstanding the fearless campaign against anti-Semitism in the pages of the Orthodox *Jüdische Presse,* the defense organizations were wholly dominated by the Reform. This preponderance reflects far more than the numerical decline of German Orthodoxy, which by the turn of the century may have amounted to a mere 10 or 15 percent of German Jewry.

At the outset of this survey, it was noted that all sectors of the German political spectrum—conservative, liberal, and radical—agreed that emancipation required conversion to Christianity. Reform spokesmen consciously or unconsciously lowered the price to a religious accommodation that would diminish and conceal Jewish religious distinctiveness. With evident sincerity and occasional concern for intellectual integrity, they labored to prepare Judaism for integration. Neo-Orthodox leaders like Samson R. Hirsch likewise overhauled traditional Judaism, especially its theology and juridical claims, to a far greater extent than they were willing to admit. But their self-deception spared them the disillusionment that struck Reform Jews when they began to realize the futility of all accommodation short of conversion. They had made the greatest investment to allay the prejudices and earn the goodwill of Germans opposed to or ambivalent about emancipation. Of all Jews, they had sacrificed the most to achieve genuine integration. Yet as far as most Germans were concerned the price remained the same. Both conservatives and liberals in different ways continued to insist on the exclusively Christian character of the German state, while a strident minority now declared that even conversion could not eradicate the racial characteristics separating Aryans and Semites. The resolve to fight anti-Semitism was made first by those Reform Jews whose personal reconstruction of Judaism made them most susceptible to bitter disappointment at the recalcitrance of German demands.

This is not to say that all Reform Jews who joined the Centralverein did so out of disillusionment. For many who were far removed from any visible Jewish practice or belief, the Centralverein provided a type of surrogate Judaism. Contemporaries like Ismar Freund and Leo Baeck were acutely aware of the religious void that the fight against anti-Semitism helped to fill. In his unpublished memoirs, Freund perceptively observed:

For a large part of assimilated Jewry in Germany, the fight against anti-Semitism was one of the strongest components of Jewish consciousness. To a great extent, many had emancipated themselves from the bonds of Jewish law. The national ideas of Judaism were rejected. [But] the will to Judaism, the Jewish feeling, existed [and] demanded expression. It required content. One found both in the political fight as conducted by the Centralverein.[8]

This was a post-emancipation phenomenon. Many who were no longer able to express their Jewishness in the limited religious forms left after the extinction of the medieval Jewish community but who remained consciously Jewish searched for new expressions of identity. Some entered the ranks of the Centralverein; others became Zionists.

One final observation seems entirely in order as a result of the cumulative experience of the defense organizations before 1914. It became increasingly evident in the course of this study that their efforts had constantly to contend with the duplicity of various and successive German governments. These confrontations between Jewry and government span the entire period from the chaplaincy controversy during the Franco-Prussian War, the expulsion of the Gemeindebund from Leipzig by the Saxon Minister of Interior, the innumerable attempts to gain the protection of the German judiciary, to the final protests before the war over the continued exclusion of Jews from the Officers Corps. Though the individual issue or case may have been inconsequential, the cumulative effect of these repeated controversies was to deprive the government of any possible educational force in bringing the mass of Germans to accept emancipation. Long after the official policy of subverting the 1812 edict of emancipation had been scuttled, the Prussian government continued to manifest its anti-Jewish sentiments in countless devious gestures and measures. Not only did it thereby fail to counter the latent medieval religious prejudices of the Christian masses, which could so easily be exploited to divert attention from the genuine causes of mass frustration and unrest, but it actually abetted them.

At the very beginning of the nineteenth century, Wilhelm von Humboldt spoke of the possible outcome of this partial, half-hearted approach to emancipation. In 1809 he submitted a perceptive memorandum on what ought to be the character of the legislation by which the Prussian government hoped to emancipate its Jewish minority. Repeatedly he emphasized that the extension of equality had to be immediate and complete. The slightest discriminatory vestige would serve to reinforce the existing deep divisions between Jews and Christians. With rare foresight, he admonished the government:

However, in a new law the Government expresses the opinion that it now holds regarding the Jews and the possibility of their civil improvement, and this opinion must necessarily be of the greatest importance in shaping the general [sentiment] of the nation. A new piece of legislation regarding the Jews which is not quite wise may thereby remove many physical detriments, but it gives rise to the possible danger of creating greater moral drawbacks—by misdirecting public opinion and strengthening old prejudices—than even their present condition presents.[9]

The adamant refusal of German governments ever to heed Humboldt's prophetic counsel contributed directly to the catastrophic failure of emancipation in Germany.

NOTES AND BIBLIOGRAPHY

ABBREVIATIONS

ALBI	Archives of the Leo Baeck Institute, New York
AZJ	*Allgemeine Zeitung des Judentums*
BLBI	*Bulletin des Leo Baeck Instituts*
C-V Zeitung	*Centralverein Zeitung*
CZA	Central Zionist Archives, Jerusalem
GB	*Geschäftsberichte des Verbandes der deutschen Juden*
IDR	*Im deutschen Reich*
IR	*Israelitische Rundschau*
JHGA	Jewish Historical General Archives, Jerusalem
JJGL	*Jahrbuch für jüdische Geschichte und Literatur*
JQR	*Jewish Quarterly Review*
JR	*Jüdische Rundschau*
KB	*Korrespondenz-Blatt des Verbandes der Deutschen Juden*
LBIYB	*Leo Baeck Institute Year Book*
MDIGB	*Mitteilungen vom Deutsch-Israelitischen Gemeindebunde*
MGWJ	*Monatsschrift für Geschichte und Wissenschaft des Judentums*
MVZADA	*Mitteilungen aus dem Verein zur Abwehr des Antisemitismus*
PAJHS	*Publications of the American Jewish Historical Society*
StB	*Stenografischen Berichte der Fünf Hauptversammlungen des Verbandes der Deutschen Juden*

NOTES

INTRODUCTION

1. Christian Wilhelm Dohm, *Über die bürgerliche Verbesserung der Juden* (Berlin and Stettin, 1781). In 1783 Dohm added a second volume of rejoinders and published it along with a slightly revised edition of Volume I in a single edition. The references below are to the combined edition (Berlin and Stettin, 1783).

2. H. E. Marcard, *Über die Möglichkeit der Juden-Emancipation im christlich-germanischen Staat* (Minden and Leipzig, 1843), pp. 39–40. See also Nathan Rotenstreich, "For and against Emancipation: The Bruner Bauer Controversy," *LBIYB*, IV (1959), 3–36.

3. Franz Reuss, *Christian Wilhelm Dohms Schrift "Über die bürgerliche Verbesserung der Juden" und deren Einwirkung auf die gebildeten Stände Deutschlands* (Kaiserslautern, 1891), p. 43.

4. Reuss, pp. 43–45, 67–69, 71–72. See also the reflections of Pastor Schwager in Dohm, II, 89–111, as well as the material collected by H. D. Schmidt, "The Terms of Emancipation, 1781–1812," *LBIYB*, I (1956), 28–39.

5. Marcard, pp. 23–26: Rotenstreich. See also Horst Fischer, *Judentum, Statt und Heer in Preussen im frühen 19. Jahrhundert* (Tübingen, 1968), pp. 151–157.

6. Dohm, I, 117–141.

7. *Idem*, II, 187–212.

8. Ismar Freund, *Die Emanzipation der Juden in Preussen*, II (Berlin, 1912), 275–276. Max J. Kohler translated this important memorandum in an appendix to his "Jewish Rights at the Congresses of Vienna (1814–1815) and Aix La-Chapelle (1818)," *PAJHS*, XXVI (1918), 103–115. (I have revised Kohler's translation of the quotation, p. 108.)

9. Franz Schnabel, *Deutsche Geschichte im neunzehnten Jahrhundert*, II (Freiburg im Breisgau, 1933), 79–86.

10. Berthold Rosenthal, *Heimatgeschichte der badischen Juden* (Bühl, 1927), pp. 257–284; Sterling, *Er Ist Wie Du*, pp. 88–101.

11. Freund, *Die Emanzipation der Juden*, II, 455–459.

12. Ludwig von Rönne and Heinrich Simon, *Die früheren und gegenwärtigen Verhältnisse der Juden in den sämmtlichen Landestheilen des Preussischen Staates* (Breslau, 1843), pp. X–XI; Schnabel, II, 278–309; Fischer, pp. 67–69.

13. Heinrich Silbergleit, *Die Bevölkerungs- und Berufsverhältnisse der Juden im deutschen Reich* (Berlin, 1930), pp. 6–7.

14. Sterling, "Der Kampf um die Emanzipation der Juden im Rheinland," in *Monumenta Judaica* (Handbuch) (Cologne, 1963), pp. 293, 299–301.

15. Leopold Auerbach, *Das Judenthum und seine Bekenner in Preussen und in den anderen deutschen Bundesstaaten* (Berlin, 1890), pp. 248–249; H. G. Reissner, "Rebellious Dilemma: The Case Histories of Eduard Gans and Some of His Partisans," *LBIYB*, II (1957), 179–193; idem, *Eduard Gans: Ein Leben im Vormärz* (Tübingen, 1965).

16. Alfred Michaelis, *Die Rechtsverhältnisse der Juden in Preussen* (Berlin, 1910), pp. 281–283; Fischer, pp. 88–89, 93.

17. Fischer, pp. 90–91.

18. *Ibid.*, pp. 151–190.

19. Sterling, "Jewish Reactions to Jew-Hatred in the First Half of the 19th Century," *LBIYB*, III (1958), 104.

20. A. Menes, "The Conversion Movement in Prussia during the First Half of the 19th Century," *Yivo Annual of Jewish Social Science*, VI (1951), 191; Reissner, "Rebellious Dilemma," pp. 179–193.

21. Sterling, "Jewish Reactions to Jew-Hatred," p. 108.

22. *Ibid.*, pp. 107–109; Schmidt, pp. 39–45.

23. This connection has, of course, been noted before, though it remains to be fully investigated. See Heinrich Graetz, *Geschichte der Juden*, XI (2nd ed.; Leipzig, 1900), 372–373; Simon Dubnow, *The World History of the Jews* (Hebrew), IX (Tel Aviv, 1958), 41–42; Max Wiener, *Jüdische Religion im Zeitalter der Emanzipation* (Berlin, 1933), pp. 87–113; Salo Baron, *A Social and Religious History of the Jews*, II (1st ed.; New York, 1937), 245–256; and especially the recent illuminating essay by Baruh Mevorah, "Messianism as a Factor in the First Reform Controversies" (Hebrew), *Zion*, XXXIV (1969), 189–218.

24. Joseph L. Blau and Salo W. Baron, eds., *The Jews of the United States 1790–1840: A Documentary History*, II (New York and Philadelphia, 1963), 559. Italics in the original.

To be sure, Napoleon had already compelled the Paris Sanhedrin of 1807 to distinguish between the religious and political commandments of Judaism, the former being absolute and eternal, the latter intended only for the duration of political independence in Palestine. But whereas Napoleon had been satisfied with a general and clearly limited statement as to what constituted the political dimension of Judaism, German opponents of emancipation steadily expanded the category to include an ever larger number of religious precepts. See Simeon J. Maslin, *Selected Documents of Napoleonic Jewry* (Cincinnati, 1957), pp. 16 ff.; M. Diogene Tama, *Transactions of the Parisian Sanhedrin* (London, 1807), pp. 149–150; Baruh Mevorah, *Napoleon and His Era* (Hebrew) (Jerusalem, 1968), pp. 88–90.

25. Moses Mendelssohn, *Jerusalem* (Frankfurt and Leipzig, 1787), *passim.* Mendelssohn's final position was somewhat more muted. He did try to reassure Michaelis, Dohm's learned critic, that religious adjustments would inevitably be made voluntarily once emancipation had been extended. Still, he bitterly contested the government's theoretical right to make such demands a precondition of emancipation. See Dohm, II, 72–77.

26. David Friedländer, *Aktenstücke die Reform der jüdischen Kolonieen in*

den Preussischen Staaten betreffend (Berlin, 1793), pp. 3–27; *idem, Sendschreiben an seine Hochwürden Herrn Oberconsistorialrath und Probst Teller zu Berlin* (Berlin, 1799), *passim; idem, Über die durch die neuen Organisation der Judenschaften in den Preussischen Staaten notwendig gewordene Umbildung* (Berlin, 1934), *passim.*

27. See also Jacob Katz, "The German-Jewish Utopia of Social Emancipation," in *Studies of the Leo Baeck Institute,* ed. by Max Kreutzberger (New York, 1967), pp. 74–75.

28. Abraham Geiger, *Das Judenthum und seine Geschichte,* I (Breslau, 1865), chs. 2, 3, and 4.

29. *Ibid.,* p. 147. The passage is taken from Charles Newburgh's translation of Geiger's book, *Judaism and Its History,* I (New York, 1911), 161.

30. Samuel Holdheim, *Über die Autonomie der Rabbinen und das Princip der jüdischen Ehe* (2nd ed.; Schwerin, 1847), Vorwort (to 1st ed.), p. vi.

31. *Idem, Gemischte Ehen zwischen Juden und Christen* (Berlin, 1850), pp. 5–7.

32. *Ibid.,* pp. 54–55. Napoleon had also forced the Assembly of Notables in 1806 to take a position on the problem of intermarriage. Its members deftly responded that, while Judaism does not forbid marriage with a Christian, a Jewish wedding ceremony would not be binding. Though a Jew does not cease to be a Jew when he intermarries, still the rabbis would bless such a union as grudgingly as priests would bless the marriage of a Catholic outside the Church. Clearly Holdheim felt compelled by the German situation to go beyond this statement. See Tama, pp. 154–156.

33. Holdheim, *Gemischte Ehen,* p. 3; Michaelis, pp. 464–465.

34. David Philipson, *The Reform Movement in Judaism,* (2nd ed.; New York, 1931), p. 150.

35. *Ibid.*

36. Michaelis, pp. 466–468.

37. Holdheim, *Gemischte Ehen,* pp. 6–7.

38. Auerbach, *Das Judenthum und seine Bekenner,* pp. 231–242.

39. Wiener, *Jüdische Religion,* pp. 87–113. In his utterly uncritical but nevertheless informative history of the Reform Movement, Philipson tried to dismiss the interpretation that many reforms were politically motivated (p. 470, n. 32). But his own narrative unwittingly provides ample evidence to confirm the relationship. See especially pp. 123, 149, 150, 234.

40. *Zur Judenfrage in Deutschland,* II (1844), 3–5.

41. Ludwig Geiger, ed., *Abraham Geiger's Nachgelassene Schriften,* I (Berlin, 1875), 453–454. The passage was taken from Max Wiener's translation of Geiger's book, *Abraham Geiger and Liberal Judaism* (Philadelphia, 1962), p. 268.

A more caustic though private pronouncement to the same effect came from Gabriel Riesser, who stood at the forefront of the emancipation struggle in the middle decades of the nineteenth century and also believed Judaism to be in need of major reforms. In a letter dated November 28, 1842, to a close friend who disagreed with him, he explained why he opposed public declarations on the nature of Judaism such as the one issued that year in Frankfurt by the newly founded Reform Society. "In this regard, my conviction, based on much experience, is that only very, very few of these reforming intellectuals are motivated by an urgent, unconditional quest for truth, which would remain the same under any circumstances. On the contrary, the great majority are moved by the discomfort caused them by the external position of Judaism. . . . How lenient have I often found these sharp critics of the most innocuous follies of Judaism in regard to their opinion about the silliness and formality which confront them from another more imposing side. Sufficient proof that they despise Judaism not so much for its lack of reason as for its oppressed state, its lack of prestige. . . ." See Ludwig Geiger, "Briefe von und an Gabriel Riesser," *Zeitschrift für die Geschichte der Juden in Deutschland*, II (1888), 59.

42. Jacob Toury, " 'Deutsche Juden' im Vormärz," *BLBI*, 1965, pp. 65–82.

43. Samson R. Hirsch, *The Nineteen Letters of Ben Uziel*, trans. by Bernard Drachman (New York, 1942), pp. 85–86, 165–168.

44. Though it ought to be noted that he made a serious effort to elucidate the underlying ethical values of Jewish civil law for his contemporaries. See Hirsch, *Horeb*, trans. by I. Grunfeld, I (London, 1962), 215–268.

45. *Idem, The Nineteen Letters of Ben Uziel*, pp. 159–162.

46. *Ibid.*, pp. 79–80. *Idem, Horeb*, I, 202.

47. *Horeb*, I, 144–147; II, 460–462.

48. Chapters 3 to 9 of *The Nineteen Letters*, which trace the origin and history of Israel's mission, bear considerable resemblance to Hegel's *Phenomenology of Mind*. Hirsch's rationalism is most evident in his treatment of prayer, which he regards solely as a pedagogic instrument. See *Horeb*, II, 471 ff.

49. Graetz, "Die Construction der jüdischen Geschichte," *Zeitschrift für die religiösen Interessen des Judenthums*, III (1846), 81–84.

50. *Ibid.*, pp. 84–90. Quotation p. 89.

51. Walter Boehlich, ed., *Der Berliner Antisemitismusstreit* (Frankfurt a.M., 1965), pp. 11, 33–47. Regarding other aspects of this important controversy between Graetz and Treitschke, see *infra*, chs. 1 and 2. Graetz remained an inveterate critic of the Reform Movement throughout his life. See S. Unna, "Briefe von H. Graetz an Raphael Kirchheim," *Jahrbuch der jüdischliterarischen Gesellschaft*, XII (1918), 320.

52. Auerbach, *Das Judenthum und seine Bekenner*, pp. 254–263, 270; A. Tänzer, *Die Geschichte der Juden im Wuerttemberg* (Frankfurt a.M., 1937), pp. 90–99; Rosenthal, pp. 292–313; Martin Philippson, *Neueste Geschichte des jüdischen Volkes*, I (2nd ed.; Frankfurt a.M., 1922), 336–341.

53. Sterling, *Er Ist Wie Du, passim*.

54. Hans Martin Klinkenberg, "Zwischen Liberalismus und Nationalismus," *Monumenta Judaica* (Handbuch), (Cologne, 1963), p. 366; Arthur Ruppin, *The Jews of Today* (London, 1913), p. 71.

55. Compiled from the data collected by Hermann Engelbert, *Statistik des Judenthums im deutschen Reiche ausschliesslich Preussens und in der Schweiz* (Frankfurt a.M., 1875), pp. 10, 36, 49, 64, 70, 90; Salomon Neumann, *Zur Statistik der Juden in Preussen von 1816 bis 1880* (Berlin, 1884), p. 27; *Handbuch der jüdischen Gemeindeverwaltung und Wohlfahrtspflege*, hrsg. DIGB (Berlin, 1913), p. 232.

56. *Israelitische Wochenschrift*, 1883, p. 411. Klinkenberg, p. 368.

57. *Statistisches Jahrbuch für das deutsche Reich*, XXXVI (1915), 4–5.

58. Esra Bennathan, "Die demographische und wirtschaftliche Struktur der Juden" in *Entscheidungsjahr 1932*, ed. by Werner E. Mosse (Tübingen, 1965), pp. 89–92.

59. *Israelitische Wochenschrift*, 1883, p. 421.

60. Klingenberg, p. 371. On the extraordinary impact of individual Jews since the emancipation on nearly every facet of Germany's cultural and intellectual life as well as on many of its financial and industrial branches, see Sidney Osborne, *Germany and Her Jews* (London, 1939); F. R. Bienenfeld, *The Germans and the Jews* (New York, 1939), pp. 126–184; and especially Siegmund Kaznelson, ed., *Juden im deutschen Kulturbereich* (3rd ed.; Berlin, 1962).

61. B. D. Weinryb, "Prolegomena to an Economic History of the Jews in Germany in Modern Times," *LBIYB*, I (1956), 298–304; Azriel Shohet, *Beginnings of the Haskalah Among German Jewry* (Hebrew) (Jerusalem, 1960), pp. 21–35.

62. Ruppin, *The Jews of Today*, pp. 53–54.

63. *Ibid.; idem, Soziologie der Juden*, I (Berlin, 1930), 376–377.

64. *Soziologie der Juden*, I, 377.

65. *Ibid.*, p. 378; *idem, The Jews of Today*, p. 54.

66. On the medieval roots of German Jewry's fragmentation, see Shohet, pp. 9–10.

67. Engelbert, pp. 1–10, 23–31, 38–44.

68. *AZJ*, 1871, pp. 109, 125–126, 150, 169–173. By the last decade of the nineteenth century, the French government was subsidizing its Jewish community of about 80,000 to the tune of 160,000 francs annually, a sum used mainly to pay the salaries of religious officials, to support the rabbinical seminary in Paris, and to finance the repairs of synagogue buildings. Michael R. Marrus, *The Politics of Assimilation: A Study of the French Jewish Community at the Time of the Dreyfus Affair* (Oxford, 1971), pp. 31, 70.

69. Max Kollenscher, *Rechtsverhältnisse der Juden in Preussen* (Berlin, 1910), pp. 28–29, 56–57; Freund, *Die Rechtstellung der Synagogengemeinden in Preussen und die Reichsverfassung* (Berlin, 1926), pp. 5–6.

70. *AZJ*, 1877, p. 778.

71. *Israelit*, 1892, p. 265.

72. *AZJ*, 1875, p. 379.

73. *Encyclopaedia Judaica*, I (Berlin, 1928), cols. 274–276.

74. *Denkschrift zur Vertheidigung des einheitlichen Rechtsverbandes der jüdischen Gemeinden in Deutschland*, hrsg. DIGB (Leipzig, 1873), p. 14.

75. Engelbert, pp. xi, 96.

76. Bernhard Jacobsohn, *Der Deutsch-Israelitische Gemeindebund nach Ablauf des ersten Decenniums seit seiner Begründung von 1869 bis 1879* (Leipzig, 1879), pp. 37–38, 51–52, 70; *MDIGB*, No. 6, pp. 59–65. See *infra*, ch. 1.

77. Ruppin, *The Jews of Today*, p. 153.

78. *Israelit*, 1869, pp. 109–110, 860, 939; *AZJ*, 1870, pp. 78–80, 86–88, 166–170.

79. Uriel Tal, "The 'Kulturkampf' and the Position of the Jews in Germany" (Hebrew), *Zion*, XXIX (1964), 236–237.

80. Hirsch, *Denkschrift über die Judenfrage in dem Gesetz betreffend den*

Austritt aus der Kirche (Berlin, 1873), pp. 4–6. Esriel Hildesheimer, the leader of the Orthodox in Berlin, repeated the same arguments in the petition to the Abgeordnetenhaus which he composed in 1875 for his congregation. See Eliav, *Rabbiner Esriel Hildesheimer Briefe* (Jerusalem, 1965), pp. 108–110.

81. *AZJ*, 1874, pp. 399–401; Hermann Makower, *Über die Gemeindeverhältnisse der Juden in Preussen* (Berlin, 1873), pp. 25–26; Tal, "The 'Kulturkampf,' " *passim*.

82. *AZJ*, 1876, pp. 268–272, 363.

83. Regarding the repercussions and effects of the legislation, see Saemy Japhet, "The Secession Movement from the Frankfurt Jewish Community under S. R. Hirsch," in *Historia Judaica*, X (1948), 99–122; Isaac Heinemann, "Supplementary Remarks," *ibid.*, pp. 123–134; Jacob Rosenheim, "The Historical Significance of the Struggle for Secession from the Frankfurt Jewish Community," *ibid.*, pp. 135–146. See also Baron, "Freedom and Constraint in the Jewish Community," in *Essays and Studies in Memory of Linda R. Miller*, ed. by Israel Davidson (New York, 1938), pp. 9–23.

CHAPTER 1

THE INITIAL REACTION: DEUTSCH-
ISRAELITISCHER GEMEINDEBUND, 1869–1881

1. Emil Lehmann, *Gesammelte Schriften* (1st ed.; Berlin, 1899), pp. 6–7. In 1865 he was elected to the Dresden town council, and in 1875, to the second chamber of the Saxon Landtag, a seat he lost in 1881. He also sat for more than thirty years on the Board of the Dresden Jewish Community.

2. *Ibid.*, p. 316.

3. Lehmann submitted to the 1869 synod of religious and lay leaders meeting in Leipzig resolutions to the effect that Judaism recognized intermarriages as long as there was no compulsion to raise the children as Christians; that when the state required a civil wedding ceremony, a religious one was not needed, though desirable; and that all matters of divorce should be handled solely by state courts. Two years later at the Augsburg synod the first resolution was tabled, the second was accepted with some modification, and the third was transferred to a committee. See *Verhandlungen der ersten israelitischen Synode* (Berlin, 1869), pp. 253–254; *Verhandlungen der zweiten israelitischen Synode* (Berlin, 1873), pp. 79–106, 109–114.

4. Lehmann, pp. 336–344. It is indicative of the change in mood wrought by anti-Semitism that in the second edition of his *Gesammelte Schriften*, published in Dresden in 1909, this essay was omitted. Lehmann died in 1898.

5. Jacobsohn, *Der Deutsch-Israelitische Gemeindebund*, pp. 6–7.

6. JHGA, M1/9.

7. *AZJ*, 1869, pp. 554–557.

8. Mark Wischnitzer, *To Dwell in Safety* (Philadelphia, 1948), pp. 25–26, 29; *AZJ*, 1869, Nos. 1–11, 14–19.

9. *AZJ*, 1869, pp. 552, 557.

10. André Chouraqui, *L'Alliance Israélite Universelle et la renaissance juive contemporaine* (Paris, 1965), pp. 25–29; Narcisse Leven, *Cinquante ans d'histoire,* I (Paris, 1911), 67–73.

11. *AZJ,* 1869, pp. 555–556. In September 1869 the Board of the Gemeindetag included the following declaration of intention in an appeal to the Jewish communities: "The beneficial idea which our French Jewish brethren embodied in the Alliance Israélite Universelle—to aid physically and spiritually those coreligionists languishing under oppression—will be embodied in the DIGB according to the feelings and views of German Jews . . ." (p. 717).

12. *AZJ,* 1869, pp. 840–841, 879–899. Because of exacting standards of selection only 300 of the 5,000 families that registered with the committee between July 1870 and July 1871 were sent to the United States. The committee was dissolved in 1873 for lack of funds. (Wischnitzer, p. 34.)

13. *AZJ,* 1869, pp. 614, 741, 857–859, 897, 963, 979. See also Zosa Szajkowski, "Emigration to America or Reconstruction in Europe," *PAJHS,* XLII (1952), 176.

14. *AZJ,* 1870, p. 26. The French defeat in 1870–71 aggravated the national tensions within the Alliance. In 1871 the English members of the Alliance asserted their autonomy in the Anglo-Jewish Association. In December 1872 some eighty-four German Jews met in Berlin to found the autonomous Israelitische Alliance in Deutschland, and, a year later, the Israelitische Allianz zu Wien appeared. In contrast to the English and Austrian organizations, which prospered, the German effort was stillborn. (Chouraqui, pp. 55–59; Leven, pp. 73–74; *AZJ,* 1872, pp. 1006–8, 1023–30; Philippson, I, 396–397.)

15. *AZJ,* 1869, pp. 940–942, 1021–22; 1870, pp. 40–41, 387; 1871, pp. 453–454, 778–779; 1872, pp. 605–607, 623–625; *MDIGB,* No. 1, pp. 15–17; No. 2, pp. 27–43. See also the anonymous pamphlet, *Das Judenthum und seine Aufgabe im neuen deutschen Reich* (Leipzig, 1871), pp. 18–23. The author of this interesting appeal to German Jews to line up behind the national organization proposed in 1869 was probably Kohner.

16. Philippson, I, 377–378. The appeal sent out by the provisional board to the Jewish communities in September 1869 confidently proclaimed: "The sorrowful days, thank God, have passed for German Israelites." (*AZJ,* 1869, p. 717.)

17. *AZJ,* 1870, pp. 823–825, 857–861, 873–874, 893, 928, 959; 1871, p. 48; *Israelit,* 1870, pp. 681–682, 1871, p. 39.

18. *AZJ,* 1871, p. 453.

19. *AZJ,* 1871, pp. 178–180, 195–196, 216–217, 380–382, 392. See especially the scathing rejoinder by Abraham Geiger published as an appendix to his *Das Judenthum und seine Geschichte,* III (Breslau, 1871), 161–200. In discussing the uproar, the Church's official organ, the *Neue Evangelische Kirchenzeitung,* pointedly addressed German Jewry as an oriental nation. Infuriated, Geiger prophetically warned, "How would it be, if in fact this eternal harassment would succeed in reawakening a long-buried nationalism, in rekindling the extinguished flame?" (p. 185).

20. *AZJ,* 1871, p. 453.

21. *AZJ,* 1871, pp. 451–454. A few months later, Kohner, or some other

spokesman of the Gemeindebund, repeated this argument with a note of ambivalence that derived from the tension between the ideal and the real. Despite the fundamentally cosmopolitan and universal nature common to both Germans and Jews, a legacy of medieval animosity persisted which succeeded in reducing Jews to the status of second-class citizens. *Das Judenthum und seine Aufgabe im neuen deutschen Reich,* pp. 3–8, 14–16. See also *supra,* p. 17 f. as well as Ludwig Philippson's series of articles, "Skizzen über die Frage: Was Haben die Juden vom Staate zu fordern?" *AZJ,* 1871, Nos. 6, 7, 8, 9, 10, 14, 15, 16, 44, 48, 49.

22. *AZJ,* 1872, p. 324.

23. On April 20, 1871, Kohner told the delegates assembled at Leipzig: "If the attempt to unite the German fatherland has succeeded, so will we succeed to unite Jewry. . . ." (*Ibid.,* 1871, p. 451.) This connection was again asserted in the address which the constituent convention of April 14, 1872, sent to Bismarck: "The unity of the German Reich ripened in us also the idea of a unification, whose purpose is to raise our German coreligionists religiously, socially and culturally." (*Ibid.,* 1872, Beilage to No. 17.)

24. Philippson, I, 17–18; Maurice Freedman, ed., *A Minority in Britain* (London, 1955), pp. 31–32; Kohler, "The Board of Delegates of American Israelites, 1859–1878," *PAJHS,* XXIX (1921), 77–84.

25. *AZJ,* 1869, pp. 325–326, 367–368; 1870, pp. 42–43.

26. *AZJ,* 1870, pp. 26–27. The report on that meeting defined the scope of the Gemeindebund thus: "It does not concern itself with politics or specifically religious questions, but rather with the preservation and organization of the communities, with institutions which could only be established by combining our resources and with uniform regulations for communal affairs."

Philippson, who was a member of the provisional committee, regarded the Gemeindebund as the fulfillment of forty years of personal commitment to the same cause: "For nearly forty years our efforts have been directed to awakening a sense of solidarity, which the Jews lost as a result of the splintering and isolation of their communities. Its absence allowed them to limit their interests to the purview of their own large or small communities, so that they became entirely incapable of pursuing a common effort or project" (p. 27).

27. Jacobsohn, *Der Deutsch-Israelitische Gemeindebund,* p. 18; *AZJ,* 1872, p. 324; *Denkschrift zur Vertheidigung des einheitlichen Rechtsverbandes der jüdischen Gemeinden in Deutschland,* pp. 15–16; *MDIGB,* No. 2, pp. 19–26; No. 3, pp. 58–59.

28. *JHGA,* M1/21. Recently Uriel Tal has suggested that Reform Jewry's opposition to the *Austrittsgesetz* must be viewed against the background of the Kulturkampf. Only initially did Reform Jews applaud the attack against an institution which they regarded as the embodiment of medievalism. But with German liberals stressing the Lutheran character of the German state and becoming increasingly intolerant of all non-Protestant minorities, Reform Jewry had second thoughts. The campaign to weaken the principle of compulsory membership suddenly appeared as a direct assault against the Jewish community. My only addition to this interpretation is that the determination to prevent communal disintegration was already one of the major reasons behind the formation of the Gemeindebund. See Tal, "The 'Kulturkampf,' " pp.

208–244; *idem, Christians and Jews in the 'Second Reich'* (*1870–1914*) (Hebrew) (Jerusalem, 1969), pp. 53–82.

29. *AZJ*, 1872, p. 324; 1876, p. 171.

30. Jacobsohn, *Der Deutsch-Israelitische Gemeindebund*, pp. 31–33.

31. *AZJ*, 1873, p. 696; 1879, p. 326; *MDIGB*, No. 37, pp. 9–11. *Supra*, pp. 18–19. The *Statistisches Jahrbuch des Deutsch-Israelitischer Gemeindebund* (Berlin, 1885) estimates a possible 2,500 Jewish communities in Germany in 1885. (See Vorwort.)

32. Jacobsohn, *Fünfzig Jahre: Erinnerungen aus Amt und Leben* (Berlin, 1912), p. 65; *idem, Der Deutsch-Israelitische Gemeindebund*, p. 3.

33. *Der Deutsch-Israelitische Gemeindebund*, p. 52.

34. *AZJ*, 1872, p. 327; *MDIGB*, No. 4, p. 10. See also the fifty-year history of the Gemeindebund in JHGA, M1/9, p. 2. The Berlin member seems to have dropped out sometime after 1872 to be replaced by Jacob Nachod of Leipzig. Originally the founders of the Gemeindebund had opened the membership to Jewish communities from German-speaking Austria as well, but at a meeting on August 24, 1873, the board limited membership to the Reich, the decisive reason being that the inclusion of Austrian Jewish communities would make the acquisition of corporate status for the Gemeindebund from the Saxon government unlikely. (*AZJ*, 1872, p. 325; *MDIGB*, No. 1, p. 14.)

35. Jacobsohn, *Der Deutsch-Israelitische Gemeindebund*, pp. 28–33, 37; *idem, Fünfzig Jahre*, pp. 65–66. Kohner was born in Bohemia in 1818. His traditional Jewish education as a child made him a knowledgeable Jew, although one committed enthusiastically to the reform of Judaism. Since 1868 he had served as president of the Jewish Community of Leipzig and in 1874 he became the first Jewish member of the town council. (*AZJ*, 1877, pp. 240–241; Jacobsohn, *Fünfzig Jahre*, p. 65.)

36. *MDIGB*, No. 4, pp. 10, 18; *AZJ*, 1877, pp. 215, 570–571, 651.

37. *MDIGB*, No. 4, p. 26; Jacobsohn, *Fünfzig Jahre*, p. 68. Born in 1814, Nachod attended the Samsonschule in Wolfenbüttel, one of the modern Jewish parochial schools. He was the partner of a Leipzig business firm which he helped to enlarge to international dimensions. In 1869 he became the vice-president of the Leipzig Jewish Community, and in 1877, its president. See *Gedenkblätter an Jacob Nachod*, hrsg. DIGB (Berlin, 1882), pp. 37–38.

38. Alphonse Levy, *Geschichte der Juden in Sachsen* (Berlin, 1900), pp. 82–83, 93, 105. By 1872–73 the Kingdom of Saxony had only 3,346 Jews. See Engelbert, p. 70; *AZJ*, 1873, p. 697.

39. *AZJ*, 1871, p. 455; *MDIGB*, No. 1, p. 2; No. 3, p. 7.

40. *MDIGB*, No. 4, pp. 3–4.

41. *MDIGB*, No. 11, pp. 2–6. In his memoirs Jacobsohn wrote: "The continuation of the Bund with its seat in Berlin is due solely to the indefatigable efforts of Nachod." (*Fünfzig Jahre*, p. 70. See *infra*, ch. 3.)

42. *AZJ*, 1872, pp. 705–708.

43. *AZJ*, 1878, p. 20.

44. See, for example, the illuminating discussion at the eleventh national convention of the Gemeindebund in 1909 on a suggested draft for the reorganization of Prussian Jewry drawn up by a mixed commission from the Gemeindebund and the Verband der deutschen Juden to be submitted to the

Prussian government. (*MDIGB*, No. 74, pp. 16–52.) At the end of the proceedings the Gemeindetag adopted a resolution which asked the commission to rewrite just about the whole draft, because the present version infringed extensively on the autonomy of the local community: "In regard to the organization of the Jewish communities of Prussia, it is only possible to create an additional organization above the local or district community insofar as it is needed for the formation and maintenance of district communities as well as for the formation of pension funds. To form a regional or state organization of communities is possible only as long as the autonomy of the community will not be infringed upon." (*Ibid.*, p. 99.)

Another draft was never forthcoming. (*Ibid.*, No. 82, p. 10.)

45. *MDIGB*, No. 22, p. 4; No. 33, p. 5; No. 37, pp. 9–11. By 1912 the membership had risen to more than 1,100 communities. (*Ibid.*, No. 82, p. 3.)

46. Felix Theilhaber, *Der Untergang der deutschen Juden* (2nd ed.; Berlin, 1921), p. 43; Jacob Picard, "Childhood in the Village," *LBIYB*, IV (1959), 285–289. See also the sketches of Jewish life in the village by Hermann Schwab, *Jewish Rural Communities in Germany* (London, 1956).

47. *Israelit*, 1869, pp. 577–581; 1870, p. 1; 1871, pp. 331–332, 344–346; Eliav, *Hildesheimer Briefe*, pp. 107, 156. On the allegiance of the *Israelit*, see Eliav, "Der *Israelit* und Erez Israel im 19. Jahrhundert," *BLBI*, VIII (1965), 275–276.

48. *Israelit*, 1872, pp. 433–434, 481–482; *AZJ*, 1872, *Beilage* to No. 17. The objectionable passage read: "Most august Prince, you have triumphantly undertaken to fight against the internal enemy with the same energy [with which you fought for German unity]. Also in this battle we stand, as far as the matter concerns us, on your side and that of the Reich. For it was precisely the former omnipotence of this foe under which many generations of our coreligionists suffered persecution, oppression and expulsion."

49. *AZJ*, 1870, pp. 78–80, 86–88, 166–170; 1872, p. 324; Hollenscher, pp. 108–110.

50. *Israelit*, 1872, p. 458.

51. See *supra*, introduction.

52. *MDIGB*, No. 2, pp. 19–26.

53. Jacobsohn, *Der Deutsch-Israelitische Gemeindebund*, p. 18.

54. A series of six articles entitled "Die Ursachen der Lebensunfähigkeit des deutsch-israelitischen Gemeindebundes," *Israelit*, 1877, Nos. 45, 46, 47, 48, 49, 50.

55. *Israelit*, 1878, p. 88. In this concluding article, Lehmann had raised the question of what was actually possible.

56. Besides the emerging disagreement between Hirsch and Hildesheimer on cooperation with the Gemeindebund, the two men differed sharply on the nature of *jüdische Wissenschaft*. Hirsch did not support Hildesheimer's Berlin *Rabbinerseminar*. (Eliav, *Hildesheimer Briefe*, pp. 207–219.)

57. *Jüdische Presse*, 1882, pp. 121, 197; 1884, pp. 23–24.

58. *MVZADA*, 1901, pp. 139–140, 148–151; *AZJ*, 1892, *Beilage* to No. 49, p. 1; Eliav, *Hildesheimer Briefe*, p. 203.

59. Eliav, *Hildesheimer Briefe*, p. 217; *AZJ*, 1892, pp. 158–159.

60. *MDIGB*, No. 16, p. 3. This obituary of David Honigmann, a Posen-

born Breslau resident, a disciple of Abraham Geiger and one of the founders of the Gemeindebund, cites a letter he wrote to Kohner in March 1872 concerning the significance of their enterprise.

In his seminal study of German anti-Semitism during the Second Reich, Tal has suggested in passing that many assimilated and alienated Jews shared the antagonism of German liberals toward Jewish efforts to preserve institutional separateness and that this viewpoint militated against the formation of an organization like the DIGB. (Tal, *Christians and Jews*, pp. 32–33.) As we shall see, this sentiment was indeed widespread and operated as a constant factor in German Jewish life. But its direct impact on the fate of the DIGB was probably minimal, because the decision to affiliate a community or not lay solely with men active in communal affairs. Their ambivalence toward the DIGB, I believe, can best be accounted for by the rampant parochialism of the German Jewish scene.

61. Johannes Ziekursch, *Politische Geschichte des neuen deutschen Kaiserreiches*, II (Frankfurt a.M., 1927), 299–303.

62. Toury, *Die politischen Orientierungen der Juden in Deutschland* (Tübingen, 1966), pp. 131–140. The major cause for concern was Prussia's long record of discrimination. In December 1868 Ludwig Philippson sent an appeal to Bismarck for the equal appointment of Jews as judges and teachers in the institutions of higher learning. Toward the end he added: "Many of my coreligionists in southern Germany are frightened by the unification of southern Germany with the North German Bund and could easily be pushed into opposing it, because of the continued denial in Prussia of that which we feel justified to claim as our constitutional right." (*AZJ*, 1869, p. 122.)

The same idea was repeated in a letter from a Jew in Württemberg a year later. (*Ibid.*, 1871, p. 43.)

63. Massing, chs. 1, 2, and 3; pp. 278–287; Kurt Wawrzinek, "Die Entstehung der deutschen Antisemitenparteien (1873–1890)," *Historische Studien*, CLXVIII (1927), chs. 2, 3, and 4; Pulzer, chs. 10 and 11; Tal, "Anti-Semitism in the Second German Reich," ch. 1. See also Fritz Stern's subtle analysis of Junker reactions to the rapid economic boom and bust which swept Germany in the aftermath of the Franco-Prussian War. Angered by their losses and plagued by feelings of guilt over having betrayed their own pre-capitalistic ethos, the Junkers succumbed to a virulent anti-Semitism which offered them the "means to regain a good conscience." Fritz Stern, "Money, Morals, and the Pillars of Bismarck's Society," *Central European History*, III (1970), 49–72. The quotation is on p. 64.

64. Stern, *The Politics of Cultural Despair*, pp. 67–70, 91–94.

65. Alex Bein, "Modern Anti-Semitism and Its Place in the History of the Jewish Question," in *Between East and West*, ed. by A. Altmann (London, 1958), pp. 164–167, 173–178. The various Treitschke essays and the most important Jewish responses are republished in Boehlich, *Der Berliner Antisemitismusstreit*.

66. JHGA, M1/15. Tal, "Anti-Semitism in the Second German Reich," p. 38; Auerbach, *Das Judenthum und seine Bekenner*, pp. 32–36; Michael Meyer, "Great Debate on Anti-Semitism: Jewish Reaction to New Hostility in Germany, 1879–1881," *LBIYB*, XI (1966), 167–170. Treitschke had been the

first to alert his countrymen to the annual influx of "pants-selling" Polish Jews, whose children and grandchildren would dominate the stock market and press. (Boehlich, pp. 9, 35.) He was immediately answered by S. Neumann in a statistical study limited to the old provinces of Prussia. Neumann argued that the rate of Jewish immigration during the period from 1822 to 1871 was proportionate to the general rate of immigration. However, Jewish emigration far exceeded proportionately the rate of general emigration, thus sharply reducing the rate of growth of Prussian Jewry. For example, from 1840 to 1871 the general population rose from 14,928,501 to 20,286,633. But emigration topped immigration by 432,287, or 2.9 percent of the total population in 1840. During the same period the Jewish population rose from 194,558 to 272,678. But Jewish emigration exceeded Jewish immigration by 35,106, or 18 percent of the Jewish population in 1840. See *Die Fabel von der jüdischen Masseneinwanderung* (Berlin, 1880), p. 9, and Anhang.

The ratio of foreign-born Jews to the Jewish population of Germany rose steadily from 1880 to 1910, though not equally in all parts of the country:

	Jewish Population		Foreign-Born		Percent	
	1880	*1910*	*1880*	*1910*	*1880*	*1910*
Reich	561,612	615,021	15,000	78,746	2.7	12.8
Prussia	363,790	415,926	10,000	48,166	2.7	11.6
Berlin	53,916	143,965	2,954	21,683	5.5	15.1
Saxony	6,516	17,578	1,000	10,378	15.3	59.0
Munich	4,144	11,083	367	3,030	8.9	27.3
Leipzig	3,265	9,434	331	6,376	10.1	67.6
Dresden	2,280	3,734	299	1,985	13.1	53.2

(S. Adler-Rudel, *Ostjuden in Deutschland 1880–1940* [Tübingen, 1959], p. 164.)

67. Auerbach, *Das Judenthum und seine Bekenner*, pp. 36–39; Wawrzinek, pp. 34–35. See also the perceptive analysis by Tal, *Christians and Jews*, pp. 24–25.

68. Auerbach, *Das Judenthum und seine Bekenner*, pp. 46–47; Ziekursch, I, 60–63.

69. Wawrzinek, p. 38. Wawrzinek dismisses as unfounded the grave doubts expressed by Jöhlinger concerning the authenticity of many of the signatures. (Otto Jöhlinger, *Bismarck und die Juden* [Berlin, 1921], pp. 42–43.)

70. Philippson, II, 29. The anti-Semites finally succeeded in having four Jews convicted as accomplices in the burning of the Neustettin synagogue. The main offender was never found. A second trial was ordered by the Reichsgericht (Supreme Court) on a minute procedural infraction, and in March 1884 the four were at last acquitted. (Auerbach, *Das Judenthum und seine Bekenner*, pp. 51–58.)

71. *MDIGB*, No. 3, pp. 52–53.

72. The statutes of 1872 read: "Wahrnehmung aller gemeinsamen Angele-

genheiten in Bezug auf die öffentliche Rechtsstellung der jüdischen Religion und ihrer Bekenner in dem deutschen Staaten." (*AZJ*, 1872, p. 324.)

The statutes of 1877 read: "Wahrnehmung aller gemeinsamen Angelegenheiten in Bezug auf die rechtliche und sociale Stellung der Bekenner der jüdischen Religion und Abwehr von Angriffen gegen dieselben." (Jacobsohn, *Die Deutsch-Israelitische Gemeindebund*, p. 56.)

73. Heinrich Henkel, *Strafverfahrensrecht: Ein Lehrbuch* (Stuttgart and Cologne, 1953), pp. 44–45, 241–242, 474–477; Franz von Liszt, "Strafrecht und Strafprozessrecht," in *Systematische Rechtswissenschaft*, ed. by Paul Hinneberg; Vol. VIII of Part Two of *Die Kultur der Gegenwart* (Berlin and Leipzig, 1906), pp. 223–233; Ernst Carsten, *Die Geschichte der Staatsanwaltschaft in Deutschland bis zur Gegenwart* (Breslau, 1932), pp. 1–57.

74. *MDIGB*, No. 5, pp. 2, 5–7, 10, 20, 23; JHGA, M1/8, M1/13, M1/14; Lehmann, pp. 219–220.

75. JHGA, M1/16; *MDIGB*, No. 3, pp. 56–57; *AZJ*, 1876, pp. 53, and 691. See Tal, *Christians and Jews*, p. 188, note.

76. Lehmann, p. 219.

77. *MDIGB*, No. 6, pp. 13–15. In June 1878 the board composed a complaint to the Saxon Minister of Justice over an anti-Semitic article in the *Allgemeine Evangelisch-Lutherische Kirchenzeitung*, ed. by C. H. Luthardt, a professor of theology at the University of Leipzig. But it was never sent! (JHGA, M1/14.)

78. Lehmann, pp. 218–219.

79. *MDIGB*, No. 6, p. 13; No. 9, pp. 30, 38; JHGA, M1/8, Vol. I. Jacobsohn, *Der Deutsch-Israelitische Gemeindebund*, p. 40.

80. JHGA, M1/13.

81. *MDIGB*, No. 9, pp. 32–33. The board even began in February 1881, in cooperation with the board of the Berlin Jewish Community, to arrange for an official audience with Bismarck.

82. JHGA, M1/8, Vol. I.

83. *MDIGB*, No. 9, pp. 1, 22–23, 36–39.

84. See *infra*, pp. 48–52.

85. *MDIGB*, No. 10, p. 20. At the beginning of the nineteenth century Leopold Zunz, the pioneer of *jüdische Wissenschaft* in Germany, had forthrightly declared that the government would extend emancipation to the Jews only to the extent that it possessed a proper understanding of Judaism. To provide the government with that information was one of the major motives behind Zunz's work. See Leopold Zunz, "Etwas über die rabbinische Literatur" (1818); in *Gesammelte Schriften* (Berlin, 1875), I, 4–5. This connection was most vigorously asserted in 1832 in his introduction to *Die Gottesdienstlichen Vorträge der Juden*, in *ibid.*, pp. 34–35. See also Ismar Schorsch, "Moritz Güdemann: Rabbi, Historian and Apologist," *LBIYB*, XI (1966), 54–55. The consistent experience of anti-Semitism in Germany throughout the nineteenth century in one form or another never permitted the practice of *jüdische Wissenschaft* to be wholly free of apologetic overtones.

86. *Hat das Judentum dem Wucherunwesen Vorschub geleistet?* hrsg. DIGB (Leipzig, 1879); JHGA, M1/14; AHW/865a; *AZJ*, 1879, pp. 405–406; *Israelit*, 1879, pp. 361–363. A more ambitious project of the same year was the

publishing of a *Lessing-Mendelssohn Gedenkbuch* to commemorate the 150th birthday of both men: "To give evidence of our gratitude for the work of these men, to revive their memory and through the presentation of their ideas and deeds to encourage and fortify the present generation in the still unfinished battle against religious hatred and intolerance of every sort—that is the objective of this book. . . ." (*Lessing-Mendelssohn Gedenkbuch*, hrsg. DIGB [Leipzig, 1879], Vorwort, p. iii.)

87. *AZJ*, 1877, pp. 31, 103, 809; *MDIGB*, No. 5, p. 29. In the debate on November 20 and 22, 1880, in the Prussian lower house, Stoecker declared Schleiden to be a Jew. When corrected by other deputies, he retorted, "Well, then he is worse than a Jew." (Auerbach, *Das Judenthum und seine Bekenner*, p. 41.)

88. *AZJ*, 1891, pp. 161–163, 173–174; M. Brann, "Verzeichniss der Schriften David Kaufmanns," in *Gedenkbuch zur Erinnerung an David Kaufmann*, ed. by M. Brann et al. (Breslau, 1900), pp. lxii, lxxiii. The article remained as relevant in 1891 as when it was first written.

89. JHGA, M1/23; AHW/865a; *MDIGB*, No. 16, pp. 19–21; *AZJ*, 1885, pp. 717–718. In a letter to Kristeller, dated July 11, 1885, Stobbe reacted to the idea of the commission. He thought the objective too limited and doubted whether much would be gained by getting scholars to search solely for sources of Jewish history. He suggested rather that all German scholars working in German history be advised that when they discover, in the course of their work, a source dealing with Jewish history, they should forward it to the commission. Stobbe urged the creation of a journal in which such items could be published, and he thought that the honorarium ought to be substantial in order to attract contributions. (JHGA, M1/23.)

90. *MDIGB*, No. 21, p. 15.

91. *Ibid.*, pp. 14–18.

92. Boehlich, pp. 7–14, 62–65, 95; Meyer, "Great Debate on Anti-Semitism," pp. 148–150. See also Reuwen Michael, "Graetz contra Treitschke," *BLBI*, IV (1961), 301–322.

93. Josef Meisel, "Historical Commission for the History of the Jews in Germany" (Hebrew), *Zion*, XIX (1954), 171–172; *MDIGB*, No. 21, p. 14. This disdain for the current theologically oriented generation of Jewish historians was again articulated in 1889 in a scathing review by Ludwig Geiger in the commission's *Zeitschrift* of a major work by Moritz Güdemann, one of Graetz's students, on the social history of German Jewry in the fourteenth and fifteenth centuries. Unlike the controversy over Graetz, this one was public, but the issue was the same. (Schorsch, "Moritz Güdemann," pp. 58–60.)

94. JHGA, M1/23.

95. *Zeitschrift für die Geschichte der Juden in Deutschland*, V, 409; *Jüdische Presse*, 1889, pp. 493–494, 505–506, 521–522; Meisel, 171–172; Meyer, "Great Debate on Anti-Semitism," pp. 157–159; Boehlich, p. 253.

96. Aside from the five volumes of its *Zeitschrift* which contain a variety of documents and essays dealing with German Jewish history, the commission sponsored such works as:

a) Julius Aronius, *Regesten zur Geschichte der Juden im fränkischen und deutschen Reiche bis zum Jahre 1273* (Berlin, 1902).

b) Robert Hoeniger, *Das Judenschreinsbuch der Laurenzpfarre zu Köln* (Berlin, 1888).

c) A. Neubauer and Moritz Stein, *Hebräische Berichte über die Judenverfolgungen während der Kreuzzüge* (Berlin, 1892).

d) Siegmund Salfeld, *Das Martyrologium der Nürnberger Memorbuches* (Berlin, 1898).

97. *MDIGB*, No. 6, pp. 13–17.

98. Ludwig Jacobowski, *Werther, der Jude* (2nd ed.; Berlin, 1893). Jacobowski's portrayal is suffused with irony, for Leo Wolff, the righteous intellectual, is quite capable of cruel selfishness in the treatment of his adoring, simple Christian girlfriend. He is driven to conquer her by fraternity pressures, but by the time she discovers her pregnancy, his attention has shifted to the far more sophisticated wife of his former Christian Gymnasium teacher. Bewildered and depressed, she commits suicide. The accuser stands condemned by his own principles!

On the widespread phenomenon of self-criticism, see Sterling, "Jewish Reactions to Jew-Hatred in the First Half of the Nineteenth Century," *LBIYB*, III (1958), 110; Emanuel Schreiber, *Die Selbstkritik der Juden* (Leipzig, [ca. 1881]). This is an entire anthology of self-criticism intended to show that in the nineteenth century Jewish leaders still continued to castigate and exhort in the prophetic spirit. See pp. vii–xvi. Another expression of this self-criticism was the extent to which Jews read the novels of Felix Dahn and Gustav Freytag with their stereotypes of the puny, cowardly, alien, treacherous Jew, and the good Jew who had become totally German and non-Jewish. See Mosse, "The Image of the Jew in German Popular Culture: Felix Dahn and Gustav Freytag," *LBIYB*, II (1957), 226–227.

99. *MDIGB*, No. 9, pp. 40–43. On February 5, 1881, a correspondent from Neustadt wrote the board that Jews had far more to fear from their own indiscretions than from the anti-Semitic petitions: ". . . thus, according to my opinion, the best way lies in influencing the sizeable Jewish press, which derides the institutions of other religions or rudely attacks individuals and thereby intensifies the passions [still further]. The Christian population will never love us; that's very clear to me. But if the Jewish population would proceed modestly, it would never lack the necessary respect, and the tirades of individual fanatics would never win such approval as is now unfortunately the case." (JHGA, M1/15.)

100. *MDIGB*, No. 9, pp. 24–25; JHGA, M1/8, Vol. I. In 1879 the board had considered sending out a similar declaration that would have been read from all pulpits on the High Holidays. It discarded the idea because such a statement would only provide grist for the anti-Semites. (*MDIGB*, No. 6, pp. 11–17.)

101. *MDIGB*, No. 3, pp. 52–53. It finally gained incorporation in 1898. (*Ibid.*, No. 82, p. 10.)

102. *MDIGB*, No. 3, pp. 52–55; No. 4, p. 31; JHGA, M1/5.

103. JHGA, M1/5.

104. *MDIGB*, No. 10, p. 11.

105. *Gedenkblätter an Jacob Nachod*, p. 43; Jacobsohn, *Fünfzig Jahre*, p. 70; JHGA, M1/9.

106. On the identity of Waldegg, see Wawrzinek, p. 46, n. 2.

107. Tal, *Christians and Jews*, p. 195, n. 32; *MVZADA*, 1894, pp. 169–171; Richard von Grumbkow, *Die Judenfrage vor Gericht* (Dresden, 1883), Vorwort.

108. Wawrzinek, pp. 46–48; Tal, "Anti-Semitism in the Second German Reich," pp. 34–37.

109. Wawrzinek, pp. 48–49; Lehmann, p. 7.

110. Levy, p. 108.

111. See the statistics cited *supra*, p. 224.

112. Philippson, II, 132.

113. Tal, "Anti-Semitism in the Second German Reich," pp. 130–132.

114. *MVZADA*, 1893, pp. 273, 415–416.

115. Tal, "Anti-Semitism in the Second German Reich," p. 130.

116. Recent students of German anti-Semitism agree that Bismarck, though opposed to the crude tactics and unconstitutional objectives of the anti-Semites, was quite willing to use the anti-Semitic parties as allies in his battle against the Progressives. (Jöhlinger, p. 112; Wawrzinek, pp. 42–43; Massing, pp. 42–43.)

117. *MDIGB*, No. 11, pp. 2–3; JHGA, M1/8, Vol. I. At the Berlin convention of 1882 all official involvement with *Abwehr* was dropped. "We omitted from the first paragraph of the old statutes the one which dealt with defense against attack. This was necessary, because otherwise we would have clashed with the law [governing the right to form] an organization, which does not allow such political discussions without police surveillance." (*MDIGB*, No. 10, p. 18.)

Thereafter the DIGB no longer submitted complaints to public prosecutors, although it stood ready to assist if called upon. This was the case in the state's prosecution of the editor of the *Westfälischer Merkur* in 1883 for having printed excerpts from the *Judenspiegel*, an anti-Semitic compilation of the same year put together by a converted Polish Jew which, among other charges, accused Jews of regarding the murder of a non-Jewish girl as a sacrifice pleasing to God. Upon request, the DIGB helped to provide the prosecutor with the necessary technical expertise. To no avail. The editor was acquitted. The court held that it had not been established that the quotations cited by the *Judenspiegel* were drawn verbatim from the *Shulhan Arukh* or that the *Shulhan Arukh* was still considered binding by all of contemporary Jewry. Secondly, despite the incendiary nature of the article, it had not been proven that by quoting this material he might incite anti-Jewish riots. In fact, none had occurred. (JHGA, M1/17; *AZJ*, 1884, pp. 793–796.)

CHAPTER 2
CONTINUED AMBIVALENCE:
THE 1880's

1. Pulzer, pp. 88–102; Massing, pp. 21–47, 173–174; Walter Frank, *Hofprediger Adolf Stoecker und die christlich-soziale Bewegung* (2nd ed.; Ham-

burg, 1935), pp. 70–123, 126. Stoecker had entered the Prussian House of Deputies in 1879, representing an election district in Westphalia. In 1884 he again won the Reichstag seat from Siegen, this time, however, only with the direct help of the local National Liberals. (Frank, pp. 70–71, 103; *AZJ*, 1884, pp. 758–760.)

2. Doris Davidsohn, "Erinnerungen einer deutsches Jüdin," *BLBI*, 1959, p. 202. See also Lehmann, pp. 223–224.

3. Hermann Robinow, "Aus dem Leben eines Hamburger Kaufmanns," ALBI, p. 16. Robinow's French phrases typify the intense attachment to things French in the best circles of Jewish society. Paris was still venerated as the center of elegance. French was often used in daily conversation, especially in the presence of the ever ubiquitous servants. If someone unwittingly began to say something in German that should not really have been heard by the servants, he was quickly reminded *"Pas en présence de la nouvelle fille. . . ."* (Curt Rosenberg, "Jugenderinnerungen," ALBI, pp. 67–68.)

4. Gustav Maier, *Mehr Licht! Ein Wort zur "Judenfrage" an unsere christlichen Mitbürger* (Ulm, 1881), p. 23.

5. *Jüdische Presse*, 1881, p. 363; 1882, pp. 67–68; *AZJ*, 1882, p. 165; 1884, pp. 148–149, 283–285, 663–666; 1889, p. 474; 1890, pp. 457–458.

6. Berthold Auerbach, *Briefe an seinen Freund Jakob Auerbach*, II (Frankfurt a.M., 1884), pp. 395, 421, 442, 452, 456, 458, 466.

7. *Ibid.*, pp. 438–439; *Jüdische Presse*, 1882, p. 68.

8. Boehlich, p. 150.

9. Hermann Cohen, *Jüdische Schriften*, I (Berlin, 1924), introduction by Franz Rosenzweig, pp. XX–XXI, XXXVI.

10. Emil Herz, *Before the Fury* (New York, 1966), p. 159.

11. Fritz Stern, "Gold and Iron: The Collaboration and Friendship of Gerson Bleichröder and Otto von Bismarck," *American Historical Review*, LXXV (1969), 37–46.

12. Jöhlinger, pp. 152–153; see especially pp. 141–153; also Frank, pp. 85–100; Massing, pp. 38–39.

13. L. Auerbach, *Das Judenthum und seine Bekenner*, p. 105.

14. Albert Lewkowitz, *Das Judentum und die geistigen Strömungen des 19. Jahrhunderts* (Breslau, 1935), p. 90; JHGA, INV/1409 (690); Lazarus, *Aus meiner Jugend* (Frankfurt a.M., 1913), pp. 1, 16, 41–45, 52–53; Josef Wohlgemuth, *Moritz Lazarus: Ein Nachruf*, Separatabdruck aus der *Jüdische Presse* (Berlin, 1903), pp. 7–12; David Baumgardt, "The Ethics of Lazarus and Steinthal," *LBIYB*, II (1957), 210; *AZJ*, 1872, pp. 1007, 1023, 1029; D. Philipson, pp. 292, 308, 382, 486. See also now the recent edition of letters thoroughly annotated and learnedly introduced by Ingrid Belke, *Moritz Lazarus und Heymann Steinthal: Die Begründer der Völkerpsychologie in ihren Briefen* (Tübingen, 1971).

15. Moritz Lazarus, *Treu und Frei: Gesammelte Reden und Vorträge über Juden und Judenthum* (Leipzig, 1887), pp. 118–119.

16. *Ibid.*, p. 69.

17. *Ibid.*, p. 71; see especially pp. 57–70; also Lewkowitz, p. 93. Hermann Cohen directed much of his aforementioned essay against Treitschke against Lazarus as well. For instance, his views on what constituted a nation were

much closer to those of Treitschke than Lazarus: "Instead of 'the *subjective* view of the members of a nation who regard themselves collectively as a nation,' I prefer the *objective faith* stemming from a common religious foundation as a *valuable criterion for a modern civilized nation.* Thereby one gains an *instrument* for the appropriation of those other conditions (which Lazarus spoke of, such as ancestry, speech, political life, etc.), each one of which alone is insufficient for the empirical concept of nationality. Now the subjective view whereby one 'belongs' to a nation becomes objective; it has now a tangible thing by which it can energetically manifest and prove itself" (Boehlich, p. 151).

18. Belke, p. 153.
19. Lazarus, *Treu und Frei,* p. 130; *AZJ,* 1880, pp. 825–826.
20. Lazarus, *Treu und Frei,* p. 139; see especially pp. 134–139.
21. *Ibid.,* pp. 118–123.
22. *Ibid.,* pp. 117, 120–121, 128; *AZJ,* 1880, pp. 825–826.
23. Lazarus, *Treu und Frei,* p. 154; see also pp. 91–93. Again Cohen disagreed fundamentally with Lazarus. Like Treitschke, he repudiated the contention that diversity enriched national life. Specifically, Cohen was willing to admit that the demands for racial unity embodied a healthy national instinct. Given the proper atmosphere, intermarriage would eventually obliterate all distinctive Jewish racial characteristics. (Boehlich, p. 144.) But Cohen did not speak for the organized Jewish community. Its spokesmen subjected his concessions to severe criticism. They sensed that he had intentionally underplayed the differences dividing Jews and Christians and thereby complicated the problem of maintaining Jewish identity. (H. Cohen, I, XXXVI; II, 470–471.) See also Lazarus' reference to this earlier fundamental clash in a poignant letter to Sigmund Maybaum, the Liberal rabbi of Berlin, in December 1899, on the occasion of a second head-on collision between Cohen and Lazarus. (Belke, pp. 228–232.)
24. Boehlich, pp. 226–227.
25. Lazarus, *Treu und Frei,* pp. 146–148; *Israelit,* 1872, p. 270. Der Hilfsverein für jüdischen Studirende in Berlin had been founded in 1841 by 43 Jewish students and 35 business friends, because stipends to the University of Berlin were available only to Christian students. By 1891 it had assisted 1,403 students with grants totaling 41,000 marks. (*AZJ,* 1891, p. 224.)
26. *AZJ,* 1881, pp. 239–240; *Israelit,* 1881, pp. 341–343.
27. MDIGB, No. 9, p. 26. Nachod had met with the leaders of the committee some time before January 4, 1881. (Eliav, *Hildesheimer Briefe,* pp. 177, 245.) Although Hildesheimer was not at all pleased with Lazarus' approval of Mommsen's essay, he agreed to help circulate copies of the two speeches delivered by Lazarus in December of 1880. Julius Bleichröder asked Lazarus whether he really intended to distribute copies of Mommsen's essay, despite its unfavorable conclusion. Lazarus answered: "Indeed I fervently hope that the Mommsen pamphlet, which is decidedly favorable to us on the *principal issue,* will be as widely distributed as possible. If at the end he gives us some advice, *we alone* shall consider whether to follow it and to what extent." (Belke, p. 154. For the full text of these two letters, see the copies of the originals in the ALBI.)

28. *AZJ*, 1881, p. 675; 1883, p. 82; Lazarus, *Treu und Frei*, p. 318. Lazarus sent a copy of his *Treu und Frei* to Crown Prince Frederick William with whom he enjoyed a personal relationship. (Belke, pp. XXXIX, 175.)

29. *Israelitische Wochenschrift*, 1882, pp. 378, 387. *An Herrn Prof. Dr. Lazarus*, von einem deutschen Juden (2nd ed.; Magdeburg, 1887), p. 4; *Jüdische Presse*, 1889, p. 338; *Im Deutschen Reich*, 1903, p. 3; Eugen Fuchs, *Um Deutschtum und Judentum* (Frankfurt a.M., 1919), p. 90; Paul Rieger, *Ein Vierteljahrhundert im Kampf um das Recht und die Zukunft der deutschen Juden* (Berlin, 1918), p. 8.

30. *AZJ*, 1880, pp. 721–723. A similar experience was related by Philippson in *AZJ*, 1884, p. 344. The date is not given, but again he called for representatives of the Jewish communities to meet to decide on a common plan of attack. This time the Berlin Board opposed him actively.

31. *Ibid.*, 1881, p. 240.

32. *Verhandlungen und Beschlüsse der Rabbiner Versammlung zu Berlin am 4. und 5. Juni 1884* (Berlin, 1885), p. 4.

33. See *supra*, ch. 1.

34. S. Leon, *Unser heutiges Judenthum: Eine Selbstkritik* (Berlin, 1890), p. 15.

35. See *supra*, introduction. The following is a table of Jewish and mixed marriages in Prussia from 1875 to 1903. It is based upon statistics compiled by the Prussian Bureau of Statistics. While the number of marriages between Jewish partners never rose above the 2,675 recorded in 1875 and in most years was several hundred lower, the number of mixed marriages over the long run steadily increased.

Year	Jewish Marriages	Mixed Marriages
1875	2,675	277
1880	2,390	228
1885	2,256	248
1890	2,513	327
1895	2,502	297
1900	2,560	474
1903	2,530	493

(M. Samter, *Judentaufen im neunzehnten Jahrhundert* [Berlin, 1906], p. 149.)

36. N. M. Gelber, "The Berlin Congress of 1878," *LBIYB*, V (1960), 221–247.

37. See also David S. Landes, "The Bleichröder Bank: An Interim Report," *LBIYB*, V (1960), 210–216.

38. B. Auerbach, II, 440.

39. *Ibid.*, II, 438–441. Ignaz Döllinger, one of Germany's foremost Catholic scholars and an authority on Church history and law, chose the birthday of Bavaria's king to address the Royal Academy of Sciences in Munich on the recent history of the Jewish people, an address in which he accused Christian-

ity of the tragedy of medieval Jewish history. Auerbach expressed his personal gratitude to Döllinger in a letter. See *AZJ*, 1881, p. 555.

40. *AZJ*, 1890, pp. 417–418. See also *ibid.*, 1875, pp. 416–418, 433–435; 1876, pp. 259–262; 1877, pp. 410–411; 1878, pp. 307–309; 1879, pp. 355–356; 1880, p. 131; 1881, pp. 519–521, 538–540; *Israelit*, 1876, pp. 933–934, 958–960; 1880, pp. 55–58, 69–71, 883–884, 923–924.

41. Boehlich, pp. 8–9, 57–60; *MDIGB*, No. 10, p. 8; Lazarus, *Treu und Frei*, pp. 120, 136. Even Graetz in his first response to Treitschke stressed the small size of the movement. (Boehlich, p. 26.) So did Philippson. (*AZJ*, 1882, pp. 101, 713–715.) See also Ludwig Bamberger's comments about the self-deception of educated Jews regarding the antipathy against their integration (Boehlich, pp. 178–179.)

42. B. Auerbach, II, p. 439; *Jüdische Presse*, 1893, pp. 49–50; *AZJ*, 1882, pp. 165–167; Lehmann, p. 108; Boehlich, p. 178.

43. *AZJ*, 1882, p. 101, 165–167, 681–683. Philippson's undaunted faith in progress was passionately reaffirmed in a long essay entitled "Die fortschreitende Entwickelung," *AZJ*, 1884, Nos. 4, 5, 6, 7, 9, 10, and 11, especially p. 66. On several occasions Philippson diagnosed German anti-Semitism in terms of the generally faction- and class-riven German scene. (*AZJ*, 1878, pp. 369–371; 1879, pp. 65–68.) He also saw it as a Conservative tactic to stay in power. (*Ibid.*, 1883, pp. 627–628; 1884, pp. 693–694.)

44. There is little doubt that countless German Jews continued to be among the most faithful adherents of the dogma of progress. See, for example, the paean by Heymann Steinthal, "Werden die Menschen immer Schlechter?" in *Über Juden und Judenthum* (2nd ed.; Berlin, 1925), pp. 142–147. The anti-Semitic revival likewise did not daunt the faith of men like Adolf Brüll (*Populär-wissenschaftliche Monatsblätter*, 1881, p. 274); Emil Lehmann (*Gesammelte Schriften*, pp. 221–222); and Jacob Nachod (*MDIGB*, No. 10, p. 8). The most outspoken deprecation of contemporary civilization expressed in the 1880's came from Heinrich Graetz, who condemned it as both morally and physically sick. [Graetz] *Briefwechsel einer englischen Dame über Judenthum und Semitismus* (Stuttgart, 1883), pp. 7–12. But Graetz remained a solitary figure. What I am suggesting is merely that this widely shared optimism in the inevitability of progress must easily have led many to diminish the proportions of German anti-Semitism and to conclude that any organized resistance was quite unnecessary. See also Adolf Leschnitzer, *The Magic Background of Modern Anti-Semitism* (New York, 1956), pp. 150–158.

45. See *supra*, ch. 1.

46. Philippson, II, 12.

47. Spiro, "Jugenderinnerungen aus hessischen Judengemeinden," ALBI, pp. 4–5; Hans Rosenberg, *Grosse Depression und Bismarckzeit* (Berlin, 1967), pp. 98–100; Tal, "Anti-Semitism in the Second German Reich," p. 238, n. 81; *idem, Christians and Jews*, p. 191.

48. Emanuel Schreiber, *Grätz's Geschichtsbauerei* (Berlin, 1881), p. 22. Boehlich, pp. 24, 139–140, 253; Lehmann, p. 223; *AZJ*, 1880, p. 20; Meyer, "Great Debate on Anti-Semitism," pp. 157–159.

49. Michael, p. 319.

50. Leon, p. 37.

51. Massing, pp. 51–59; *AZJ*, 1885, pp. 777–779; 1887, p. 503. "In 1887, Boeckel was elected to the Reichstag. He was the first ant-Semitic deputy who remained independent from the Conservative Party, the founder of an autonomous anti-Semitic Reichstag group. . . ." (Massing, p. 88.)

52. *AZJ*, 1877, p. 283; 1888, pp. 739–740; *Israelit*, 1888, p. 1471.

53. JHGA, Kn II/A III 2. I suspect that this memorandum from Breslau was written by Graetz for Kristeller. What has survived in the archives is only the introduction to what appears to have been suggestions for the new statutes of the Gemeindebund. A letter dated February 16, 1882, and following in the files immediately after the memorandum, which was dated January 29, 1882, seems to be Kristeller's answer to Graetz. It is not clear to whom the letter was sent, but Kristeller refers to the suggestions made, and urgently requests his correspondent to attend the deliberations. However, from another Kristeller letter dated March 6, 1882 to someone else, it appears that at the time Graetz was suffering from an eye infection which prevented him from reading and writing, and therefore most likely also from traveling. This circumstantial evidence is buttressed by the fact that the views expressed in the memorandum certainly dovetailed with the views Graetz expressed a year later in his *Briefwechsel einer englischen Dame*, pp. 7–12, 20–26.

54. A. Asch and J. Philippson, "Self-Defence at the Turn of the Century: the Emergence of K.C.," *LBIYB*, III (1958), 121–125, 134–135; Ernest I. Jacob, "Life and Work of B. Jacob (1862–1945)," in *Paul Lazarus Gedenkbuch* (Jerusalem, 1961), p. 94; *Israelitische Wochenschrift*, 1889, pp. 167–170, 177. The enthusiastic response to anti-Semitism among university students upset many contemporary observers. See Maier, pp. 15–16; *AZJ*, 1881, p. 35; 1882, p. 23; 1886, pp. 484–487; 1888, pp. 170, 425; 1890, p. 275. Between 1878 and 1886 the majority of German fraternities were in theory opposed to anti-Semitism, though in practice few accepted Jews. In 1896 the convention of German fraternities officially adopted the policy not to admit Jews. See Asch, *Geschichte des K.C.* (n.p., 1964), pp. 9–10, 56.

55. Belke, pp. LXXIII–LXXX, 164–165, 172–174, 211–224, 229–232; Lewkowitz, pp. 113–114; Lazarus, *The Ethics of Judiasm*, trans. by H. Szold (2 vols.; Philadelphia, 1900–1901). The *Jüdische Presse* repudiated the project because of Lazarus' well-known Reform affiliations. (1884, pp. 191–193)

56. David Hoffmann, *Der Schulchan-Aruch und die Rabbinen über das Verhältnis der Juden zu Andersgläubigen* (2nd ed.; Berlin, 1894), pp. iv–v.

57. *Supra*, p. 66; *AZJ*, 1884, pp. 321–322, 360–363, 405–407, 425, 438; *Verhandlungen und Beschlüsse*, pp. 17–18; Eliav, *Hildesheimer Briefe*, pp. 195, 198–199, 259–260; *Jüdische Presse*, 1884, pp. 227–229, 271–272; *Israelit*, 1884, pp. 783, 843–844.

58. *MDIGB*, No. 23, pp. 1–10; No. 31, pp. 6–9; No. 33, p. 16; Samuel Kristeller, *Liebe deinen Nächsten wie dich selbst* (Berlin, 1891); *idem, Belegstellen zu den Grundsätzen der jüdischen Sittenlehre* (Berlin, 1891). Lazarus, who had drafted the final version himself, was strongly opposed to the marshaling of proof texts. The ultimate validity of these principles, he contended in a long letter to Kristeller, derived from the fact that they accorded entirely with the spirit of contemporary Jewry. (Belke, pp. 175–181.) These *Grundsätze* were still invoked in the more vicious and vulgar polemics of the Wei-

mar era. See, for example, Hermann Strack, *Jüdische Geheimgesetze?* (*Berlin,* *1921*), pp. *15–16.*

59. L. Auerbach, *Das Judenthum und seine Bekenner,* pp. 212–229.

60. *AZJ,* 1896, pp. 361–362.

61. Adolph Brüll, "Der Deutsch-Israelitische Gemeindebund und sein Wirken," *Populär-wissenschaftliche Monatsblätter,* 1888, pp. 121–122. The reference is to Jeremiah 2:28. The decade was punctuated with appeals to organize for self-defense. See *Israelitische Wochenschrift,* 1879, pp. 401–402, 410–411, 442–443; 1880, pp. 375–376; 1882, pp. 9–10, 65–66, 73–74, 377–378; *Israelit,* 1880, pp. 25–26; *AZJ,* 1883, pp. 81–83; 1888, pp. 659–660; *Populärwissenschaftliche Monatsblätter,* 1888, pp. 12–14.

62. Leopold Auerbach, *Das jüdische Obligationenrecht* (Berlin, 1870); Werner Sombart, *The Jews and Modern Capitalism,* trans. by M. Epstein (Glencoe, Ill., 1951), pp. 80, 375. The information on Auerbach is regrettably sparse. On the basis of his legal study and a lecture delivered in 1890 on the significance of the belief in divine revelation for Judaism, I am inclined to identify Auerbach's religious position with that of Frankel and Graetz, though his work on Jewish law seems to have been ignored by that school's *Monatsschrift.* In any event, in that lecture he argued that the revelation at Mount Sinai was the beginning and foundation of Judaism. It was indispensable for a belief in the existence and unity of God, concepts which defy rational or empirical proof. The purpose of Judaism was to teach mankind the meaning of God's unity, creation, and omnipotence. Auerbach warned Jews not to fear enunciating their beliefs or admitting that Judaism rested on dogmas. *Jüdisches Literatur-Blatt* (literary supplement to the *Israelitische Wochenschrift*), 1890, pp. 177–178, 181–182.

63. L. Auerbach, *Das Judenthum und seine Bekenner,* pp. 288–289, 301–304, 331.

64. *Ibid.,* pp. 273–274.

65. *Ibid.,* pp. 425–426.

66. *Ibid.,* pp. 419–420, 450–454. Auerbach was talking only of Prussia and not of Germany, since religion was a matter of state jurisdiction.

67. *AZJ,* 1889, pp. 771–773; *Populär-wissenschaftliche Monatsblätter,* 1889, pp. 286–287.

68. L. Auerbach, *Das Judenthum und seine Bekenner,* pp. 423, 450–451, 456–488.

69. *Israelitische Wochenschrift,* 1889, pp. 379–380; *Israelit,* 1889, pp. 1437–39, 1494–96, 1535–36, 1555–56, 1607–8, 1622–24.

70. The reviews of Auerbach's book appeared in *Jüdische Presse,* 1889, pp. 473–474, 487–488, 513–514, 553–554, 586–587; 1890, pp. 21–22. The earlier proposal appeared in *Jüdische Presse,* 1889, pp. 305–306, 325–326, 337–338, and it was endorsed, pp. 345–346.

71. Reprinted in *Israelit,* 1889, pp. 1439–41. See also *Israelitische Wochenschrift,* 1889, p. 379.

CHAPTER 3
HELP FROM OUTSIDE:
VEREIN ZUR ABWEHR
DES ANTISEMITISMUS,
1891–1914

1. Mendelssohn, *Gasammelte Schriften,* ed. by G. B. Mendelssohn, V (Leipzig, 1844), 640; see especially pp. 639–640.

2. *Supra,* ch. 2.

3. Toury, "Jüdische Parteigänger," *BLBI,* 1961, pp. 327–328; Lazarus, *Treu und Frei,* pp. 159–180.

4. Tal, "Anti-Semitism in the Second German Reich," pp. 3–4; Massing, pp. 87–90; *Antisemiten-Spiegel,* hrsg. *VZADA* (Danzig, 1890), pp. 18–25. The *Antisemiten-Spiegel* put the anti-Semitic vote at 50,000.

5. Massing, pp. 288–294.

6. *IDR,* 1902, pp. 670–671.

7. Carlheinz Gräter, *Theodor Barths politische Gedankenwelt* (University of Würzburg, 1963), p. 14.

8. *Die Nation,* 1890, pp. 667–669.

9. *MVZADA,* 1892, p. 1; *AZJ,* 1891, pp. 49–50.

10. JHGA, Kn II/A II 3; *MVZADA,* 1893, pp. 439–441.

11. JHGA, TD–475; *MVZADA,* 1893, pp. 439–441; 1898, pp. 57–58; 1901, p. 36.

12. *MVZADA,* 1893, pp. 1, 439–441; 1904, p. 122; JHGA, Rh/Nw/35.

13. *AZJ,* 1891, Beilage to No. 24, p. 2; *MVZADA,* 1892, p. 355; 1893, p. 440; 1895, pp. 205–206; 1896, p. 188; 1899, p. 172; 1908, pp. 329, 370; *Jüdische Presse,* 1893, pp. 139–140; *Israelit,* 1891, pp. 415–416; 1892, pp. 769–771; JHGA, Kn II/A II 3. On Austrian anti-Semitism see Pulzer, *passim.*

14. JHGA, Kn/II/A II 3; Rh/Nw/35; *MVZADA,* 1892, pp. 41–42; 1893, pp. 439–441; 1897, p. 74; 1899, pp. 241–242.

15. *MVZADA,* 1893, pp. 399–401; JHGA, Kn II/A II 3.

16. Katz, "The German-Jewish Utopia," pp. 65–72.

17. *Supra,* pp. 47–48, 69–71.

18. *MVZADA,* 1895, pp. 57–58, 65–66.

19. *Ibid.,* 1894, p. 334; 1896, pp. 187–188; *Die Nation,* 1892, pp. 511–512. Hermann Bahr, *Der Antisemitismus* (Berlin, 1894), pp. 14–15.

20. *MVZADA,* 1893, pp. 255–257; 1897, pp. 33–34, 73; 1898, pp. 27, 185; 1901, p. 35; 1903, pp. 177–178; 1904, p. 122; 1907, pp. 74–75; 1909, p. 321. According to *IDR,* one of the members was Dr. Georg Winter, the vice-president of the Verein (1909, p. 4).

21. *MVZADA,* 1892, pp. 41–42; 1910, p. 373.

22. *MVZADA,* 1893, pp. 439–441; 1899, pp. 225–226, 241–242; 1908, p. 331; 1913, p. 188; *Antisemiten-Spiegel* (Danzig, 1891), p. 2; JHGA, Rh/Nw/35.

23. *MVZADA*, 1895, p. 233; *AZJ*, 1895, No. 31, Beilage, p. 1; Schnabel, II, 184–191; Ziekursch, II, 257–264.

24. *MVZADA*, 1895, pp. 453–454; Ziekursch, II, 348, 366; Max Schwarz, *Biographisches Handbuch der Reichstage* (Hanover, 1965), p. 437; *AZJ*, 1902, pp. 529–530. See also the obituary in the *General-Anzeiger*, November 6, 1902, p. 1.

25. Gräter, p. 14; Friedrich Sell, *Die Tragödie des deutschen Liberalismus* (Stuttgart, 1953), pp. 288–290; *MVZADA*, 1909, pp. 170–172; *IDR*, 1903, pp. 457, 691. As a young Hamburg lawyer, Barth was deeply influenced by a close friendship with Ludwig Bamberger, whose bust decorated Barth's desk for the rest of his life. (Gräter, pp. 9–10.)

26. Schwarz, p. 327; Georg Gothein, *Der deutsche Aussenhandel* (Berlin, 1901); also *idem*, "Die Wirkungen des Schutzzollsystems in Deutschland," *Volkswirtschaftliche Zeitfragen*, 1909, Heft 243/244.

27. Sell, pp. 272–273.

28. Schnabel, II, 90–173, and especially 104–105 and 132.

29. *AZJ*, 1895, No. 31, Beilage, p. 1; *Die Nation*, 1892, pp. 143–144; *MVZADA*, 1894, pp. 305–306; 1895, pp. 113–114, 297–298; Georg Winter, *Der Antisemitismus in Deutschland*, hrsg. VZADA (Magdeburg, 1896), pp. 22–58. One of the most unscrupulous and vicious anti-Semitic theoreticians of the second half of the nineteenth century, who constantly combined his anti-Jewish tirades with an equally uncompromising repudiation of liberalism, was Paul de Lagarde. See Stern, *The Politics of Cultural Despair*, pp. 91–97.

30. *Die Nation*, 1892, pp. 143–144; Winter, pp. 68–71, 119–120; *MVZADA*, 1893, pp. 311–312; 1907, pp. 313–315, 323–326.

31. Bahr, pp. 12–14. Quotation p. 12.

32. *Antisemiten-Spiegel* (Danzig, 1891), p. 3; *MVZADA*, 1904, p. 122; 1907, p. 299; *Die Juden im Heere*, hrsg. VZADA (Berlin, ca. 1909), pp. 86–88.

33. *MVZADA*, 1901, p. 37.

34. *Antisemiten-Spiegel* (Danzig, 1890), pp. 8–10; *Antisemiten-Spiegel* (Berlin and Frankfurt a.M., 1911), pp. 5–7; *MVZADA*, 1897, p. 73; 1907, pp. 396–398; 1910, p. 142; 1913, p. 188.

35. Quoted in *MVZADA*, 1909, p. 147, and also *Die Juden im Heere*, p. 40. See also *MVZADA*, 1901, p. 51; 1904, pp. 122–125; 1909, pp. 88–90; 1912, pp. 181–184; 1913, pp. 66–67, 107–109. On the decline of political anti-Semitism after 1907, see Tal, "Anti-Semitism in the Second German Reich," pp. 150–153.

36. *MVZADA*, 1901, pp. 51, 76, 147–148; 1904, p. 125; 1909, pp. 175–176; 1911, pp. 157–160; 1912, pp. 85–87.

37. Ernest Hamburger, "Jews in Public Service under the German Monarchy," *LBIYB*, IX (1964), 206–238.

38. Lysbeth W. Muncy, *The Junker in the Prussian Administration under William II, 1888–1914* (Providence, 1944), pp. 104, 109–110, 191, 230–234; Tal, "Anti-Semitism in the Second German Reich," pp. 160–161; Sell, p. 252; Gräter, p. 21; Carl E. Schorske, *German Social Democracy 1905–1917* (New York, 1965), pp. 146–196; J. C. G. Röhl, "Higher Civil Servants in Germany, 1890–1900," *Journal of Contemporary History*, II (1967), 109–110.

39. *AZJ,* 1891, pp. 37–38; 1892, pp. 26–27, 38; 1893, p. 315; *Israelit,* 1891, pp. 89, 255, 353, 787–788; 1893, pp. 766–767; 1894, pp. 271–272; *Jüdische Presse,* 1893, pp. 521–523; 1895, pp. 301–302.

40. JHGA, Kn II/A II 3.

41. *MVZADA,* 1892, p. 312; 1893, pp. 1–2, 72, 175–176; JHGA, Rh/Nw/35.

42. *IDR,* 1902, p. 672.

43. JHGA, Rh/Nw/35; A/202; A/33.

44. *Statistisches Jahrbuch des DIGB* (Berlin, 1895), p. 1; JHGA, Kn II/A II 3.

45. *Statistisches Jahrbuch des DIGB* (Berlin, 1895), p. 46; JHGA, Rh/Nw/35. On the Xanten blood libel, see M. Philippson, II, 48–50.

46. *MVZADA,* 1908, pp. 134–135. *Israelitisches Familienblatt,* 1908, No. 18, p. 6. Despite his large contributions to aid Russian Jews and colonization, he was an active anti-Zionist. *Correspondenz No. 7 der Zionistischen Vereinigung für Deutschland;* Henriette H. Bodenheimer, *Im Anfang der zionistischen Bewegung* (Frankfurt a.M., 1965), p. 66.

47. *Supra,* p. 47.

48. *MVZADA,* 1900, pp. 385–387; *AZJ,* 1892, p. 38; 1900, Beilage to No. 49, p. 1; *IDR,* 1907, p. 172; Fred B. Stern, "Ludwig Jacobowski, der Author von *Werther, der Jude," BLBI,* III (1964), 101–137. See also the critical review of the book by Dubnow in his "Letters on Old and New Judaism," in *Nationalism and History,* ed. by Koppel S. Pinson (Philadelphia, 1958), pp. 146–149. In July of 1891 Jacobowski sounded a new note of Jewish belligerency, which became increasingly audible within German Jewry after 1890, and eventually led to the founding of the Centralverein:

"For a decade we have silently let the raging waves of anti-Semitism sweep over us. Our patience and endurance are now at an end. Now comes the fight.

"A young Jewish generation is preparing itself, which is and feels like a German, as only a blond head with blue eyes can, but which will not suffer those brutal attacks by street urchins simply because it has not tasted any holy water. . . . This young generation has not yet stirred itself. But there are already signs. It will come." (Jacobowski, *Offene Antwort eines Juden auf Herrn Ahlwardt's "Der Eid eines Juden"* [Berlin, 1891], pp. 5, 31.)

49. *MVZADA,* 1901, p. 33; 1904, pp. 225–226; 1911, p. 157. For a time the young Kurt Eisner also worked for the Marburg bureau of the Abwehrverein. In 1893 he was an editor of a Marburg paper. The Leo Baeck Institute in New York has recently received two receipts signed by Eisner for sums of 275 marks each. They are dated September 1, and October 1, respectively. These large sums were paid to Eisner by the Marburg bureau of the Verein, perhaps to pay for some of the expenses incurred during the campaign against anti-Semitic candidates in the Reichstag elections of June 6, 1893. See file of Kurt Eisner in the Archives.

50. MVZADA, 1891, pp. 1–4; Curt Bürger, *Deutschtum und Judentum* (Berlin, 1913), pp. 50–51, 58. The rejection of the decidedly anti-Christian motifs of racial anti-Semitism by the Abwehrverein was categorical. (*MVZADA,* 1892, p. 425; 1894, pp. 177–178; 1895, pp. 210–11; 1897, pp. 161–162.

51. *MVZADA,* 1892, pp. 253–255; 1894, p. 59; 1895, pp. 33, 50–51, 57–58, 65–66; 1897, pp. 73–76; 1899, pp. 57–58.

52. *Ibid.,* 1893, pp. 471–473. For the background of this viewpoint, see *supra,* pp. 2–3; and *infra,* p. 99.

53. *Ibid.,* 1894, pp. 5, 19–21.

54. *Ibid.,* 1894, pp. 9–10.

55. *Ibid.,* 1897, p. 123; 1900, pp. 401–403; 1903, pp. 276–278, 281–283.

56. *Ibid.,* 1894, pp. 373–374; 1897, p. 293; 1898, pp. 74–75; 1903, pp. 305–307.

57. *Ibid.,* 1897, pp. 282–284, 291–293; 1903, pp. 289–292; Bürger, p. 58. ". . . Jew-baiting (*Judenhetze*) alone has produced these hotheaded Jews (*Hetzjuden*). Zionism is the reaction to anti-Semitism. They are equal in their senseless onesidedness and blind injustice." (*MVZADA,* 1897, p. 284.)

58. *Ibid.,* 1897, p. 293; 1903, pp. 299–301; 1912, p. 191.

59. See *supra,* Introduction.

60. Boehlich, pp. 212–227. See also Tal, *Christians and Jews,* pp. 26–27, 30–31. Mommsen had been one of the original founders of the Abwehrverein. See *MVZADA,* 1897, p. 387. According to Fritz Haber, the Nobel Prize winning chemist who had converted to Christianity as a student, Mommsen's article exercised a decisive influence on him and his friends. See Rudolf A. Stern, "Fritz Haber: Personal Recollections," *LBIYB,* VIII (1963), 88.

61. JHGA, INV-124-1, pp. 100, 104, 106; INV-124-2, pp. 2, 34, 69, 107, 116, 139; *MVZADA,* 1911, p. 25. Other references to contact between the two organizations and comments by one about the other reveal little information about substantive differences. See *IDR,* 1895, pp. 111–114; 1897, p. 190; 1899, p. 225; 1900, pp. 163–164; 1902, pp. 601–603; 1907, pp. 229–234; *MVZADA,* 1896, pp. 187–188; 1903, pp. 38–39; 1911, p. 23; 1913, p. 194; *Antisemiten-Spiegel* (Berlin and Frankfurt a.M., 1911), p. 445.

62. Tal, *Christians and Jews,* chs. 1 and 4; *idem,* "Anti-Semitism in the Second German Reich," pp. 196–200, 207, 210–211, 221; *idem,* "Liberal Protestantism and the Jews in the Second Reich 1870–1914," *Jewish Social Studies,* XXVI (1964), 23–41; *idem,* "The Intellectual Elite in Germany and Its Position on the Jews in the Period of Bismarck" (Hebrew), in *Elites and Leading Groups* (Hebrew) (Jerusalem, 1966), pp. 98–130; especially p. 127 for two statements by Gneist, made in 1875 and 1881, on the necessary dissolution of German Jewry for complete integration. On the basis of an 1899 address by Rickert, Tal suggests that his position was identical with that of Mommsen. He quotes two passages: ". . . Protestantism is the major economic and moral force in the swift-moving industrial revolution of our time. . . . Liberal Protestantism is the crucial ideological and political protagonist of the national renaissance of our time. . . . It is the basis of the new society that is now being brought into existence." ("Liberal Protestantism," p. 27.) ". . . whilst as true liberals we will never deny the Jews' right to exist, still the continued existence of liberal Judaism seems incomprehensible to some of us" (p. 36).

One further example might be cited to indicate the extent to which the animosity of the Abwehrverein toward Jewish survival corresponded to the attitude of individual members. In 1907 Otto Caspari, a professor of philosophy at the University of Heidelberg and one of the signers of the 1891 declaration announcing the formation of the Verein, expressed his belief that the root cause of anti-Semitism was the racial difference between Semite and Aryan. Only the total disappearance of the Jews through intermarriage with Germans would ultimately resolve the racial antagonism: "If the mixing of blood and the crossing of races (i.e., marriage with a Christian) is only achievable through religious conversion, then let this be done in a mood of idealistic sacrifice. Only through this most profound willingness to sacrifice can the mutual racial hatred be extinguished in the course of many centuries." To eradicate every trace of former Jewish identity, Caspari recommended that at the time of marriage the Jewish partner always should adopt the family name of his Christian mate. (Julius Moses, ed., *Die Lösung der Judenfrage* [Berlin-Leipzig, 1907], pp. 84–85.)

CHAPTER 4
TIME TO ACT: 1893

1. Philippson, II, 48–50.

2. *Gutachten über das jüdisch-rituelle Schlachtverfahren* (Berlin, 1894), p. iii. The agitation against kosher slaughtering had already been intense during the mid-1880's. In 1886 the League of German Societies for the Protection of Animals petitioned the Reichstag for a law requiring the prior stunning of all animals that were to be slaughtered. The petition, however, never left the committee. That same year Bavaria passed such a law, but specifically exempted the Jewish community. A similar petition reached the Reichstag floor in 1887. This time the Reichstag specifically excluded kosher slaughtering from its deliberations. See Philippson, II, 130–131; Eliav, *Hildesheimer Briefe,* pp. 224–228, 271–273; *Jüdische Presse,* 1887, pp. 195–199. In Switzerland a referendum on August 20, 1893, amended the Constitution so as to require stunning before slaughtering. (*Gutachten,* p. iii.) This amendment still remains part of the Constitution today. (*Jewish Exponent* [Philadelphia], May 5, 1967, p. 1.)

3. Tal, "Anti-Semitism in the Second German Reich," pp. 127–132; Massing, pp. 71–72.

4. Massing, p. 66; Frank, pp. 229–234. In May 1893 Manteuffel defended the plank in terms of expediency: "The Jewish question was unavoidable, if one did not wish to leave to the demagogic anti-Semites the full force (Wind) of the movement, with which they would have simply sailed right by us." (Frank, p. 234.)

5. *Israelit,* 1889, pp. 285–287; 1890, pp. 805–807; *Jüdische Presse,* 1893, pp. 21–22, 53–55, 61–62; *Israelitische Wochenschrift,* 1892, pp. 161–166, 185–186; *AZJ,* 1892, p. 349; 1893, pp. 1, 13–15, 157, 289, 301, 385, 421.

6. *AZJ,* 1893, pp. 218, 241–243, 253, 266, 505; *Jüdische Presse,* 1893, pp. 231–233, 469–470.

7. *Israelitische Wochenschrift,* 1891, pp. 49–51.

8. Hermann Strack, *Der Blutaberglaube in der Menschheit: Blutmorde und Blutritus* (2nd ed.; Munich, 1892), pp. vii–x.

9. Paul Nathan, *Der Prozess von Tisza-Eszlár* (Berlin, 1892), pp. v–vi,

viii–xxxix; *idem, Xanten-Cleve: Betrachtungen zum Prozess Buschhof,* Separat-Abdruck aus der *Nation* (Berlin, 1892), p. 16.

10. Reported in *MVZADA*, 1892, pp. 312–313 (quotation p. 312).

11. Hermann Strack, *Die Juden, dürfen sie "Verbrecher von Religions wegen" genannt werden?* (Berlin, 1893), p. 8; see especially pp. 5–8, 23–30. See also *Jüdische Presse*, 1893, pp. 41–43, and *AZJ*, 1893, p. 38, for expressions of gratitude.

12. [Raphael Löwenfeld], *Schutzjuden oder Staatsbürger? von einem jüdischen Staatsbürger* (3rd ed.; Berlin, 1893), p. 8.

13. *Ibid.,* pp. 8–14.

14. *Ibid.,* pp. 26–27.

15. *Ibid.,* pp. 17–25.

16. "Die antisemitische Bewegung in Deutschland," *Populär-wissenschaftliche Monatsblätter,* 1881, pp. 4–7; Leon, pp. 15, 37.

17. *Israelit,* 1881, pp. 17–18; 1886, pp. 371–372, 401, 438–441; 1890, pp. 821–822; 1891, pp. 90, 145–146, 411–413; 1892, pp. 17–19; 1893, pp. 41–43, 79–81.

18. *Israelit,* 1891, pp. 643–645, 651–652, 755–757, 865–866; 1892, pp. 377–379. Such an appeal for unity had been issued by the *AZJ,* 1892, p. 73.

19. The term *Akum* is an acronym of the Hebrew words *Obday Kokhavim u-Mazalot* (worshippers of stars and constellations of the Zodiac). Although appearing in numerous Talmudic and Rabbinic texts, it is definitely not a Talmudic word. On the contrary, it is a term invented by the papal inquisition of the sixteenth century and used by its censors of Hebrew books. Required to expurgate every allegedly anti-Christian appellation and statement, the censors indiscriminately replaced countless references to *Goy* (gentile), *Nokhri* (non-Jew), and *Obed Abodah Zarah* (idolater) with *Akum,* a term that could not possibly be misunderstood as referring to Christians. Nevertheless, in the nineteenth century, even after the origins of this acronym had been elucidated, many anti-Semites continued to insist that it also referred to Christians. (M. Mortara, "Die Censor hebräischer Bücher in Italien und der *Canon purificationis* [*Sefer Ha-Zikuk*]," *Hebräische Bibliographie,* V [1862], 72–77, 96–101; Hoffmann, pp. 129–141.) On the by no means monolithic attitude of medieval rabbinic authorities on Christianity and Jewish relations with Christians, see Jacob Katz, *Exclusiveness and Tolerance* (Oxford, 1961).

20. *Jüdische Presse,* 1893, pp. 83–87; *AZJ,* 1893, pp. 73–75, 85; *Israelitische Wochenschrift,* 1893, pp. 73–74; *Israelit,* 1893, p. 287. In contrast to the leaders of German Reform, who regarded the Oral Law as the product of a long historical development, the spokesmen of Neo-Orthodoxy vigorously reasserted the divinity of the entire corpus of Jewish law. See A. Geiger, *Das Judenthum und seine Geschichte,* I, 73–75; Hirsch, *The Nineteen Letters of Ben Uziel,* pp. 194–195; *idem, Horeb,* I, Forward.

21. Marcus Hirsch, *Kulturdefizit am Ende des 19. Jahrhunderts* (Frankfurt a.M., 1893). Hirsch did consider the 1891 Abwehrverein a hopeful start (p. 139). Still, the gravity of the moment strained his belief in the ultimate triumph of liberalism. "The ultimate victory of the ideas of the liberty, equality and fraternity of mankind is certain. But as the advance of the unholy movement steadily deepens the cultural depression in which we unfortunately find ourselves at the end of the nineteenth century, the ultimate triumph of

civilization (*Kultur*), the ultimate reconciliation of opposites is steadily pushed back" (p. 116).

22. L. Auerbach, *Wie ist die Judenhetze mit Erfolg zu bekämpfen?* (Berlin, 1893).

23. James Simon, *Wehrt Euch* (Berlin, 1893), pp. 1, 13–24; Fritz Auerbach, *Der Antisemitismus und das freisinnige Judentum* (Frankfurt a.M., 1893), pp. 5–7, 13–14; "James Simon: Industrialist, Art Collector, Philanthropist," *LBIYB*, V (1965), 3–23.

24. *AZJ*, 1890, pp. 225–226.

25. *Ibid.*, 1892, pp. 97, 458; 1893, pp. 421, 457, 482.

26. Eliav, *Jewish Education in Germany*, pp. 345–347; Cf. [Jakob Thon], *Die jüdische Gemeinden und Vereine in Deutschland* (Berlin, 1906), pp. 21–22.

27. *Israelit*, 1893, pp. 1685–86, 1758; *AZJ*, 1888, p. 104; Ismar Elbogen, "Aus der Frühzeit der Vereine für jüdische Geschichte und Literatur," in *Festschrift zum 70. Geburtstage von Moritz Schaefer* (Berlin, 1927), p. 50.

28. Elbogen, "Aus der Frühzeit der Vereine," p. 50; *AZJ*, 1892, No. 9, Beilage, p. 1; No. 10, Beilage, p. 1; *Die Welt*, 1909, p. 688.

29. *AZJ*, 1894, No. 32, Beilage, p. 2. The historical allusion is to Nehemiah 4:11.

30. *AZJ*, 1893, p. 541; Elbogen, "Aus der Frühzeit der Vereine," p. 51.

31. *JJGL*, 1900, p. 282; *IDR*, 1904, pp. 448–449; Elbogen, "Aus der Frühzeit der Vereine," pp. 52–53.

32. *JJGL*, hrsg. vom Verbande der Vereine für jüdische Geschichte und Literatur in Deutschland, 1898–1938.

33. *JJGL*, 1900, p. 282.

34. *AZJ*, 1895, pp. 433–434.

35. *Ibid.*, 1895, p. 553.

36. *AZJ*, 1893, Beilage to No. 4, p. 1.

37. *Jüdische Presse*, 1893, p. 63; *AZJ*, 1893, Beilage to No. 7, p. 1; *MVZADA*, 1893, p. 72. This is the sequence of events as reported by all three of the contemporary sources cited above. However, according to Eugen Fuchs, the major Centralverein figure before the war, in an address in 1903, the committee was formed by about two dozen notables on June 30, 1892, in the house of Julius Isaac in Berlin. (*Um Deutschtum und Judentum* [Frankfurt, a.M., 1919], p. 91). Paul Rieger, the historian of the Centralverein's first twenty-five years, accepts this date, probably on the authority of Fuchs. (*Ein Vierteljahrhundert im Kampf um das Recht und die Zukunft der deutschen Juden* [Berlin, 1918], p. 12.) If the date is correct, and there is no contemporaneous confirmation, it is at least evident that the committee did not come out in the open until January 1893.

38. *MVZADA*, 1893, pp. 36, 72.

39. JHGA, Kn II / A II 3.

40. Rahel Straus, *Wir lebten in Deutschland* (Stuttgart, 1961), pp. 60–62. This portrait of Löwenfeld, whose pamphlet led directly to the founding of the Centralverein, is drawn by his niece.

41. *AZJ*, 1893, Beilage to No. 5, pp. 1, 134–135; *Israelit*, 1893, p. 251; Rieger, pp. 18–19.

42. *AZJ*, 1893, p. 135.

43. Rieger, p. 19.
44. *Ibid.*, pp. 18–19.
45. Shortly before the Reichstag elections in June 1893, the committee sent out a circular urging rabbis and teachers to attend local election meetings to refute anti-Semitic vilifications, an act that suggests that the committee had still not relinquished the field to the Centralverein. See *Israelitische Wochenschrift*, 1893, p. 183.
46. *Gutachten über das jüdisch-rituelle;* Paul Nathan, ed., *Die Kriminalität der Juden in Deutschland* (Berlin, 1896); *Die Juden als Soldaten* (Berlin, 1897). As to the nature of the arguments presented in the first two and in similar Jewish rebuttals of racial accusations, see Tal, "Anti-Semitism in the Second German Reich," pp. 116–27.

The committee and Centralverein did cooperate in fighting the anti-Semites. They worked together on the Konitz blood libel of 1900. See JHGA, INV-124-1, pp. 102–103. In October 1902 the Centralverein reluctantly gave the committee a sorely needed 2,000 marks. See JHGA, INV-124-2, p. 56.

The major financial support for the committee's publications seems to have come from individual contributions and the Jewish communities. On April 8, 1894, Nathan wrote to the Königsberg Board criticizing its meager contribution of 300 marks to help fight the campaign against kosher slaughtering. Frankfurt had given, in contrast, 5,000 marks. See JHGA, Kn II/A II 3.

47. Fuchs, p. 91. I have found no evidence that Nathan was even a member of the Centralverein. None of the three membership lists for the years 1902, 1905, and 1908 published by the Centralverein includes his name. See *Mitgliederverzeichnis*, Berlin: 1902, 1905, 1908. In contrast, he was actively involved in the Verein zur Abwehr des Antisemitismus. In 1901 he sat on the enlarged board (*MVZADA*, 1901, p. 33), and according to Max Bodenheimer, the first president of the German Zionist Organization, he was for a time editor of the Verein's Mitteilungen. (M. Bodenheimer, *Prelude to Israel* [New York, 1963], p. 80.)

Nathan's reserve toward the Centralverein may also have resulted from ideological differences. His biographer insists that Nathan saw the struggle against anti-Semitism in terms of justice and culture, not as a defense of Jewish interests. (Ernst Feder, *Politik und Humanität: Paul Nathan* [Berlin, 1929], pp. 74–75.) Like so many other coreligionists, Nathan did not renounce his belief in progress and the ultimate resolution of the Jewish problem. In 1907 he wrote: "The course of history is certainly not unilinear nor does it advance steadily upwards. Moreover, it moves in different countries at different speeds . . . The education of mankind is torturous and gruesome and yet in retrospect it reveals progress. The constantly ascending development will the more triumphantly set in, the larger the number of those who believe in it and the more intelligently their energy is employed to clear the way for it." (Moses, *Die Lösung der Judenfrage*, pp. 26–27.)

48. Adolf Lewin, *Geschichte der badischen Juden seit der Regierung Karl Friedrichs, 1738–1909* (Karlsruhe, 1909), p. 372.

CHAPTER 5
SELF-DEFENSE: CENTRALVEREIN
DEUTSCHER STAATSBÜRGER JÜDISCHEN
GLAUBENS, 1893–1914

1. The formulation "deutscher Staatsbürger jüdischen Glaubens" was first proposed by [Löwenfeld], *Schutzjuden oder Staatsbürger?*, p. 26. See also Bernhard Breslauer, "Erinnerung" in *Festschrift zum 70 Geburtstage*, pp. 19–20.

2. *IDR*, 1909, pp. 231–232. See also Emil Lehmann's revision of Löwenfeld's original six principles, which was adopted at the second public meeting of the Centralverein on September 27, 1893. (*MVZADA*, 1893, p. 379.)

3. Martin Mendelsohn, *Die Pflicht der Selbstvertheidigung* (Berlin, 1894), pp. 5–9, 17; Fuchs, pp. 50–54. The Abwehrverein itself had criticized this incomprehensible silence on several occasions. See *MVZADA*, 1892, p. 312; 1893, pp. 1–2, 175–176.

4. See *supra*, chs. 1 and 2.

5. Mendelsohn, pp. 6, 7, 9, 17, 31; *IDR*, 1896, p. 460.

6. Hans-Jürgen Puhle, *Agrarische Interessenpolitik und preussischer Konservatismus im wilhelminischen Reich (1893–1914)* (Hanover, 1966), pp. 32–35, 46, 125–133.

7. Mildred S. Wertheimer, *The Pan-German League* (New York, 1924), pp. 22–48; Pulzer, pp. 219–221.

8. Rieger, p. 21.

9. *IDR*, 1895, p. 3; 1902, pp. 389–390, 1912, pp. 1–10; *C-V Zeitung*, 1924, p. 6.

10. JHGA, INV-124-1, pp. 36–38; A/33; *IDR*, 1897, pp. 645–646; *C-V Zeitung*, 1924, pp. 5–6.

11. *An die deutschen Staatsbürger jüdischen Glaubens: Ein Aufruf* (Berlin, 1893). Thus, for example, Gustav Karpeles, the editor of the *Allgemeine Zeitung des Judentums*, was an Austrian citizen and never became a member of the Centralverein. (*IDR*, 1909, pp. 509–510.) Likewise immigrants from eastern Europe, who in most instances failed to receive citizenship, which was a state jurisdiction, never became members. See Ludwig Foerder, *Die Stellung des Centralvereins zu den innerjüdischen Fragen in den Jahren 1919–1926* (Breslau, 1927), p. 8.

12. *IDR*, 1896, pp. 285–286; 1903, p. 12; Fuchs, p. 291. By 1932 the Centralverein comprised some 60,000 individual members, organized into 23 regional branches and 634 local chapters. Its operations were directed by the Berlin headquarters, with a budget of 1,000,000 marks, and 15 regional bureaus. After the Nazi takeover, it survived until November 10, 1938, when its offices were closed and its rich library of Anti-semitica confiscated by the Gestapo. See Arnold Paucker, "Der jüdische Abwehrkampf," in *Entscheidungsjahr 1932*, ed. by Werner E. Mosse (Tübingen, 1965), pp. 424–425; Hans Reichmann, "Der Centralverein deutscher Staatsbürger jüdischen Glaubens,"

in *Festschrift zum 80. Geburtstag von Leo Baeck* (London, 1953), pp. 63, 71, 73.

13. Ernst Herzfeld, "Lebenserinnerungen," ALBI, pp. 68–71. *IDR*, 1900, pp. 115, 167, 363; 1906, pp. 7–9, 201, 677–679; 1907, pp. 202–207; 1909, pp. 144–162, 231–236; 1910, pp. 112–120, 173–181; 1911, p. 312. A revision of the law of association by the Reichstag in 1908 permitted women to join political organizations. Earlier, women were legally forbidden even to attend Centralverein meetings, since political issues were frequently discussed, though the police never bothered to interfere. After 1908 women could become full members, a decision welcomed by the Centralverein. See *ibid.*, 1903, pp. 468–469; 1908, pp. 288–289. During these middle years of the first decade of the twentieth century, the Centralverein began to look for a full-time legal adviser (syndic). In 1907 or 1908 Ludwig Hollaender, a young Munich lawyer, accepted the post. After the war he became the Executive Director of the organization. See Alfred Hirschberg, "Ludwig Hollaender, Director of the C. V.," *LBIYB*, VII (1962), 43–44, 52–53.

14. JHGA, INV-124-1, pp. 6–7, 9; *IDR*, 1895, p. 3; 1900, p. 116; 1902, p. 178; 1913, p. 52.

15. *Israelit*, 1894, pp. 1778–79; JHGA, INV-124-1, p. 44.

16. JHGA, INV-124-2, p. 153; *IDR*, 1905, p. 143; 1909, pp. 224, 380; 1910, pp. 470–471, 623; 1913, p. 323.

17. *IDR*, 1905, p. 141; *General-Anzeiger*, February 9, 1908, p. 2. The table is compiled from statistics provided by Thon, pp. 56, 58.

18. *Jüdische Presse*, 1893, pp. 13–14, 22–23, 49–51; 1895, pp. 43–44; *IDR*, 1896, pp. 200–210; 1897, p. 110–113; 1903, p. 243; Rieger, p. 53. Throughout 1894 the *Jüdische Presse* simply ignored the Centralverein, with the exception of a single brief report. (*Jüdische Presse*, 1894, pp. 507–508.)

19. *Israelit*, 1893, pp. 77–79, 117–119, 1863–65; 1894, pp. 831–832; 1896, pp. 215–217, 457–458, 489–492; *IDR*, 1896, p. 286; 1913, pp. 450–455. See also *Ein Wort an die deutschen Staatsbürger jüdischen Glaubens* (Mainz, 1896). For the earlier period, see *supra*, pp. 108–109.

20. *Israelitische Wochenschrift*, 1893, pp. 342–343; *AZJ*, 1893, p. 470; 1894, pp. 37–38, 613; 1897, pp. 253–254; 1898, pp. 301–302. The Centralverein desired better relations with the Jewish press, but was wary of becoming too closely identified with any organ, because each represented a distinct religious position. At a December 1894 general meeting Horwitz said: "The Board itself desires contact with the Jewish press, but that requires caution, because the organization must not align itself with the viewpoint of a religious party." (*AZJ*, 1894, p. 594.)

21. *Israelitische Wochenschrift*, 1893, pp. 325–326; *AZJ*, 1896, p. 37; *IDR*, 1907, p. 395; 1910, pp. 771–777; Fuchs, pp. 3–4, 92.

22. Paul Billerbeck, "Vereinsorganisationen innerhalb der Judenschaft Deutschland," *Nathanael*, XXI (1905), 7. In the 1920's he and Hermann Strack collaborated to publish their epoch-making *Kommentar zum Neuen Testament aus Talmud und Midrash*, 4 vols. (Munich, 1922–28).

23. Fuchs, pp. 3–4, 22; *IDR*, 1896, pp. 489–490; 1902, p. 209.

24. [Maximilian Parmod], *Antisemitismus und Strafrechtspflege* (3rd ed.; Berlin, 1894), pp. 2–4, 6–7, 44, 98–101, 111–121; R. H. Gage and A. J. Wa-

ters, *Imperial German Criminal Code* (Johannesburg, 1917), pp. 30, 43, 49, 91–93. Parmod was actually a pseudonym for Dr. Max Apt, a member of the legal department. The pamphlet sought to demonstrate that the demands of the Centralverein were justified by the existing criminal code. See Rieger, pp. 26, 47. However, the pamphlet made no direct reference to the Centralverein. Consequently it was warmly approved even by the *Israelit* (1894, pp. 1541–42); also the *Jüdische Presse* (1894, pp. 411–412). In 1940 Ambrose Doskow and Sidney B. Jacoby wrote an informative survey of the legal efforts made by the Centralverein to combat German anti-Semitism. The bulk of the essay is devoted to the Weimar period, but the criminal code was still that of the Empire, so that some of their discussion pertains to the earlier period. Ambrose Doskow and Sidney B. Jacoby, "Anti-Semitism and the Law in pre-Nazi Germany," *Contemporary Jewish Record*, III (1940), 498–509.

25. Fuchs, pp. 45–46.

26. *Jüdische Presse*, 1893, pp. 501–503. On the various interpretations as to what constituted a church institution or practice according to Section 166, see especially Ignaz Ettinger, "Zur Lehre von den Religionsvergehen," *Strafrechtliche Abhandlungen*, CCIII (1919), 78–79.

27. Parmod, pp. 68–69, 98–101.

28. Reprinted by *Jüdische Presse*, 1895, pp. 99–100. For concurring Jewish statements, see also *Jüdische Presse*, 1893, pp. 501–503, and *AZJ*, 1894, p. 159.

29. [Löwenfeld], *Schutzjuden oder Staatsbürger?*, p. 26.

30. On the Strack pamphlet, see *supra*, pp. 106–107; Parmod, pp. 4, 25–31, 53–63.

31. *IDR*, 1895, p. 40; Fuchs, pp. 3–50; *C-V Zeitung*, 1924, pp. 8–9; Hirschberg, pp. 52, 57; Adolph Asch, "Posener und Berliner Erinnerungen 1881–1931," ALBI, in chapter on "Berlin 1914–1915."

32. *IDR*, 1895, p. 40; Fuchs, pp. 159–168; Rieger, p. 24.

33. *AZJ*, 1891, pp. 121–122; 1894, p. 613; 1895, pp. 146, 440; 1896, pp. 86, 507; 1898, pp. 301–302. The *Jüdische Presse*, on the other hand, never wavered in its support of prosecution. See *Jüdische Presse*, 1894, pp. 475–476, 491–492; 1895, pp. 127–128.

34. *AZJ*, 1895, pp. 160–161.

35. *IDR*, 1896, pp. 492–493.

36. Fuchs, pp. 177–194; *AZJ*, 1895, pp. 183–185; *IDR*, 1896, pp. 72, 494; 1899, p. 537; 1902, p. 202. The accusation that Jews rendered meat to be sold to gentiles unfit for consumption by urinating on it was part of the broader medieval suspicion that Jews contrived, whenever possible, to poison Christians. See Joshua Trachtenberg, *The Devil and the Jews* (New York and Philadelphia, 1961), pp. 100–101.

37. *IDR*, 1902, pp. 201–202.

38. *Ibid.*, 1900, pp. 120–121, 396–397; 1903, p. 7.

39. *Ibid.*, 1896, p. 70.

40. *IDR*, 1899, pp. 294–298, 534–536.

41. *Ibid.*, pp. 309–317, 608; 1900, pp. 405–408.

42. L. Auerbach, *Das Judenthum und seine Bekenner*, pp. 304–305.

43. Israel Davidson, "Kol Nidre," *American Jewish Year Book*, XXV

(1923), 180–194; Zunz, "Vorschriften über Eidesleistung der Juden," in *Gesammelte Schriften*, II, 241–264; Michaelis, p. 150.

44. *MVZADA*, 1895, pp. 137–138.

45. *Supra*, p. 127. See also *Jüdische Presse*, 1895, pp. 127–128, 144–145, 169–170; *AZJ*, 1895, pp. 145–146, 218–219.

46. *IDR*, 1899, pp. 113–114.

47. *Ibid.*, pp. 112–113.

48. *MVZADA*, 1901, pp. 106, 113, 153, 239; *IDR*, 1902, p. 204.

49. *IDR*, 1902, p. 203; see especially 1896, p. 70; 1907, p. 56.

50. *Ibid.*, 1899, pp. 112–113.

51. *Ibid.*, p. 537; 1900, p. 122.

52. *IDR*, 1911, pp. 47–49, 83. Except for a brief period after the assassination of Rathenau, the record of the German judiciary during the Weimar Republic did not improve. It remained reluctant to convict or to impose a heavy sentence: "The fines that were imposed were wholly ineffective as deterrents. They came to be regarded by agitators as business expenses, to be reckoned as part of the cost of continuing a profitable enterprise." (Doskow and Jacoby, "Anti-Semitism and the Law," p. 507. See also Paucker, "Der jüdische Abwehrkampf," pp. 441–448.)

The 1924 essay by Ludwig Foerder of the Centralverein, *Antisemitismus und Justiz* (Berlin, 1924), read much like the 1894 essay on the same subject by Max Apt of the Centralverein. This depressing sameness underscores the unaltered exposed position of the Jewish minority in German society.

53. Massing, pp. 127–148; Pulzer, pp. 118–126; Tal, "Anti-Semitism in the Second German Reich," pp. 150–153; Fuchs, p. 63; *IDR*, 1896, pp. 460–461; 1897, pp. 573–574; 1901, pp. 298–299; 1907, pp. 56–57; 1911, pp. 321–322.

54. *Jüdische Presse*, 1895, pp. 522–523.

55. *AZJ*, 1895, p. 49; *IDR*, 1903, pp. 316–318, 363, 500–503; 1905, pp. 73–79, 131–132.

56. *IDR*, 1905, p. 243.

57. *Ibid.*, 1900, pp. 124–125.

58. *Ibid.*, 1901, pp. 571–605; *Die Gutachten der Sachverständigen über den Konitzer Mord, nach den amtlichen Akten* (Berlin, 1903).

59. *IDR*, 1896, p. 459; 1907, p. 214; 1912, pp. 305–317.

60. *IDR*, 1904, pp. 639–646; 1905, pp. 260–266; 1907, pp. 34–39.

61. The Centralverein itself regarded the vigorous utilization of the courts as its most important operation. See *ibid.*, 1899, p. 168.

62. *An die deutschen Staatsbürger jüdischen Glaubens; IDR*, 1895, p. 6.

63. Mendelsohn, pp. 29–30; *IDR*, 1897, pp. 498–500; 1898, pp. 235–241; *AZJ*, 1898, pp. 253–254; Toury, *Die politischen Orientierungen*, p. 207; Fuchs, pp. 66–68.

64. Fuchs, pp. 66–83; Toury, *Die politischen Orientierungen*, p. 207. Two Jewish deputies were actually elected in that election, but neither had received the open support of the Centralverein. (Toury, p. 207.)

65. JHGA, INV-124-2, p. 72; *IDR*, 1906, pp. 563–564; 1907, pp. 141–147. As a result of this political activity, the German authorities regarded the Centralverein as a political organization. (*IDR*, 1906, p. 560.)

66. George D. Crothers, *The German Elections of 1907* (New York, 1941), pp. 113, 115, 145, 162–163.

67. *IDR*, 1911, pp. 115, 183. See *supra*, pp. 99–100.

68. Toury, *Die politischen Orientierungen*, pp. 211–212; Selma Spier, "The Fatherland," *LBIYB*, IV (1959), 306; Richard Lichtheim, *A Remnant Will Return* (Hebrew) (Tel Aviv, 1953), p. 44.

69. Crothers, p. 174.

70. Toury, *Die politischen Orientierungen*, pp. 210–211, 269–270; *IDR*, 1903, pp. 620–621; 1909, p. 225.

71. Toury, *Die politischen Orientierungen*, pp. 284–294, 339–342; *idem*, "Plan for a Jewish Political Organization in Germany" (Hebrew), *Zion*, XXVIII (1963), 164–205.

72. *Idem*, Die politischen Orientierungen, pp. 204–205, 293–294.

73. *Ibid.*, pp. 207, 340.

74. Fuchs, pp. 70–71; *IDR*, 1906, pp. 559–564; 1907, pp. 102–103.

75. *Infra*, ch. 7.

76. *Infra*, ch. 6.

77. *IDR*, 1907, pp. 394–400.

78. *Ibid.*, 1909, pp. 231–232.

79. *IDR*, 1897, pp. 187–192; 1900, pp. 186–190; 1907, pp. 400–410.

80. *Ibid.*, 1895, pp. 33, 199; 1902, p. 210; *AZJ*, 1895, No. 12, Beilage, p. 1.

81. *IDR*, 1902, pp. 195–196; JHGA, INV/751. See *supra*, pp. 47–48.

82. *AZJ*, 1896, p. 37; *IDR*, 1900, pp. 189–190.

83. JHGA, INV/751.

84. *IDR*, 1906, pp. 279–298.

85. *Ibid.*, 1899, pp. 183–184.

86. *JR*, 1903, p. 13.

87. *IDR*, 1906, pp. 281–286.

88. *Ibid.*, 1899, pp. 9, 65–69.

89. See *infra*, pp. 162–168.

90. On the conversion movement of the first decades of the century, see Menes, pp. 187–205; Michael Meyer, *The Origins of the Modern Jew* (Detroit, 1967), pp. 85–114.

91. Ruppin, *Soziologie der Juden*, I, 299, 303; see also *Zeitschrift für Demographie und Statistik der Juden*, 1914, p. 117. At the beginning of 1902 German Jewry was agitated by a report that shortly before the previous Christmas thirty Jews, mainly students, lecturers, and assistant professors, had converted as a group in Breslau. (*Israelitische Rundschau*, 1902, No. 7, p. 10; *Die Welt*, 1902, No. 21, p. 1.) Aside from the numerical and intellectual losses, the financial loss to the Jewish community was often considerable. Before the war twelve Berlin millionaires had left the Jewish community. (Theilhaber, p. 116.)

92. *Die Welt*, 1912, p. 351.

93. Theilhaber, pp. 117–118.

94. Abraham A. Fraenkel, *Lebenskreise* (Stuttgart, 1967), p. 97; Flora Meyer, "Erinnerungen aus meinem Leben in Berlin," ALBI, pp. 1, 3; Margarete Susman, *Ich habe viele Leben gelebt* (Stuttgart, 1964), pp. 70–71. The

quotation appears in A. Landsberger, ed., *Judentaufen* (2nd ed.; Munich, 1912), p. 76.

95. *IDR*, 1899, pp. 228–229.

96. *IDR*, 1899, pp. 228–229; 1900, p. 129; 1908, pp. 395–402; 1910, pp. 65–76, 487.

97. See *supra*, pp. 56–57.

98. H. Cohen, II, 345. Abraham Fraenkel, who studied at Marburg shortly before the war and knew Cohen during his last lonely years at the university, related in his memoirs that in Cohen's later years he absolutely refused to enter a house where either husband or wife was a converted Jew. (Fraenkel, p. 97.)

99. *IDR*, 1911, pp. 189–197. On the Friedländer proposal, see Meyer, *The Origins of the Modern Jew*, pp. 70–78.

100. Gustav Levinstein, *Zur Ehre des Judentums* (Berlin, 1911), p. 80. This collection of polemics was published by the Centralverein after his death. The table of contents conveys the tone of the book quite accurately: "Die Taufe, Warum die Juden nicht Christen werden können, Über die Erlösung des Judentums, Jüdische Kindertaufen. . . ."

101. *IDR*, 1908, pp. 718–720; 1909, pp. 162–172.

102. JHGA, INV-124-1, p. 112.

103. JHGA, INV-124-2, p. 161.

104. *IDR*, 1910, pp. 171, 485–534, 807–811; 1911, pp. 100–102, 286–287, 349–350.

105. *IDR*, 1909, pp. 1–7. A motion to force the pro-Mugdan member of the Executive Committee (Lövinson) to resign was defeated by only twenty votes at a regular meeting of the Centralverein on February 22, 1909. (*Ibid.*, pp. 237–261.)

106. *IDR*, 1909, pp. 109–111, 123–125, 129–143; *JR*, 1909, pp. 122, 137.

107. *IDR*, 1909, pp. 198–221; 1911, pp. 183, 253–256; 1912, p. 266; 1913, pp. 131–132.

108. *Ibid.*, 1910, p. 487; Theilhaber, pp. 118–119.

109. *Preussische Jahrbücher*, CII–CIII (1900–1901), 140.

110. *Ibid.*, pp. 131–140, 510–516.

111. Jakob Fromer, *Vom Ghetto zur modernen Kultur* (Heidelberg, 1906), *passim*.

112. *Idem*, "Das Wesen des Judenthums," *Die Zukunft*, 1904, pp. 440–456. The essay was reprinted by Fromer in his *Vom Ghetto*, pp. 195–236. The Centralverein published an uncompromising refutation. (*IDR*, 1904, pp. 377–386, 517–522, 546–547.)

113. Fromer, *Vom Ghetto, passim*. Theodor Nöldeke, the world-famous Orientalist, wrote a review of Fromer's book which appeared first in a Munich paper and was then reprinted in Strasbourg. In the review, Nöldeke, who had trained many Jewish students in the course of a brilliant career, contested the right of emancipated Jewry, and above all of its Reform component, to preserve a separate identity. He demanded of educated Jews that they at least should make it possible for their children to join the "dominant society" by having them baptized. At the request of the *Allgemeine Zeitung des Judentums*, Hermann Cohen responded with a hard-hitting, incisive rebuttal. As a

committed Reform Jew, Cohen attacked precisely the underlying refusal of liberal Protestants to recognize the religious sincerity of liberal Judaism. "The fundamental mistake here is the skepticism regarding liberal Judaism. There is either faith or lack of faith. In liberal Judaism, lack of faith dominates. Thus religion is unimportant. Thus the dark power of the 'dominant society' can legitimately make its demands. In a similar fashion, Theodor Mommsen in the role of our defender also gave us the worst advice." (H. Cohen, II, 374.)

Again Cohen repeated the warning that converts were Jewry's greatest enemy. Their opportunism was taken to prove the absence of religious conviction among liberal Jews and their personal sacrifice was used to reprove those Jews who failed to show similar concern for the national welfare. (*Ibid.*, II, 369–377.)

Margarete Susman also reviewed Fromer's book in the *Frankfurter Zeitung*, contending that in light of Judaism's capacity to develop, the emancipation from the ghetto and its ritualistic form of religion did not necessarily entail the dissolution of Judaism. See H. L. Goldschmidt, "Leben und Werk Margarete Susmans," in *Auf gespaltenem Pfad*, ed. by Manfred Schlösser (Darmstadt, 1964), pp. 36–37.

See also the review by R. Urbach, "Zwei Bücher über das Wesen des Judentums," *MGWJ*, L (1906), 129–151, in which Fromer's work is critically compared to that of the same name by Leo Baeck.

114. One other noteworthy example was the novelist Jakob Wassermann. In 1904 he had already depicted sympathetically the dimensions of the problem facing the emancipated Jew in Germany. Jakob Wassermann, "Das Los der Juden," in *Die Neue Rundschau* (August, 1904), pp. 940–948.

In 1921 he published the record of his personal commitment to the fusion of German and Jew: *Mein Weg als Deutscher und Jude* (Berlin, 1921). In contrast to the earlier essay, this was a book frequently bordering on despair. Moreover, by 1921 his condemnation of the Jew as the guilty party was unmitigated. He railed against the formalism of Judaism, bereft of beauty, spirit, and piety. He denounced its concept of God as a phantom and its sense of chosenness as a major obstruction to assimilation. He had not the slightest sense of kinship with Jews outside of Germany. Nevertheless, he remained a Jew. When asked by an old friend whether he was still a confirmed Jew, he answered: "A confirmed Jew? I really don't know what to do with that adjective. I am a Jew. With that everything is said. I cannot change it; I do not want to change it" (p. 94). See also pp. 15–16, 54, 102–103, 106–107, 119.

For a biographical description of this dualism produced by emancipation and anti-Semitism, see Solomon Liptzin, *Germany's Stepchildren* (New York and Philadelphia, 1961).

115. JHGA, K Ge 2/17. At the time Rathenau may have contemplated conversion. The judicial declaration preserved in Jerusalem would at least indicate that he did withdraw from the organized Jewish community, a step certainly in accord with his general antipathy toward organized religion. See especially Rathenau's pamphlet, *Eine Streitschrift vom Glauben* (Berlin, 1919). However, I have been unable to find any confirmation of such a withdrawal in the literature on Rathenau.

116. W. Hartenau, "Höre, Israel," *Die Zukunft*, 1897, pp. 455–456.

117. *Ibid.,* pp. 454–462. The editor of this important periodical was Maximilian Harden, a friend of Rathenau's who had himself converted to Protestantism at the age of sixteen, because it appeared to him to correspond more closely to the culture of his advanced civilization. Although a monarchist and an intense nationalist, he was a bitter critic of William II. See Toury, *Die politischen Orientierungen,* p. 268; Erich Gottgetreu, "Maximilian Harden: Ways and Eros of a Publicist," *LBIYB,* VII (1962), 237; Harry Young, *Maximilian Harden: Censor Germaniae* (Hague, 1959), pp. 10–15. Several years later, as we have seen, Harden published the controversial essay by Fromer. Thus periodically he offered his respected journal as a public forum for a discussion of the Jewish question. The charge of Jewish femininity was not uncommon during this period. In 1903 Otto Weininger, an unstable young baptized Jew, published a philosophic study on *Geschlecht und Charakter* in which he condemned Judaism as the very embodiment of the feminine principle of existence. (Liptzin, pp. 184–189.) To counter the charge, the early Zionists devoted considerable attention to physical fitness. See Adolf Böhm, *Die zionistische Bewegung,* I (2nd ed.; Berlin, 1935), 202–203; *JR,* 1908, pp. 491–492; 1912, p. 222.

118. *General-Anzeiger,* January 22, 1911, p. 1.

119. *Ibid.,* p. 2; see also Harry Kessler, *Walther Rathenau: His Life and Work* (New York, 1930), pp. 51–52. Rathenau's criticism of the government's Jewish policy provoked a defense by a Prussian aristocrat. In his subsequent answer, Rathenau, who during the war organized the government's procurement of raw materials, agreed that the present policy reflected the determination of the Prussian aristocracy to retain control. But even this policy would eventually be overcome by the needs of the new industrial state. This state required all the talent it could attract and it could ill afford to exclude the middle class and the Jews. (*General-Anzeiger,* February 5, 1911, pp. 1–2; February 12, 1911, pp. 1–2.)

120. *C-V Zeitung,* 1923, p. 218. Rathenau's concept of Judaism was most clearly delineated in his 1917 rejection of an invitation to convert. By then the urgency of war had driven the government to relax its discriminatory policy, and Rathenau's ethical objection to conversion had been obviated. Instead he now extolled Judaism as a free community of monotheists whose religion was purely spiritual. In contrast to both types of Christianity, it possessed neither dogma nor ecclesiastical organization. The essay was really an assault against all forms of organized religion, and Rathenau tried hard to depict Judaism as a wholly spiritual and voluntary alternative. (Rathenau, *Eine Streitschrift vom Glauben,* pp. 10–14, 16 ff.; see also Leo Baeck's sympathetic portrayal of Rathenau in "Types of Jewish Self-Understanding," *Judaism,* IX [1960], 159–163.)

121. *IDR,* 1902, p. 464; Fuchs, pp. 236–238, 272; JHGA, INV-124-2, p. 99. See also *infra,* ch. 7.

122. *Impressionen* (Leipzig, 1902), pp. 3–20; *IDR,* 1897, pp. 187–192; 1902, pp. 527–528; JHGA, INV-124-2, p. 53. In 1901 Löwenfeld withdrew from the Executive Committee of the Centralverein. No reason was recorded, although the resignation may not have been unrelated to the unfolding concern of the leadership for Jewish identity. (JHGA, INV-124-2, pp. 13, 17.) Löw-

enfeld did remain a member of the Centralverein. See *Mitglieder Verzeichnis* (Berlin, 1908), p. 51.

123. Fuchs, pp. 228, 237; *IDR*, 1903, p. 712; *C-V Zeitung*, 1924, pp. 1–3. Both Fuchs and Horwitz were Reform Jews. (*C-V Zeitung*, 1924, p. 3; Fuchs, p. 165.)

124. Ludwig Hollaender, *Deutsch-Jüdische Probleme der Gegenwart* (Berlin, 1929), pp. 5–23; Hirschberg, p. 67.

CHAPTER 6
A SECOND "FRONT": VERBAND DER
DEUTSCHEN JUDEN, 1904–1914

1. *MVZADA*, 1898, pp. 201–202, 209; 1903, pp. 201–202; *Der politische Antisemitismus*, hrsg. VZADA (Berlin, 1907), p. 10; Massing, pp. 71, 190; Tal, "Anti-Semitism in the Second German Reich," p. 8. In 1907 the anti-Semitic parties did manage to send seventeen deputies to the Reichstag, although their total vote was only 267,205 votes. (*Ibid.*)

2. *IDR*, 1901, pp. 571–605; Philippson, II, 61–64. Max Liebermann von Sonnenberg's *Der Blutmord in Konitz* (7th ed.; Berlin, 1901) went through six editions between December 1900 and February 1901. The Centralverein responded to the charge with *Der Gutachten der Sachverständigen über den Konitzer Mord, nach den amtlichen Akten* (Berlin, 1903). In his unpublished memoirs Sammy Gronemann, a Hanover lawyer, Zionist, and author, claimed to have uncovered evidence pointing to a Konitz "Schulmann." The man had allegedly caught the boy with his daughter and killed him in a fit of rage. (Sammy Gronemann, "Erinnerungen," ALBI, pp. 201–202.)

3. *MVZADA*, 1901, p. 43.

4. *Ibid.*, p. 44.

5. *Ibid.* Schönstedt provided some illuminating statistics on the number of Jews in the legal profession. Between 1887 and 1900 the percentage of Jewish lawyers in Prussia had risen from 20.4 percent to 26.8 percent of the total. In Berlin, out of 851 lawyers, 526 were Jews; and out of 176 notaries, there were 65 Jews (*ibid.*, p. 43). Theodor Barth, who in 1902 became president of the Abwehrverein, accused Schönstedt of subverting the Constitution. How was public sentiment to be measured? Every official could interpret it to suit his end, and the conduct of public affairs would become subjective and arbitrary (*ibid.*, p. 44).

At the beginning of 1902 the Catholic Center in Bavaria complained that Jews constituted 2.8 percent of the judges in Bavaria, although constituting only 1 percent of the population. Both houses passed a resolution asking the King to observe this ratio in appointing Jews to the judiciary. However, he rejected the request as an invasion of a royal prerogative. (*IDR*, 1902, pp. 1–7, 212–213.)

6. Fuchs, pp. 197–214. See also (Aron ?) Ackermann, *Vogelfrei* (Brandenburg a.H., 1901), pp. 11–18; *IDR*, 1901, pp. 81–82, 101, 236–237.

7. Fuchs, pp. 273–275.

8. Breslauer, "Erinnerung," p. 20; *IDR*, 1904, pp. 422–423; *Lexikon für Theologie und Kirche*, VI (Freiburg, 1961), cols. 69–72. The Katholikentag remained the vehicle for Catholic protest during the Kulturkampf after the German government dissolved the national Mainz Verein der Deutschen Katholiken in 1876. (Johannes B. Kissling, *Geschichte des Kulturkampfes im deutschen Reich*, III [Freiburg, 1916], 128–135. Regarding the influence of the Katholikentag on the Judentag proposal see also *AZJ*, 1900, pp. 601–602.) Philippson's article appeared in the *AZJ*, 1900, pp. 459–461; and the *Jüdische Presse*, 1900, pp. 425–426. A short obituary for Philippson was written by Ludwig Geiger in the *AZJ*, 1910, p. 616.

9. *Ost und West*, 1901, col. 86.

10. *IDR*, 1904, p. 76.

11. *AZJ*, 1900, pp. 482, 485–486, 495–497, 557–558, 585; *JJGL*, 1901, pp. 1–6; 1902, pp. 1–6; *IDR*, 1901, p. 101; 1902, pp. 257–259.

12. *Israelit*, 1900, pp. 1723–26. This article also reflected the position of the Freie Vereinigung für die Interessen des orthodoxen Judentums founded by Hirsch in 1885. The opposition of the separatistic Orthodox actually intensified once the idea of a Judentag had been dropped in favor of a *Gesamtorganisation* at the end of 1900. (JHGA, Kn II/A II 4.)

13. *AZJ*, 1900, pp. 557–558; M. Bodenheimer, *Zionismus und Judentag* (Cologne, [ca. 1901]), pp. 17–22; *Die Welt*, 1909, p. 941; *Ost und West*, 1901, cols. 87–89.

14. H. Bodenheimer, *Im Anfang der zionistischen Bewegung*, p. 187.

15. *Ibid.*, pp. 185–187, 194.

16. *Die Welt*, 1900, No. 41, p. 3.

17. Fuchs, p. 272; JHGA, INV-124-1, p. 117.

18. JHGA, Kn II/A II 4. See also Majorie Lamberti, "The Attempt to Form a Jewish Bloc: Jewish Notables and Politics in Wilhelmian Germany," *Central European History*, III (1970), 82–83.

19. *Die Welt*, 1901, No. 2, pp. 2–3; No. 5, pp. 5–6; No. 7, p. 5; *MVZADA*, 1901, pp. 17–18, 26–27; H. Bodenheimer, *Im Anfang der zionistischen Bewegung*, pp. 201–203; *IDR*, 1901, pp. 42–43.

20. This was Bodenheimer's opinion as well. (H. Bodenheimer, *Im Anfang der zionistischen Bewegung*, p. 206; see also *Die Welt*, 1909, pp. 941–942. On German Jewry's reaction to Zionism, see *infra*, ch. 7.)

21. JHGA, Kn II/A II 4; *Die Welt*, 1909, p. 942.

22. *IDR*, 1902, pp. 421–423.

23. See *supra*, pp. 113–114.

24. *AZJ*, 1901, pp. 541–542; JHGA, Kn II/A II 4; M 1/9 (*Zur Geschichte des DIGB*, pp. 36–40); *MDIGB*, No. 58, pp. 36–43; *IDR*, 1904, p. 257. There was also substantial opposition to the proposal from southern Germany. According to the delegate from Munich: "We southern Germans are not at all sympathetic toward the proposal. We have a government with which we can be legitimately satisfied, and we have no need to receive directives from a common center in Berlin or Königsberg." (*MDIGB*, No. 58, p. 40.)

25. JHGA, M 21/2; Kn II/A II 4; *IDR*, 1903, pp. 727–728; 1904, pp. 73–86, 253–265; *Jüdische Presse*, 1904, pp. 69–70, 171–174; *Die Welt*, 1904, No. 19, p. 2; *StB*, No. 1, p. 68. Bodenheimer and Alfred Klee represented the

Zionists, who continued to participate thereafter. See *Jüdische Presse*, 1904, p. 173; *Die Welt*, 1908, No. 23, p. 9; Walter Breslauer (son of Bernhard Breslauer), "Der Verband der Deutschen Juden," *BLBI*, VII (1964), p. 352. The failure of Walter Breslauer to consult the unpublished sources scattered in the files of the JHGA seriously limits the value of his account. See also the somewhat partisan account of the origin of the Verband by Jacob Toury, "Organizational Problems of German Jewry," *LBIYB*, XIII (1968), 57–72, as well as the more judicious analysis by Lamberti, pp. 73–93.

26. Friedländer, *Akten-Stücke*, p. 8; Tama, *passim*; Baron, *A Social and Religious History of the Jews*, V, 126; *idem, History and Jewish Historians* (Philadelphia, 1964), pp. 241, 442; Gerson D. Cohen, "Esau as Symbol in Early Medieval Thought," in *Jewish Medieval and Renaissance Studies*, ed. by Alexander Altmann (Cambridge, 1967), p. 35; Moshe Rinott, "Gabriel Riesser," *LBIYB*, VII (1962), 32–33.

The name of the Verband went through three discernible stages. The original draft of the constitution read: "Der Verband der Israeliten Deutschlands bezweckt die Vertretung der Gesamtinteressen der Israeliten Deutschlands." (JHGA, Kn II/A II 4.)

Fuchs proposed that this sentence ought to read: "Die Organisation der deutschen Juden bezweckt die Vertretung der israelitischen Gesamtinteressen der Juden Deutschlands." (*Ibid.*)

The final constitution, however, read: "Der Verband der deutschen Juden bezweckt die Vertretung aller den Juden Deutschlands gemeinsamen Interessen." (*Ibid.*)

27. Gronemann, p. 90.

28. Fuchs, pp. 281–282, 288–289; JHGA, M 21/2; *General-Anzeiger*, May 23, 1904, pp. 1–2; *StB*, No. 1, pp. 64–65; *KB*, No. 1, pp. 1–2; *Israelitisches Familienblatt*, 1908, No. 43, p. 2.

29. *Israelitisches Familienblatt*, 1908, No. 3, p. 1; JHGA, M 21/2; M 4/2; Kn II/A II 4; Kn II/A II 5; Kn II/A II 6; *GB*, No. 5, p. 14; No. 7, p. 16.

30. W. Breslauer, pp. 351, 359; *JR*, 1913, pp. 473, 525; *StB*, No. 2, p. 6; No. 4, pp. 4–6; No. 5, pp. 5, 7.

31. *StB*, No. 1, p. 69; *GB*, No. 7, p. 7. The board had the right to invite additional individuals to join. Thus in November of 1911 the full board had eighty-two members; the working board had only nineteen. (*GB*, No. 7, pp. 6–9.)

32. JHGA, Kn II/A II 4; Kn II/A II 5; *IDR*, 1904, p. 421; *GB*, No. 5, pp. 1–2.

33. JHGA, Kn II/A II 6.

34. JHGA, Kn II/A II 5; Kn II/A II 6; *GB*, No. 6, pp. 24–25.

35. *StB*, No. 1, p. 53; Felix Makower, *Bericht über die Tätigkeit des Verbandes der deutschen Juden bei der Vorbereitung des preussischen Volksschulunterhaltungsgesetzes von 1906* (Berlin, 1907), *passim; KB*, No. 12, pp. 1–22.

36. W. Breslauer, pp. 352–354.

37. *Israelitisches Familienblatt*, 1908, No. 43, pp. 2–3.

38. JHGA, M 21/2. The centrifugal forces fragmentizing German Jewry again undermined the efforts of the Gemeindebund. The most that could be achieved was a Federation of Prussian Jewish Communities (Preussischer Lan-

desverband jüdischer Gemeinden), representing 97 percent of Prussian Jewry. Its General Assembly was elected by direct vote. Though the Federation never received official government recognition, it operated from 1925 to 1933 with varying success. See Kurt Wilhelm, "The Jewish Community in the Post-Emancipation Period," *LBIYB*, II (1957), 65–67; Ahron Sandler, "The Struggle for Unification," *ibid.*, 76–84; Freund, *Die Rechtstellung*, pp. 28–36.

39. *KB*, No. 1, pp. 3–7. These eighty-two correspondents were located in thirty cities and fifty-two districts.

40. *Ibid.*, No. 4, p. 4; *GB*, No. 8, p. 7.

41. *KB*, No. 2, pp. 1–6. The conclusions of later reports merely confirmed and refined this original assessment. See *ibid.*, No. 4, pp. 6–7; No. 6, pp. 6–9; No. 8, p. 5; No. 10, p. 5. Unfortunately the reports themselves were never published. Only a summary of the major conclusions appeared. For a highly instructive personal account of the overtly hostile Jewish-Gentile relations in the small towns of Hesse at the end of the century, see the unpublished memoirs of S. Spiro.

42. *GB*, No. 7, pp. 17–18; *StB*, No. 5, pp. 13–14.

43. Hirsch Hildesheimer, ed., *Neue Gutachten über das jüdisch-rituelle Schlachtverfahren* (Berlin, 1908).

44. Adler-Rudel, p. 20; Helmut Neubach, *Die Ausweisungen von Polen und Juden aus Preussen 1885/86* (Wiesbaden, 1967), pp. 18–21, 122–129. Neubach, the most recent historian of the expulsions from 1884 through 1887, has concluded that Prussian policy was at least partially determined by muted anti-Semitic motives. At the time, Bismarck protested that the only objective was to rid the Eastern provinces of unwanted recent Polish immigrants. However, Neubach submits that the intention was also to protect the German *Mittelstand* and *Kleinbürgertum* against Polish Jewish competition as well as to rid the country of revolutionary Jewish intellectuals. (Neubach, pp. 219–220.)

45. Adler-Rudel, pp. 20–21, 24. Of the few cases of naturalization reported in Germany, only 36 percent occurred in Prussia, which in 1910 had 48,000 foreign-born Jews. (*Ibid.*, p. 21; *KB*, No. 8, p. 3.) The issue of Jewish immigration generated as much controversy in the final decades of the Empire as it had done in the days of Treitschke and the anti-Semitic petition. See Bahr, p. 68; Landsberger, pp. 15, 21, 37–38, 52, 75–76, 79–80, 109, 115.

46. *KB*, No. 10, p. 2; *GB*, No. 7, pp. 23–24; No. 8, pp. 16–18; *StB*, No. 5, p. 17; W. Breslauer, pp. 370–371; Ernst Rudolf Huber, *Dokumente zur Deutschen Verfassungsgeschichte*, II (Stuttgart, 1964), 249–253, 382–389.

47. Ziekursch, II, 237–241, 382–383; III, 189–190.

48. B. Breslauer, *Die Abwanderung der Juden aus der Provinz Posen* (Berlin, 1909); *StB*, No. 3, pp. 35–46; W. Breslauer (p. 369) agrees that general economic factors exerted a more decisive influence than the Verband was willing to admit. See *JR*, 1905, pp. 629–631; 1906, pp. 105–108; Richard Wonser Tims, *Germanizing Prussian Poland* (New York, 1966), pp. 210–211. In 1905, although the Jews of Posen constituted only 4 percent of the population, they still paid 25 percent of the Prussian income tax collected in the city. (Tims, p. 210.) A. Asch, who was born in the city of Posen in 1881, offers a valuable description of the city's social structure and the position of its Jewish population at the end of the century in his unpublished memoirs. He relates that as

far as promoting lawyers to notaries in Posen, the government maintained three separate lists: one for German Christians, a second for Jews, and a third for Poles. New appointments were always equally distributed among the three lists. But since the list of Jewish contenders was by far the longest, individual Jewish lawyers were of course seriously disadvantaged. (Asch, chapter on Posen.)

    49. *GB*, No. 6, pp. 24–25; No. 7, pp. 20–21, 37–39; *StB*, No. 4, p. 16; JHGA, Kn II/A II 5.

    50. B. Breslauer, *Die Zurücksetzung der Juden an den Universitäten Deutschlands* (Berlin, 1911), pp. 12–13. Many of the Jewish faculty members objected strongly to Breslauer's study. "Many of them did not want the investigation at all. Some feared that the result would cause the proper authorities to push back the Jews still further than [they had been] up to now. All possible objections were raised in this connection. One [man] felt that the present questions had nothing to do with anti-Semitism; another feared the impossibility of arriving at a reliable conclusion. In short, the information was refused for every possible reason" (p. 5). For the Conservatives' defense of government policy, see Tal, *Christians and Jews,* pp. 97–101.

    51. *KB*, No. 6, pp. 1–2. These restrictions must be measured against the extraordinary number of young Jews entering the secondary schools and universities of Germany. The following table represents those children out of the total population of school-age children receiving a secondary education:

State	Year	Percentage of Christians	Percentage of Jews
Prussia	1906–1907	7.9	58.9
Bavaria	1905–1906	5.5	39.6
Baden	1905–1906	7.1	45.2
Hamburg	1906–1907	20.9	95.6
Berlin	1906	14.1	67.5
Frankfurt	1906	26.5	86.6

In 1905–1906, Jews represented 6.97 percent of all students studying at Prussian universities. They represented 16.14 percent of those in medicine, 9.35 percent of those in law, and 4.88 percent of those in philosophy. Yet in 1905, the 409,501 Jews in Prussia constituted only 1.1 percent of the total Prussian population. (Ruppin, *The Jews of Today,* pp. 39, 126, 130.)

    52. *StB*, No. 4, pp. 28–29; see also *StB*, No. 1, pp. 42–43, 45; *IDR*, 1905, p. 572; Röhl, "Higher Civil Servants in Germany," p. 111. Röhl quotes the following observation from the memoirs of Alexander von Hohenhole, a Junker critic of the Prussian Court: "If the father or grandfather had allowed himself to be baptised . . . and if the son had refurbished the tarnished glory of some noble family with his inherited wealth by marrying one of the daughters, then people were prepared to disregard his race so long as this was not all too obvious in his facial features" (p. 111).

    The rich memoir literature of the period poignantly translates the statistics compiled by the Verband into personal terms. There is little doubt that academic discrimination was a well-known constant of Jewish life, dissuading many from embarking on certain careers and frustrating many of those brave enough to try. Generally, advancement awaited only the exceptional or baptized Jew. See, for example, Fraenkel, pp. 75–89, 103–104; Herz, pp. 180–181, 191–192; E. G. Lowenthal, "Wie Ich zum Geographen Wurde," *BLBI*, 1965, p. 102; Eduard Isaac, "Aus Meinem Leben," ALBI, pp. 22, 34; Rosenberg, p. 104.

53. Freund, "Staat, Kirche und Judentum in Preussen," *JJGL*, XIV (1911), 109–111, 138. Graetz had concluded the first edition of Volume XI of his *Geschichte der Juden*, which brought his narrative up to the 1848 revolutions, with an undisguised reference to his own day: "The recognition of Jews as equal members is already largely realized; the recognition of Judaism, however, still faces tough opposition" (p. 582).

This remark was one of the many in the volume attacked by Treitschke in his critical essay of 1879 (Boehlich, pp. 45–46). M. Brann, who edited a second edition of Graetz's eleventh volume in 1900, omitted the passage along with a number of others that Treitschke had found offensive. (Graetz, *Geschichte der Juden*, XI [2nd ed., ed. by M. Brann; Leipzig, 1900], pp. vii–viii.)

54. *StB*, No. 2, pp. 26–27.

55. Freund, "Staat, Kirche und Judentum in Preussen," pp. 130–132. See also *idem, Die Rechtsstellung*, pp. 219–226.

56. Freund, "Staat, Kirche und Judentum in Preussen," p. 132; *idem, Die Rechtsstellung*, p. 231.

57. *MVZADA*, 1909, pp. 50–54.

58. F. Makower, *Bericht über die Tatigkeit des Verbandes*, pp. 26–30; Freund, *Die Rechtsstellung*, pp. 11–12, 229–232. Because of the accumulation of legislation and ministerial edicts in the various provinces during the course of the nineteenth century, it was by no means a simple task to determine what exactly was the status quo in any one area. Since the 1906 law left unchanged all matters concerning the opening, financing, and administration of public Jewish *Volksschulen*, the hiring of Jewish teachers at Christian *Volksschulen*, and the offering of Jewish religious instruction at Christian *Volksschulen*, the Verband commissioned Freund to establish what precisely constituted present practice and law. The result was his comprehensive *Die Rechtsstellung;* see Vorwort.

59. Freund, *Die Rechtsstellung*, pp. 236–237.

60. JHGA, M 4/2; *MVZADA*, 1909, pp. 50–54; *GB*, No. 7, pp. 31–36; No. 8, pp. 13–14; No. 9, p. 18; *StB*, No. 5, p. 14.

61. H. Cohen, II, 354–356.

62. Ferdinand Weber, *System der altsynagogalen palästinischen Theologie aus Targum, Midrash und Talmud* (Leipzig, 1880); Emil Schürer, *Geschichte der jüdischen Volkes im Zeitalter Jesu Christi* (3 vols., 3rd ed.; Leipzig, 1898–1902); D. Wilhelm Bousset, *Jesu Predigt in ihrem Gegensatz zum Judentum* (Göttingen, 1892); *idem, Die Religion des Judentums im neutestamentlichen Zeitalter* (Berlin, 1903). See especially George Foot Moore, "Christian Writers on Judaism," *Harvard Theological Review*, XIV (1921), 228–254;

also Israel Abrahams, *Studies in Pharisaism and the Gospels, First and Second Series*, with prolegomenon by Morton S. Enslin (New York, 1968), pp. v–xxiv.

63. Adolf Harnack, *Das Wesen des Christentums* (3rd ed.; Leipzig, 1900), pp. 69–70, 109–110, 116–117, 119; Josef Eschelbacher, "Die Vorlesungen Adolf Harnack's über das Wesen des Christenthums," *MGWJ*, XLVI (1902), 137–138; Felix Perles, "What Jews May Learn from Harnack," *JQR*, XIV (1902), pp. 523, 540.

64. Abrahams, "Professor Schürer on Life under the Jewish Law," *JQR*, XI (1899), 628, 630–631; Perles, *Bousset's Religion des Judentums in neutestamentlichen Zeitalter kritisch untersucht* (Berlin, 1903), pp. 6–18, 22–24; Moritz Güdemann, "Das Judentum im neutestamentlichen Zeitalter in christlicher Darstellung," *MGWJ*, XLVII (1903), 236–249. Jewish critics were angered by the caution that Christian theologians advised in using the works of Jewish scholars. Witness Perles' bitter comment on Schürer: "Schürer sticks in a similar warning in his history, when he marks the works of Jewish scholars in the bibliography (Vol. I, pp. 4 ff.) with an asterisk, whereby one is unintentionally reminded of the yellow patch, by means of which Jews in former times could be recognized already from a great distance" (p. 7).

65. Perles, *Bousset's Religion des Judentums*, pp. 21–22. Güdemann, "Das Judentum im neutestamentlichen Zeitalter," pp. 247–249.

66. Güdemann, "Das Judentum im neutestamentlichen Zeitalter," pp. 120–136, 231–235; Baeck, "Harnack's Vorlesungen über das Wesen des Christenthums," *MGWJ*, XLV (1901), 107; Eschelbacher, "Die Vorlesungen Adolf Harnach's," pp. 229–235; *idem, Das Judentum im Urteile der modernen protestantischen Theologie* (Leipzig, 1907), pp. 3–11, 31–34; Abrahams, "Professor Schürer," pp. 632–639, 641.

67. Friedrich Delitzsch, *Babel und Bibel: Ein Vortrag* (Leipzig, 1902); *idem, Zweiter Vortrag über Babel und Bibel* (Stuttgart, 1904). For a list of the literature provoked by the first lecture, see *Zweiter Vortrag*, pp. 43–47. See also Jacob J. Finkelstein, "Bible and Babel," *Commentary*, XXVI (1958), 431–444.

68. Benno Jacob, "Das Judenthum und die Ergebnisse des Assyriologie," *AZJ*, 1902, pp. 187, 211–212, 222–225; *idem*, "Prof. Delitzsch' Zweiter Vortrag über Babel und Bibel," *AZJ*, 1903, pp. 197–198; Baeck, *Das Wesen des Judentums* (Berlin, 1905), pp. 6–8; I. Münz, *Dr. Wilhelm Münz: Ein Gedenkblatt* (n.p., n.d., [1917?]), pp. 14–16.

69. In addition to the articles by Abrahams and Perles already mentioned, see, among many others, Solomon Schechter's earlier review of Harvard Professor C. H. Toy's *Judaism and Christianity, a Sketch of the Progress of Thought from Old Testament to New Testament* in *JQR*, III (1891), 754–766; also C. G. Montefiore, "Rabbinic Judaism and the Epistles of St. Paul," *JQR*, XIII (1901), 161–217.

70. Schechter, *Seminary Addresses and Other Papers* (New York, 1959), p. 37; see also pp. 35–39.

71. R. Travers Herford, *The Pharisees* (New York, 1924), pp. 11–17; Moore, "Christian Writers on Judaism," pp. 252–253; *idem, Judaism in the First Centuries of the Christian Era*, I (Cambridge, 1954), 125–134; Herbert

F. Hahn, "Wellhausen's Interpretation of Israel's Religious History: A Reappraisal of His Ruling Ideas," in *Essays on Jewish Life and Thought*, ed. Joseph Blau et al., (New York, 1959), pp. 299–308. The most recent, expansive, and penetrating analysis of the tense dialectic relationship between Jewish and Protestant scholarship in Germany on the inter-testamental period is by Tal, *Christians and Jews*, pp. 134–171.

72. H. Cohen, II, 134. See also *IDR*, 1902, pp. 386–388, 474; *AZJ*, 1902, pp. 73–74, 342; 1903, pp. 37, 39; 1905, p. 85; Eschelbacher, *Das Judentum im Urteile*, p. 24; Güdemann, *Jüdische Apologetik* (Glogau, 1906), pp. viii, 228; A. Samter, pp. 94–144; R. Urbach, "Judentum und Christentum," *MGWJ*, L (1906), 257–288. In this 1907 essay, Cohen proposed to the B'nai B'rith that it raise funds to pay Jewish *Dozenten* to teach Judaica at German universities. Since such men were doomed by the system to remain unsalaried instructors, the Jewish community had to ensure them a respectable income. The reasoning behind this proposal had not changed since the days of Zunz, who had also fought in vain to gain entry for Jewish studies into the sacred halls of the university.

"What Zunz wrote remains true: 'The equality of the Jew in practice and life will derive from the equality extended to the scholarly study of Judaism [Wissenschaft des Judentums].' The extension of equality to our scholarly endeavor is the indispensable prerequisite for the genuine achievement of social equality. But equality for scholarship, at least in Germany, can . . . only be achieved at the university. . . . German scholarship has developed predominantly at the universities." (H. Cohen, II, 139.)

73. See *supra*, pp. 7–8, 10–11, 44–47, 111–113.

74. Leopold Lucas, "Zum 25jährigen Jubiläum der Gesellschaft zur Förderung der Wissenschaft des Judentums," *MGWJ*, LXXI (1927), 321–331; Elbogen, "Zum Jubiläum der Gesellschaft zur Förderung der Wissenschaft des Judentums," *ibid.*, LXXII (1928), 1–5; *AZJ*, 1902, pp. 532–533; 1903, pp. 565–566.

75. Baeck, *Das Wesen des Judentums*, pp. 9–17, 25, 32–36, 93–112; Eschelbacher, *Das Judentum und das Wesen des Christentums*, (2nd ed.; Berlin, 1908).

76. Güdemann, *Jüdische Apologetik*, pp. 8, 9, 18, 28, 31, 44–45. Already four years earlier, Güdemann, the chief rabbi of Vienna, had countered Harnack with *Das Judenthum in seinen Grundzügen und nach seinen geschichtlichen Grundlagen dargestellt* (Vienna, 1902).

77. Some of the early important publications were:

Wilhelm Bacher, *Tradition und Tradenten in den Schulen Palästinas und Babyloniens* (Leipzig, 1914).

Georg Caro, *Sozial- und Wirtschaftsgeschichte der Juden im Mittelalter und der Neuzeit* (2 vols.; Leipzig, 1908–1920).

Ismar Elbogen, *Der jüdische Gottesdienst in seiner geschichtlichen Entwicklung* (Leipzig, 1913).

Samuel Krauss, *Talmudische Archaeologie* (3 vols.; Leipzig, 1910–1912).

Nikolaus Müller, *Die jüdische Katakombe am Monteverde zu Rom* (Leipzig, 1912).

78. JHGA Kn II/A II 4. The original draft read: "Die Erörterung religiö-

ser, kultureller und ritueller Fragen ist nur insoweit statthaft, als es sich um die Abwehr von Angriffen Andersgläubiger handelt." However, at a meeting on November 29, 1903, those present unanimously voted to strike the word *Andersgläubiger.*

79. *StB*, No. 1, p. 31.

80. *Berliner Tageblatt,* Morgen-Ausgabe, October 31, 1905; copy in JHGA, Kn II / A II 4.

81. *StB*, No. 2, p. 6; No. 3, pp. 15–17, 22–23. From 1881 to 1886 Count von Zedlitz-Trützscheler was Regierungspräsident in Oppeln. At the time of the expulsions in 1885 from the Eastern provinces, he informed the Prussian government in a memorandum on the subject that he considered the Jews to be a "veritable scourge of the province." From 1886 to 1891 he served as Oberpräsident of Posen, and from 1903 to 1909, as Oberpräsident of Silesia. (Neubach, pp. 59–60.)

82. *Die Welt,* 1909, pp. 941–942; JHGA, Kn II / A II 5; *StB,* No. 4, p. 6; No. 5, p. 7.

83. JHGA, Kn II / A II 4. Nevertheless, the apologetic work of the Verband was carried on almost solely by the rabbis and scholars of non-Orthodox German Jewry (Ismar Elbogen, Leo Baeck, Hermann Cohen, Joseph Eschelbacher, Albert Lewkowitz, Heimann Vogelstein, Sigmund Maybaum, Jakob Guttmann, Moritz Güdemann, among others), and hence the image of Judaism projected was definitely not Orthodox.

84. *KB*, Nos. 1–14, 1907–1914; JHGA, Kn II / A II 5; Guttmann's speech, "Die Idee der Versöhnung im Judentum," was reprinted in *Vom Judentum* (Heft, No. 2).

85. JHGA, M 4 / 2; Kn II / A II 5; *KB,* No. 3, pp. 7–8; No. 10, pp. 11–12; *GB,* No. 6, p. 20.

86. *KB*, No. 14, p. 13; *Soziale Ethik im Judentum* (Frankfurt a.M., 1913).

87. *Die Lehren des Judentums nach den Quellen,* 5 vols., ed. by Simon Bernfeld (I–IV) and Fritz Bamberger (V) (Leipzig, 1920–1929). See the reviews by Isaac Heinemann, *MGWJ,* 1925, pp. 113–117; 1929, pp. 419–420.

88. JHGA, M 4 / 2; Kn II / A II 5; *KB,* No. 3, pp. 3–4; *GB,* No. 5, p. 16; *MVZADA,* 1903, p. 298. Inducing Jews to read this literature was by no means a simple matter. (JHGA, Kn II / A II 4.) On the medieval disputations, see Baron, *A Social and Religious History of the Jews,* V, 112.

CHAPTER 7

INTERNAL DISCONTENT, 1897–1914

1. *IDR*, 1913, p. 200.

2. *Ibid.,* 1896, pp. 193–195.

3. *MVZADA,* 1897, p. 299.

4. Fuchs, pp. 227–229. He had stressed the Centralverein's disagreement with Zionism as early as 1895. (*Ibid.,* p. 58.)

5. *IDR,* 1899, pp. 230–231.

6. JHGA, INV-124-2, pp. 60, 153–154, 168; *IDR,* 1913, pp. 234–235.

7. *IDR,* 1902, p. 464; Fuchs, p. 272. Fuchs was probably the most decisive

moderating influence on the Executive Committee. To the occasional chagrin of others on the committee, he openly admitted that Zionism was making some positive contributions to the German Jewish scene. Without accepting the national viewpoint of Ahad Ha-Am, he did come to favor the idea that Palestine ought to become "a spiritual, religious center for all Jews," and he supported colonization toward that end. The Zionist leaders recognized him as a friend, and one suggested that if Fuchs had been born twenty years later he would have been a Zionist. The confrontation with Zionism was certainly one of the factors leading to the development of his own concept of Judaism. Committed to the ideal of unity, Fuchs tried hard to avoid the conflict that erupted in 1913. (JHGA, INV-124-2, p. 99; *JR*, 1913, p. 187; *C-V Zeitung*, 1924, p. 4. See also *supra*, pp. 147–148.)

8. See *supra*, pp. 97–98.

9. H. Bodenheimer, *The History of the Basle Program* (Hebrew) (Jerusalem, 1947), pp. v, ix–xii, xvi, xxix–xxx, xxxiii–xxxiv; Werner J. Cahnman, "Munich and the First Zionist Congress," *Historia Judaica*, III (1941), 7–23.

10. JHGA, M 4/1; *AZJ*, 1897, p. 333. See also the more general treatment of non-Zionist and anti-Zionist reactions in Western Europe by Ben Halpern, *The Idea of the Jewish State* (Cambridge, 1961), pp. 131–176.

11. Gronemann, pp. 81, 84, 86, 101, 104–106, 146.

12. Sandler, p. 77; Lichtheim, *A Remnant Will Return*, p. 139.

13. Wilhelm, "Der Zionistische Rabbiner," in *In Zwei Welten*, ed. by Hans Tramer (Tel Aviv, 1962), pp. 61–62. In 1902 the administration of the Reform Rabbinical Seminary in Berlin forced the dissolution of the National-jüdische Verein der Hörer an der Lehranstalt für die Wissenschaft des Judentums. (*Ibid.*, pp. 65–67.) One of its members was the young American Judah L. Magnes. (Norman Bentwich, *For Zion's Sake* [Philadelphia, 1954], pp. 25–26.) The administration of Hebrew Union College, the Reform seminary in the United States, was equally antagonistic toward Zionists within its ranks. Between 1904 and 1907 at least five members of the faculty who strongly sympathized with Zionism resigned under administration pressure. (Naomi W. Cohen, "The Reaction of Reform Judaism in America to Political Zionism [1897–1922]," *PAJHS*, XL [1950–1951], 372–382.)

14. *JR*, 1907, pp. 167–171, 177–179, 189, 198, 205, 209–211; Emil Cohn, *Die Geschichte meiner Suspension* (Berlin, April 1907); *idem, Mein Kampf ums Recht* (Berlin, May 1907). See also now the interesting personal file of Emil Cohn on this case in the ALBI, which includes a warm letter of support to Cohn from Leo Baeck.

From Cohn's account of the discussion, the views of the director, Dr. Przygode, who proudly posed as a philo-Semite, on the Jewish question were typical of the latent anti-Semitism which German Jews so often heard from their "friends." "The man calls himself a philo-Semite. . . . He hopes for the complete disappearance of the Jews into Germanism. He favors intermarriage and sees nothing dishonorable in conversion, even if it is not the result of conviction. . . . At any rate he is delighted with every Jewish father who sends his child to Christian religious instruction, and he is proud that at his school there are more than a few of this type." (Cohn, *Die Geschichte meiner Suspension*, pp. 4–5.)

15. H. Bodenheimer, *Im Anfang der zionistischen Bewegung*, pp. 20–21, 34–36. In 1894 Bodenheimer and David Wolffsohn had formed a small National-jüdische Vereinigung in Cologne. Its principles asserted that the Jews constituted a national entity and that the ultimate solution of the Jewish problem demanded the erection of a Jewish state. (*Ibid.*, pp. 15, 22.)

16. *Ibid.*, p. 60. On September 20, 1897, Bodenheimer had reported to Herzl: "The hunt [*Hetzjagd*] has begun. From all sides the dogs are digging their teeth into our loins. Hopefully we will soon find the strength to smash the entire pack. The lodges are working systematically [against us]; likewise the defense organizations and the organization of German Citizens of the Jewish Confession [sic]" (p. 57).

17. *IDR*, 1897, p. 479.

18. *Die Referate der Herren Schach und Dr. Schauer über Organisation und Agitation*, hrsg. ZVfD; *Protokol des III Delegiertentags der deutschen Zionisten*, p. 1.

19. *IR*, May 30, 1902, *JR*, 1904, p. 222; also Lichtheim, *The History of Zionism in Germany* (Hebrew) (Jerusalem, 1951), p. 99; *idem, A Remnant Will Return*, p. 137. One year after the death of Herzl, the leadership of the international Zionist movement passed into German hands. The Seventh Zionist Congress, meeting in Basle in the Summer of 1905, elected two German delegates, David Wolffsohn and Otto Warburg, as members of the seven-man Executive Committee, and Wolffsohn as president of the organization. The new president, who resided in Cologne, immediately transferred the offices of the Central Bureau and *Die Welt*, the Zionist weekly, there. When Warburg became the third president of the organization in 1911, both offices were moved to Berlin, where they remained until the outbreak of the war. Thus one may legitimately designate the years 1905–14 as the period of German leadership. (Böhm, I, 313–319.)

20. CZA, A 15/19.

21. *Zionistisches A-B-C- Buch* (Berlin, 1908), pp. 85–86; *IR*, May 9, 1902, p. 19; *JR*, 1904, pp. 254–255. Although *Die Welt* was published in German, Loewe had felt as early as 1898 that it could not serve effectively the direct needs of the German Zionists. In a long letter to Wolffsohn, he proposed a separate paper for the German Zionist Federation. (CZA, A 15/VII 5 [L-M].) Loewe retired as editor at the end of 1908 in the face of rising criticism within the organization. Thereafter the scope of the paper was gradually circumscribed to Zionist matters alone. The radicalization had begun. (CZA, A 15/VII 21.)

The use of the adjective *jüdische* in the title was probably influenced by Herzl's declaration in the first issue of *Die Welt* (June 3, 1897): "Our weekly is a Jew-paper (*Judenblatt*). . . . We are taking this word, which is supposedly a term of abuse, and we shall transform it into a word of honor." (Böhm, I, 179.)

22. Lichtheim, *The History of Zionism in Germany*, pp. 98, 116–117; Kurt Blumenfeld, *Erlebte Judenfrage* (Stuttgart, 1962), p. 50.

23. *Die Referate der Herren Schach und Dr. Schauer*. In the well-known exchange of letters in 1897 between Bodenheimer and Hermann Schapira, a professor of mathematics at Heidelberg and an old supporter of Palestinian

colonization (*Hibbat Zion*), Schapira warned of splitting German Jewry still further by waving the flag of Jewish nationalism. At that time Bodenheimer already regarded the warning more sympathetically than some other German Zionists. (H. Bodenheimer, *The History of the Basle Program*, pp. xx, xxv–xxvi, xlii.)

24. *Der Nationaljude als Staatsbürger*, Flugblatt No. 2, hrsg. ZVfD, 1897.

25. *Was Will der Zionismus?*, hrsg. ZVfD (Berlin, 1903), p. 12. Paradoxically, the criterion for nationality was identical with that proposed by Moritz Lazarus back in 1879—that is, popular will.

26. *Unser Programm*, Flugblatt No. 4, hrsg. ZVfD ([ca. 1897]). *JR*, 1903, p. 45; Max Nordau, "Der Zionismus der westlichen Juden," *JR*, May 26, 1903, Sonderausgabe; *Was Will der Zionismus?*, pp. 17–18; Fabius Schach, *Über die Zukunft Israels* (Berlin, 1904), p. 13.

27. *JR*, 1904, pp. 222–223; *Die Welt*, 1904, No. 23, p. 8.

28. *JR*, 1904, pp. 225–228; Gronemann, p. 77. The Basle Program read: "Zionism strives to create for the Jewish people a home in Palestine secure of public law. The Congress contemplates the following means to the attainment of this end:

1. The promotion on suitable lines, of the colonization of Palestine by Jewish agricultural and industrial workers.

2. The organization and binding together of the whole of Jewry by means of appropriate institutions, local and international, in accordance with the laws of each country.

3. The strengthening and fostering of Jewish national sentiment and consciousness.

4. Preparatory steps toward obtaining Government consent, where necessary, to the attainment of the aim of Zionism." (Oscar I. Janowsky, *Foundations of Israel* [New York, 1959], p. 134.)

29. *Die Welt*, 1904, No. 24, pp. 3–5. On February 26, 1899, Bodenheimer informed Adolf Friedemann of his personal reasons for resisting the pressure to settle in Berlin: "My moving to Berlin is scarcely conceivable, since I would have to give up here a fairly decent practice, and this [I] could [do] only if I could figure on at least the same income in Berlin.

"If you should discover in your area an opportunity, I would be delighted. I could not bring myself merely to settle there as an attorney, since I would have to invest years of energetic legal work to reach—confidentially—my current practice of about 20,000 marks, and then [I] would be unable to devote to the [Zionist] cause either time or strength." (CZA, A 15 / I 9.)

30. *Die Welt*, 1910, pp. 139–143; Franz Oppenheimer, *Erlebtes, Erstrebtes, Erreichtes: Lebenserinnerungen* (Düsseldorf, 1964), p. 210. See also Herzl's defense of Oppenheimer in a letter to Bodenheimer dated June 16, 1903, in H. Bodenheimer, *Im Anfang der zionistischen Bewegung*, pp. 280–281.

31. H. Bodenheimer, *Im Anfang der zionistischen Bewegung*, p. 63; *JR*, May 26, 1903, Sonderausgabe; 1904, pp. 50, 264–265, 277–278; 1905, pp. 85, 115–116, 119; 1907, pp. 93–94, 318–319, 541–545. In 1902 Bodenheimer submitted a *Denkschrift* to the German government in an effort to interest it in supporting the creation of a Jewish homeland in Palestine. Based upon the Herzlian assumption that a Jewish state would contribute to the alleviation of

internal tensions and therefore interest European governments, the *Denkschrift* suggested that a Jewish state would terminate the immigration from Eastern Europe, withdraw idealistic Jewish youth from Socialism, and remove from German society the religious and national elements unwilling to assimilate. Herzl lauded the *Denkschrift* as a masterpiece. (H. Bodenheimer, *Im Anfang der zionistischen Bewegung*, pp. 218–227.)

32. *Der Zionismus*, Flugblatt No. 1, hrsg. ZVfD, 1897; *Die Welt*, 1902, No. 22, pp. 2–4; No. 23, pp. 3–5; *JR*, 1908, pp. 151–153, 393–394.

33. Bernhard Cohn, *Jüdisch-politische Zeitfragen* (Berlin, 1899), pp. 43–44; M. Bodenheimer, *Zionismus und Judentag* (Cologne, [ca. 1901]), p. 8; *JR*, 1903, p. 153.

34. Regarding the Centralverein, see *supra*, p. 147.

35. M. Bodenheimer, *Zionismus und Judentag*, p. 12.

36. *Die Welt*, 1900, No. 41, p. 2; 1901, No. 2, p. 3; 1902, No. 28, pp. 4–6.

37. *IDR*, 1903, p. 187; *JR*, 1908, p. 219; *Zionistisches A-B-C- Buch*, pp. 274, 279, 288–289. It should be noted that by 1908 the amicable relations with the Centralverein were part of a broader reconciliation with the major sectors of German Jewry initiated by the Zionist Federation. The convention of 1908 officially welcomed "the work of the other large Jewish organizations, in so far as it serves the structure and unity of Jewry as a whole as well as strengthening Jewish identity and national consciousness." (*JR*, 1908, p. 223.) The major motive seems to have been to tap non-Zionist financial resources for immediate colonization, especially since after the Uganda controversy the prospects for a charter had dimmed. (*JR*, 1907, pp. 275–277; 1908, pp. 220–221, 245–246, 263–266; *Zionistisches A-B-C- Buch*, p. 175.)

38. *JR*, 1903, pp. 267–268; 1905, pp. 663–664; 1907, pp. 65–66; 1908, pp. 60, 127–128; Toury, *Die politischen Orientierungen*, pp. 209–210, 276–294.

39. On relations in Posen, see *JR*, 1903, pp. 521–522, 532; 1908, pp. 61, 75–76, 298; Toury, *Die politischen Orientierungen*, pp. 340–342. On relations in Hamburg, see *JR*, 1904, pp. 174–175, 191–192; *Israelitisches Familienblatt*, 1908, No. 27, p. 3; CZA, A 15/VII 21.

40. Witness Richard Lichtheim's letter of April 1, 1908, to Arthur Hantke: "Nothing is really of much value when the leadership fails to heed the dictates [of the National Convention]. It is also vital that in purely Zionist questions the Zionists [themselves] should receive instructions, which today are totally wanting. . . . Zionism must not suffer because of Bodenheimer. I have pity for this old man. But if the lack of direction continues, all the discontented students will soon depart." (CZA, A II/32/9.)

41. *JR*, 1908, pp. 234–235, 246–247, 255–257; 1909, p. 461.

42. CZA, A 15/VII 21; A 15/VII 22; A 102/12/4; A 102/12/3/1; Blumenfeld, *Erlebte Judenfrage*, pp. 16–17.

43. Blumenfeld, *Erlebte Judenfrage*, pp. 67–68.

44. *Ibid.*, pp. 59–60.

45. CZA, A 15/VII 25.

46. *JR*, 1912, p. 222.

47. *Ibid.*, p. 206.

48. *Ibid.*, 1914, p. 270.

49. *JR*, 1914, p. 267.

50. CZA, A 15/VII 25.

51. *Ibid.*, A 15/VII 27; see also CZA, A 142/237; A 102/12/6.

52. *JR*, 1914, p. 271.

53. Hans Kohn, ed., *Nationalism and the Jewish Ethic: Basic Writings of Ahad Ha-Am* (New York, 1962), pp. 44–154; Leon Simon, *Ahad Ha-Am* (Philadelphia, 1960), pp. 169–194; Alex Bein, *Theodore Herzl* (Philadelphia, 1956), p. 165.

54. Böhm, pp. 485–503, 594–603.

55. Both the Russian and Austrian Zionist organizations in 1906 adopted platforms calling for Jewish nationality rights in their respective countries. With the prospects of a charter receding, both groups concentrated upon developing a national consciousness among the Jewish masses by working for nationality rights. The promise of a Duma in Russia and the assurance of universal suffrage in Austria made the internal conditions for such *Gegenwartsarbeit* quite favorable. (Oscar Janowsky, *The Jews and Minority Rights (1898–1919)* [New York, 1933], pp. 98–113, 137–140.)

In America before the war, the Federation of American Zionists "never encouraged the *aliyah* of American youth to aid in rebuilding the desolate land. In practical terms, early American Zionists were asked for no more than financial contributions and loyalty to a political ideal." (N. Cohen, "The *Maccabaean's* Message: A Study in American Zionism until World War I," *Jewish Social Studies*, XVIII, [1956], 177.)

56. M. Bodenheimer, *Prelude to Israel*, pp. 60–98, 134–135; Oppenheimer, pp. 210–215; Lichtheim, *The History of Zionism in Germany*, pp. 92–95; *Die Welt*, 1902, No. 46, pp. 3–5; 1903, No. 3, pp. 1–2; *JR*, 1902, pp. 65–67, 73–74; 1903, pp. 49–51. Early Zionist literature did, however, cite the tenacity of German anti-Semitism as one more reason for becoming a Zionist. (*Deutsche Juden*, Flugblatt No. 6; *Was Will der Zionismus?*, p. 16.) Furthermore, some early Zionists clearly joined in bitter protest against German anti-Semitism. Yet the despondency of Bernhard Cohn, a physician for many years in a small Berlin suburb who was eventually driven out by anti-Semitism, was not typical. In his 1896 pamphlet *Vor dem Sturm* (Berlin), he recommended emigration, for German Jewry was in the midst of "a real war situation . . . in which the legal question is no longer even considered" (p. 12). By 1899 Cohn had become a fervent Zionist. See his *Jüdisch-politische Zeitfragen*, which also contained a thoroughly negative critique of the Centralverein (pp. 24–39). Cohn was the father of Emil Cohn, the young liberal Zionist rabbi dismissed by the Berlin Jewish Community in 1907. (*Supra*, p. 181 f.; Hans Tramer, "Bernhard und Emil Cohn," *BLBI*, VIII (1965), 340–345.) First-generation Zionists like Fabius Schach and Adolf Friedemann likewise joined in protest against a painful dualism created by anti-Semitism. (*IDR*, 1900, pp. 437–442; *Die Welt*, 1910, pp. 304–305.)

57. Lichtheim, *The History of Zionism in Germany*, p. 102; *IR*, September 26, 1902; Böhm, pp. 485–486; M. Bodenheimer, *Prelude to Israel*, pp. 39–40; Straus, pp. 43–44, 47–53, 77–80, 100, 170; Robert Weltsch, "Deutscher Zionismus in der Rückschau," in Tramer, *In Zwei Welten*, pp. 31–32; Salo Translateur, "Erinnerungen aus meiner ersten zionistischen Tätigkeit in Breslau, Schlesien, von 1898 bis 1904," *ALBI*, p. 1; Spiro, p. 40; Herz,

p. 178; Elias Auerbach, *Pioneer der Verwirklichung* (Stuttgart, 1969), pp. 71–72, 98–99.

58. *IR*, March 21, 1902; May 2, 1902; August 8, 1902; *JR*, 1906, p. 587; 1907, pp. 86–88. The entire Zionist movement at the time appealed overwhelmingly to students. (Hans Kohn, *Martin Buber* [2nd ed., Cologne, 1961], pp. 23–24.)

59. Blumenfeld, *Erlebte Judenfrage*, pp. 27–35.

60. Lichtheim, *A Remnant Will Return*, pp. 20–24, 51–55, 132–133.

61. Blumenfeld, *Zionistische Betrachtungen* (Berlin, 1916), pp. 8, 12, 14–15, 25; Lichtheim, *A Remnant Will Return*, pp. 131–135; see also Saul Esh, "Kurt Blumenfeld on the Modern Jew and Zionism," *Jewish Journal of Sociology*, VI (1964), 232–242; Weltsch, pp. 32–35.

62. *IDR*, 1900, pp. 437–442; *Die Welt*, 1903, No. 47, p. 12.

63. *JR*, 1909, pp. 390–392. For a similar analysis, see M. Calvary, *Die Aufgabe des deutschen Zionismus*, Sonder-Abdruck aus dem *Jüdischen Studenten*, IX, No. 6 (1912).

64. Max Mayer, "A German Jew Goes East," *LBIYB*, III (1958), 344–345; Gronemann, p. 123.

65. Kohn, *Martin Buber*, pp. 16–25, 37–42.

66. Martin Buber, "Das Judentum und die Juden," in *Drei Reden über das Judentum* (Frankfurt a.M., 1920), pp. 11–31. This use of racial ideology to substantiate the claim of Jewish nationhood fully discredited Zionism in the eyes of anti-Zionists. To quote but one rebuttal: "One should imagine that a theory from which every hatred, every hostility, every evil against the Jews has taken its weapons for so long could not provide at the same time the arguments for an organization that allegedly should rescue Judaism. Would a defender of capitalism choose the Marxian theory of value as an article of faith?" See *Zionistische Taktik*, hrsg. Antizionistische Komitee (Berlin, [ca. 1913]), p. 12.

See also George L. Mosse, "The Influence of the Völkisch Idea on German Jewry," in *Studies of the Leo Baeck Institute*, ed. by Max Kreutzberger (New York, 1967), pp. 81–114.

67. Moritz Goldstein, "German Jewry's Dilemma," *LBIYB*, II (1957), 236–254.

68. *Idem*, "Deutsch-jüdischer Parnass," *Der Kunstwart*, (March 1912), pp. 281–294.

69. H. Bodenheimer, *The History of the Basle Program*, pp. v, ix, xi–xii, xvi, xxix–xxx, xxxiii–xxxiv, xl; *Zionistische Taktik*, pp. 17–18. For a striking example of how an anti-Semitic author exploited Zionist arguments to prove that Jews were a foreign race, see Massing, pp. 246–247, n. 40.

70. *IDR*, 1912, pp. 411, 437–450.

71. Werner Sombart, *The Jews and Modern Capitalism*; idem, *Die Zukunft der Juden* (Leipzig, 1912), *passim*.

72. CZA, A 15/VII 25; *JR*, 1912, pp. 207–208; *Die Welt*, 1911, pp. 1361–63. In 1912 Sombart also offered some trenchant criticism of Jews who converted for materialistic advantage. Such characterless citizens, he argued, endangered the very moral fiber of society. The contribution of the Zionist movement was that it instilled Jews with pride and self-respect. "From the

viewpoint of character, a national Jew is indeed an entirely different guy [Kerl] [than a self-effacing assimilated Jew], whom you may hate, but whom you must also respect. And I regard the significance of the Jewish national movement . . . above all in its character-building power. . . ." (Landsberger, p. 17.)

73. Fuchs, pp. 121–140; *JR*, 1912, p. 473.

74. Now the anti-Zionists reemphasized: "The concept '[a home in Palestine] secured by public law' includes, despite all attempts at disguise, the idea of national sovereignty. But the essence of sovereignty is exclusiveness, and to serve two masters loyally remains eternally impossible." (*Zionistische Taktik*, p. 15.)

On the Moroccan crisis and German reaction, see Ziekursch, III, 229–244; Sell, pp. 347–349.

75. CZA, A 15/VII 25.

76. Ibid.

77. See *supra*, pp. 142–143.

78. CZA, A 15/VII 25; see also *ibid.*, A 15/VII 26. The articles appeared in *Die Welt*, 1912, pp. 1261–62; *JR*, 1912, p. 390.

79. *Die Welt*, 1912, p. 1556; *JR*, 1912, p. 483. According to the Zionist report of the reconciliation meeting held on December 12, 1912, Hollaender was a member of the Antizionistische Komitee; Fuchs and Horwitz were not. (CZA, A 15/VII 25.)

80. *Israelitisches Familienblatt*, 1913, No. 14, p. 1; Fuchs, pp. 230–246; *IDR*, 1913, pp. 194–200, 309.

81. *IDR*, 1913, pp. 236–238, 246–247; *Israelitisches Familienblatt*, 1913, No. 14, p. 1. Fuchs was the only non-Zionist who had some favorable comments to offer about Zionism. He praised its contribution to the revival of Jewish self-respect, and it is quite likely that the moderation of the resolution was the result of his influence. (*IDR*, 1913, p. 246.)

82. *JR*, 1913, pp. 177–178, 187; CZA, A 15/VII 26. The *Israelitisches Familienblatt*, 1913, No. 29, p. 1, already noted the paradox. The organization was finally named the Reichsverein deutscher Juden. Its first major undertaking was a series of protest meetings in October 1913 against the Beiliss trial in Russia. Horwitz' opposition to these public protests gave the Zionists yet another opportunity to denounce the Centralverein. (*JR*, 1913, p. 485; *Die Welt*, 1913, pp. 1472, 1534.) In the Spring of 1914 the Reichsverein defended alien Jews (mainly Orthodox Jews or Zionists) in Duisburg (Rhineland) against the Board of the Jewish Community which sought to deprive them of the right to vote. The Prussian Minister of Interior, whose approval was required, rejected the proposal. (CZA, A 142/327.) These seem to have been the only significant actions of a very insignificant organization.

83. Most of the debate centered on fixing responsibility for the break. For their part the Zionists claimed that the rapid growth of the Zionist Federation frightened the Centralverein into terminating its neutrality. The Zionists affirmed their patriotism and condemned the Centralverein for its willingness to dispense with most of Judaism for the sake of equality and acceptance. See *JR*, 1913, pp. 135–136, 148, 187–189, 251–254; 1914, pp. 3–4, 12; *Die Welt*,

1913, pp. 429–432, 585–586; *Israelitisches Wochenblatt,* 1913, p. 232; *IDR,* 1913, pp. 201–213, 296–304, 402–408; 1914, pp. 220, 298–302, 309–319. By May 30, 1913, the Centralverein claimed that only 197 Zionists had left the organization. (*IDR,* 1913, p. 299.)

84. *JR,* 1913, pp. 197, 230–231, 297; *IDR,* 1913, pp. 304–314. After the failure to unseat the Centralverein, Blumenfeld and Hantke preferred that all Zionists withdraw; Klee and Motzkin advised their continued participation. (CZA, A 15/VII 26.) The circulars sent by Hantke on November 13 and December 31, 1913, stressed that the battle against the assimilationists must be fought by raising the youth in the atmosphere of Zionist thought and labor. (CZA, A 102/12/6.)

85. *IDR,* 1913, pp. 547–555; 1914, pp. 289–302; Walter Laqueur, "The German Youth Movement and the Jewish Question," *LBIYB,* VI (1961), 193–200.

86. *Zionistisches A-B-C- Buch,* pp. 66–69; Böhm, I, 470–476; Lichtheim, *The History of Zionism in Germany,* pp. 110–113; CZA, A 102/12/6. By 1914, the Alliance Israélite Universelle also had 10 schools with some 1,800 students in Palestine. Zionists had likewise not failed to condemn their use of French rather than Hebrew as the language of instruction. See Böhm, I, 466; Chaim Weizmann, *Trial and Error* (New York, 1949), pp. 142–143; Chouraqui, pp. 192–193, 259.

87. Lichtheim, *The History of Zionism in Germany,* p. 113; Weizmann, p. 143; *JR,* 1914, pp. 11, 23, 24.

88. CZA, Z 3/34. See also the revealing exchange of letters between Emil Fränkel, a Munich *Justizrat,* and Hermann Cohen as to why Cohen saw fit to afix his signature to this declaration (*JR,* 1914, pp. 67, 111–112).

89. *Ibid.,* A 15/VII 27.

90. Böhm, I, 475; *IDR,* 1914, p. 339; *JR,* 1914, p. 343. While apparently the overwhelming majority of German Jews and German Zionists responded to the outbreak of the war with the same jubilation as their countrymen (*IDR,* 1914, p. 370; Walter Gross, "The Zionist Students' Movement," *LBIYB,* IV [1959], 150), one young Zionist at least seemed permanently influenced by the radical rhetoric of the second generation. In a letter written sometime after the outbreak of hostilities, Kurt Ittmann, a law student, defended his resolve not to volunteer: "I would like to state in advance that I am a Zionist, and as such [I] am of the opinion that for us Jews there are perhaps concerns still more important than this war. Of course as soon as I am drafted I will fight as bravely for Germany as anybody else, in order to show by deed my gratefulness to this country, which offers me hospitality and which I love for that reason. But as long as I can, I will fight for an issue that must lie much closer to us Jews, namely our Jewish future." (CZA, A 15/VII 27.)

AN APPRAISAL

1. Tal, "Anti-Semitism in the Second German Reich," p. 153.
2. Kaznelson, pp. 579, 820.

3. Billerbeck, 1904, p. 34; 1905, pp. 29–30.

4. Robert F. Byrnes, *Antisemitism in Modern France* (New Brunswick, 1950), pp. 99–104; Chouraqui, pp. 139–141; Marrus, pp. 141–154, 196–242.

5. Hannah Arendt, *The Origins of Totalitarianism* (2nd ed.; New York, 1958), pp. 23–25, 54.

6. *Ibid.,* p. 24. On the underlying philosophic views which inform Miss Arendt's judgments, see the incisive analysis of her life's work by Benjamin I. Schwartz, "The Religion of Politics," *Dissent,* March–April 1970, pp. 144–161.

7. H. Cohen, II, 228.

8. JHGA, P 2 / Me 19, p. 6; Hirschberg, p. 43. For a different interpretation of the same phenomenon, see Wiener, *Jüdische Religion,* pp. 267–271.

9. Revision of the translation by Kohler, "Jewish Rights at the Congress of Vienna," p. 115; original in Freund, *Die Emanzipation der Juden,* II, 282.

BIBLIOGRAPHY

ARCHIVES

Archives of the Leo Baeck Institute, New York

Asch, Adolph. "Posener und Berliner Erinnerungen 1881–1931."
File of Emil Cohn.
File of Kurt Eisner.
Gronemann, Sammy. "Erinnerungen."
Herzfeld, Ernst. "Lebenserinnerungen."
Isaac, Eduard. "Aus meinem Leben."
Meyer, Flora. "Erinnerungen aus meinem Leben in Berlin."
Robinow, Hermann, "Aus dem Leben eines Hamburger Kaufmanns."
Rosenberg, Curt. "Jugenderinnerungen 1876–1904."
Spiro. "Jugenderinnergungen aus hessischen Judengemeinden."
Translateur, Salo. "Erinnerungen aus meiner ersten zionistischen Tätigkeit in Breslau, Schlesien, von 1898–1904."

The Central Zionist Archives, Jerusalem

Files of Max Bodenheimer, A 15:
A 15/I 9   Letters from Bodenheimer to Friedemann, 1897–1900.
A 15/VII 5   Correspondence, 1898.
A 15/VII 21   Correspondence, 1908.
A 15/VII 22   Correspondence, 1909.
A 15/VII 25   Correspondence, 1912.
A 15/VII 26   Correspondence, 1913.
A 15/VII 27   Correspondence, 1914.

Files of Arthur Hantke, A 11:
A 11/32/9   Letters from Richard Lichtheim, 1907–1911.

Files of Alfred Klee, A 142:
A 142/327   Voting rights for foreign nationals in the Jewish communities in Germany.

Files of Hugo Schachtel, A 102:
A 102/12/3/1   Correspondence.
A 102/12/4   Correspondence.
A 102/12/6   Correspondence.

Files of Central Zionist Office, Berlin, Z 3:
Z 3 /34   Antizionistische Kundgebungen in Deutschland, 1913–1915.

Jewish Historical General Archives, Jerusalem

Centralverein deutscher Staatsbürger jüdischen Glaubens:
INV/124/1   Protokolle des Vorstandssitzungen des Centralvereins, 1895–
                1905, Vol. I.
INV/124/2   Protokolle des Vorstandssitzungen des Centralvereins, 1894–
                1905, Vol. II.
INV/751/3   Two public appeals issued by the Centralverein in 1907.

Deutsch-Israelitischer Gemeindebund:
M 1/5   Übersiedelung Leipzig-Berlin.
M 1/8   Circulare, 1871–1886, 1902–1922.
M 1/9   Zur Geschichte des Deutsch-Israelitischen Gemeindebundes,
                1869–1919.
M 1/13   Strafanträge, 1876–1881.
M 1/14   Verein gegen Wucher, 1878–1888.
M 1/15   Antisemitismus—Petition, 1879–1881.
M 1/16   Strafanträge, 1876–1881.
M 1/17   Process Contra Justus.
M 1/21   Lasker'sche Austrittsgesetz.
M 1/23   Historische Kommission.

Rabbinerverband in Deutschland:
M 4/1   Protokolle, Korrespondenz, 1896–1899.
M 4/2   Briefwechsel, 1909–1911.

Verband der deutschen Juden:
M 21/2   Korrespondenz, Aufrufe, 1904–1922.

Verein zur Abwehr des Antisemitismus:
TD-475   Statut, Aufrufe, Einladung zur ausserordentlicher Mitglieder-
                versammlung.

Altona-Hamburg-Wandsbek:
AHW/865a   Deutsch-Israelitischer Gemeindebund, 1869–1913.

Berlin:
K Ge 2/17   Walther Rathenau: Austritt aus dem Judentum, 26 Januar 1895.

Königsberg:
Kn II/A II 3   Verein zur Abwehr des Antisemitismus, 1891–1922.
Kn II/A II 4   Gesamtorganisationen der deutschen Juden, 1901–1907.
Kn II/A II 5   Ausschuss des Verbandes der deutschen Juden, 1907.
Kn II/A II 6   Ausschuss des Verbandes der deutschen Juden, 1911.

Neuwied:
Rh/Nw/35   Verein zur Abwehr des Antisemitismus, 1893–1895.

Regensburg:
A/202   Akt Betreffend den Verein zur Abwehr des Antisemitismus,
                1902.
A/33   Emancipation und Abwehr des Antisemitismus, 1813–1900.

PRIMARY SOURCES

Abrahams, Israel. "Professor Schürer on Life under the Jewish Law." *JQR,* XI (1899), 626–642.

——. *Studies in Pharisaism and the Gospels, First and Second Series.* Prolegomenon by Morton S. Enslin. New York, 1968.

Ackermann, (Aron?). *Vogelfrei.* Brandenburg, a.H., 1901.

Allgemeine Zeitung des Judentums. Leipzig and Berlin, 1869–1914.

An Herrn Prof. Dr. Lazarus. Von einem deutschen Juden. 2nd ed. Magdeburg, 1887.

Antizionistische Komitee. *Der Zionismus, seine Theorien, Aussichten und Wirkungen.* Berlin, n.d. [ca. 1912].

——. *Zionistische Taktik.* Berlin, n.d. [ca. 1912].

Aronius, Julius. *Regesten zur Geschichte der Juden im fränkischen und deutschen Reiche bis zum Jahre 1273.* Berlin, 1902.

Auerbach, Berthold. *Briefe an seinen Freund Jakob Auerbach.* Edited by Jakob Auerbach. 2 vols. Frankfurt a.M., 1884.

Auerbach, Elias. *Pioneer der Verwirklichung.* Stuttgart, 1969.

Auerbach, Fritz. *Der Antisemitismus und das freisinnige Judentum.* Frankfurt a.M., 1893.

Auerbach, Leopold. *Das Judenthum und seine Bekenner in Preussen und in anderen deutschen Bundesstaaten.* Berlin, 1890.

——. *Das jüdische Obligationenrecht.* Berlin, 1870.

——. *Wie ist die Judenhetze mit Erfolg zu Bekämpfen?* Berlin, 1893.

Bach, Albert. *Die Lösung der Judenfrage und die Aufgabe des Centralvereins deutscher Staatsbürger jüdischen Glaubens.* Reprint from *Nord und Süd,* 1912.

Baeck, Leo. "Harnacks Vorlesungen über das Wesen des Christenthums." *MGWJ,* XLV (1901), 97–120.

——. *Das Wesen des Judentums.* Berlin, 1905.

Bahr, Hermann. *Der Antisemitismus.* Berlin, 1894.

Belke, Ingrid. *Moritz Lazarus und Heymann Steinthal: Die Begründer der Völkerpsychologie in ihren Briefen.* Tübingen, 1971.

Berliner, E., ed. *Professor Dr. M. Lazarus und die öffentliche Meinung.* Berlin, 1887.

Bernfeld, Simon, and Bamberger, Fritz, eds. *Die Lehren des Judentums nach den Quellen.* 5 vols. Leipzig, 1920–1929.

Billerbeck, Paul. "Vereinsorganisationen innerhalb der Judenschaft Deutschland." *Nathanael,* XX (1904), 33–61, 65–92; XXI (1905), 1–31.

Blau, Joseph L., and Baron, Salo W., eds. *The Jews of the United States 1790–1840: A Documentary History.* 3 vols. New York and Philadelphia, 1963.

Blumenfeld, Kurt. *Erlebte Judenfrage.* Stuttgart, 1962.

——. *Zionistische Betrachtungen.* Berlin, 1916.

Bodenheimer, Henriette Hannah, ed. *Im Anfang der zionistischen Bewegung.* Frankfurt a.M., 1965.

Bodenheimer, Henriette Hannah, ed. *Toldot Tokhnit Basel* ("The History of the Basle Program"). Jerusalem, 1947.

Bodenheimer, Max. *Prelude to Israel*. New York, 1963.

———. *Zionismus und Judentag*. Cologne n.d. [ca. 1901].

Boehlich, Walter, ed. *Der Berliner Antisemitismusstreit*. Frankfurt a.M., 1965.

Bousset, D. Wilhelm. *Jesu Predigt in ihrem Gegensatz zum Judentum*. Göttingen, 1892.

———. *Die Religion des Judentums im neutestamentlichen Zeitalter*. Berlin, 1903.

Breslauer, Bernhard. *Die Abwanderung der Juden aus der Provinz Posen*. Berlin, 1909.

———. "Erinnerung." In *Festschrift zum 70 Geburtstage von Moritz Schaefer*. Berlin, 1927.

———. *Die Zurücksetzung der Juden an den Universitäten Deutschlands*. Berlin, 1911.

Brüll, A. "Der Deutsch-Israelitische Gemeindebund und sein Wirken." *Populär-wissenschaftliche Monatsblätter*, (1888), pp. 121–129.

Buber, Martin. *Drei Reden über das Judentum*. Frankfurt a.M., 1920.

Bürger, Curt, ed. *Antisemiten-Spiegel*. Berlin and Frankfurt a.M., 1911.

———. *Deutschtum und Judentum*. Berlin, 1913.

C-V Zeitung. Berlin, 1923–1924.

Calvary, M. *Die Aufgabe des deutschen Zionismus*. Sonder-Abdruck aus dem *Jüdischen Studenten*, Vol. IX, No. 6 (1912).

Centralverein deutscher Staatsbürger jüdischen Glaubens. *An die deutschen Staatsbürger jüdischen Glaubens: Ein Aufruf*. Berlin, May 1893.

———. *Die Gutachten der Sachverständigen über den Konitzer Mord*. Berlin, 1903.

———. *Mitglieder-Verzeichnis*. Berlin, 1902.

———. *Mitglieder-Verzeichnis*. Berlin, 1905.

———. *Mitglieder-Verzeichnis*. Berlin, 1908.

Cohen, Hermann. *Jüdische Schriften*. 3 vols. Berlin, 1924.

Cohn, Bernhard. *Jüdisch-politische Zeitfragen*. Berlin, 1899.

———. *Vor dem Sturm*. Berlin, 1896.

Cohn, Emil. *Die Geschichte meiner Suspension*. Berlin, April 1907.

———. *Mein Kampf ums Recht*. Berlin, May 1907.

Comité zur Abwehr antisemitischer Angriffe in Berlin. *Gutachten über das jüdisch-rituelle Schlachtverfahren*. Berlin, 1894.

———. *Die Juden als Soldaten*. Berlin, 1897.

Davidsohn, Doris. "Erinnerungen einer deutsches Jüdin." *BLBI*, 1959, pp. 193–205.

Delitzsch, Friedrich. *Babel und Bibel: Ein Vortrag*. Leipzig, 1902.

———. *Zweiter Vortrag über Babel und Bibel*. Stuttgart, 1904.

Deutsch-Israelitischer Gemeindebund. *Denkschrift zur Vertheidigung des einheitlichen Rechtsverbandes der jüdischen Gemeinden in Deutschland*. Leipzig, 1873.

———. *Gedenkblätter an Jacob Nachod*. Berlin, 1882.

———. *Handbuch der jüdischen Gemeindeverwaltung und Wohlfartspflege*. Berlin, 1913.

——. *Hat das Judenthum dem Wucherunwesen Vorschub geleistet?* Leipzig, 1879.

——. *Lessing-Mendelssohn-Gedenkbuch.* Leipzig, 1879.

Dohm, Christian Wilhelm. *Über die bürgerliche Verbesserung der Juden.* 2 vols. Berlin and Stettin, 1783.

Dubnow, Simon. *Nationalism and History.* Edited by Koppel S. Pinson. Philadelphia, 1958.

Ein Wort an die deutschen Staatsbürger jüdischen Glaubens. Mainz, 1896.

Eliav, Mordechai. *Rabbiner Esriel Hildesheimer Briefe.* Jerusalem, 1965.

Engelbert, Hermann. *Statistik des Judenthums im Deutschen Reiche ausschliesslich Preussens und in der Schweiz.* Frankfurt a.M., 1875.

Eschelbacher, Josef. *Das Judentum im Urteile der modernen protestantischen Theologie.* Leipzig, 1907.

——. *Das Judentum und das Wesen des Christentums.* 2nd ed. Berlin, 1908.

——. "Die Vorlesungen Adolf Harnacks über das Wesen des Christenthums." *MGWJ,* XLVI (1902), 119–141, 229–239, 407–427; XLVII (1903), 53–68, 136–149, 249–263, 434–446, 514–534.

Foerder, Ludwig. *Antisemitismus und Justiz.* Berlin, 1924.

——. *Die Stellung des Centralvereins zu den innerjüdischen Fragen in den Jahren 1919–1926.* Breslau, 1927.

Fraenkel, Abraham A. *Lebenskreise.* Stuttgart, 1967.

Freund, Ismar. *Die Emanzipation der Juden in Preussen.* 2 vols. Berlin, 1912.

——. *Die Rechtsstellung der Juden im preussischen Volksschulrecht.* Berlin, 1908.

——. *Die Rechtstellung der Synagogengemeinden in Preussen und die Reichsverfassung.* Berlin, 1926.

——. "Staat, Kirche und Judentum in Preussen," *JJGL,* XIV (1911), 109–138.

Friedländer, David. *Akten-Stücke die Reform der jüdischen Kolonieen in den preussischen Staaten betreffend.* Berlin, 1793.

——. *Sendschreiben an seine Hochwürden Herrn Oberconsistorialrath und Probst Teller zu Berlin.* Berlin, 1799.

——. *Über die durch die neuen Organisation der Judenschaften in den Preussischen Staaten notwendig gewordene Umbildung.* Berlin, 1934.

Fromer, Jakob [Elias Jakob]. "Das Wesen des Judenthums." *Die Zukunft,* 1904, pp. 440–456.

——. *Vom Ghetto zur modernen Kultur.* Heidelberg, 1906.

Fuchs, Eugen. *Um Deutschtum und Judentum.* Frankfurt a.M., 1919.

Gage, R. H., and Waters, A. J. *Imperial German Criminal Code.* Johannesburg, 1917.

Geiger, Abraham. *Judaism and Its History.* Translated by Charles Newburgh. 2 vols. New York, 1911.

——. *Das Judenthum und seine Geschichte.* 3 vols. Breslau, 1865–1871.

Geiger, Ludwig, ed. *Abraham Geiger's Nachgelassene Schriften.* 5 vols. Berlin, 1875–1878.

——. "Briefe von und an Gabriel Riesser." *Zeitschrift für die Geschichte der Juden in Deutschland,* II (1888), 47–75.

General-Anzeiger für die gesamten Interessen des Judentums. Berlin, 1903–1910.

Geschäftsberichte des Verbandes der deutschen Juden. Berlin, 1905–1914.

Goldstein, Moritz. "Deutsch-jüdischer Parnass." *Der Kunstwart,* March 1912, pp. 281–294.

——. "German Jewry's Dilemma." *LBIYB,* II (1957), 236–254.

Gothein, Georg. *Der deutsche Aussenhandel.* Berlin, 1901.

——. "Die Wirkungen des Schutzzollsystems in Deutschland." *Volkswirtschaftliche Zeitfragen,* Heft 243 / 244 (1909).

[Graetz, Heinrich.] *Briefwechsel einer englischen Dame über Judenthum und Semitismus.* Stuttgart, 1883.

Graetz, Heinrich. "Die Construction der jüdischen Geschichte." *Zeitschrift für die religiösen Interessen des Judenthums,* III (1846), 81–97, 121–132, 361–381, 413–421.

——. *Geschichte der Juden.* 11 vols. 2nd and 4th eds. Leipzig, 1900–1909.

Grumbkow, Richard von. *Die Judenfrage vor Gericht.* Dresden, 1883.

Güdemann, Moritz. *Das Judenthum.* 2nd ed. Vienna, 1902.

——. "Das Judentum im neutestamentlichen Zeitalter in christlicher Darstellung." *MGWJ,* XLVII (1903), 38–53, 120–136, 231–249.

——. *Jüdische Apologetik.* Glogau, 1906.

Harnack, Adolf. *Das Wesen des Christentums.* 3rd ed. Leipzig, 1900.

Hartenau, W. [Walther Rathenau]. "Höre, Israel." *Die Zukunft,* 1897, pp. 454–462.

Heinemann, Isaac. "Besprechung: *Die Lehren des Judentums nach den Quellen.*" *MGWJ,* LXIX (1925), 113–117.

——. "Besprechung: *Die Lehren des Judentums nach den Quellen.*" *MGWJ,* LXXIII (1929), 419–420.

Herz, Emil. *Before the Fury.* New York, 1966.

Hildesheimer, Hirsch, ed. *Neue Gutachten über das jüdisch-rituelle Schlachtverfahren.* Berlin, 1908.

Hirsch, Marcus. *Kulturdefizit am Ende des 19. Jahrhunderts.* Frankfurt a.M., 1893.

Hirsch, Samson R. *Der Austritt aus der Gemeinde.* Frankfurt a.M., 1876.

——. *Denkschrift über die Judenfrage in dem Gesetz betreffend den Austritt aus der Kirche.* Berlin, 1873.

——. *Horeb.* Translated by I. Grunfeld. 2 vols. London, 1962.

——. *The Nineteen Letters of Ben Uziel.* Translated by Bernard Drachman. New York, 1942.

Hoeniger, Robert. *Das Judenschreinsbuch der Laurenzpfarre zu Köln.* Berlin, 1888.

Hoffmann, David. *Der Schulchan-Aruch und die Rabbinen über das Verhältnis der Juden zu Andersgläubigen.* 2nd ed. Berlin, 1894.

Holdheim, Samuel. *Gemischte Ehen zwischen Juden und Christen.* Berlin, 1850.

——. *Über die Autonomie der Rabbinen und das Princip der jüdischen Ehe.* 2nd ed. Schwerin, 1847.

Hollaender, Ludwig. *Deutsch-Jüdische Probleme der Gegenwart.* Berlin, 1929.

Huber, Ernst Rudolf. *Dokumente zur deutschen Verfassungsgeschichte.* Vol. II, Stuttgart, 1964.

Im deutschen Reich. Berlin, 1895–1914.

Der Israelit. Mainz and Frankfurt a.M., 1869–1914.

Israelitische Rundschau. Berlin, 1901–1902.

Israelitische Wochenschrift. Breslau and Magdeburg, 1870–1894.

Israelitisches Familienblatt. Hamburg, 1898–1914.

Israelitisches Wochenblatt. Berlin, 1913.

Jacobowski, Ludwig. *Offene Antwort eines Juden auf Herrn Ahlwardt's "Der Eid eines Juden."* Berlin, 1891.

——. *Werther, der Jude.* 2nd ed. Berlin, 1893.

Jacobsohn, Bernhard. *Der Deutsch-Israelitische Gemeindebund nach Ablauf des ersten Decenniums seit seiner Begründung von 1869 bis 1879.* Leipzig, 1879.

——. *Fünfzig Jahre: Erinnerungen aus Amt und Leben.* Berlin, 1912.

Jahrbuch für jüdische Geschichte und Literatur. Vols. I to XVII (1898–1914).

Jüdische Presse. Berlin, 1870–1914.

Jüdische Rundschau. Berlin, 1903–1914.

Kohler, Max J. "Jewish Rights at the Congresses of Vienna (1814–1815) and Aix-La-Chapelle (1818)." *PAJHS,* XXVI (1918), 32–125. (Includes translation of Wilhelm Humboldt's memorandum of July 17, 1809.)

Kohn, Hans, ed. *Nationalism and the Jewish Ethic: Basic Writings of Ahad Ha-Am.* New York, 1962.

Kollenscher, Max. *Rechtsverhältnisse der Juden in Preussen.* Berlin, 1910.

——. *Zionismus oder Liberales Judentum.* Berlin, 1912.

——. *Zionismus und Staatsbürgertum.* Berlin, n.d.

Korrespondenz-Blatt des Verbandes der deutschen Juden. Berlin, 1907–1914.

Kristeller, Samuel, ed. *Belegstellen zu den Grundsätzen der jüdischen Sittenlehre.* Berlin, 1891.

——. *Liebe deinen Nächsten wie dich selbst.* Berlin, 1891.

Landsberger, A., ed. *Judentaufen.* Munich, 1912.

Lazarus, Moritz. *Aus meiner Jugend.* Frankfurt a.M., 1913.

——. *The Ethics of Judaism.* Translated by H. Szold. 2 vols. Philadelphia, 1900–1901.

——. *Treu und Frei: Gesammelte Reden und Vorträge über Juden und Judenthum.* Leipzig, 1887.

Lehmann, Emil. *Gesammelte Schriften.* Berlin, 1899.

Leon, S. *Unser heutiges Judenthum: Eine Selbstkritik.* Berlin, 1890.

Levinstein, Gustav. *Zur Ehre des Judentums.* Berlin, 1911.

Levita, Benedictus. "Die Erlösung des Judenthums." *Preussische Jahrbücher,* CII–CIII (1900–1901), 131–140.

Lichtheim, Richard. *Das Programm des Zionismus.* Berlin, 1911.

——. *Shear Yashuv* ("A Remnant Will Return"). Tel Aviv, 1953.

Liebermann von Sonnenberg, Max. *Der Blutmord in Konitz.* 7th ed. Berlin, 1901.

[Löwenfeld, Raphael.] *Schutzjuden oder Staatsbürger?* 3rd ed. Berlin, 1893.

Lowenthal, E. G. "Wie Ich zum Geographen Wurde." *BLBI,* 1965, pp. 89–106.

Maier, Gustav. *Mehr Licht! Ein Wort zur "Judenfrage" an unsere christlichen Mitbürger.* Ulm, 1881.

Makower, Felix. *Bericht über die Tätigkeit des Verbandes der deutschen Ju-*

den bei der Vorbereitung des preussischen Volksschulunterhaltungsgesetes von 1906. Berlin, 1907.

Makower, Hermann. *Über die Gemeindeverhältnisse der Juden in Preussen.* Berlin, 1873.

Marcard, H. E. *Über die Möglichkeit der Juden-Emancipation im christlich-germanischen Staat.* Minden and Leipzig, 1843.

Maslin, Simeon J. *Selected Documents of Napoleonic Jewry.* Cincinnati, 1957.

Mendelsohn, Martin. *Die Pflicht der Selbstvertheidigung.* Berlin, 1894.

Mendelssohn, Moses. *Gesammelte Schriften.* Edited by G. B. Mendelssohn. Vol. V. Leipzig, 1844.

———. *Jerusalem.* Frankfurt and Leipzig, 1787.

Mevorah, Baruh. *Napoleon u-Tekufato* (Napoleon and His Era). Jerusalem, 1968.

Michaelis, Alfred. *Die Rechtsverhältnisse der Juden in Preussen.* Berlin, 1910.

Mitteilungen aus dem Verein zur Abwehr des Antisemitismus. Berlin, 1891–1914.

Mitteilungen vom Deutsch-Israelitischen Gemeindebunde. Leipzig and Berlin, 1873–1914.

Montefiore, C. G. "Rabbinic Judaism and the Epistles of St. Paul." *JQR,* XIII (1901), 161–217.

Moses, Julius, ed. *Die Lösung der Judenfrage.* Berlin-Leipzig, 1907.

Nathan, Paul, ed. *Die Kriminalität der Juden in Deutschland.* Berlin, 1896.

———. *Der Prozess von Tisza-Eszlár.* Berlin, 1892.

———. *Xanten-Cleve: Betrachtungen zum Prozess Buschhof.* Separat-Abdruck aus der *Nation.* Berlin, 1892.

Die Nation. Berlin, 1890, 1892.

Neubauer, A., and Stein, Moritz. *Hebräische Berichte über die Judenverfolgungen während der Kreuzzüge.* Berlin, 1892.

Neumann, Salomon. *Die Fabel von der jüdischen Masseneinwanderung.* Berlin, 1880.

———. *Zur Statistik der Juden in Preussen von 1816 bis 1880.* Berlin, 1884.

Oppenheimer, Franz. *Erlebtes, Erstrebtes, Erreichtes: Lebenserinnerungen.* Reprinted. Düsseldorf, 1964.

Ost und West. Berlin, 1901–1914.

Parmod, Maximilian (Max Apt). *Antisemitismus und Strafrechtspflege.* 3rd ed. Berlin, 1894.

Perles, Felix. *Bousset's Religion des Judentums im neutestamentlichen Zeitalter kritisch untersucht.* Berlin, 1903.

———. "What Jews May Learn from Harnack." *JQR,* XIV (1902), 517–542.

Picard, Jacob. "The Childhood in the Village." *LBIYB,* IV (1959), 273–293.

Populär-wissenschaftliche Monatsblätter zur Belehrung über das Judentum. Frankfurt a.M., 1880–1890.

Rathenau, Walther. *Eine Streitschrift vom Glauben.* Berlin, 1919.

———. *Impressionen.* Leipzig, 1902.

Referate über die der ersten israelitischen Synode zu Leipzig überreichten Anträge. Berlin, 1871.

Rönne, Ludwig von, and Simon, Heinrich. *Die früheren und gegenwärtigen Verhältnisse der Juden in den sämmtlichen Landestheilen des preussischen Staates.* Breslau, 1843.

Sachse, Heinrich [Heinrich Loewe]. *Antisemitismus und Zionismus.* Berlin, n.d. [1894?].

Salfeld, Siegmund. *Das Martyrologium der Nürnberger Memorbuches.* Berlin, 1898.

Schach, Fabius. *Über die Zukunft Israels.* Berlin, 1904.

Schechter, Solomon. "Higher Criticism—Higher Anti-Semitism." *Seminary Addresses and Other Papers.* New York, 1959.

——. "The Law and Recent Criticism." *JQR,* III (1891), 754–766.

Schreiber, Emanuel. *Grätz's Geschichtsbauerei.* Berlin, 1881.

——. *Die Selbstkritik der Juden.* Leipzig, n.d. [ca. 1881].

Schürer, Emil. *Geschichte der jüdischen Volkes im Zeitalter Jesu Christi.* 3rd ed. 3 vols. Leipzig, 1898–1902.

Simon, J. *Wehrt Euch.* Berlin, 1893.

Sombart, Werner. *The Jews and Modern Capitalism.* Translated by M. Epstein. Glencoe, Illinois, 1951.

——. *Die Zukunft der Juden.* Leipzig, 1912.

Spier, Selma. "The Fatherland." *LBIYB,* IV (1959), 294–308.

Statistisches Jahrbuch des Deutsch-Israelitischen Gemeindebundes. Berlin, 1885, 1895.

Steinthal, Heymann. *Über Juden und Judenthum.* 2nd ed. Berlin, 1925.

Stenographische Berichte über die fünf Hauptversammlungen des Verbandes der deutschen Juden. Berlin, 1905–1914.

Strack, Hermann. *Der Blutaberglaube bei Christen und Juden.* Munich, 1891.

——. *Der Blutaberglaube in der Menschheit: Blutmorde und Blutritus.* 2nd ed. Munich, 1892.

——. *Die Juden, dürfen sie "Verbrecher von Religions wegen" genannt werden?* Berlin, 1893.

——. *Jüdische Geheimgesetze?* Berlin, 1921.

Straus, Rahel. *Wir lebten in Deutschland.* Stuttgart, 1961.

Susman, Margarete. *Ich habe viele Leben gelebt.* Stuttgart, 1964.

Tama, M. Diogene. *Transactions of the Parisian Sanhedrin,* London, 1807.

[Thon, Jakob.] *Die jüdische Gemeinden und Vereine in Deutschland.* Berlin, 1906.

Unna, S. "Briefe von H. Graetz an Raphael Kirchheim." *Jahrbuch der Jüdisch-literarischen Gesellschaft,* Vol. XII (1918).

Urbach, R. "Judentum und Christentum." *MGWJ,* L (1906), 257–288.

——. "Zwei Bücher über das Wesen des Judentums." *MGWJ,* L (1906), 129–151.

Verband der deutschen Juden. *Soziale Ethik im Judentum.* Frankfurt a.M., 1913.

——. *Vom Judentum.* Nos. 1–6. Berlin, n.d.

Verein zur Abwehr des Antisemitismus. *Antisemiten-Spiegel.* Danzig, 1890.

——. *Antisemiten-Spiegel.* 2nd ed. Danzig, 1891.

——. *Die Juden im Heere.* Berlin, n.d. [ca. 1909].

——. *Der politische Antisemitismus von 1903–1907.* Berlin, 1907.

Verhandlungen der ersten israelitischen Synode. Berlin, 1869.

Verhandlungen der zweiten israelitischen Synode. Berlin, 1873.

Verhandlungen und Beschlüsse der Rabbiner Versammlung zu Berlin am 4. und 5. Juni 1884. Berlin, 1885.

Wassermann, Jakob. "Das Los der Juden." *Die neue Rundschau,* August 1904, pp. 940–948.

——. *Mein Weg als Deutscher und Jude.* Berlin, 1921.

Weber, Ferdinand. *System der altsynagogalen palästinischen Theologie aus Targum, Midrash und Talmud.* Leipzig, 1880.

Weizmann, Chaim. *Trial and Error.* New York, 1949.

Die Welt. Vienna, Cologne, and Berlin, 1897–1914.

Wiener, Max, ed. *Abraham Geiger and Liberal Judaism.* Philadelphia, 1962.

Winter, Georg. *Der Antisemitismus in Deutschland.* Magdeburg, 1896.

Zeitschrift für Demographie und Statistik der Juden. Vols. I to IX (1905–1914).

Zionistische Vereinigung für Deutschland. *Correspondenz No. 7.* N.p., n.d.

——. *Deutsche Juden.* Flugblatt No. 6. N.p., n.d.

——. *Der Nationaljude als Staatsbürger.* Flugblatt No. 2. N.p., n.d.

——. *Protokol des III delegiertentags der deutschen Zionisten.* N.p., n.d.

——. *Die Referate der Herren Schach und Dr. Schauer über Organisation und Agitation.* N.p., n.d.

——. *Unser Programm.* Flugblatt No. 4. N.p., n.d.

——. *Was Will der Zionismus?* Berlin, 1903.

——. *Der Zionismus.* Flugblatt No. 1. N.p., n.d.

——. *Der Zionismus und die jüdische Religion.* Flugblatt No. 3. N.p., n.d.

——. *Zionistisches A-B-C- Buch.* Berlin, 1908.

Zunz, Leopold. *Gesammelte Schriften.* 3 vols. Berlin, 1875–1876.

Zur Judenfrage in Deutschland. Breslau, 1843–1844.

SECONDARY SOURCES

Adler-Rudel, S. *Ostjuden in Deutschland 1880–1940.* Tübigen, 1959.

Arendt, Hannah. *The Origins of Totalitarianism.* 2nd ed. New York, 1958.

Asch, Adolph. *Geschichte des K.C.* N.p., 1964.

——, and Philippson, J. "Self-Defence at the Turn of the Century: The Emergence of K.C." *LBIYB,* III (1958), 122–139.

Baeck, Leo. "Types of Jewish Self-Understanding." *Judaism,* IX (1960), 159–163.

Baron, Salo W. "Freedom and Constraint in the Jewish Community." In *Essays and Studies in Memory of Linda R. Miller.* Edited by Israel Davidson. New York, 1938.

——. *History and Jewish Historians.* Philadelphia, 1964.

——. *A Social and Religious History of the Jews.* 1st ed. Vol. II. New York, 1937.

——. *A Social and Religious History of the Jews.* 2nd ed. Vol. V. Philadelphia, 1957.

Baumgardt, David. "The Ethics of Lazarus and Steinthal." *LBIYB,* II (1957), 205–217.

Bein, Alex. "Modern Anti-Semitism and Its Place in the History of the Jewish Question." In *Between East and West.* Edited by A. Altmann. London, 1958.

——. *Theodore Herzl*. Philadelphia, 1956.

Bennathan, Esra. "Die demographische und wirtschaftliche Struktur der Juden." In *Entscheidungsjahr 1932*. Edited by Werner E. Mosse. Tübingen, 1965.

Bentwich, Norman. *For Zion's Sake*. Philadelphia, 1954.

Bergmann, Hugo. "Eduard von Hartmann und die Judenfrage in Deutschland." *LBIYB*, V (1960), 177–197.

Bienenfeld, F. R. *The Germans and the Jews*. New York, 1939.

Böhm, Adolf. *Die zionistische Bewegung*. 2nd ed. Vol. I. Berlin, 1935.

Brann, Marcus. "Verzeichniss der Schriften David Kaufmanns." In *Gedenkbuch zur Erinnerung an David Kaufmann*. Edited by M. Brann et al. Breslau, 1900.

Breslauer, Walter. "Der Verband der Deutschen Juden (1904–1922)." *BLBI*, VII (1964), 345–380.

Byrnes, Robert F. *Antisemitism in Modern France*. New Brunswick, 1950.

Cahnman, Werner J. "Munich and the First Zionist Congress." *Historia Judaica*, III (1941), 7–23.

Carsten, Ernst. *Die Geschichte der Staatsanwaltschaft in Deutschland bis zur Gegenwart*. Breslau, 1932.

Chouraqui, André. *L'Alliance Israélite Universelle et la renaissance juive contemporaine*. Paris, 1965.

Cohen, Gerson D. "Esau as Symbol in Early Medieval Thought." In *Jewish Medieval and Renaissance Studies*. Edited by A. Altmann. Cambridge, 1967.

Cohen, Naomi W. "The *Maccabaean's* Message: A Study in American Zionism until World War I." *Jewish Social Studies*, XVIII (1956), 163–178.

——. "The Reaction of Reform Judaism in America to Political Zionism (1897–1922)." *PAJHS*, XL (1951), 361–394.

Crothers, George Dunlap. *The German Elections of 1907*. New York, 1941.

Davidson, Israel. "Kol Nidre." *American Jewish Year Book*, XXV (1923), 180–194.

Doskow, Ambrose, and Jacoby, Sidney B. "Anti-Semitism and the Law in Pre-Nazi Germany." *Contemporary Jewish Record*, III (1940), 498–509.

Dubnow, Simon. *Dibray Y'may Am Olam* ("The World History of the Jews"). Vol. IX. Tel Aviv, 1958.

Elbogen, Ismar. "Aus der Frühzeit der Vereine für jüdische Geschichte und Literatur." *Festschrift zum 70. Geburtstage von Moritz Schaefer*. Berlin, 1927.

——. "Zum Jubiläum der Gesellschaft zur Förderung der Wissenschaft des Judentums." *MGWJ*, LXXII (1928), 1–5.

Eliav, Mordechai. *Ha-Hinukh Ha-Yehudi be-Germania bimay Ha-Haskalah ve-ha-Emancipazia* ("Jewish Education in Germany in the Period of the Enlightenment and the Emancipation"). Jerusalem, 1960.

——. "Der Israelit und Erez Israel im 19. Jahrhundert." *BLBI*, VIII (1965), 273–301.

Encyclopaedia Judaica. Vol. I. Berlin, 1928.

Esh, Saul. "Kurt Blumenfeld on the Modern Jew and Zionism." *Jewish Journal of Sociology*, VI (1964), 232–242.

Ettinger, Ignaz. "Zur Lehre von den Religionsvergehen." *Strafrechtliche Abhandlungen,* Vol. CCIII (1919).
Feder, Ernst. *Politik und Humanität: Paul Nathan.* Berlin, 1929.
Finkelstein, J. "Bible and Babel." *Commentary,* XXVI (1958), 431–444.
Fischer, Horst. *Judentum, Staat und Heer in Preussen im frühen 19. Jahrhundert.* Tübingen, 1968.
Frank, Walter. *Hofprediger Adolf Stoecker und die christlich-soziale Bewegung.* 2nd ed. Hamburg, 1935.
Freedman, Maurice, ed. *A Minority in Britain.* London, 1955.
Gelber, N. M. "The Berlin Congress of 1878." *LBIYB,* V (1960), 221–247.
Goldschmidt, H. L. "Leben und Werk Margarete Susmans." In *Auf gespaltenem Pfad.* Edited by Manfred Schlösser. Darmstadt, 1964.
Gottgetreu, Erich. "Maximilian Harden: Ways and Eros of a Publicist." *LBIYB,* VII (1962), 215–246.
Gräter, Carlheinz. *Theodor Barths politische Gedankenwelt.* Würzburg, 1963.
Gross, Walter. "The Zionist Students' Movement." *LBIYB,* IV (1959), 143–164.
Hahn, Herbert F. "Wellhausen's Interpretation of Israel's Religious History: A Reappraisal of His Ruling Ideas." In *Essays on Jewish Life and Thought.* Edited by Joseph Blau et al. New York, 1959.
Halpern, Ben. *The Idea of the Jewish State.* Cambridge, Mass., 1961.
Hamburger, Ernest. "Jews in Public Service under the German Monarchy." *LBIYB,* IX (1964), 206–238.
Heinemann, Isaac. "Supplementary Remarks on 'The Secession from the Frankfurt Jewish Community under S. R. Hirsch.'" *Historia Judaica,* X (1948), 123–134.
Henkel, Heinrich. *Strafverfahrensrecht: Ein Lehrbuch.* Stuttgart and Cologne, 1953.
Herford, Travers R. *The Pharisees.* New York, 1924.
Hirschberg, Alfred. "Ludwig Hollaender, Director of the C.V." *LBIYB,* VII (1962), 39–74.
Howard, Burt Estes. *The German Empire.* New York, 1906.
Jacob, Ernest I. "Life and Work of B. Jacob (1862–1945)." In *Paul Lazarus Gedenkbuch.* Jerusalem, 1961.
"James Simon: Industrialist, Art Collector, Philanthropist." *LBIYB,* X (1965), 3–23.
Janowsky, Oscar. *Foundations of Israel.* New York, 1959.
——. *The Jews and Minority Rights (1898–1919).* New York, 1933.
Japhet, Saemy. "The Secession from the Frankfurt Jewish Community under S. R. Hirsch." *Historia Judaica,* X (1948), 99–122.
Jewish Exponent. Philadelphia, May 5, 1967.
Jöhlinger, Otto. *Bismarck und die Juden.* Berlin, 1921.
Katz, Jacob. *Exclusiveness and Tolerance.* Oxford, 1961.
——. "The German-Jewish Utopia of Social Emancipation." In *Studies of the Leo Baeck Institute.* Edited by Max Kreutzberger. New York, 1967.
Kaznelson, Siegmund, ed. *Juden im deutschen Kulturbereich.* 3rd ed. Berlin, 1962.

Kessler, Count Harry. *Walther Rathenau: His Life and Work.* New York, 1930.

Kissling, Johannes B. *Geschichte des Kulturkampfes im deutschen Reich.* Vol. III. Freiburg, 1916.

Klinkenberg, Hans Martin. "Zwischen Liberalismus und Nationalismus." In *Monumenta Judaica.* Handbuch. Cologne, 1963.

Kohler, Max J. "The Board of Delegates of American Israelites, 1859–1878." *PAJHS,* XXIX (1921), 75–135.

Kohn, Hans. *Martin Buber: Sein Werk und Seine Zeit.* 2nd ed. Cologne, 1961.

Lamberti, Majorie. "The Attempt to Form a Jewish Bloc: Jewish Notables and Politics in Wilhelmian Germany," *Central European History,* III (1970), 73–93.

Landes, David S. "The Bleichröder Bank: An Interim Report." *LBIYB,* V (1960), 201–220.

Laqueur, Walter. "The German Youth Movement and the Jewish Question" *LBIYB,* VI (1961), 193–204.

Leschnitzer, Adolf. *The Magic Background of Modern Anti-Semitism.* New York, 1956.

Leven, Narcisse. *Cinquante ans d'histoire: l'Alliance Israélite Universelle.* 2 vols. Paris, 1911.

Levy, Alphonse. *Geschichte der Juden in Sachsen.* Berlin, 1900.

Levy, Ze'ev. "The Role of Apologetics in the Central Union of German Jews during the First Years of Its Existence" (Hebrew). *Yalkut Moreshet,* No. 12 (August 1970), pp. 63–86.

Lewin, Adolf. *Geschichte der badischen Juden seit der Regierung Karl Friedrichs (1738–1909).* Karlsruhe, 1909.

Lewkowitz, Albert. *Das Judentum und die geistigen Strömungen des 19. Jahrhunderts.* Breslau, 1935.

Lexikon für Theologie und Kirche. Vol. VI. Freiburg, 1961.

Lichtheim, Richard. *Toldot Ha-Zionut be-Germania* ("The History of Zionism in Germany"). Jerusalem, 1951.

Liptzin, Solomon. *Germany's Stepchildren.* New York and Philadelphia, 1961.

Liszt, Franz von. "Strafrecht und Strafprozessrecht." In *Systematische Rechtswissenschaft.* Vol. VIII of Part Two of *Die Kultur der Gegenwart.* Edited by Paul Hinnenberg. Berlin-Leipzig, 1906.

Lucas, Leopold. "Zum 25jährigen Jubiläum der Gesellschaft zur Förderung der Wissenschaft des Judentums." *MGWJ,* LXXI (1927), 321–331.

Marrus, Michael. *The Politics of Assimilation: A Study of the French Jewish Community at the Time of the Dreyfus Affair.* Oxford, 1971.

Massing, Paul. *Rehearsal for Destruction.* New York, 1949.

Mayer, Max. "A German Jew Goes East." *LBIYB,* III (1958), 344–357.

Meisel, Josef. "The Historical Commission for the History of the Jews in Germany" (Hebrew). *Zion,* XIX (1954), 171–172.

Menes, A. "The Conversion Movement in Prussia during the First Half of the 19th Century." *Yivo Annual of Jewish Social Science,* VI (1951), 187–205.

Mevorah, Baruh. "Messianism as a Factor in the First Reform Controversies" (Hebrew). *Zion,* XXXIV (1969), 189–218.

Meyer, Michael A. *The Origins of the Modern Jew.* Detroit, 1967.

Michael, Reuwen. "Graetz contra Treitschke." *BLBI,* IV (1961), 301–322.

Moore, George Foot. "Christian Writers on Judaism." *Harvard Theological Review,* XIV (1921), 197–254.

———. *Judaism in the First Centuries of the Christian Era.* Vol. I. Cambridge, 1954.

Mortara, M. "Die Censor hebräischer Bücher in Italien und der *Canon purificationis* (*Sefer Ha-Zikuk*)." *Hebräische Bibliographie,* V (1862), 72–77, 96–101.

Mosse, George L. *The Crisis of German Ideology.* New York, 1964.

———. "The Image of the Jew in German Popular Culture: Felix Dahn and Gustav Freytag." *LBIYB,* II (1957), 218–227.

———. "The Influence of the Völkisch Idea on German Jewry." In *Studies of the Leo Baeck Institute.* Edited by Max Kreutzberger. New York, 1967.

Muncy, Lysbeth W. *The Junker in the Prussian Administration under William II, 1888–1914.* Providence, R.I., 1944.

Münz, I. *Dr. Wilhelm Münz: Ein Gedenkblatt.* N.p., n.d. [1917?].

Neubach, Helmut. *Die Ausweisungen von Polen und Juden aus Preussen 1885/86.* Wiesbaden, 1967.

Osborne, Sidney. *Germany and Her Jews.* London, 1939.

Paucker, Arnold. "Der jüdische Abwehrkampf." In *Entscheidungsjahr 1932.* Edited by Werner E. Mosse. Tübingen, 1965, pp. 405–499.

Philippson, Martin. *Neueste Geschichte des jüdischen Volkes.* 2nd ed. 3 vols. Frankfurt a.M., 1922–1930.

Philipson, David. *The Reform Movement in Judaism.* 2nd ed. New York, 1931.

Pinson, Koppel S. *Modern Germany.* New York, 1954.

Puhle, Hans-Jürgen. *Agrarische Interessenpolitik und preussischer Konservatismus im wilhelminischen Reich (1893–1914).* Hanover, 1966.

Pulzer, Peter G. J. *The Rise of Political Anti-Semitism in Germany and Austria.* New York, 1964.

Reichmann, Eva G. *Hostages of Civilisation.* Boston, 1951.

Reichmann, Hans. "Der Centralverein deutscher Staatsbürger jüdischen Glaubens." In *Festschrift zum 80. Geburtstag von Leo Baeck.* London, 1953.

Reichmann-Jungmann, Eva. "Der Centralverein deutscher Staatsbürger jüdischen Glaubens." Sonderabdruck aus dem Septemberheft 1930 der *Süddeutschen Monatshefte: Die Judenfrage.*

Reissner, H. G. *Eduard Gans: Ein Leben im Vormärz.* Tübingen, 1965.

———. "Rebellious Dilemma: The Case Histories of Eduard Gans and Some of His Partisans." *LBIYB,* II (1957), 179–193.

Reuss, Franz. *Christian Wilhelm Dohms Schrift "Über die bürgerliche Verbesserung der Juden" und deren Einwirkung auf die gebildeten Stände Deutschlands.* Kaiserslautern, 1891.

Rieger, Paul. *Ein Vierteljahrhundert im Kampf um das Recht und die Zukunft der deutschen Juden.* Berlin, 1918.

Rinott, Moshe. "Gabriel Riesser." *LBIYB,* VII (1962), 11–38.

Röhl, J. C. G. "Higher Civil Servants in Germany, 1890–1900." *Journal of Contemporary History,* II, No. 3 (1967), 101–102.

Rosenberg, Hans. *Grosse Depression und Bismarckzeit*. Berlin, 1967.

Rosenheim, Jacob. "The Historical Significance of the Struggle for Secession from the Frankfurt Jewish Community." *Historia Judaica*, X (1948), 135–146.

Rosenthal, Berthold. *Heimatgeschichte der badischen Juden*. Bühl and Baden, 1927.

Rotenstreich, Nathan. "For and against Emancipation: The Bruno Bauer Controversy." *LBIYB*, IV (1959), 3–36.

Ruppin, Arthur. *The Jews of Today*. New York, 1913.

———. *Soziologie der Juden*. Vol. I. Berlin, 1930.

Samter, M. *Judentaufen im neunzehnten Jahrhundert*. Berlin, 1906.

Sandler, Ahron. "The Struggle for Unification." *LBIYB*, II (1957), 76–84.

Schmidt, H. D. "The Terms of Emancipation 1781–1812." *LBIYB*, I (1956), 28–47.

Schnabel, Franz. *Deutsche Geschichte im neunzehnten Jahrhundert*. 4 vols. Freiburg im Breisgau, 1933–1937.

Schorsch, Ismar. "Identity or Integration—Which?" (Review of Uriel Tal, *Christians and Jews in the 'Second Reich' 1870–1914*.) *Judaism*, XIX (1970), 373–377.

———. "Moritz Güdemann: Rabbi, Historian and Apologist." *LBIYB*, XI (1966), 42–66.

Schorske, Carl E. *German Social Democracy 1905–1917*, New York, 1965.

Schwab, Hermann. *The History of Orthodox Jewry in Germany*. London, 1950.

Schwartz, Benjamin I. "The Religion of Politics." *Dissent*, March–April 1970, pp. 144–161.

Schwarz, Max. *Biographisches Handbuch der Reichstage*. Hanover, 1965.

Sell, Friedrich C. *Die Tragödie des deutschen Liberalismus*. Stuttgart, 1953.

Shohet, Azriel. *Im Hilufay Tekufot* ("Beginnings of the Haskalah Among German Jewry"). Jerusalem, 1960.

Silbergleit, Heinrich. *Die Bevölkerungs- und Berufsverhältnisse der Juden im deutschen Reich*. Berlin, 1930.

Simon, Leon. *Ahad Ha-Am*. Philadelphia, 1960.

Statistisches Jahrbuch für das deutsche Reich. Vol. XXXVI (1915).

Sterling, Eleonore. *Er Ist Wie Du*. Munich, 1956.

———. "Jewish Reactions to Jew-Hatred in the First Half of the 19th Century." *LBIYB*, III (1958), 103–121.

———. "Der Kampf um die Emanzipation der Juden im Rheinland." *Monumenta Judaica*. Handbuch. Cologne, 1963.

Stern, Fred B. "Ludwig Jacobowski, der Author von *Werther, der Jude*." *BLBI*, III (1964), 101–137.

Stern, Fritz, "Gold and Iron: The Collaboration and Friendship of Gerson Bleichröder and Otto von Bismarck." *American Historical Review*, LXXV (1969), 37–46.

———. "Money, Morals, and the Pillars of Bismarck's Society." *Central European History*, III (1970), 49–72.

———. *The Politics of Cultural Despair*. Garden City, 1965.

Stern, Rudolph A. "Fritz Haber: Personal Recollections." *LBIYB*, VIII (1963), 70–102.

Szajkowski, Zosa. "Emigration to America or Reconstruction in Europe." *PAJHS*, XLII (1952), 157–188.

Tal, Uriel. *Christians and Jews in the 'Second Reich' (1870–1914)* (Hebrew). Jerusalem, 1969.

——. "Ha-Antishemiyut ba-Reich ha-Germani ha-Sheni, 1870–1914" ("Anti-Semitism in the Second German Reich, 1870–1914"). Unpublished Ph.D. dissertation, Hebrew University, 1963.

——. "The Intellectual Elite in Germany and Its Position on the Jews in the Period of Bismarck" (Hebrew). *Kebusot Ilit Ve-Shikhvot Manhigot* ("Elites and Leading Groups"). Jerusalem, 1966.

——. "The 'Kulturkampf' and the Position of the Jews in Germany" (Hebrew). *Zion*, XXIX (1964), 208–242.

——. "Liberal Protestantism and the Jews in the Second Reich 1870–1914." *Jewish Social Studies*, XXVI (1964), 23–41.

Tänzer, A. *Die Geschichte der Juden im Wuerttemberg.* Frankfurt a.M., 1937.

Theilhaber, Felix A. *Der Untergang der deutschen Juden.* 2nd ed. Berlin, 1921.

Tims, Richard Wonser. *Germanizing Prussian Poland.* New York, 1966.

Toury, Jacob. " 'Deutsche Juden' im Vormärz." *BLBI*, 1965, pp. 65–82.

——. "Jüdische Parteigänger des Antisemitismus." *BLBI*, 1961, pp. 323–335.

——. "Organizational Problems of German Jewry." *LBIYB*, XIII (1968), 57–90.

——. "Plan for a Jewish Political Organization in Germany" (Hebrew). *Zion*, XXVIII (1963), 164–205.

——. *Die politischen Orientierungen der Juden in Deutschland.* Tübingen, 1966.

Trachtenberg, Joshua. *The Devil and the Jews.* New York and Philadelphia, 1961.

Tramer, Hans. "Bernhard und Emil Cohn." *BLBI*, VIII (1965), pp. 326–345.

Wawrzinek, Kurt. "Die Entstehung der deutschen Antisemitenparteien (1873–1890)." *Historische Studien*, CLXVIII (1927).

Weinryb, B. D. "Prolegomena to an Economic History of the Jews in Modern Times." *LBIYB*, I (1956), 279–306.

Weltsch, Robert. "Deutscher Zionismus in der Ruckschau." In *In Zwei Welten.* Edited by Hans Tramer. Tel Aviv, 1962.

Wertheimer, Mildred S. *The Pan-German League.* New York, 1924.

Wiener, Max. *Jüdische Religion im Zeitalter der Emanzipation.* Berlin, 1933.

Wilhelm, Kurt. "The Jewish Community in the Post-Emancipation Period." *LBIYB*, II (1957), 47–75.

——. "Der Zionistische Rabbiner." In *In Zwei Welten.* Edited by Hans Tramer. Tel Aviv, 1962.

Wischnitzer, Mark. *To Swell in Safety.* Philadelphia, 1948.

Wohlgemuth, Josef. *Moritz Lazarus: Ein Nachruf.* Separatabdruck aus der *Jüdische Presse.* Berlin, 1903.

Young, Harry F. *Maximilian Harden: Censor Germaniae.* Hague, 1959.

Ziekursch, Johannes. *Politische Geschichte des neuen deutschen Kaiserreiches.* 3 vols. Frankfurt a.M., 1927–1932.

INDEX

Abrahams, Israel, 171
Ahad Ha-Am, 190-91, 260 n.7
Ahlwardt, Hermann, 84
Akum, 240 n.19
Alienation from Judaism, 138-39, 143-47, 192-93
Alldeutscher Verband, 118, 131
Allgemeine Zeitung des Judentums, 64, 68, 87, 92, 105, 111, 114, 122, 126-27, 243 n.11, 248 n.113
Allgemeiner Rabbinerverband in Deutschland, 160, 181
Alliance Israélite Universelle, 25-26, 60, 158, 205, 219 n.11, 219 n.14, 267 n.86
Anglo-Jewish Association, 219 n.14
Anti-Semitism: among liberals, 2-3, 98-99, 207, 238 n.62; at universities, 72, 165, 194, 233 n.54; Berlin Movement, 54-55, 69; blood libels, 94, 103-06, 128, 130, 132, 150, 152, 237 n.45; economic discrimination, 132, 134, 143, 164; expulsion of Eastern Jews, 163; faction in Reichstag, 104; government discrimination, 27, 162-68; in Saxony, 48-52, 225 n.77; kosher slaughtering, 51, 104, 115, 132, 163, 239 n.2; petition to Bismarck, 38; racial, 40, 80, 207; social, 90, 143
Antizionistische Komitee, 199, 202, 266 n.79
Apt, Max (Maximilian Parmod), 125, 245 n.24, 246 n.52
Arendt, Hannah, 205
Auerbach, Berthold, 56, 61, 67, 69, 76-78

Auerbach, Fritz, 110
Auerbach, Leopold, 74-76, 110, 232 n.39, 234 n.62, 234 n.66
Augusta (Queen), 68
Austrittsgesetz, 20, 39

"Babel und Bibel" controversy, 170-71
Baeck, Leo, 171, 173, 207, 249 n.113, 259 n.83
Barth, Jakob, 61
Barth, Theodor, 81-82, 84-85, 87-88, 90, 142, 236 n.25, 251 n.5
Bärwald, Hermann, 44
Bauer, Bruno, 2
Berliner, Abraham, 45
Berliner Tageblatt, 174
Bernfeld, Simon, 176
Biedermann, Karl, 82
Billerbeck, Paul, 204
Bismarck, Otto von, 13, 17, 19, 29, 33, 37-38, 58, 68, 71, 87-88, 164, 220 n.23, 223 n.62, 228 n.116, 254 n.44
Bleichröder, Gerson von, 58-59, 67, 230 n.27
Blumenfeld, Kurt, 188-89, 192-94, 198, 267 n.84
B'nai B'rith, 134, 149, 159, 202, 258 n.72
Board of Deputies of American Israelites, 29, 158
Bodenheimer, Max, 154, 182-86, 188-89, 191-92, 242 n.47, 261 n.15, 261 n.16, 261 n.23, 262 n.29, 262 n.31, 263 n.40
Boeckel, Otto, 80-81, 233 n.51

Börne, Ludwig, 5
Bousset, D. Wilhelm, 169-70
Breslau School, 234 n.62
Breslauer, Bernhard, 152, 155, 253
    n.25, 255 n.50
Breslaur, Emil, 61
Bresslau, Harry, 44-46, 61
Brodnitz, Julius, 130
Buber, Martin, 193-94
Bülow, Bernhard von, 133
Bund der Landwirte, 118, 131

Caspari, Otto, 82, 238 n.62
Cassel, David, 45
Centralverein deutscher Staatsbürger
    jüdischen Glaubens, 1, 12, 20, 115,
    121, 126, 149-55, 160-61, 179, 195,
    202, 208, 241 n.37, 241 n.40, 242
    n.45, 242 n.46, 243 n.2, 243 n.11,
    244 n.13, 244 n.18, 244 n.20, 245
    n.24, 246 n.52, 246 n.61, 246 n.65,
    248 n.100, 248 n.105, 250 n.112,
    251 n.2; connection with Verband
    der Deutschen Juden, 158, 160,
    206; fight against conversion, 117,
    138-46; finances, 120-21; ideology,
    100, 117, 119, 126, 136-37, 148;
    Im deutschen Reich, 120; origins,
    114-15; political activities, 132-33,
    135, 142-43; recourse to courts, 122-
    31, 206; relations with Abwehrver-
    ein, 99-100, 113-14, 133; relations
    with Zionists, 134-35, 147, 179-80,
    182, 186-87, 195-201, 206, 259 n.4,
    260 n.7, 263 n.37, 266 n.82, 266
    n.83, 267 n.84; significance of, 1, 12-
    13, 78, 205-06; size, 119, 122, 243
    n.12; structure, 118, 120; surrogate
    Judaism, 207-08
Christian Social Workers' Party, 37,
    54
Cohen, Hermann, 56-57, 74, 140, 156,
    168, 172, 205, 229 n.17, 230 n.23,
    248 n.98, 248 n.113, 258 n.72, 259
    n.83, 267 n.88
Cohn, Bernhard, 264 n.56
Cohn, Emil, 181, 260 n.14

Comité zur Abwehr antisemitischer
    Angriffe, 113, 156, 242 n.46
Conservative Party, 54, 85, 91, 100,
    104, 118, 255 n.50

Dahn, Felix, 227 n.98
Darwin, Charles, 138
Delitzsch, Friedrich, 170-71
Deutsch-Israelitischer Gemeindebund,
    19, 28, 34, 36, 39, 42, 53, 60-61, 66,
    69, 71, 73, 118, 136, 156, 158, 160-
    62, 219 n.11, 220 n.21, 220 n.26,
    220 n.28, 221 n.34, 221 n.44, 253
    n.38; apologetica, 42-47; Historical
    Commission, 44, 46; message for
    German Jewry, 30, 47-48; origins,
    24-26, 30-33, 42; recourse to courts,
    39-41, 47, 228 n.117; relations with
    Saxon government, 23, 32, 49-52,
    208, 221 n.34; response of Orthodox
    Jewry, 29, 34-35; structure, 30-31;
    welfare programs, 27, 35, 52
Deutscher Handlungsgehilfen Verband,
    118, 131
Disunity of German Jewry, 30-36
Dohm, Christian Wilhelm, 1-2, 79, 96,
    213 n.1, 214 n.25
Döllinger, Ignaz, 231 n.39
Dreyfus Affair, 168, 204
Drumont, Edouard, 77, 204
Dühring, Eugen, 37

Eger, Akiba, 114
Eisner, Kurt, 237 n.49
Elbogen, Ismar, 259 n.83
Eschelbacher, Josef, 173, 259 n.83

Feivel, Berthold, 193
Fichte, Johann Gottlieb, 70
Fischer, Senator, 95
Foerder, Ludwig, 246 n.52
Forckenbeck, Maximilian, 37, 82
Förster, Bernhard, 37
Fraenkel, Abraham, 138, 234 n.62,
    248 n.98
Fränkel, Emil, 267 n.88
Frankfurter Zeitung, 91, 249 n.113
Frederick William III, 4-5

Frederick William IV, 4-5
Freie Vereinigung für die Interessen des orthodoxen Judenthums, 161, 252 n.12
French Jewry, 204-5, 217 n.68
Freund, Ismar, 161, 166, 207, 256 n.58
Freund, William, 9-10
Freytag, Gustav, 82, 227 n.98
Friedemann, Adolf, 183, 189-90, 262 n.29, 264 n.56
Friedemann, Edmund, 81, 93, 113, 115
Friedländer, David, 7, 141, 157
Fritsch, Theodor, 131
Fromer, Jacob, 144-45, 248 n.113, 250 n.117
Fuchs, Eugen, 119, 125-26, 132-33, 135, 146-48, 151-52, 154-55, 160, 180, 197-99, 206, 241 n.37, 251 n.123, 253 n.6, 259 n.7, 266 n.81

Gans, Eduard, 5
Geiger, Abraham, 7-8, 25, 42, 170, 219 n.19, 223 n.60
Geiger, Ludwig, 44, 226 n.93, 252 n.8
German Jewry: demography, 13-16, 51; immigrants, 25, 51, 163, 223 n.66; local Jewish communities, 17-21, 65, 71, 75-77, 94, 113, 154, 156-57, 161, 167, 221 n.34, 221 n.44, 225 n.81, 247 n.91, 264 n.56, 266 n.82; occupational distribution, 14-15; organizational proliferation, vi, 149, 204-5; preference for Christian spokesmen, vi, 43, 79-80, 87, 114, 196-97; prosperity, 15-16; reluctance to resist, 65-71, 122
German People's Association, 37
German Reform Party, 37, 50
German Social Anti-Semitic Party, 81
Gesellschaft zur Beförderung des Christentums unter den Juden, 5
Gesellschaft zur Förderung der Wissenschaft des Judentums, 149, 172-73
Ginsberg, Adolf, 113
Glagau, Otto, 36
Gneist, Rudolf von, 30, 86-87, 238 n.62

Goldmann, Felix, 141
Goldschmidt, Levin, 80
Goldstein, Moritz, 194, 196
Gothein, Georg, 88
Graetz, Heinrich, 10-11, 43-46, 70-72, 158, 165, 170, 232 n.44, 233 n.53, 234 n.62, 256 n.53
Gronemann, Sammy, 158, 181, 185, 192, 251 n.2
Güdemann, Moritz, 173-74, 226 n.93, 259 n.83
Guttmann, Jakob, 175, 181, 259 n.83

Haber, Fritz, 238 n.60
Haeckel, Ernst, 138
Haehnle, Hans, 82
Hallgarten, Charles, 93-95
Hantke, Arthur, 183, 186-87, 190-91, 198, 263 n.40, 267 n.84
Harden, Maximilian, 250 n.117
Hardenberg, Karl von, 4
Harnack, Adolf, 169-70, 173
Hartmann, Eduard von, 197
Hegel, G. W. F., 216 n.48
Henrici, Ernst, 37
Herford, R. Travers, 171
Herzfeld, Ernst, 119-20
Herzfeld, Levi, 170
Herzl, Theodor, 154, 180, 182, 186, 188, 190, 261 n.16, 261 n.19, 261 n.21, 262 n.30, 263 n.31
Heymann, Hans Gideon, 183, 198
Hibbat Zion, 190
Hildesheimer, Esriel, 33, 35, 73, 109, 218 n.80, 222 n.56, 230 n.27
Hildesheimer, Hirsch, 95, 113, 121
Hilfsverein der deutschen Juden, 149
Hilfsverein für jüdischen Studirende in Berlin, 230 n.25
Hirsch, Isaac, 77
Hirsch, Marcus, 109-10, 240 n.21
Hirsch, Samson Raphael, 10, 19-20, 33, 35, 77, 109, 121, 153, 207, 216 n.44, 216 n.48, 222 n.56
Hirschberg, Julius, 61
Hirschen, Baron, 79
Hochschule für die Wissenschaft des Judentums, 73

Hoffmann, David, 73
Hohenhole, Alexander von, 255 n.52
Holdheim, Samuel, 8
Hollaender, Ludwig, 141, 148, 198-99, 244 n.13, 266 n.79
Honigmann, David, 42, 222 n.60
Horovitz, Marcus, 109
Horwitz, Maximilian, 126, 132, 135, 152, 154-55, 160, 175, 198, 206, 244 n.20, 251 n.123, 266 n.82
Humboldt, Wilhelm von, 3, 208-9

Imperial Union for Combating Social Democracy, 133
Intermarriage, 8-9
Isaac, Julius, 113-14, 241 n.37
Der Israelit, 77, 109, 121, 153, 245 n.24
Israelitische Alliance in Deutschland, 60, 219 n.14
Israelitische Allianz zu Wien, 219 n.14
Israelitische Wochenschrift, 122
Ittmann, Kurt, 267 n.90

Jacob, Benno, 72, 171, 175
Jacobowski, Ludwig, 47, 95, 227 n.98, 237 n.48
Jacobsohn, Bernhard, 30, 41, 50
The Jewish Committee of December 1, 1880, see Das judische Comité vom 1 Dezember 1880
Jost, Isaac M., 158
Der Jude, 158
Judentag, 135, 154-55, 183, 252 n.8, 252 n.12
Judiciary, 39-40
Das jüdische Comité vom 1 Dezember 1880, 59-65; activities, 64-65; ideology, 62-63; origins, 53, 59-61
Jüdische Frauenbund, 159
Jüdische Presse, 73, 77, 105, 121, 206, 244 n.18, 245 n.24, 245 n.33
Jüdische Rundschau, 183, 198
Junkers, 12, 89-92, 223 n.63, 255 n.52

Karpeles, Gustav, 111-13, 243 n.11
Kartell Convent, 72, 97, 149

Kaufmann, David, 43-44
Klee, Alfred, 187, 192, 198, 200
Kohner, Moritz, 25, 28-31, 33, 48, 206, 219 n.15, 219 n.21, 220 n.23, 221 n.35, 223 n.60
Kristeller, Samuel, 35, 46, 61, 67, 113, 206, 226 n.89, 233 n.53, 233 n.58

Lachmann, Edmund, 160
Lagarde, Paul de, 37, 236 n.29
Lazarus, Moritz, 31, 51, 53, 59-69, 72-73, 80, 118, 136, 206, 229 n.17, 230 n.23, 230 n.27, 233 n.58, 262 n.25
League of Anti-Semites, 37
Lehmann, Emil, 24, 33, 41, 47, 49-50, 122, 127, 129, 206, 218 n.1, 218 n.3, 218 n.4, 222 n.55, 243 n.2
Lehmann, Markus, 33-34, 222 n.55
Leszinsky, Eduard, 186
Levinstein, Gustav, 141
Levita, Benedictus, 143-44
Lewin, Carl, 190
Lewkowitz, Albert, 259 n.83
Lichtheim, Richard, 192, 263 n.40
Loewe, Heinrich, 183
Loewe, Ludwig, 61, 192, 261 n.21
Löwenfeld, Raphael, 108, 114, 121-22, 125, 206, 241 n.40, 243 n.2, 250 n.122
Lucas, Leopold, 172
Luther, Martin, 70, 173

Maier, Gustav, 56
Marr, Wilhelm, 36-37
Mauthner, Fritz, 56, 139
Maybaum, Sigmund, 181, 230 n.23, 259 n.83
Mendel, Emanuel, 61
Mendelsohn, Martin, 126
Mendelssohn, Moses, 7, 79, 214 n.25
Meyer, Flora, 138
Meyer-Cohen, Heinrich, 95-96, 113
Mommsen, Theodor, 37, 63-64, 82, 96, 99, 230 n.27, 238 n.60, 238 n.62, 249 n.113
Monatsschrift für Geschichte und Wissenschaft des Judentums, 173

Montefiore, Claude, 171
Moore, George Foot, 171
Mosse, Rudolf, 95
Mortara, Edward, 25, 29
Motzkin, Leo, 198
Mugdan, Otto, 142, 198, 248 n.105

Nachod, Jacob, 30-31, 35, 48-52, 68, 206, 221 n.37, 221 n.41, 230 n.27
Napoleon, 4, 29, 203, 214 n.24, 215 n.32
Nathan, Paul, 95, 105-6, 113, 115, 206, 242 n.46, 242 n.47
Nathanael, 105
Nation, 81, 88, 106, 125
National-jüdische Verein der Hörer an der Lehranstalt für die Wissenschaft des Judentums, 260 n.13
National-jüdische Vereinigung für Deutschland, *see* Zionistische Vereinigung für Deutschland
National Liberal Party, 71, 87, 134, 229 n.1
Navy League, 133
Neumann, Salomon, 113, 224 n.66
Nöldike, Theodor, 248 n.113
Nothnagel, Hermann, 83

Oppenheim, Juda, 57
Oppenheimer, Franz, 186, 189, 190, 192, 262 n.30
Orthodox Judaism, 8, 10, 19-20, 33-34, 57, 73, 77-78, 92, 108-9, 114, 121-22, 142, 146, 156, 163, 166, 206-7, 218 n.80, 240 n.20, 252 n.12

Paris Sanhedrin, 214 n.24
Parmod, Maximilian, *see* Apt, Max
Peltasohn, Martin, 151
Philippson, Ludwig, 25-26, 64-65, 69, 220 n.26, 223 n.62, 232 n.41, 232 n.43
Philippson, Martin, 69, 95, 152-56, 160-61, 173, 252 n.8
Pinkert, Alexander (Egon Waldegg), 37, 50-51
Pinsker, Leon, 69
Preussische Jahrbücher, 143

Preussischer Landesverband jüdischer Gemeinden, 253 n.38
Progressive People's Party, 132, 135, 142
Progressive Union, 87-88, 142
Progressives, 77-78, 81, 84-86, 92, 104, 134, 151, 160, 187
Pückler, Count, 128-29

Rathenau, Walther, 145-47, 203, 246 n.52, 249 n.115, 250 n.117, 250 n.119, 250 n.120
Reform Judaism, 6-10, 19-20, 24, 33-34, 60, 76, 78, 92, 108-9, 121-22, 153, 166, 179, 206-7, 215 n.41, 216 n.51, 220 n.28, 240 n.20, 248 n.113, 251 n.123, 260 n.13
Reichsverein deutscher Juden, 266 n.82
Richter, Eugen, 77, 87, 132, 135
Rickert, Heinrich, 81, 87-88, 90, 93, 114, 238 n.62
Rieger, Paul, 115, 241 n.37
Riesser, Gabriel, 158, 215 n.41
Robinow, Hermann, 55
Rohling, August, 50
Rülf, Isaac, 192

Schach, Fabius, 264 n.56
Schapira, Hermann, 261 n.23
Schauer, Rudolf, 184, 192
Schechter, Solomon, 171
Schleiden, Matthias Jakob, 43-44, 226 n.87
Schönstedt, Karl Heinrich von, 151, 251 n.5
Schleiermacher, Friedrich, 141
Schürer, Emil, 169-70, 257 n.64
Self-criticism, 47-48, 67-70, 135-36, 227 n.98
Simon, James, 110-11, 113
Simonson, Emil, 186
Social Democratic Party, 54, 58, 85, 92, 104, 131, 150
Social Reich Party, 37
Sombart, Werner, 16, 75, 196-97, 199, 265 n.72

Sonnenberg, Max Liebermann von, 37, 81
Stein, Baron vom, 4
Steinschneider, Moritz, 44
Steinthal, Heymann, 59, 61
Stobbe, Otto, 44, 226 n.89
Stoecker, Adolf, 37, 50, 54, 57-58, 68, 71, 80-81, 89, 226 n.87, 229 n.1
Strack, Hermann, 105-6, 125
Strassman, Wolf, 61
Susman, Margarete, 139, 249 n.113
Suttner, Baron von, 83

Tal, Uriel, v, vi, 100, 220 n.28
Teller, William Abraham, 141
Tirpitz, Alfred von, 197
Tolstoy, Count Leo, 114
Toury, Jacob, 134-35
Treitschke, Heinrich, 37, 54, 56, 60-61, 63-64, 68, 89, 99, 140, 143-44, 197, 223 n.66, 229 n.17, 230 n.23, 254 n.45
Treitschke-Graetz controversy, 11, 45-46, 62, 70, 232 n.41, 256 n.53
Trietsch, Davis, 193

Verband der Deutschen Juden, 135, 161-62, 165, 206, 221 n.44, 253 n.26, 256 n.52, 256 n.58; apologetica, 169-77, 259 n.81; national conventions, 159-60, 164; origins, 150-58; purpose, 150, 158-60; relations with government, 162-68; significance of name, 157-58; structure, 159
Verband der jüdischen Jugendvereine Deutschlands, 149, 200-1
Verband der Vereine für jüdische Geschichte und Literatur, 112-13, 149, 159
Verband für jüdische Wohltätigkeitspflege, 159
Verband national-jüdischer Turnvereine, 97
Verein für Cultur und Wissenschaft der Juden, 5
Verein jüdischer Studenten, 97

Verein zur Abwehr des Antisemitismus (Austria), 83
Verein zur Abwehr des Antisemitismus (Germany), 79, 82-85, 98, 113-14, 122, 133, 180, 237 n.49, 237 n.50, 238 n.62, 240 n.21, 242 n.47, 243 n.3, 251 n.5; committment to Rechtsstaat, 86, 89-91, 100; Jewish component, 92-95; leadership, 82, 86-87, 89; Mitteilungen, 85-86, 95-97, 242 n.47; origins, 80, 82, 88, 238 n.60; problem of usury, 84; rejection of legal defense, 84; size, 82-83; structure, 82-83; views on Judaism, 95-101
Vereinigung Badischer Israeliten, 115
Vereinigung für das liberale Judentum, 149, 199
Vogelstein, Hermann, 259 n.83

Waldegg, Egon, see Pinkert, Alexander
Wandervogel, 201
Warburg, Otto, 191, 261 n.19
Wassermann, Jakob, 249 n.114
Wattenbach, Wilhelm, 44
Weber, Albrecht, 82, 96-97
Weber, Ferdinand, 169
Weber, Max, 196
Weininger, Otto, 250 n.117
Weizäcker, Julius, 44
Weizmann, Chaim, 193
Wellhausen, Julius, 170
Werner, Mose Cossman, 174, 181
William I, 37, 58, 64, 68
William II, 107, 110, 171, 197, 250 n.117
Wissenschaft des Judentums, 43-47, 111-13, 169-77, 225 n.85, 258 n.72
Wolffsohn, David, 188, 192, 261 n.15, 261 n.19

Zedlitz-Trützschler, Count von, 175, 259 n.81
Zionism in Germany, 98, 134-35, 147, 154-55, 158-59, 179-80, 187, 191, 198-99, 201-2, 208, 250 n.117, 251 n.2, 262 n.29, 263 n.40, 264 n.56, 265 n.58, 265 n.66, 265 n.69,

265 n.72, 266 n.79; Basle Program, 185, 190-91, 262 n.28; Blau-Weiss Vereine, 201; First generation, 182, 189-92, 199-200; Jewish reactions to, 179-82; organization, 154, 183-84, 186, 188, 190-91; Posen resolution, 189-91, 195, 198; propaganda, 184-86; racial overtones, 192; relations with Hilfsverein der Deutschen Juden, 201-2; second generation, 191-95, 199, 267 n.90; views on Anti-Semitism, 187, 191, 193; *Die Welt,* 154, 186-87, 197-98, 261 n.19, 261 n.21

Zionistische Vereinigung für Deutschland, 182-83, 261 n.15

Zunz, Leopold, 44, 225 n.85, 258 n.72